Atlantic Canada's Irish Immigrants

ALSO BY LUCILLE H. CAMPEY

Ignored but Not Forgotten:
Canada's English Immigrants

Seeking a Better Future:
The English Pioneers of Ontario and Quebec

Planters, Paupers, and Pioneers:
English Settlers in Atlantic Canada

An Unstoppable Force:
The Scottish Exodus to Canada

"A Very Fine Class of Immigrants":
Prince Edward Island's Scottish Pioneers, 1770–1850

"Fast Sailing and Copper-Bottomed":
Aberdeen Sailing Ships and the Emigrant Scots They Carried to Canada, 1774–1855

The Silver Chief:
Lord Selkirk and the Scottish Pioneers of Belfast, Baldoon and Red River

After the Hector:
The Scottish Pioneers of Nova Scotia and Cape Breton, 1773–1852

The Scottish Pioneers of Upper Canada, 1784–1855:
Glengarry and Beyond

Les Écossais:
The Scottish Pioneers of Lower Canada, 1763–1855

With Axe and Bible:
The Scottish Pioneers of New Brunswick, 1784–1874

All published by Natural Heritage/Dundurn Press, Toronto

Lucille Campey has three websites:
www.englishtocanada.com
for her books on English emigration to Canada

www.irishtocanada.com
for her books on Irish emigration to Canada

www.scotstocanada.com
for her books on Scottish emigration to Canada

THE IRISH IN CANADA

Atlantic Canada's Irish Immigrants

A Fish and Timber Story

Lucille H. Campey

DUNDURN
TORONTO

Editor: Allison Hirst
Design: Laura Boyle
Cover design: Courtney Horner
Printer: Webcom
Front cover image: *Halifax Harbour at Sunset*, circa 1853. Oil painting by John O'Brien, 1831–91. Courtesy of the Art Gallery of Nova Scotia. Gift of the Halifax Chamber of Commerce, 2007.
Back cover image: View of the port of Londonderry from an original sketch by John Nixon, circa 1790. Reproduced courtesy of the National Library of Ireland ET B38.

Library and Archives Canada Cataloguing in Publication

Campey, Lucille H., author
    Atlantic Canada's Irish immigrants : a fish and timber story / Lucille H. Campey.

(The Irish in Canada)
Includes bibliographical references and index.
Issued in print and electronic formats.

ISBN 978-1-4597-3023-6 (paperback).--ISBN 978-1-4597-3024-3 (pdf).--ISBN 978-1-4597-3025-0 (epub)

    1. Irish--Atlantic Provinces--History. 2. Immigrants--Atlantic Provinces--History. 3. Fisheries--Atlantic Provinces--History. 4. Lumber trade--Atlantic Provinces--History. 5. Atlantic Provinces--Emigration and immigration--History. 6. Ireland--Emigration and immigration--History. I. Title. II. Series: Campey, Lucille H. Irish in Canada.

FC2020.I6C34 2016   971.5004'9162   C2016-903095-4
                                                  C2016-903096-2

1   2   3   4   5   20   19   18   17   16

We acknowledge the support of the **Canada Council for the Arts** and the **Ontario Arts Council** for our publishing program. We also acknowledge the financial support of the **Government of Canada** through the **Canada Book Fund** and **Livres Canada Books,** and the **Government of Ontario** through the **Ontario Book Publishing Tax Credit** and the **Ontario Media Development Corporation.**

Care has been taken to trace the ownership of copyright material used in this book. The author and the publisher welcome any information enabling them to rectify any references or credits in subsequent editions.
— *J. Kirk Howard, President*

The publisher is not responsible for websites or their content unless they are owned by the publisher.

Printed and bound in Canada.

VISIT US AT
Dundurn.com | @dundurnpress | Facebook.com/dundurnpress | Pinterest.com/dundurnpress

Dundurn
3 Church Street, Suite 500
Toronto, Ontario, Canada
M5E 1M2

To Geoff

CONTENTS

LIST OF MAPS

All maps are © Geoff Campey, 2016

LIST OF TABLES

ACKNOWLEDGEMENTS

I am indebted to a great many people. First, I wish to gratefully thank the Foundation for Canadian Studies in the U.K. for their grant, which I used toward my research and travel costs.

I would like to begin by thanking the archivists and librarians in Canada and Ireland who have helped me in locating material. In particular, I wish to thank Janice Cook at the New Brunswick Archives for the trouble she took in digging out very wide-ranging sources for me to study during my visit. I also owe a special thanks to Debby Andrews at the Centre for Newfoundland Studies, Memorial University, St. John's, who located obscure sources that I could not have found on my own. I also thank John Boylan at the Public Archives of Prince Edward Island for his assistance.

I am grateful to the many people who helped me to locate and obtain illustrations. In particular, I thank the historian Harold E. Wright, who lives in Saint John, for his permission to use photographs from his extensive collection. An expert on Partridge Island's history, Harold's help was invaluable to me in piecing together how the quarantine facilities operated during the Great Irish Famine. I also thank the president of the Miramichi Branch of the New Brunswick Genealogical Society for his help in tracking down a photograph of Dr. John Vondy, who died treating immigrants during the famine period. I am also grateful to Joshua Green of the Provincial Archives of New Brunswick, who went to a lot of trouble to locate the New Brunswick illustrations used in this book.

The writing of this book has depended on the help and forbearance of my husband, Geoff. We are a team, and without him this and my other books would never have been written. He produces the tables, maps, and appendices, locates the illustrations, helps with the research, and guides me through my rough patches. I am also greatly indebted to Allison Hirst for her meticulous labour in turning my manuscript into a book and I thank my longstanding friend, Jean Lucas, who continues to proofread my work and offer guidance.

This book is dedicated to Geoff, with all my love.

PREFACE

*A*tlantic Canada's Irish Immigrants: A Fish and Timber Story* is the first
of three books on the Irish in Canada, this one concentrating on the
ones who settled in Newfoundland, Nova Scotia, New Brunswick, and
Prince Edward Island. The Irish presence was experienced earliest and to
a very enduring extent in the four Atlantic provinces. They were the largest immigrant group in Newfoundland and New Brunswick by the 1850s
and ranked second only to the Scots in Prince Edward Island.

My primary objectives in writing this book have been to determine
what prompted people to leave Ireland in the first place and to discover
why they chose various destinations in Atlantic Canada. In considering
their settlement choices, I identified the pull factors that drove this saga.

This will be a departure from the doom-laden approach, adopted by
some commentators, which would have us believe that the Irish who
arrived on our shores were helpless exiles, lacking in ambition, who
went in a lemming-like way to wherever they were told to go. This is, of
course, preposterous.

The Irish should not be mourned as victims. They took the logical
response of people who were caught up in dire economic circumstances.
They emigrated to achieve a better standard of living and to be part of a

more egalitarian society. Their location choices in Atlantic Canada were made following a careful consideration of the various opportunities that were available in the different locations across the region. Even during the distressing period of the Great Irish Famine of the mid-1840s, when the number of Irish arrivals suddenly skyrocketed, the issue of where to settle had salience. By this time the immigration saga was reaching the finish line. The Irish had been coming to Atlantic Canada for some one hundred years, and most arrived before the famine struck.

I will begin with a study of eighteenth-century immigration to Newfoundland, Nova Scotia, and Prince Edward Island, some of which was driven by the fishing trade. I will then describe how the timber trade took over in the following century, turning New Brunswick into an Irish colony and also creating farming and job opportunities in the other Maritime provinces. A consideration of the famine years is followed by an examination of the shipping services used by the Irish. Fortunately, the quality of the shipping used to take them across the Atlantic can be assessed by consulting the Lloyd's Shipping Register. Still in use today, the register provides irrefutable evidence that the Irish generally sailed in seaworthy ships. Far from being put in rickety old barges, as is frequently alleged, the Irish had access to some of the best ships of the day. "Coffin ship" mythology is not supportable by the evidence.

I was fortunate in having access to Cecil J. Houston and William J. Smyth's book *Irish Emigration and Canadian Settlement*, which gave me an excellent grounding on the subject. On a provincial level, Terrence Punch's many detailed studies of Nova Scotia's Irish were of immense help, as was Brendan O'Grady's work on Prince Edward Island. Peter Toner's detailed studies of Irish immigration to New Brunswick and John Mannion's comprehensive investigation of specific Irish communities in Newfoundland were indispensable. However, my loudest plaudit goes to the New Brunswick Archives for having established the "Irish Portal" website, which provides access to an amazing array of immigrant letters, government reports, newspaper reports, census data, and a multiplicity of other records.

A serious limitation on any study of immigration to Atlantic Canada is the incompleteness of the customs and shipping data. Accurate figures on the numbers who came from Ireland cannot be given. This is especially the case for New Brunswick, whose customs records were lost in 1877 in the great fire of Saint John.

The task of quantifying Irish immigration statistics was made even more difficult in Newfoundland by the fact that settlement had long been discouraged in order to safeguard the interests of the merchants who controlled the province's economy.

Religion was a constant theme and there were plenty of factors that worked against the process of settlement. The unsuccessful attempts by the ruling classes to establish feudal landholding regimes in Prince Edward Island retarded settlement as did the elitist and bigoted behaviour of government officials against Irish Catholics in Nova Scotia. The early take-up of much of Nova Scotia's good agricultural land by the late eighteenth century meant that it attracted relatively few Irish immigrants who mainly arrived after 1820. And as better transport systems developed, the Maritime provinces faced increasing competition from Upper Canada's much better land, and few immigrants from Ireland and Great Britain came to Atlantic Canada after the mid-nineteenth century.

We must not forget that the real story is about the immigrants themselves. A primary objective of this book was to give them a voice. Their descriptions of the conditions they encountered give us a flavour of the challenges they faced when they arrived. There were plenty of stumbling blocks and they were not always made to feel welcome, but the Irish were outstandingly successful pioneers. And that success greatly benefited the development of Atlantic Canada.

ABBREVIATIONS

DCB	*Dictionary of Canadian Biography*
DRO	Devon Record Office
LAC	Library and Archives Canada
LMS	*London Missionary Society Papers*
MCFMS	Mellon Centre for Migration Studies
MMS	*Methodist Missionary Society Papers*
NAB	National Archives of Britain
NAI	National Archives of Ireland
NLI	National Library of Ireland
NSARM	Nova Scotia Archives and Records Management
PANB	Provincial Archives of New Brunswick
PANL	Provincial Archives of Newfoundland and Labrador
PAPEI	Provincial Archives and Records Office of Prince Edward Island
PP	British Parliamentary Papers
PRONI	Public Record Office, Northern Ireland
RHL	Oxford University, Rhodes House Library
SOAS	University of London, School of Oriental and African Studies
STRO	Staffordshire County Record Office
WRO	Worcestershire Record Office

CHAPTER 1

Fish, Timber, and Hope

It is to the credit of the great majority of [Irish] immigrants that once given a fair start in this country, they rapidly rose from want to comfort and often to affluence.[1]

Professor William Ganong's observation, made in his "Origins of Settlement in the Province of New Brunswick," published in 1904, seems blindingly obvious, but it needed to be said. Many of the Irish who came to live in Atlantic Canada were not given a fair start. Not only that, their important contribution to Atlantic Canada's development has been belittled and misconstrued. Their story is not a tragic epic in which victims of famine were forced to flee their homeland. The truth is otherwise. It is a tale of how hope and hard work gave Atlantic Canada its stalwart Irish population.

Irish Catholics suffered discrimination from the moment they arrived. Rather than being welcomed as useful additions to the local population, they were treated with contempt by the Protestant elite who governed the region. Because Catholics owed their religious allegiance to Rome, their loyalty to the British Crown was questioned. Another mark against the Irish was their poverty. When large numbers of penniless Irish began arriving in Nova Scotia in 1816, officials complained about the drain they would be on the public purse. There was certainly no question of them being welcomed as useful settlers. They were just riff-raff. Unfortunately this imagery of the sad, bedraggled, and unwanted Irish immigrant has moved centre stage. It has enveloped the entire emigration saga. A mythology attributing all Irish emigration to poverty, disease, and forced exile has come into existence and it is rarely challenged. Far from being a great tragedy full of pitiful victims, this saga is about thrusting, brave, and well-organized people who grabbed their opportunities in Canada to the benefit of it and themselves.

The high death toll associated with the immigration that took place during the period of the Great Irish Famine in the 1840s became the story. By then, Ireland's population had reached around 8.5 million — double that of today. Being reliant on a good potato crop, it was just a matter of time before hunger and disease struck, which happened in the early 1840s when the crop failed, creating the most traumatic event in the history of modern Ireland.[2] However, the immigration that took place during the period of the Great Irish Famine was, in fact, the later stage of the influx of Irish settlers to Atlantic Canada. The sudden surge in numbers during the famine period represented the tail end of an immigrant stream, not its beginning. After 1855 the stream reduced to a trickle.[3]

Between the end of the Napoleonic Wars in 1815 and the 1840s, half a million Irish arrived in Canada (initially British North America), representing 60 percent of the total, with the Scots and English making up the rest. In other words, at that time the Irish were Canada's principal colonizers. By the late 1850s they were the largest immigrant group in both Newfoundland and New Brunswick and equalled the Scots in Prince Edward Island. Only in Nova Scotia, where they were eclipsed by the earlier Scottish takeover of much of the province, were the Irish in the minority.[4]

For nearly a century the Irish left their native country in search of the better life that Atlantic Canada offered. Few were compelled by force or famine to leave Ireland.[5] They deliberately chose to emigrate. Their chief limitation on being able to leave their homeland was their ability to pay for their relocation costs. With a rapidly growing population and an increasing subdivision of its land holdings, Ireland's agricultural

Irish cabin scene, Glenbeigh, county Kerry, circa 1865–1914.

system had become unsustainable. People were stuck with the age-old problems of unproductive land and overpopulation. Conditions were also desperate for Ulster textile workers. Because theirs was a cottage-based, labour-intensive industry, they were particularly vulnerable to the structural changes taking place in the early nineteenth century as a result of increasing mechanization. Thousands of Ulster linen weavers were thrown out of work or had to survive on pitiable rates of pay, thus creating another massive stimulus for emigration.[6]

The Irish frequently came to Canada in small, well-organized groups and were supreme networkers. Contacts with family and friends already established in North America helped them to assess where their best opportunities lay. They collected information, weighed alternatives, and headed for a particular location. Once settled, they were valued for their skills and work ethic, and they attracted other followers, often sending money back home to cover the transport costs of relatives and friends. That said, their woes as struggling immigrants have been far better chronicled than their obvious success in adapting to the testing conditions of pioneer life.

Map 1: Reference Map of Ireland When United with Great Britain (pre - 1922)

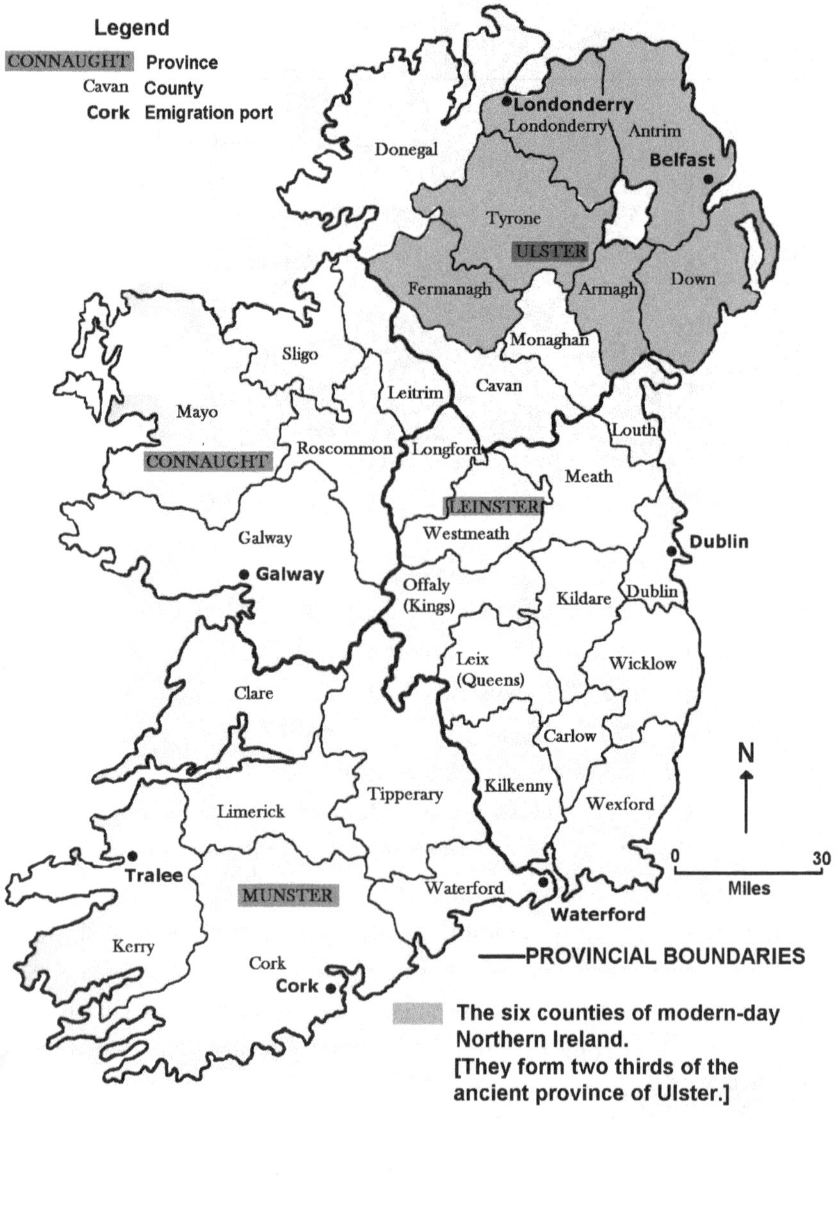

Legend

CONNAUGHT Province
Cavan County
Cork Emigration port

Londonderry
Londonderry
Antrim
Donegal
Belfast
Tyrone
ULSTER
Fermanagh
Armagh
Down
Monaghan
Sligo
Leitrim
Cavan
Mayo
Louth
Roscommon
Longford
CONNAUGHT
Meath
LEINSTER
Galway
Westmeath
Dublin
Galway
Offaly
(Kings)
Kildare
Dublin
Leix
(Queens)
Wicklow
Clare
Carlow
Kilkenny
Tipperary
Wexford
Limerick
Tralee
MUNSTER
Waterford
Waterford
Kerry
Cork
Cork

N

0   30
Miles

——PROVINCIAL BOUNDARIES

The six counties of modern-day
Northern Ireland.
[They form two thirds of the
ancient province of Ulster.]

Extended Irish families spread themselves widely across North America, with many choosing the United States. For example, having relocated from county Armagh to the Saint John River Valley region of New Brunswick in 1816, Mr. Laurence Hughes continued to receive letters from brothers in Boston, Pennsylvania, Iowa, and a brother-in-law in Minnesota, all extolling the benefits to be had from farming in their part of the United States.[7] While he resisted these siren calls, most of his brothers and sisters headed south.

Arriving in the Miramichi region from Cork at about this time, John McCarthy could compare notes with two brothers already settled in Michigan and Wisconsin.[8] Similarly, having worked for a while in the city of Saint John, probably as a labourer, Martin Dyer, from county Sligo, found employment in Rhode Island and shortly after that went to work on the York and Erie Railroad. Gerald Dougherty followed a similar pattern, working first in Prince Edward Island, moving to Boston a year later, and two years later working on a railroad in Maine.[9] People steadily worked their way up the employment ladder, which sometimes meant abandoning the Atlantic region for the better-paid jobs that the United States offered.

The Irish did not have the backing of wealthy proprietors in establishing their communities as had been the case with many Scots.[10] They had to organize their sea crossings, find a job or acquire land, if they were going into farming, and learn how to adjust to a completely new physical environment on their own. Family and friends who had been through the experience could help, and there was also a plethora of "emigrant guides" that pointed the way, this extract being typical:

> An emigrant is generally so poor on his arrival that he can seldom afford to purchase a lot of land; but after the lapse of four years, with care and industry, he is generally able to effect that object.... An emigrant, therefore, on his arrival here, will prudently engage with a farmer as a labourer for the first year, in order to acquire the means of improving land and the mode of cultivating it.[11]

Pioneer conditions were gruelling and required considerable toughness and determination. Early arrivals had to transform the huge tracts
of wilderness that awaited them into settled communities:

> For the man who has been accustomed to work in good
> clear land ... the gloomy forest presents rather a strange
> appearance when he enters upon his grounds ... the
> entire surface of the earth being covered with innu-
> merable trees ... a solitary settler builds his little shanty
> amidst the stumps, the walls of his dwelling are large
> logs piled on each other and dovetailed at the corners
> with a square hole cut through for a door and another
> for a window, the cracks are filled with moss; this fabric
> is covered with the bark of a tree secured by long poles
> and with the furniture inside all of his own making.[12]

A winter scene in York County, New Brunswick, showing a load of logs being drawn
by a team of horses.

The challenges facing the Reverend Samuel Bacon were quite different. Having been appointed in 1821 to serve as an Anglican missionary in the Miramichi region of New Brunswick, he planned his departure from Ireland carefully. His cousin advised him to take £30 to £40 "to furnish yourself with a moderate portion of those comforts, which that rigorous climate will render absolutely necessary," and to bring plenty of clothing. He should take: "2 hats, 3 suits of clothes, a good great coat, 6 pairs of new boots or shoes, 6 pairs of worsted or lamb's wool stockings, 6 pairs of cotton hose, 12 good shirts, 6 good flannel waistcoats, 12 neck cloths, 12 pocket handkerchiefs, a flannel and cotton dressing gown." He was also advised to have "a thick rough loose great coat" and an old hat to wear on the sea crossing.

This dealt with his material comforts, but to help him cope with the inevitable "attacks of ennui," he was advised that he should also take books describing the "many trees, shrubs and flowers and insects that will engage your attention."[13] His moments of leisure were all very well, but for most new arrivals, pioneer life revolved around back-breaking and never-ending physical labour.

Meanwhile, Irish Catholics continued to receive negative press, often being portrayed as ignorant and rowdy types who frequently got drunk and enjoyed having a good punch-up. Drunkenness was a widespread social problem in early Canada. Descriptions abound of early settlers who ended up in a drunkard's grave. Although the problem was not exclusive to the Irish, they seemed to fall prey to alcohol's addictive charms more than most.[14] As if to demonstrate their determination to succeed as colonizers, families from counties Cork and Kerry actually founded what they termed a "teetotal settlement" in New Brunswick. The demon drink was not going to impede their progress! However, the cheapness of rum and whiskey and the isolation and hardships of pioneer life remained a lethal combination for many Irish, bringing misery and often an early death.

By the mid-nineteenth century, Irish Catholics had a pro-Catholic newspaper, the *Saint John Weekly Freeman*, which provided a forum for challenging anti-Catholic prejudices and enhancing their reputation in the city. In 1859 the paper asked its readers why it was that the arrival of eighty immigrants from Galway had gone unreported in the other newspapers. The answer it gave was that "these mere Irish are not of that better class so longed for" — had they been Scottish, "what poems would have been sung!"[15] However, this slight probably mattered very little. As the Cork-born journalist and politician John Maguire observed when he visited Halifax in the 1860s, prosperity had arrived: "In no city of the American continent do the Irish occupy a better position or exercise a more deserved influence than in Halifax.... The Irish element is everywhere discernible in every description of business and in all branches of industry, in every class and in every condition of life, from the highest to the lowest."[16]

Each of the four Atlantic provinces has its own individual story. The fishing trade with Britain attracted the Irish to Newfoundland from the eighteenth century, while the timber trade brought the main immigrant stream to Nova Scotia, New Brunswick, and Prince Edward Island a century later.

Newfoundland's Irish were Catholics from the southeast of Ireland who first took up employment in the cod fishery as seasonal workers.[17] John Francis O'Leary's fishing contract, stating that he was to have as his wages "half the fish he catches, rations and cuffs (fingerless mittens) in the winter," was hardly very generous.[18] Despite the poor remuneration and tough working conditions, those Irish with an eye to the future could see the benefits of remaining and becoming permanent residents, with most settling in the Avalon Peninsula.

Later, Irish Catholics would seek work in New Brunswick's lumber camps and Nova Scotia's coal mines, where jobs were also onerous and badly paid. But, for the poorest of the poor, these were stepping stones to the better life that the New World could offer.

Because of the limitations of Newfoundland's agriculture and overall economy, many Irish fishery workers set their sights on moving to more advantageous locations. By simply crossing to the other side of the Gulf of St. Lawrence, they could procure much better farmland and have access to the better-paid jobs that were to be had in eastern Nova Scotia, Cape Breton, Prince Edward Island, and the Miramichi River region of New Brunswick (see Map 2). This they did, and their letters home to family and friends ensured that other groups of immigrants from the southeast of Ireland continued to arrive. As a result, these regions became settlement strongholds for Irish Catholics who had originated from counties Waterford, Kilkenny, Wexford, Carlow, and Tipperary.[19]

The next group from Ireland could not have been more different. Ulster Presbyterians, who could trace their ancestry back to the Lowlands of Scotland, had been relocating to North America since the mid-eighteenth century to escape religious discrimination in Ireland and to benefit from the New World's enticing farming opportunities. In keeping with this spirit of enterprise, the New Hampshire–born Alexander McNutt, a man of Ulster ancestry, took it upon himself to organize the relocation of between four and five hundred Ulster people to Nova Scotia in the 1760s. Having obtained a large tract of land in the Cobequid Bay region (later in Colchester County) from the Nova Scotia government, McNutt located his recruits in the Ulster counties of Donegal, Tyrone, and Londonderry. With his help they went on to establish successful farming communities in Truro, Londonderry, and Onslow Townships. However, his venture did not attract as many followers as had been anticipated. The settlements were in the wrong locations for what was to follow. The region's timber trade, which was firmly established by 1815, became focused on Saint John, New Brunswick. It was the principal port from which ships, loaded with timber cargoes, left for Great Britain and Ireland, and was the primary destination to which immigrants from Great Britain and Ireland sailed. Reaching Cobequid Bay in Nova Scotia required a substantial onward voyage by steamer, making this location far less desirable.

Although their earliest major settlements were in Nova Scotia, it was New Brunswick that would eventually attract the majority of the Irish. With its semi-feudal land system, Prince Edward Island was less appealing. While settlers could acquire leaseholds from landlords, they could not easily purchase land, prompting many Irish to bypass it all together or to eventually leave.[20] As a result, the island became a well-trodden staging post for people seeking onward settlement in other parts of the Maritimes. But that situation changed in the 1830s when a Catholic priest organized the departures of more than two thousand Irish people originating from county Monaghan who were then residing in Glasgow.

The explosive growth in the Maritime region's timber trade had made sea travel affordable for the masses.[21] The ports of Londonderry and Cork began trading regularly with New Brunswick, offering space in their vessels to immigrants as they set off to cross the Atlantic to collect timber cargoes. The timber trade became the driving force behind local

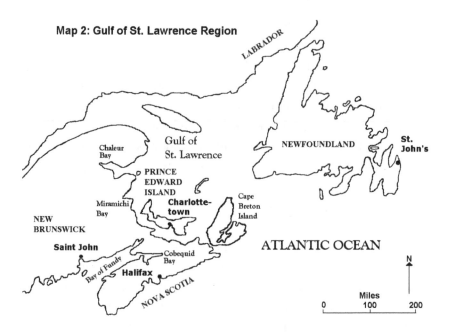

Map 2: Gulf of St. Lawrence Region

economies, and for the poor it provided the means to earn money to purchase land, although in New Brunswick there were plenty of lumbermen
who never became farmers. Despite being regularly plunged into boom
and bust, according to fluctuations of business cycles in Britain, the timber trade offered diverse employment opportunities and was often a vital
component of an immigrant's livelihood.[22]

The earliest Irish arrivals to Nova Scotia had come mainly from the
ancient province of Ulster, consisting of counties Antrim, Armagh,
Down, Fermanagh, Londonderry, and Tyrone, in what is now called
Northern Ireland (in the U.K.), and from the counties of Cavan, Donegal,
and Monaghan, now in the Republic of Ireland (see Map 1).[23] However,
the main Irish influx to the Atlantic region began with the end of the
Napoleonic Wars in 1815, when the British Isles were plunged into a deep
economic and agricultural depression, drawing people from across Ireland.
Agricultural workers, farmers, tradesmen, craftsmen, miners, fishermen,
general labourers, and others came with differing prospects. Although
those who emigrated were not just the poor, they were the ones who had

St. Patrick's Day Parade, Halifax, 1919. Attracting a very large crowd, the parade was led by "three beautiful white horses which wore green saddles as well as [green] ribbon streamers" (*Halifax Herald, March 18*).

most to gain initially. Irrespective of the type of employment they sought, the shortage of labour in the Atlantic region worked to their advantage, since they could command much higher wages than was possible in Ireland. Forest clearance and farming in New Brunswick brought great numbers of Irish to its river valleys.

The timber trade provided the impetus to the province's economic development and greatly influenced settlement choices. Irish Protestants predominated in the Saint John River Valley in the southwest, while Irish Catholics came in considerable numbers to the Miramichi River in the northeast part of the province. And later on, as the focus of the timber trade moved slowly northward and eastward, it drew Irish Protestants and Catholics to the Chaleur Bay and Richibucto regions, where they established agricultural and fishing communities.[24]

Irish immigration began primarily as a Protestant movement, but as the nineteenth century wore on, it became increasingly Catholic, with large numbers settling in the cities of Saint John and Halifax, where they constituted the largest part of the urban work force.[25] In New Brunswick,

Saint John's Irish Catholics primarily originated from counties in Ulster and county Cork, while many of Halifax's Irish Catholics came from the southeastern counties of Waterford, Tipperary, Kilkenny, Carlow, and Wexford.[26] The fishing and timber trades created these two different settlement patterns. The Newfoundland Irish had used Halifax as a safe haven once they completed their employment contracts at the fishery. This gave Halifax its intake from the southeast of Ireland. Meanwhile, Saint John acquired most of its Irish via Londonderry and Cork, the two main ports in Ireland from which ships left regularly to collect timber cargoes. Later on, in the 1830s and 1840s, ports in the south and west of Ireland provided an ever larger proportion of the outflow.

In spite of having reasonable quantities of good fertile land, New Brunswick's agricultural development was slow and fraught with difficulties. The province oscillated between offering free land grants and insisting on land sales, as it searched for the best compromise between attracting colonizers, discouraging speculators, and fostering good relations with various mercantile interests and the elite families who essentially governed the province. Settlements eventually materialized from a chaotic mishmash of part land grants and part land sales and from settlers

View of the port of Londonderry from an original sketch by John Nixon, circa 1790.

circumventing the law by seizing possession of their lands through squatting.[27] In the end the Irish did succeed, not necessarily due to any practical skills that they brought with them, but because of their toughness, immense courage, and ability to cope with harsh conditions.

Religion often brought comfort to immigrants struggling to cope with a new and challenging environment. However, Irish settlers in Atlantic Canada were not as well served by their religious leaders as were the Scots and English. Presbyterian Scots were supported by the Glasgow Colonial Society, a body that was dedicated to building and supporting Church of Scotland congregations across Canada,[28] while Church of England worshippers were well served by Anglican missionaries sent by the London-based Society for the Propagation of the Gospel, a body that spent considerable funds overseas.[29] Irish Protestants had no equivalent support system.[30] Church of Ireland worshippers had to join the Anglican Church, where they would have been seen as outsiders.[31] Meanwhile, Irish Catholics were served by a few priests, scattered across considerable distances, with their churches and religious services having to be funded entirely by local communities. Churches were erected only where and when populations could provide for a priest.[32]

Sometimes the Anglican missionaries were Irish, as was the case with the Cork-born John McGivern, who, in 1849, was appointed by the Society for the Propagation of the Gospel to serve the parish of St. George in Charlotte County, New Brunswick. He remained in the post until his death in 1866.[33] However, the missionaries were mainly English, as was the case with Samuel Bacon who was based in the Miramichi region. His congregation consisted of English and Irish "labourers and mechanics, connected with the mills and shipyards" of the timber trade, many being "migratory."[34] The Reverend Bacon complained that the Irish members of his congregation wanted to adopt the more free-and-easy ways of the Methodists and other nonconformist sects, which were growing in popularity. The instructions for choosing Reverend Bacon's replacement following his death (which he may have written) stipulated that only staunch Anglicans should be allowed to vote.[35] However, the Reverend Bacon was out of touch with what ordinary people wanted.

Despite being the official religion in Atlantic Canada, the Church of England attracted relatively few followers. Anglican clergymen were regarded as remote figures who adhered to rigid hierarchical structures and seemed not to appreciate the hunger of their congregations for kind words and a smile. Methodist and Baptist preachers fared much better. Trudging huge distances speaking of God's love and salvation, they had far greater appeal.[36] Donegal-born Reverend Matthew Richey, based in Parrsboro (Kings County), Nova Scotia in the early 1820s as a Methodist preacher, embraced "the wilderness and solitary place" where he came to live, travelling many miles to tend to his flock.[37] There were many more like him.

In many ways, Catholic priests were more supportive in that they occasionally offered practical help to their parishioners. For example, concerned about the squalid conditions being endured by some Irish families, John Sweeney, the Roman Catholic Bishop of Saint John, organized a major colonization scheme on their behalf. With his help, fifty families moved from Saint John to Carleton County on the west side of the province, where they established the thriving farming community of Johnville, named after the bishop. When John Maguire visited the settlement with Bishop Sweeney in 1862, he found comfortable dwellings, spacious barns, and cleared fields. The ordinary man no longer "had to accept that poverty shall be his doom — that he shall die in the condition in which he was brought into the world and that he shall transmit hard toil and scanty remuneration as a legacy to his children."[38]

It was much the same in the Monaghan settlement just south of Fort Augustus in Prince Edward Island, which Maguire also visited. Its Irish settlers, who originated from county Monaghan in Ulster, had been living in great penury in Glasgow. They were assisted by their priest, Father John MacDonald, who owned the land on which they settled. He helped them to raise the necessary funds for their relocation, travelled with them to the island, and helped them to find their bearings. Arriving in the 1830s and 1840s, they were highly successful. Twenty years later Maguire met the settlers who "had long since passed the log-cabin stage and were occupying substantial and commodious frame houses." All around him during a circuit of sixty miles, there was "an air of neatness and comfort."[39]

Given the tensions that existed between Irish Catholics and Protestants, it is hardly surprising that religion would occasionally become a source of provocation. The Reverend David Fitzgerald, from county Kerry, who served as the Anglican rector of St. Paul's Church in Charlottetown for thirty-eight years, used the pulpit to rail against what he called the "corruptions" and "heathen" nature of the Roman Catholic faith.[40] He was a lifelong member of the Orange Order, holding the office of chaplain to the Charlottetown lodge for many years. With its anti-Catholic jibes and oaths, the Orange Order was always going to provoke tensions. The Orangemen's parades, which commemorate the victory of the Protestant King William over the Catholic King James at the Battle of the Boyne in 1690, incited riots from time to time, particularly in New Brunswick. However, when the Orange Order expanded beyond its Irish origins in Canada, to eventually embrace all Protestants, it transformed itself into a British men's social club, whose principal role was to extol British values and provide mutual support to its members.

From the 1830s on, as it acquired its internal routes and became more accessible to immigrants, Upper Canada became a prime destination of the Irish. Not being able to compete with Upper Canada's much better land and job prospects, Atlantic Canada increasingly lost many of its already-established Irish settlers to it. And yet, when the Great Irish Famine struck, New Brunswick suddenly became a prime destination, with seventeen thousand Irish arriving at Saint John in 1847.[41] Despite occurring at the end of this mass movement of people, the high death toll associated with the famine period dominates modern thinking. The brutal oppression of the Irish by the English in the distant past is brought to mind by people wishing to see a sinister role for the British government in this event.[42] Some commentators even suggest that it willfully caused the famine tragedy to happen.[43]

Despite having a happy ending, the Irish to Atlantic Canada story is overshadowed by demons and myths that concentrate on wicked plots and forced expulsions. While most Irish eagerly grasped the escape route from extreme poverty that emigration offered, they are portrayed as reluctant victims of landlord cruelty. The inescapable conclusion of this study is that most emigration was voluntary and self-financed. The Irish did not leap into the dark, but instead chose particular locations on the strength of a careful deliberation of their economic prospects. Nor did they sail in coffin ships, as is frequently alleged. Shipping data reveals that they generally sailed in good ships. There was a high death toll at sea, but this was due to disease and not generally to failings in the quality of the shipping service.

Irish Catholics may have had to struggle with Protestant intolerance and organized bigotry, but this did not dent their ardour in exploiting Atlantic Canada's abundant fishing, farming, mining, and forestry opportunities. Pressures at home had not forced them into exile as is commonly claimed. Whether Catholic or Protestant, the Irish made a conscious choice to leave.

The Irish had a major impact on Atlantic Canada's development. They dominated the major cities and towns, established farming and fishing communities across all four provinces, and helped to shape the region's economic, social, and cultural development. Their story follows.

CHAPTER 2

❦

Early Irish Settlers

This morning I got up early and took a long walk on the rising grounds over this village, placed at the top of the Basin of Minas.... On my right lay the townships of Onslow and Londonderry, which appeared as if one continued village, laying for 10 or 12 miles around the Bay, and in a circular amphitheatre; on my left, again, a similar view of Truro township, stretching to the mouth of the Shubenacadie river, the whole forming a gay lively picture.[1]

When Lord Dalhousie, the lieutenant governor of Nova Scotia, visited the Cobequid Bay region in 1817, he observed a sprawling settlement that had been founded some fifty-six years earlier by Irish people. The original settlers had come either from the province of Ulster[2] in Ireland or from the southern colonies of North America.

On their tour of Nova Scotia in 1774, John Robinson and Thomas Rispin, two Yorkshire farmers, remarked that the rural townships were "chiefly inhabited by Irish ... [who] were the best farmers [they had] seen in this country."[3] Those who came from the southern colonies had fathers or grandfathers who had originated from Ulster. Throughout the previous century, Ulster had lost a great many of its people to Pennsylvania and the other American colonies. Between 1718 and 1775 — the year that the American War of Independence began — a quarter of a million Ulster people emigrated to the North American colonies.[4] Religious grievances dating back to yet another century had helped to propel this great exodus.

These were the descendents of the many Lowland Scots who had been moved into Ulster in the seventeenth century.[5] Their ancestors had settled on land that had been confiscated from Irish Catholics, this being a manoeuvre carried out by the English Crown to strengthen its interests in Ireland. However, because of their Presbyterian faith, the Ulster arrivals were treated with disdain by the Irish Episcopal establishment. They were regarded as dissidents and, as a result, denied civil and military office.[6] Far from being the chosen ones, they suffered discrimination. Harassed by prejudice and facing poor and uncertain economic prospects, they could see obvious advantages in moving to North America. As glowing reports filtered back of the better life to be had abroad, Ulster people left in droves.

Meanwhile, Britain had been consolidating its hold over Acadia (peninsular Nova Scotia) after acquiring it from France in 1713. Facing ongoing hostilities, it was concerned that Acadia might side with France in any future conflicts. So it took steps to augment its population with politically reliable British and foreign Protestants. After establishing Halifax as the capital of the province, the government sanctioned public funds to finance the relocation costs of more than 2,500 British people, who arrived in 1749. The Halifax immigrants, recruited in London, included ex-soldiers and sailors, some of whom were of Irish descent, and tradesmen who worked in a wide range of occupations.[7] They were brought out by Governor Edward Cornwallis in 1749 to build the new capital, but the extremely tough conditions forced many to leave.[8] However, around 1,500 of the hardiest remained and founded the town, as was intended. They were soon joined by large numbers of merchants and other settlers from New England who had correctly anticipated Halifax's potential as a future economic hub. Shortly after establishing Halifax's population in 1749, the British government brought around 2,700 so-called Foreign

Protestants — chiefly Germans, Swiss, and French Huguenots — to the province. They, too, received free passage, land, and a year's subsistence.[9]

By 1755, Britain's continuing hostilities with France were causing it to revise its military strategy in Nova Scotia. Acadians were now regarded as potential accomplices of the French. The British solution was immediate and brutal.[10] It took the unprecedented step of actually expelling thirteen thousand Acadians in two separate deportations that were carried out in 1755 and 1758. The Acadian expulsions certainly undermined French power and fighting ability in the region, but the policy was exceedingly inhumane for the people who were displaced. And to assist the process of colonization even further, the hunting and fishing territories of the Native Peoples were also seized.[11]

Having deported the Acadian population, New Englanders were then brought in to take their place.[12] Providing a generously funded relocation scheme, the government recruited eight thousand New Englanders, known as Planters,[13] who mainly originated from Massachusetts, Connecticut, and Rhode Island. Arriving between 1759 and 1762, they came in large family groups and sometimes as entire communities, with farmers settling mainly on the former Acadian lands in the Annapolis Valley and fishermen along the southwestern coastline.[14] Included in their number, whose communities would take shape along Cobequid Bay, were some New Hampshire and Massachusetts people, all of Ulster ancestry (see Map 3).

The Cobequid Bay settlers had been recruited by Alexander McNutt, a man of Ulster ancestry who had come from New Hampshire.[15] He, like many other enterprising Americans, spotted the rewards that could be made from assisting the Nova Scotia government in finding people to settle its vast acreages. Having served at Fort Cumberland (near Sackville, New Brunswick) as a Massachusetts provincial captain, he was familiar with the rich marshlands to be found in the Cobequid Bay region. His proposal to recruit settlers was accepted by the government, which promised to give him one hundred acres of land for every five hundred that were granted to his colonizers.[16] Beginning with modest ambitions, he developed a grandiose plan to relocate thousands of Ulster people to Nova Scotia, but this plan was never realized. All the same, he and his recruits had a profound impact on the early settlement of the province.

McNutt adopted a two-pronged approach.[17] In the spring of 1761 he organized the relocation of fifty New Hampshire and Massachusetts families of Ulster extraction to Onslow and Truro Townships.[18] The highly fertile land was incentive enough for them to move, despite the government's rejection of the settlers' request for funds to pay relocation costs.[19] Already familiar with North American farming conditions and techniques, the settlers adapted quickly to their new surroundings. Stage two was the recruitment of Ulster people directly from Ireland. A shared ancestral link would bind both groups together during the early phases of colonization. An added bonus was the availability of vacant Acadian farms. The first arrivals at Truro Township were greeted by 1,036 acres of "dyked marsh," 390 acres of "cultivated upland," and 200 acres of "cleared intervale. Several orchards were also in full vigour, and some of them still produce fruit." Not only were there no vast forests to clear; the drudgery of preparing land for cultivation had already been done.[20]

To find his recruits, McNutt undertook a vigorous advertising campaign in Ireland, centred on the port of Londonderry. Before chartering the necessary ships to take people to Nova Scotia, he went to London to secure official backing. The British government was in a quandary. It needed loyal immigrants for its North American colonies, but it feared that immigration would seriously deplete its workforce and armed services. Yet, despite these concerns, it succumbed to McNutt's persuasive powers. Because he offered to fund the transport costs of his settlers, the British government was not committing itself to any immediate expense, although the Nova Scotia government would have to fund their initial settling-in costs.

McNutt travelled to Londonderry in Ireland that same year to take charge of arrangements. He launched his campaign with an advertisement in the *Belfast Newsletter*, inviting "industrious farmers and useful mechanics" to move to Nova Scotia, offering two hundred acres to the head of each family and fifty to each member.[21] He also offered fifty acres to indentured servants upon completion of their work contracts and increased that offer later to two hundred acres.[22] The response was greater than anticipated in that he had to charter two ships rather than one. The *Jupiter* sailed first in early July 1761, followed by the *Hopewell*, which sailed in mid-August. In total, the two ships transported between two hundred and four hundred people.[23]

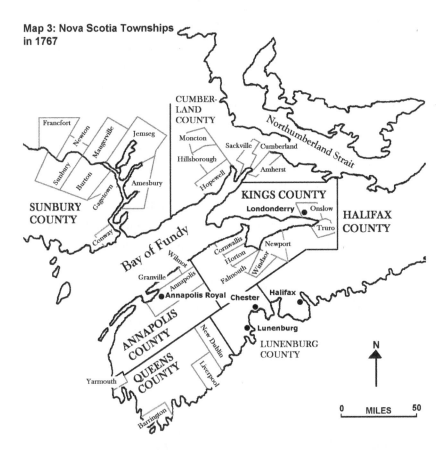

Map 3: Nova Scotia Townships in 1767

Unlike the fairly well-heeled New Hampshire farmers who came in the first group, these settlers were of limited means. Over the winter the Ulster immigrants worked in Halifax, relying on financial support from the Nova Scotia council. The following spring, the council procured a vessel to take them to Cobequid Bay and also offered the settlers provisions, seed corn, and building materials. Most would settle in Londonderry Township.[24]

At this point McNutt suddenly introduced his bold plan to ship between seven and eight thousand Ulster people to Nova Scotia. Alarm bells rang. The British government, already uneasy about the loss of Irish people to the colonies, decided enough was enough. However desirable the settlement of Nova Scotia might be, it decreed that "the migration from Ireland of such great numbers of his majesty's subjects must be attended with dangerous consequence to that kingdom." The governor of Nova Scotia could not grant land to people from Ireland, "except to those who have lived there [Nova Scotia] or in another Colony for five years."[25] McNutt ignored the ruling and in 1762 signed up another 170 Ulster settlers.[26] His use of a highly favourable letter written by the previous year's recruits that claimed that "the soil of this country [Nova Scotia] is much richer and bears everything larger and in greater abundance than in Pennsylvania" no doubt swayed many.[27]

Meeting resistance from Lieutenant Governor Belcher when the group reached Halifax, McNutt threatened to take his colonists to Philadelphia. Belcher relented. Provisions were supplied and the settlers were taken to New Dublin, west of Lunenburg, but by 1770 most had moved on[28] (see Map 3). However, McNutt could not keep up the pretense that he had access to land any longer, although his business partners in Londonderry sent out three ships — the *Hopewell*, *Falls*, and *Admiral Hawke* — in 1768, which took settlers to Nova Scotia.[29]

All the while, McNutt seemed remarkably disinterested in the well-being of his Nova Scotia recruits. He appears never to have visited their communities, preferring to spend time during the 1760s with his brother Benjamin on McNutt Island (Shelburne County) at the southern end of the peninsula and later tending to his timber trade activities in the town of Truro.[30] Had McNutt gone to Onslow Township, he would have realized that his recruits were suffering severe privations. When Charles Morris, the provincial surveyor, visited Cobequid Bay in 1763 he discovered that the fifty Onslow families were struggling to stay alive.[31] "If they are not relieved this winter there will be real danger of their starving or quitting the colony." They had a relatively small proportion of stock and very few people had "any substance [resources] among them."[32] The news was far better for the sixty families in Truro Township and the fifteen families in Londonderry whom Morris described as doing extremely well.[33] Seven years later there were still large concentrations of Irish settlers in Londonderry and Truro Townships but only a tiny number in Onslow.[34] However, by 1829, when Thomas Haliburton visited Cobequid, Truro, Onslow, and Londonderry Townships, each had around 1,400 residents who were clearly prospering.[35]

In all, McNutt appears to have persuaded between four hundred and five hundred people to emigrate from Ireland to Nova Scotia, most from the counties of Donegal, Tyrone, and Londonderry.[36] Even so, the American colonies continued to attract far more Ulster immigrants than did Nova Scotia.[37] Quite simply, the pull of joining long-established extended families in Pennsylvania and the other southern colonies would have outweighed any incentives that the newly opened Cobequid Bay region could offer.[38] McNutt's settlements were not greatly enlarged by later emigration from Ireland since Nova Scotia was largely bypassed during the large exodus of the 1820s and 1830s. By this time shipping services between Ireland and the Maritimes were being propelled by the timber trade, which was mainly centred at Saint John, New Brunswick.

Thomas Desbrisay was another colourful character who, being Irish-born, sought Irish immigrants to settle on his land in the Island of St. John, later renamed Prince Edward Island. Having been appointed the island's lieutenant governor in 1769 and purchasing large tracts of land near Charlottetown (in lots 31 and 33) he was well placed to begin his search for settlers.[39] Much of the island's land had been sold to wealthy proprietors two years earlier in a lottery, with Desbrisay having purchased his land from one of the grantees.[40] But he was different from most of the other proprietors who simply sat back and waited for their land to increase in value despite the settlement obligations that were attached to their grants. Desbrisay made strenuous efforts to attract settlers from the north of Ireland.[41] His stumbling block was that, unlike Alexander McNutt, who offered land purchases, he sought to make his profits from the rents paid by tenants.[42]

Desbrisay's advertisements in the *Belfast Newsletter* in 1771 stressed the fertility of the land and the island's plentiful natural resources: "A man at his leisure hours may supply his family by his gun and fishing."[43] Yet the most important selling point was his offer to fund sea crossings. Despite this incentive, Desbrisay only attracted nine families, who sailed in the *Hopewell* from Londonderry in August of that year.[44] Said to be mostly Presbyterians of "remarkably decent and orderly appearance," they were mainly farmers and tradesmen who settled on Lot 33.[45] This disappointing beginning can be attributed to a lack of interest in

Late-eighteenth-century portrait of Irish-born Walter Patterson, who became Prince Edward Island's first governor in 1769. Patterson's corrupt and incompetent handling of land transactions following the 1767 lottery made him a controversial figure, and after seventeen years as governor he was forced to leave office.

leaseholds, an obstacle that Desbrisay was able to overcome the following year after glowing accounts of life on the island appeared in the *Belfast Newsletter*.[46] His agents went to work seeking recruits from the estates of the earls of Hertford and Hillsborough in the north of Ireland, while Desbrisay organized an extensive newspaper campaign.

He signed up 188 Ulster people on this, his second attempt, with most originating from counties Antrim, Down, and Armagh.[47] As was the case with the 1771 group, the heads of households were mainly farmers and tradesmen, the latter including many linen weavers.[48] No longer was a free passage on offer, although the fares at the time, set at one guinea (£1.1s.), were remarkably low.[49] The group sailed in May 1772 from Belfast and Newry in the *John and James*, enduring a lengthy voyage of ten and a half weeks, which exhausted the provisions store on what was an overcrowded ship. One passenger claimed later that when the vessel reached Charlottetown, no provisions were to be found anywhere, and, despite their pleas to the captain to be taken to Nova Scotia, "they were left there [Charlottetown] to starve"[50] Soon after arriving, another passenger wrote a scathing account of life on the island:

As for this place, it is not fit for any Christian to live in; as there are six months of a severe winter in it of frost and snow, we cannot put anything into the ground before the middle of May soonest; and mice there are as large as your rats, without any tails, destroying everything as soon as it comes to perfection. The land is very good if it was not for the long winter. I hope if God spares us days that we will go for Philadelphia or some other place about one year from this time.[51]

To add to his problems, Desbrisay was then ordered to stop recruiting tenants from Ireland by Lord Hillsborough, the colonial secretary on whose estates he had been most active. On being told to confine his recruitment to foreign Protestants and Americans, he came up against the same restrictions that had beset Alexander McNutt.[52] Like him, he only attracted a tiny fraction of the immigrant stream from Ulster, which continued to flow to the southern colonies. He brought a total of around 250 Ulster people to the island and all the while engaged in questionable land dealings.[53] At one stage he sold land in Lot 31 to ten Ulstermen, who would discover when they arrived on the island in 1774 that he had mortgaged the land and therefore could not convey title to them.[54] Nevertheless, despite his roguish and sometimes illegal behaviour, Desbrisay can be credited with having recruited Prince Edward Island's earliest Irish settlers, many of whom left surnames behind that still survive in modern times.[55]

Despite the growing belief in government circles that immigration from Britain should be discouraged, if not stopped all together, the influx continued to increase. Between 1772 and 1775 some nine hundred or so mainly Yorkshire people settled in Nova Scotia and what would become the separate province of New Brunswick. Having been enticed to the Chignecto isthmus by no less a figure than Lieutenant Governor Michael Francklin, they joined the New Englanders who had already established themselves at Amherst, Cumberland, and Sackville.[56] Meanwhile, several hundred people from the Highlands and Islands of Scotland headed for Prince Edward Island, Pictou, and other places on the east side of Nova Scotia and Cape Breton at this time, having been assisted by various proprietors and a land company.[57] Nevertheless, the settled population consisting mainly of New Englanders, Scots, English, Irish, Acadians, and Germans was woefully small. Oddly enough, the outcome of the American War of Independence, which began in 1775 and ended in 1783, worked to the region's advantage. Having lost the war, the British government relocated large numbers of Loyalists from the United States to Atlantic Canada, thus beginning a new chapter in Atlantic Canada's economic development.

Following Britain's defeat in the American Revolutionary War, officially recognized by the Treaty of Paris in 1783, around forty thousand people who had taken the British side (known collectively as Loyalists) fled from what became the independent country of the United States and sought sanctuary in the British-held northern colonies. The Loyalist influx had an explosive impact on the Atlantic region's population. Receiving land grants and financial help under the British Loyalist Assistance program, about thirty-five thousand refugees moved to Nova Scotia, while another five thousand went to the old province of Quebec.[58] When New Brunswick was divided from the peninsula as a separate colony in 1784, around fifteen thousand Loyalists would find themselves in it and nineteen thousand would be in Nova Scotia. Taken together, Loyalists doubled the population of peninsular Nova Scotia and swelled the population count north of the militarily important Bay of Fundy nearly fivefold.[59]

Men who had seen action in earlier military campaigns, once resettled, could provide some form of backup should the need arise. But the policy of moving large numbers of loyal settlers into areas judged by the government to have military importance had its drawbacks. A soldier's training and experience did not necessarily prepare him and his family for the rigours of pioneer farming. Having to farm land chosen for its military value, not its soil quality, also had its perils. Inferior land created dissatisfaction and discouraged settlers from staying, although some Loyalists clearly found good land and prospered. However, most Loyalists had to contend with poorly administered land grant procedures and some cold-shouldering from local people who felt resentful over their provisioning and other advantages. Greatly disillusioned, many simply gave up. By the late 1780s, many thousands would be returning to the United States.[60]

Around half of the thirty-five thousand Loyalists who came to the Maritime region were civilian refugees. The other half were disbanded British soldiers and provincial soldiers[61] who had served in regiments raised in North America, including: the Volunteers of Ireland (105th Regiment), Loyal Nova Scotia Volunteers, the British Legion Regiment, the King's Orange Rangers,[62] the Nova Scotia Regiment, New Jersey Volunteers, King's American Regiment, Queen's Rangers, Loyal American Regiment, and the Prince of Wales Volunteers.[63] Because many of its recruits were Irish immigrants living at the time in North America, the involvement of the Volunteers of Ireland Regiment must have increased the Irish population in the Maritime region once the war was over. Moreover, since the Volunteers of Ireland Regiment had previously been merged with the Roman Catholic Volunteers Regiment, formed in Pennsylvania, the disbanded soldiers from the combined regiments would have raised the Catholic element of the population as well.

Men from the provincial corps were known as the "Provincials" to distinguish them from civilian refugees, although the difference was not always clear since many civilians had also served during the war in regiments.[64] Most civilians went to Nova Scotia while the Provincials were mainly sent to New Brunswick. In addition to being provided with free land, Loyalists could also claim provisions and other help from the government. Former soldiers were granted land according to their rank, with the usual amount ranging from as many as one thousand acres for officers to one hundred acres for privates. Civilians normally received one hundred acres for each head of family and fifty additional acres for every person belonging to the family.

Loyalists were widely dispersed in the southwestern peninsula of Nova Scotia,[65] but in New Brunswick they were mainly concentrated along the Saint John River Valley and its tributaries (see Map 4).[66] By 1785, Halifax had acquired about 1,200 Loyalists. Another 2,000 were settled in the Annapolis Valley and another 1,000 were scattered about the fertile Minas Basin. Around 1,300 went to Digby while Shelburne (formerly Port Roseway) suddenly gained 10,000 Loyalists, making it the fourth-largest town in North America, after Philadelphia, New York, and Boston. There were further Loyalist population clusters near the earlier

Plaque marking the Loyalist (Provincials) Burial Ground at St. Anne's (later Fredericton), New Brunswick. Ex-servicemen and their families spent their first winter in 1783 at this, the site of an early Acadian settlement. The extreme cold, miserable living conditions, and inadequate food contributed to many deaths.

Map 4: Locations of Loyalists in the Maritimes, 1785

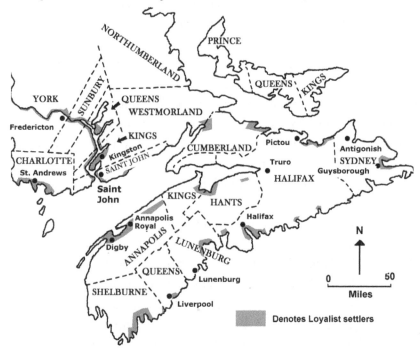

Ulster Irish settlements, founded at Truro Township in Hants County, and on the east side of the province, especially at Pictou,[67] Merigomish, and Guysborough (formerly New Manchester). The largest reported Irish intake occurred in the Antigonish area when disbanded soldiers from the Nova Scotia Volunteers[68] acquired their land grants. Many were Roman Catholic Irishmen who had enlisted at New York.[69] Timothy Hierlihy, their former commander, led around eighty-six officers and men from this unit to Antigonish Harbour, where they established a settlement at Town Point, later renamed Dorchester. The ex-soldiers gradually moved upriver to the present site of Antigonish.[70] With their surviving Irish surnames[71] and a local priest's observations in 1787 that large Roman Catholic congregations were likely to be formed, men from the Nova Scotia Volunteers Regiment clearly made a significant contribution to the Catholic population.[72]

While mainland Nova Scotia and New Brunswick received most of the Loyalists, Prince Edward Island and Cape Breton acquired relatively few. Only about four hundred moved to Cape Breton, created as a separate colony in 1785, with many settling in Sydney.[73] Anxious to protect its coal-mining interests there, the British government was reluctant to see it colonized and made Cape Breton as inaccessible as possible to settlers by restricting freehold grants to Loyalists and fish merchants. About five hundred Loyalists obtained land in Prince Edward Island, but many left because of its chaotic land ownership regime, which caused considerable confusion over land titles and encouraged tenancies rather than freeholds.[74] Whatever their final number, Loyalists mainly took up residence in the isthmus between Malpeque Bay and Bedeque in Prince County (Lots 16, 17, 19, 25, and 26).[75] Smaller groups were to be found in Queens County at Lots 32, 35, and 65, in the middle of the Island, and at Lots 49 and 50 along the upper reaches of Orwell Bay.[76]

The high-profile actions of the government and various proprietors greatly increased the number of settlers from the British Isles in the Maritime provinces; but another much less obtrusive influx was also taking place. It was being driven by long-standing trading links between southern Ireland and Newfoundland. From the eighteenth century, Irish workers, living in counties Wexford, Kilkenny, Waterford, Tipperary, and Cork,

Plaque in Waterford recording the place where Irish workers set sail for Newfoundland. Trade between Waterford and Newfoundland contributed greatly to the city's economy during the eighteenth century. By the beginning of the following century Newfoundland came to be known as "merely Waterford parted by the sea."

were being recruited year after year to work during the summer in the Newfoundland fisheries. This brought a steady flow of itinerant Irish workers across the Atlantic, some of whom settled permanently. Beginning around 1670, and particularly between 1750 and 1830, Newfoundland received large numbers of Irish immigrants.

The slow accumulation of former fishery workers gave Newfoundland's population a significant boost. And once these Irish settlers discovered the far greater land and employment opportunities to be had in nearby Nova Scotia, Cape Breton, Prince Edward Island, and New Brunswick, they crossed the Gulf of St. Lawrence in search of more advantageous locations. Their preferred destinations initially were Halifax, Saint John, New Brunswick, St. John's, Newfoundland, and the fishing bays of Cape Breton and Prince Edward Island.

CHAPTER 3

The Newfoundland Irish

St. John's was first and foremost a fishery and not an official colony and permanent settlement on the island [Newfoundland] was not encouraged until the eighteenth century.[1]

By the late eighteenth century about five thousand Irish people were migrating to Newfoundland each spring, and growing numbers were settling permanently.[2] The majority headed for the town of St. John's and other parts of the Avalon Peninsula.[3] The Irish had long responded to the employment opportunities that were on offer at the Newfoundland fishery, with their ability to fill such jobs made possible by the fact that English vessels called at Waterford on their outward journey to purchase provisions. This provided an opportunity for people from southeast Ireland to take up jobs during the summer months in what was essentially an English fishery. In fact, the fishery's labour and provisions were supplied entirely from England and Ireland, lining the pockets of the English merchants and providing jobs for West Country and Irish seasonal workers.[4] Thus, "fortified by religion at home and rum in Newfoundland, generations of men sailed off to the fishery. To the poor it provided a living and for the lucky, a chance to rise; the spirited country boy found a chance of adventure and the ne'er-do-well found a refuge."[5]

This trading link brought a steady flow of Irish workers to Newfoundland throughout the eighteenth and nineteenth centuries, most originating from the counties of Wexford, Waterford, Kilkenny, and Tipperary.[6] The English merchants needed "winter men" to remain in Newfoundland when the thousands of workers who had fished during the summer returned to Britain, and they generally selected Irish workers for such jobs. It was then a small step for the workers to remain on the island permanently. However, unlike the great surge in Irish immigration that occurred between 1800 and 1820, this was a gradual influx. A family would often clear land, build a house, and run a fishing station, then possibly move to a good farming location somewhere else in Atlantic Canada, leasing their property to a new arrival who might decide to remain. A combination of temporary and permanent settlements, together with the natural increase in the already-established population, caused many of the best fishing harbours along the eastern and southern shores of the Avalon Peninsula gradually to acquire small Irish and English populations.[7]

The Newfoundland Company, founded by English businessmen in 1610, had sought to promote the colonization of the island, although its very existence was opposed by the merchants who wanted to exploit the island solely as a fishing base. With settlers would come government and unwelcome regulations that might interfere with the smooth running of a venture that was designed solely as a wealth creator for England.[8] John Guy, the first governor of the colony, led forty Bristol settlers to Cupids Cove on the southwest end of Conception Bay that same year, and eleven years later Sir George Calvert (Lord Baltimore) brought settlers to Ferryland on the Avalon Peninsula, south of St. John's. In 1623, Lucius Bentinck Cary (Lord Falkland) is believed to have founded an Irish colony in the same area, while Ferryland was also the destination of Sir David Kirke's one hundred colonists who came in 1639.[9]

But encountering enormous difficulties, the settlers floundered and required ongoing financial support from the company just to survive.[10] Nevertheless, settlements did become firmly established soon afterward. This happened because seasonally employed fishery workers chose to remain on the island, not because of any colonization schemes.[11] Those who stayed added significantly to the Irish and English population, while the trading links of the merchants who employed them influenced where they settled.

Anglican clergymen often stressed the severe challenges that came with living in Newfoundland. People did not normally seek a better life there, but chanced upon the place for work-related reasons. According to Anglican Bishop Edward Feild, it was more a case of asking what its people could do for it rather than the other way around:

> I am still more in want of men than of friends and if you know any good man who would rather be useful in his generation than comfortable and be a blessing to others, rather than be himself preferred, let him come to Newfoundland.[12]

Although workers were meant to return home, some decided to remain in Newfoundland, and in doing so increased the permanent population of the island, much to the annoyance of the colonial authorities. Permanent residency was officially discouraged, if not banned altogether, but the enforcement of this regulation was highly selective. While the authorities pretended not to notice the English Protestants from the West Country who were taking up residency, they were vehemently opposed to having Irish Catholics as permanent residents. Nevertheless, many Irish and English workers refused to comply with imperialistic wishes and became Newfoundlanders.[13]

Confining themselves mainly to the eastern shore of the Avalon Peninsula initially, English and Irish residents settled separately from the already-established French inhabitants who occupied the southern shore.[14] But following Britain's victories over France in wars fought during the late 1690s and early 1700s, French settlers were required to leave their Newfoundland homes on the south shore.[15] Under the Treaty of Utrecht (1713), which resolved a number of European conflicts, France was forced to relinquish all sovereign rights in Newfoundland in return for maintaining its fishing rights on the south shore.[16] Irish fishermen soon

Map 5: Irish Concentrations in the Avalon Peninsula, 1857

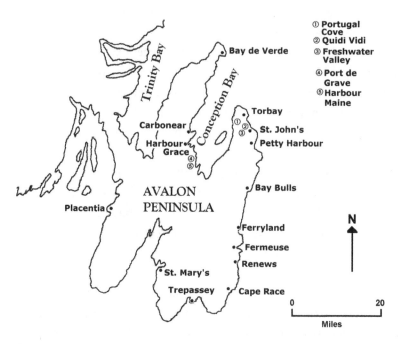

① Portugal Cove
② Quidi Vidi
③ Freshwater Valley
④ Port de Grave
⑤ Harbour Maine

replaced the departed French settlers on the southern shore. In 1725, "some hundreds" of Irishmen were said to be located at Placentia, on the western shore of the Avalon Penninsula, having replaced the substantial French community that had once lived there.[17] In 1742, the Irish outnumbered English residents in the harbours between Placentia and St. John's, especially at Ferryland. By this time the Irish formed roughly 50 percent of the population of St. John's. The transition to a permanently settled Irish population had well and truly been made (see Map 5).[18]

This was a gradual break with the past, not the outcome of some long-deliberated plan. It was more of an afterthought. Although the fishery offered employment, prospective settlers had plenty of obstacles to overcome. The island's agricultural potential was poor; the climate was harsh; jobs were poorly paid and mainly limited to the fishery.[19] There was also a shortage of women, thus making it difficult for people to marry and raise families. Despite these drawbacks, the Irish were predominant in many parts of the Avalon Peninsula:

By 1753, all the major communities on the Avalon Peninsula had Irish majorities; neither the English settlers nor the English government had anticipated this. They [the Irish] had begun to settle at the beginning of the century; within fifty years, the Irish settlers probably constituted nearly half of the total population.[20]

While many were servants, the settled Irish population also included shopkeepers, tavern owners, tradesmen, and fishing boat owners, the so-called planters, who obtained equipment and supplies on credit from merchants and hired a crew from fishermen registered with a firm.[21]

A partial census of the District of St. John's, taken in 1794–95, reveals that, in addition to the town of St. John's, the Irish were concentrated at nearby Portugal Cove, Southside, Torbay, and Quidi Vidi, as well as at Petty Harbour (see Map 5).[22] In addition to these settlements on the eastern and northern shores of the Avalon Peninsula, the Irish were also well represented at this time along Conception Bay, on the northern shore, and at Placentia and St. Mary's along the southern and western shores.

Summer fishing station at Newfoundland. Photograph by G.F. Briggs, date unknown.

Meanwhile, the efforts being made by the Irish to establish homes for themselves on the island were viewed with increasing alarm within government circles. While West Country Protestants might be tolerated, Irish Catholics were classed as undesirables. Once they began to predominate in the Avalon Peninsula, edicts were issued to force them to return home, and if they remained, to restrict their freedom to practise their religion, hold jobs, and own property. This was out-and-out religious persecution:

> The authorities tried to ensure that all those brought out to fish were taken back. They tried to prohibit the holding of Mass by imposing exorbitant fines on those participating and by destroying the property used for religious purposes. They refused to permit Roman Catholics to operate public houses; they limited the number of Irish allowed to live in any one household. They discouraged the practice of bringing out Irish women to get work.[23]

The hope was that they would give up and return to Ireland, but they showed remarkable forbearance and generally stayed put. The Irish were used to being spurned. This was nothing new.

Ireland had been overrun repeatedly by the British. The Irish had their lands taken from them and their Roman Catholic religion had been proscribed. When they came to Newfoundland, the Irish probably expected to be mistreated, and this meant steeling themselves against widespread bigotry and religious persecution. Little wonder that they despised British authority in all of its forms and occasionally spoke with their fists. However, despite being treated shamefully, many Irish managed to possess property, operate public houses, and practise their Catholic faith. And, by 1783, the prohibitions against the Irish were gradually being removed.

The American Revolutionary War, which began in 1775, marked a major turning point in Newfoundland's development, since it broke the merchant's monopoly. Because the war destabilized their participation in the fishing trade, Newfoundland people had greater access to fishery jobs, thus boosting the local economy. They were now allowed to import goods from the United States.[24] The war also created a sudden demand for other forms of labour beyond fishing. The migratory workforce slowly died out and increasingly the labour demands of the fishery were met from the local population, thus giving the island's economy an enormous boost. With the end of the war in 1784, Father James Louis O'Donel arrived, becoming Newfoundland's first Catholic bishop. He built a chapel in St. John's, thus giving added encouragement to Irish people to remain behind.[25] By the end of the eighteenth century, when the fur trade and seal hunting had been established as winter pursuits, the island offered greater incentives for year-round habitation.

Progress, however, was painfully slow. When William Dyott sought refuge near Ferryland during a bad storm in 1787, he observed that there "are very few inhabitants who remain here all the year." The ones who did "are principally Irish of the lowest class.... The country is quite a desert — nothing but rocks, spruce and fir. I did not see an animal of any sort. They [the residents] build up small wooden houses just to serve the season and the Irish fishermen have small cabins; they live on salt provisions and sea biscuit."[26]

Understandably, religious strife flared up from time to time. Feelings ran high in Ferryland in 1788 when two Catholic clergymen fell out over religious protocol. It is thought that Father Patrick Power from Kilkenny (Leinster Province) refused to accept Father James O'Donel's authority as the Vicar Apostolic (or Bishop) of Newfoundland. O'Donel, who hailed from Munster Province, excommunicated him, thus sparking off a major riot.[27] Well over a hundred men representing the Leinster and Munster factions of the population were convicted of "riotously and unlawfully assembling to the great terror and injury of all his Majesty's subjects," receiving sentences ranging from forfeiting their wages, fines, lashes, and transportation.[28]

In addition to having to deal with occasional outbreaks of riotous behaviour, the authorities also feared that disaffected Irish settlers might side with the French in any future conflicts between France and Britain.[29] Many suspected them of having Irish republican sympathies. Given that the United Irishmen Rebellion of 1798 had been led by people from county Wexford, and that many of Newfoundland's Irish had Wexford origins, there were understandable fears that the rebellion would cross the Atlantic.

Such fears were realized two years later when soldiers serving in the Royal Newfoundland Regiment conspired to lead an insurrection in St. John's in support of the United Irish Movement, which sought Ireland's release from British rule.[30] Inadequate food and clothing and poor wages had helped to fuel the rebellion, as did the soldiers' disdain for their commanding officer, Brigadier-General John Skerrett, who was a strict disciplinarian.[31] In April 1800, between forty and fifty men of the regiment deserted and assembled near Fort Townshend with the intention of taking up arms against anyone who tried to stop them; but they were apprehended. The plot was foiled and retribution was swift.[32] Bishop O'Donel, who had played a pivotal role in defusing the crisis, may have acted behind the scenes to alert the authorities. If he did, he ensured that the uprising in Newfoundland was no more successful than the one in Ireland had been two years earlier.[33] A plaque commemorating the mutiny explains how the plot was hatched:

> An army powder shed which occupied this site was chosen as the place of rendezvous by fifty United-Irish mutineers of the Royal Newfoundland Regiment on the night of 25 April, 1800. Nineteen men stationed on Signal Hill deserted their posts and met as planned, but others from Fort William and Fort Townshend were prevented from joining. In June 1800 five of the mutineers were hanged on gallows erected on this site after being found guilty of mutiny by a general court-martial.[34]

Many people at the time must have wondered about the intended political objectives of the mutiny in the St. John's garrison. British authority had been flouted in support of Irish self-rule — a cause that had little bearing on how Newfoundland functioned.[35] Given that Bishop O'Donel actually favoured British rule, he was never going to side with the mutineers, although part of the price that had to be paid afterward was that Irish Catholics in St. John's had to endure even greater restrictions. And, surprisingly, despite the brutal methods that were used to quell the rebellion, anti-British feeling did not resurface to any great extent. In fact, one

Plaque at Belvedere Street, St. John's, marking the site of the Royal Newfoundland Regiment Mutiny of 1800. An oak tree brought from county Wexford was planted on the site in 2000 by members of the Irish Newfoundland Association.

hundred years later, the Newfoundland Regiment would fight with commendable bravery in both world wars. Loyalty to the British Empire was at high ebb in Newfoundland, as it was across Canada:

Looking back, life went on pretty normally after the uprising, although religious and ethnic tensions continued to surface. When he visited St. John's in 1800, Governor William Waldegrave was shocked by the widespread poverty that was helping to fuel these tensions:

Soldiers of the First Newfoundland Regiment marching in a church parade in 1914. The unit suffered very heavy losses on July 1, 1916, the first day of the Battle of the Somme, and since then the day is observed as a memorial day in Newfoundland and Labrador. In recognition of its valour during the battles of Ypres in 1917, the unit was renamed the Royal Newfoundland Regiment by King George V.

> The very first object which attracted my attention on my landing in the town of St. John's was the wretchedness and apparent misery of its inhabitants. It instantly occurred to me that if such were their state in the height of summer whilst money (relatively speaking) must be flowing in upon them from their active labours, what must be their wants in the frigid season.[36]

The population of St. John's was increasing rapidly. Six hundred and seventy Irish immigrants landed in the town in 1804, but hard times were around the corner.[37] The island's economy collapsed when the Napoleonic Wars ended in 1815. This precipitated an economic depression, while a fire that swept through St. John's the following year — burning more than 130 homes and merchants' premises — added to the misery. Peter Strange, a provisions merchant in county Wexford who supplied "provisions and passengers to the fishery at Your Majesty's Island of Newfoundland," complained how "the destructive fires" had destroyed his business even though he was living in Ireland.[38] An Anglican minister noted how "families, which at 10 o'clock were in affluent and respectable circumstances, were reduced to poverty and many of them to absolute beggary," later that same day.[39] The overall state of the town was grim:

> The streets are now filled with beggars of the lower order by day and those of the Middle Class of society by night who are yet ashamed to acknowledge themselves reduced to a state of mendacity while it be light — poverty and disease are now constantly in view and the number of paupers having lately doubled, the funds of the Public Charitable Institutions are almost exhausted. This town now relieves upwards of 1,800 persons daily and chiefly by voluntary contributions ...[40]

The accelerating slide into crisis produced a lawless gang, "consisting in public of about 100 men," and an "Armed Association" was formed to deal with the threat it posed to people and property: "The inhabitants ... keep up a regular patrol and about 35 persons parade the streets all night to check depredations which otherwise would be constantly committed and to prevent unlawful assemblages."[41]

However, to offset this gloom were the benefits being gained by the increasing use of local labour in the fishery.[42] Despite the near state of collapse and general misery, eleven thousand Irish people came to St. John's between 1814 and 1815.[43] Some had sailed without paying their passages, presumably on the understanding that they would get jobs in the fishery on arrival and use their wages to finance their debts. But judging from the numerous notices in the *Royal Gazette and Newfoundland Advertiser* listing the names of men who had sailed on specific ships and had not yet paid their fares, deception was widespread (see Table 1).[44] While ship captains threatened action against them in Ireland, there was probably little that they could do to recover their funds. In the meantime, most of

TABLE 1

Irish Passengers Who Sailed from Waterford to St. John's, Newfoundland, between 1809 and 1816 Without Paying Their Fares

[PANL: Mildred Howell Collection, 1810–1814, *Newfoundland Ancestor* 9, no. 1, 39]

1. NOTICE to the undermentioned persons who arrived in the Brigs ***Daphne***, Thomas HARRIS, Master, **1809** and ***The Thomas***, Thomas BULLEY, Master, **1811 & 1812**. If their passage is not paid to subscriber immediately, and made acquainted where and with whom those serve, arriving this year on or before the 10th of next month, necessary steps will be taken to recover same from their sureties in Ireland.

Per *Daphne*, 1809	Per *Thomas*, 1811
Edward Walsh	Patrick Reardon
Daniel McCarthy	Thomas Bold
John Daly	Michael Connolly
William Harrington	William Sullivan
Patrick Meagher	John Wall
Patrick Thomas	Patrick Henrick
Richard Burns	**1812**
Walter Flemming	John Gaught
John Dooling	Patrick Collings
Andrew Higgings	Richard Doyle
Paul Higgings	John Connelly
	John Congdon
	Peter Power
	Edmund Power (July 2)

2. LAST NOTICE: Undermentioned persons who came as passengers in the Brig *Joyce* from Ireland in the years **1809, 1810, and 1811**, have not accounted for their passage. If not paid before Oct. 1st, their respective sureties in Ireland will be sued.

Pater Coady	Richard Sinnott	Patrick O'Rourke
James Coady	Thomas Murphy	John Cullin
Martin Grace	Patrick Lambert	James Neal
John Nevill	Patrick Murphy	John Doolin
Matthew Brien	Anthony Kent	Thomas Rourke
Thomas Hayden	James Hanrick	Patrick Farrell

Dennis Cosgrove
Judith Quigley
Patrick Cearful
Margaret Furlong
Edward Walsh
Ellen Hanrick
Nick Kenaught
Eleanor Byrne
Peter Grady
Martin Tobin
Bridget Rourke
Judith Rourke

Elizabeth Mackey
John Forrestall
Mary Walsh
Patrick Foley
Mary Hogan
Thomas McGuire
Johanna Grady
Roger Fitzpatrick
Catherine Moran
Johannah Power
John Hannevery
Thomas Murphy

Thomas Denniess
Catherine Neale
Thomas Shean
Mary Keane
Richard Kelly
Catherine Power
Edward Byrne
Anne Warren
Darby Burn
Dennis Reddy
Betty Ryan

Signed: Patrick MORRIS, St. John's, July 30, 1812.

3. NOTICE to the undermentioned persons who arrived last Spring in the ship **Laura**, William Warren, Master from Wexford, are requested to make payment of their passage by September 20th next.

Patrick Butter
John Lynch, Snr.
James Lynch
Thomas Walsh
Thomas Lonergen

Laurence Forrestall
Frank Dunn
Daniel Reddy
John Power
Thomas Shea

John Queenlan
Patrick Meagher
Dennis Bryan
James Barrett
Dennis Fogerty

St. John's, July 30

4. NOTICE: The undermentioned persons arrived in the ship **Laura**, William Warren, master from Waterford in **1812 & 1813**. If payment of passage is not paid, necessary steps will be taken to recover [funds] from their sureties in Ireland.

1812
John Collins
Maurice Hearn
John Kiely
John Lynch, Snr.

1813
John Ball
James Brougham
Michael Buckley
Michael Burn

John Lynch, Jnr.   Thomas Carroll
Philip Mulcahy   Patrick Connell
John Queenlen   Patrick Meagher
Philip Reddy   Timothy Carey
James Lahart   Thomas Connelly
Thomas Stack   Thomas Dunn

Signed: Warren & Babb, St. John's, August 12, 1813.

5. The undermentioned passengers per the brig **Good Intent**, Thomas Fox, Master from Waterford to this port (St. John's), in the Spring, **1816,** are hereby informed that unless their Passage Notes are paid to the Subscribers, on or before the 20th proximo, they will indiscriminately be sent home to recover from their respective Sureties.

Oct. 17, 1817. Bulley, Job & Cross.

John Grechy   Joseph Redmond
Michael Birmingham   Thomas Scott
W.A. Hearn   David Kyly
Daniel Lynagh   Roger M'Grath
John Turney   John Keefe
Catherine Wells   John Kennedy
William Christopher   John Clancey
Thomas Martin   William Burke
Nicholas Hall   Richard Flood
Francis Higgins   Thomas Dunn
John Power   Andrew Cain
Edward Doyle   Patrick Tobin
Edward Flannigan   Patrick Ryan
John Maher   Patrick Kyley
Michael Power   Mary Phelan
John Hayes   Bridget Asper
Betsy Shallow   Mary Brophy
Bridget Hall   James Harris
John Wright   Ellen Finnagan
Edward Walsh   Thomas Boland
John Kelly   Thomas Whelan

the men with outstanding debts had probably moved on smartly to Nova Scotia, where employment opportunities would have been far better.

Many, like the small group of twelve from Ballyscullion Parish, in county Londonderry, simply settled in St. John's.[45] The others would have headed for the bays on the eastern, southern, and western shores of the Avalon Peninsula. Those who left Inistioge Parish in county Kilkenny to settle in Logy Bay, just north of St. John's, managed to transplant whole communities. Between 1784 and 1844, ninety-four Inistioge people moved to Newfoundland. This was not, however, a migration of married couples, in that people emigrated as individuals and married after settling in Newfoundland. Gradually many acquired sufficient resources to establish a farm or a small independent fishery.[46] In addition, the Irish also became predominant at Placentia Bay and St. Mary's Bay on the southern and western shores, although they were but a fraction of the number who went to St. John's and the eastern shore. St. John's Irish element consisted of fourteen thousand in 1836, representing a sevenfold increase since 1794.

Meanwhile, the chance survival of a passenger list for the crossing of the *Thomas Farrall* in 1825 from New Ross in county Wexford to St. John's reveals that out of the 164 Irish workers shown as going to work in the fishery, some 38 percent were women (see Table 2).[47] Women would also have found employment in the various towns, working as domestic servants for merchants and other well-to-do people. No doubt, their presence contributed to the growth of permanent settlement in Newfoundland, although they were still in relatively short supply. Even as late as 1830, there were twice as many males as females in Newfoundland.[48] Predictably, Newfoundland governors had tried to ban female immigration, but their orders were never enforced and Irish females continued to settle on the island, particularly in St. John's.[49]

With its excellent port and stone-covered beaches, well-suited for drying fish, the town of Placentia developed into an important fishing and trading centre. A Waterford merchant family led by Pierce Sweetman, together with the Poole-based Saunders family, dominated the Placentia fishing trade from the late eighteenth century and annually brought hundreds of Irishmen to the area, some of whom

TABLE 2

Passenger List: Crossing of *Thomas Farrall*, Captain Thomas Barry, from New Ross to St. John's, Newfoundland, May 1825
[NAB CO 194/71, 322–23]

1. James McDaniel
2. Thomas Connors
3. Catherine Connors
4. Daniel Clancy
5. John Clancy
6. Kearn [Kieran] Clancy
7. Richard Holland
8. Catherine Hollan
9. Thomas Cahill
10. Thomas Behan
11. Bridget Behan
12. Moses Doyle
13. Simon Ryan
14. Thomas McDaniel
15. Judy Ryan
16. John Bolger
17. Alley Grady
18. John Buggy
19. Thomas Barnet
20. Anastasia Barnet
21. Martin Moore
22. Anne Brennan
23. John Brennan
24. James Costigan
25. Bridget Costigan
26. James Kehoe
27. Richard Stanton
28. Jane Stanton
29. William Walker
30. Elizabeth Walker
31. William Dixon
32. Alley Dixon
33. Hanna Brien
34. Mary Brien
35. Joshua Bobicar
36. Margaret Bobicar
37. Joshua Bobicar

38. John Bobicar
39. Thomas Bobicar
40. George Sparks
41. Sarah Sparks
42. Margaret Bobicar
43. Nicholas Ryan
44. James Ryan
45. John Downey
46. David Phelan
47. Charles Kavanagh
48. Elen Kavanagh
49. John Scallian
50. William Scallian
51. Pat Cleary
52. John Longford
53. Judith Boyle
54. Patrick Carroll
55. Catherine Carroll
56. Patrick Neal
57. John McGlennan
58. Marg't McGlennan
59. Joseph Walsh
60. Edward Nowlan
61. Pat Cantwell
62. Michael Nolan
63. Robert Wilson
64. Jane Wilson
65. John Wilson
66. Maria Wilson
67. Darby Wilson
68. Casper Wilson
69. Anne Wilson
70. Anne Bradley
71. John Howlett
72. William Payne
73. John Holden
74. Michael Holden

75. Mary Finn
76. Kearn Brennan
77. Catherine Brennan
78. James Fitzgerald
79. Nancy Fitzgerald
80. Pat Purcell
81. Nancy Purcell
82. Margaret Ryan
83. John Grace
84. Richard Walsh
85. Judith Walsh
86. James Kinshellow
[Kinsella]
87. Anne Kinshellow
88. Timothy Finlan
89. Elenor Finlan
90. Joseph Burrows
91. Marg't Burrows
92. Judith Dempsey
93. Anne Dempsey
94. Sarah Dempsey
95. William Henecy
[Hennessey]
96. Honor Henecy
97. Elenor Browne
98. Samuel Boyle
99. Elizabeth Bates
100. Pat Broderick
101. Anty Broderick
102. Martin Hogan
103. Elen Hogan
104. James Berigin
105. Daniel Boyle
106. Judy Boyle
107. John Boyle
108. William Smyth
109. Ann Smyth

110. Edward Dillon	128. Margaret Bobicar	146. Peter Kinshellow
111. Jane Dillon	129. Margaret Wickham	147. Eliza Kinshellow
112. Adam Jackson	130. John Fennall	148. Thomas Dempsey
113. Daniel Brennan	131. Mary Fennall	149. Robert Dempsey
114. Stephen Ryan	132. Ann Wilson	150. William Dempsey
115. Judith Ryan	133. Robert Wilson	151. Mary Broderick
116. Andrew Shore	134. Jane Wilson	152. Judy Broderick
117. Simon Coogan	135. Thomas Wilson	153. John Broderick
118. Lawrence Doyle	136. John Fitzgerald	154. Kitty Hogan
119. William Kealy	137. Pat Fitzgerald	155. Anne Hogan
120. Murtagh Brennan	138. Mary Fitzgerald	156. Eliza Hogan
121. Mary Brennan	139. Bridget Fitzgerald	157. Ellen Brennan
122. Martin Reed	140. Kitty Fitzgerald	158. Alley Brennan
123. Eliza Behan	141. Michl Purcell	159. Pat Brennan
124. William Behan	142. Thomas Purcell	160. James Brennan
125. Johanna Behan	143. John Purcell	161. John Bryan
126. Anne Holland	144. John Kinshellow	162. David Wells
127. Anty Holland	145. Walter Kinshellow	163. Catherine Kealy
		164. Thos Kehoe

I certify that passengers are going on the Brig *Thomas Farrell* Thos Barry Master to Newfoundland solely for the purpose of prosecuting the fishery.

remained and settled permanently.[50] Thomas Saunders, who, along with his brother William, ran the firm until 1788, spoke well of the "Irish boys" who came out each summer from Waterford:

> We have been very lucky in having no runaways this spring [1786] we have lost but two men and an Irish Boy. I would advise you never to send out more English young-sters than will just clear the vessels. The most of all that ran away from here the winter before this were English youngsters and boys. They never any of them stick to the place or have any attachment to it; but for hard labour one Irish youngster is worth a dozen of them.[51]

When Pierce Sweetman took charge in 1789, only a third of the labour was being supplied from overseas, with most employees being resident

TABLE 3

**Boat Owners in Placentia Employed by Pierce Sweetman in June 1789
[PANL MG49.40]**

Captain James Salmon, Placentia, June 2, 1789

	Shallops	Jacks
Richard Kelly	2	
Richard Burnhan	2	
Christopher St. Croix	1	1
Thos. Farrell	2	
Andrew Duggan	1	1
Thos. Viguss	2	1
Wm. Collins	1	
Timy. Crawley		1
Peter Landell		1
Harris Fuller		1
Wm. Kelly		1
Wm. Lamb	1	
Wm. Murphy	1	1
Thos. Muckleroy	1	
Geo. Blanch	1	1
F. Blanch	1	
M. Blanch		1
Jon. Moran		1
Chas. Jewell		1
Thos. Miller	1	
Wm. Lawler	1	
Wm. Davies		1
G. Reilly	1	1

fishermen/boat owners or overwintering servants. Judging from the surnames of some of the boat owners Sweetman employed in 1789, most were Irish (see Table 3).[52] And yet the influx of migratory workers continued. Close to six hundred passengers were recorded as arriving directly from Ireland at the harbour of Great Placentia between 1811 and 1827, most being indentured servants.[53] Many would have stayed on the island, mainly settling in Placentia Bay, although in any one year they accounted for only a tiny fraction of the total workforce.

Genealogical evidence indicates that only a few immigrant Irish families had settled at Placentia before 1810 and that they attracted a steady trickle of followers until the late 1830s.[54] Thirty-four Irish families have been identified as having established farms in the Placentia/ St. Mary's area by 1836 (see Map 5).

Placentia town had a handful of wealthy merchants — men like John Power, who had "a fine situation" at the north side of the harbour, having "a dwelling house and gardens, well stocked with fruit trees, a barn and cooperage, two stores and both two stories high, with fifty or sixty acres of land."[55] Although most people in the area originated from Ireland, some also came from the West Country in England.[56]

Meanwhile, other immigrant families from Ireland sought the farming opportunities to be had at this time near St. John's, settling at Freshwater Valley, just west of the city. Like those at Placentia, they mostly originated from counties Wexford, Waterford, Kilkenny, and Tipperary.

With continuing immigration from Ireland and England during the first half of the nineteenth century, Newfoundland's population continued to grow. In the 1830s Bouchette noted that settlements were concentrated at the heads of bays: "On the whole shore of Conception Bay, thence to St. John's and southward to Cape Race [east of Trepassey] the settlements are numerous and populous. The principal [ones] are besides St. John's, the Bay of Bulls, Brigus, Cape Broyle Harbour, Ferryland, Fermore [Fermeuse], and Renowes [Renews]" (see Map 5).[57] He was essentially describing many of the places being inhabited by the Irish. In 1840, roughly half of the province's population had Irish origins, with nearly 75 percent concentrated at or near St. John's. The Irish continued to be the predominant ethnic group in St. John's in 1857.[58] They dominated the southern shore between Ferryland and Placentia and were the largest part of the population at Harbour Main, Port de Grave, Harbour Grace, and Carbonear along Conception Bay.[59]

View of Placentia from a hill overlooking the harbour, circa 1892 to 1904. Photograph by Robert Edwards Holliday.

However, it would seem that the benefits of immigration had not necessarily reached the Irish Catholics who chose an urban way of life in St. John's. When he toured Newfoundland in 1835, the Reverend Edward Wix, an Anglican missionary, was struck by the friendliness of the Placentia Irish.[60] In stark contrast were the St. John's Irish, whom he claimed "are excited to frequent breaches of the peace by the most seditious Romish priesthood."[61] Their ugly mood was probably due more to poverty than any religious differences they may have had with the Reverend Wix. The Irish in Placentia had been able to establish farms and small fishing enterprises, thus giving themselves far better economic prospects than their equivalents in St. John's, who were probably living in abject poverty as labourers and servants. On his travels, the Reverend Wix was struck by "the marked dissimilarity between the descendents of Jersey-men, Frenchmen, Irish, Scotch and English people." He observed the mainly Irish inhabitants of Conception Bay, whom he thought differed from the mostly English inhabitants of Trinity Bay, "as much as if they were of a distant nation," although only a short distance separated them; "the same can be said of the difference between those [Irish] who live in Placentia and those [English] who live in Fortune Bay."[62]

The Reverend Wix railed against the "foul origin" of some of the people, who by implication were Irish Catholics, and he failed to understand their frustrations and grievances. It is true that the Irish occasionally let off steam, as was witnessed in 1830 in Arichat, Cape Breton, when "a lawless and merciless mob of Irishmen, many of them just arrived from Newfoundland and a great number yet expected," caused mayhem. Following violent disturbances with their fellow Scots over an election result, a request went out from the residents of Arichat for military protection, since, while "the Scotch have all gone home, the Irish [are] left to act as they please."[63]

Thirty years later, violence broke out during the 1861 elections in Harbour Grace and Harbour Main in response to charges of undue Catholic influence in the Liberal government. Several lives were lost and many people were wounded as troops had to be called in to restore order.[64]

Religious and political tensions helped to fuel these violent outbreaks, but an ongoing resentment of misdeeds attributed to the British may also have contributed to this aura of social discontent. A French diplomat, Joseph Arthur, the Comte de Gobineau, commented in 1861 on the longstanding bitterness felt by the Newfoundland Irish toward the British: "The fisherman preserves tales of violent deeds and frightful depredations which are probably not very historically founded but which keep alive in him an unshakeable ill-will for the British nation."[65]

There is no doubt that Irish Catholics were treated badly, but despite the obstacles placed in their way, they readily adopted Newfoundland as their new home and anti-British feelings were never strong enough to halt this influx. By the mid-eighteenth century, the province's permanent population was predominately Irish Catholic.[66] The Irish supplied the cheap labour that had made the fishery so profitable to the merchants. Even when the labour demands of the fishery were being met adequately by the native-born population, they continued to arrive, not as fishery workers, but as prospective farmers, tradesmen, and labourers.

Newfoundland's meagre agricultural resources and limitations to its fishing economy led many of its Irish inhabitants to seek greener pastures elsewhere. The fishery had brought them to Newfoundland, and once they acquired capital and an understanding of New World opportunities and farming methods, they ventured across the Gulf of St. Lawrence to seek better locations elsewhere in Atlantic Canada. They would found new communities in Cape Breton, in southeastern Nova Scotia, the Miramichi in New Brunswick, and parts of Prince Edward Island. However, this migration of already-settled Irish Catholics to other parts of Atlantic Canada must be seen in a far wider context. In 1816, with the arrival of the timber trade, Irish immigration to Atlantic Canada went up several gears. The timber trade revolutionized immigrant travel and propelled a growing stream of immigrants from Ireland to the Maritimes.

The spotlight now moves away from the Catholics who originated from southeast Ireland and settled in Newfoundland. It now shines on all parts of Ireland. The timber trade brought Protestants and Catholics to the Maritime provinces in ever greater numbers from across the length and breadth of Ireland. Their story follows.

CHAPTER 4

Nova Scotia's Irish and Their Links with Newfoundland

> Emigrants from Ireland to Nova Scotia were farmers, fishermen, small traders, cottagers and itinerant labourers. Few of them achieved mention in contemporary public records.[1]

The humble folk from Ireland who made Nova Scotia their home left few records behind and simply faded into the background. Shipping records show that between 1815 and 1838 some 37,500 immigrants arrived in Nova Scotia from the British Isles, of whom nearly 22,000 were Scots, 13,000 were Irish, and 2,000 were English.[2] The large influx of Scottish Highlanders, which began in the late eighteenth century, ensured that Scots predominated in both mainland Nova Scotia and Cape Breton, as is evident from these figures. Nevertheless, the Irish had a significant presence in the province. They were mainly Catholics who originated from the southeast of Ireland, while a substantial but much smaller group of Presbyterians came from Ulster in the north of the country. Most of the Catholic arrivals were very poor, some arriving in a destitute state. Where documentation survives, it refers to the disgruntlement of Halifax residents who objected to having to repeatedly subsidize large numbers of poverty-stricken immigrants. Their continuing arrival was a sore point over many years.

Irish Catholics were attracted by the prospect of finding employment in or near Halifax and by the longer-term hope of acquiring land in the eastern stretches of the province, which in most cases was taken by squatting. They sought little but the means of subsistence, but, lacking many of the relevant skills and without much in the way of capital, life was a constant struggle. On the other hand, Nova Scotia's Ulster farmers generally arrived with adequate means. Their impact can be seen in the thriving settlements they left behind in Colchester and Hants counties on the west side of the province.

Despite being treated with indifference, and in some cases hostility, many Irish Catholics remained in Nova Scotia and prospered. Since they generally came with very little money, the province's anti-Catholic legislation forbidding them from owning land was not a serious obstacle.[3] In any case, a critical factor in Nova Scotia's appeal to these people was its proximity to the Newfoundland fishery. Having taken up seasonal employment there, workers often sought the much better land prospects and good fishing opportunities to be had in eastern Nova Scotia or Cape Breton. Although crossing the Gulf of St. Lawrence was very hazardous, it was a relatively short distance to travel.

In fact, most of the Irish Catholics who settled in Nova Scotia during the eighteenth century had not come directly from Ireland, but had instead relocated from Newfoundland.[4] A typical example was the Waterford-born Michael Fitzgerald, who, after a brief period of employment in Newfoundland, came to Halifax in 1798, eventually settling at nearby Portuguese Cove.[5] Most Irish arrivals were like Michael in making a beeline for Halifax. In 1760, one third of the town's population of nearly three thousand was Irish and Roman Catholic. Seven years later, two thousand of the province's twelve thousand or so residents were Irish-born, and half of those lived in Halifax. There was plenty of construction work in both the town and its port, thus ensuring that it continued to attract Irish arrivals. In fact, the south end of Halifax, where many of the Irish eventually settled, came to be known as Irishtown.[6]

Halifax's later prosperity is revealed in this winter scene of George Street painted in 1875 by F.E. Wilmot.

However, the steady influx of desperately poor Irish people from Newfoundland alarmed the Nova Scotia government. In 1806, Governor Sir John Wentworth complained bitterly about the "useless Irishmen" who "pass annually from Newfoundland through this province, where some of them remain one, two or perhaps three years, and then proceed onward to the United States."[7] Seemingly unaware of the extent of their poverty, he could not appreciate that they were slowly lifting themselves up by their bootstraps. Having worked in St. John's, they found better-paying jobs in Halifax before moving to an American city where their prospects would have been even brighter. It never occurred to Governor Wentworth that Nova Scotia had to offer hope and encouragement to such people if it were to retain them.

There were two Irish groups in Nova Scotia, and they could not have been more different. There were the many Catholics from southeastern

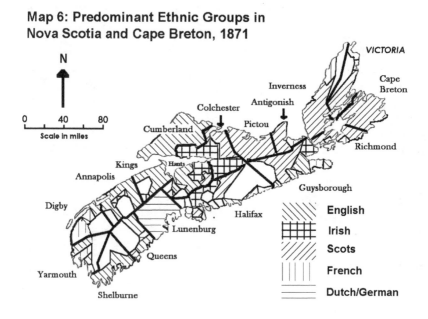

Map 6: Predominant Ethnic Groups in
Nova Scotia and Cape Breton, 1871

Ireland who mainly originated from counties Wexford, Carlow, Waterford, Kilkenny, and Tipperary.[8] Most of these settled in Halifax County, though some also went to Guysborough and Antigonish Counties and to the fishing and coal-mining areas of Cape Breton. Meanwhile, having established themselves in the Cobequid Bay region during the 1760s, a smaller group of Ulster people from the north of Ireland colonized a large swathe of Colchester County and parts of neighbouring Hants County on the west side of the province (see Map 6). They mainly came from counties Donegal, Tyrone, and Londonderry in west Ulster.

Surprisingly, although the Ulster settlers had laid the foundations of their settlements many decades earlier, they attracted only a relatively small retinue of followers in the early nineteenth century.[9] One reason for this was the explosive growth in New Brunswick's timber trade. By the time immigration resumed after the Napoleonic Wars ended in 1815, the trade was increasingly becoming centred at Saint John. While a total of 1,500 or so Ulster people sailed from Londonderry and Belfast to Halifax between 1817 and 1821, they were the only ones to do so. They were the sum total of the nineteenth-century passenger trade from Ulster to Nova Scotia (see Appendix I).[10] The Ulster immigrant stream to Atlantic Canada changed direction in the 1820s, and New Brunswick was the beneficiary.

There were other factors that discouraged Ulster people from settling in their long-established Nova Scotia communities. Upon arriving at Halifax or Saint John, they would have had the added expense of having to travel to the Cobequid Bay. In addition, the final approach to the port of Halifax was along a craggy and dangerous coastline. Before the arrival of reliable lighthouses, captains frequently misjudged the rocky ledges near the shore or were blown onto rocks on the approach to Halifax. As happened to many other vessels, the *Alexander Buchanan*, which sailed from Londonderry in June 1818, became wrecked off Cape Sable, while the *Fame*, sailing from Belfast with 114 passengers, went ashore at Cole Harbour.[11] Although in both of these cases all of the passengers were rescued, shipwrecks with extensive loss of life were regular occurrences along this southern coast.

Another issue was the fact that much of the province's best agricultural land had already been granted to New England Planters and Loyalists, this having happened in the late eighteenth century. Nevertheless, if Philip Martin from county Fermanagh is to be believed, plenty of people from the north of Ireland relocated to Nova Scotia. After serving with the 81st Regiment during the 1820s, he asked to be admitted to the Royal Hospital in Chelsea (London) on the grounds that "during my time in the service ... my friends all emigrated to Nova Scotia, so that I am left desolate among strangers."[12]

Certainly, by 1871 the Ulster Irish had become ensconced across much of Colchester and Hants Counties, particularly in places along or near the Minas Basin shores (see Map 7).[13] The greatest concentrations were at Truro, Londonderry, Economy, and Upper Stewiacke in Colchester County and at Maitland, Noel, Rawdon, Ste. Croix, and Windsor in Hants County.

Presbyterianism was still strong in Colchester County in 1871, but less so in Hants County, where Methodism had widespread support.[14] Some of the residents were descended from people who just happened on the place. John and Catherine Smiley, together with John's brother,

Map 7: Ulster Irish Settler Locations in Colchester and Hants Counties

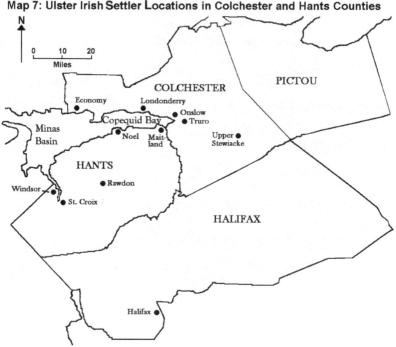

Joseph, and his wife, Margaret, and their respective families had sailed in the *Dispatch* in 1828 from Londonderry to Quebec. Among the people who survived a shipwreck near Newfoundland, they were taken to Halifax and, being "too frightened to ever travel on a ship again," they decided to "remain on the firm land of Nova Scotia."[15] Both families settled in Ardoise to the east of Ste. Croix.[16]

According to the Reverend John Mulholland,[17] who was living in Windsor in 1849, "most of the people here are from the North of Ireland." Some had originated from Ballymena (county Antrim) and Coleraine (county Londonderry), while others came from Crumlin and Antrim (county Antrim). He also stated that "they first landed, as is general for North of Ireland emigrants, at Saint John, New Brunswick and then came in this direction.... Some of them are very wealthy now."[18] While Colchester and Hants Counties became Ulster strongholds, Cumberland County to the north of Colchester attracted settlers equally from the north and south of Ireland.[19]

Meanwhile, life was much tougher for the many Catholic Irish who settled in Nova Scotia. Their poverty was often extreme and affected their transport arrangements. Significantly, many sailed to Halifax via St. John's, Newfoundland. Desperate to emigrate and having few resources, the poorest of the poor chose the most basic form of transport they could find. With the passing of the Passenger Act of 1803, most vessels providing transatlantic crossings were beyond their reach. The vessels now had to adhere to strict space allocations for passengers, and this inevitably led to an increase in fares.[20] However, being exempt from this legislation, Newfoundland shippers were able to take as many passengers as they wished in their vessels and were thus able to offer much cheaper passage. No questions were asked about overcrowding or safety.

Thus, in 1815, vessels normally used to transport fish and provisions along the Newfoundland route took out "over 3,600 persons, almost all of them from Ireland and very poor."[21] These fishing vessels were probably ill-adapted for carrying passengers, but in that year, when shipping was in demand, they provided a vital means for poor people to leave Ireland.

Most left from Waterford, but some ships were advertised as sailing from Belfast. Some, like the Irish passengers who sailed in the *Speculator* that year from Waterford to St. John's, had not even paid their passages.[22] Although a great many would move on to other parts of British North America and the United States, a significant number of Irish people who arrived at this time from Newfoundland settled in Nova Scotia.[23] Many found jobs in Halifax and remained there.

By 1827, 80 percent of Nova Scotia's Irish Catholics were accommodated in the town of Halifax or in the surrounding area.[24] The attractions were many: The town offered regular employment to new arrivals. And the nearby coastline enabled those who came as fishermen to resume their traditional way of life. According to Father James Jones, who lived in the area between 1785 and 1800, "most of the Irish in Halifax had come here from Placentia."[25] Eight years earlier another priest, based in Halifax, had reported that the Irish "are engaged in fishing along our shores."[26] In 1815, Bishop Joseph Octave Plessis actually visited the forty Irish families living in Prospect, Ketch Harbour, and Herring Cove, and was told that they had been visited by Father Jacques for a period of twenty-five

Old St. Patrick's Roman Catholic Church, Brunswick Street, Halifax, circa 1880. The church, built in 1840, was demolished in 1883 and was replaced two years later by a larger Gothic-style brick and stone building.

years.[27] Thus the earliest Irish Catholic settlement had been established by at least 1790, if not before. These coves had probably attracted Irish fishermen long before priests came to minister to their needs. Looking ahead to the 1850s, the Kilkenny-born Thomas Maher would establish himself as a storekeeper at nearby St. Margarets Bay, purchasing herring, mackerel, cod, haddock, and salmon from local fishermen, many of whom were Irish.[28]

Yet in 1816, there were few people like Thomas Maher. Most arrivals had a limited objective of simply landing a job as a labourer or fisherman in the Halifax area or in Cape Breton. Such jobs would hardly bring much of an improvement in their standard of living in the short term, but at least they might be a first step to future economic self-betterment. However, the Nova Scotia authorities had other plans for them. In 1816, Charles Morris, the surveyor-general, advised that they should be "instantly sped off to a place of settlement" so that they can become "valuable" settlers; but this was impractical because of their extreme poverty:

> The difficulties experienced by the recent settlers in Nova Scotia were in part owing to their inability to defray the expenses incidental to the survey and granting of such portions of land as might be authorized by Government, many of them on their arrival being destitute of the necessities of life, and their kindred folk and friends already settled on the eastern section of the Province having suffered much from very uncommon frosts and the devastation committed by the mice were unable to assist them and promote their establishment as has been the case in preceding years."[29]

Another difficulty, according to Morris, was that recent arrivals had to go "into the interior to look for a settlement on account of all the lands on the sea coast, Harbours and places of easy access having been already granted." Moreover, "as almost all the Lands adapted for settlement … within the district of Pictou and county of Sydney are disposed of," it will be necessary to direct new arrivals to the western part of the province, "where there are many thousand acres of land sufficient to accommodate many thousand families of Emigrants."[30]

Morris recommended that the Irish be sent to Shelburne County, which, following the severe downturn in its economy, was rapidly losing its residents. But all of his suggestions were unsuitable.[31] Regardless of his advice, the Irish sought locations on the eastern side of the province. That was where their kinsfolk had settled, and that is where they would settle. As John Young, a Halifax merchant, observed in 1818, the many poor immigrants arriving at Halifax, irrespective of whether or not they were Irish, were moving on to other destinations. They were almost being treated like unwelcome intruders:

> The tide of emigration, which for the last two years set in upon our shores, has mocked us with delusive hopes and we have had the mortification to see it race past us to fill the creeks and harbours of the United States. Those strangers who visited us in quest of settlement were taken under the care and direction of no body of men, and after wandering through our streets — the outcasts of the old world and intruders on the new — they averted their eye from our inhospitable reception and sought in other regions that rest that was denied them here.[32]

While the immediate needs of the poor immigrants who streamed into Halifax were met, often rather begrudgingly, little thought was being given to their future role as settlers. No one considered how best to encourage them or to assist them in assimilating into the communities that were sprouting up across the province. In fact, instead of seeing them as welcome additions to Nova Scotia's population, those in authority regarded them as useless riff-raff. Anti-Catholic prejudices were almost certainly to blame. Had there been any joined-up thinking, no one in their right mind would have suggested sending them to the western side of the province when their compatriots who had preceded them had settled on the eastern side. This explains why the military settlement founded in 1816 at Sherbrooke (now New Ross) in Lunenburg County, on the west, was an utter fiasco.

Nearly three hundred disbanded soldiers from the Royal Newfoundland Fencibles and Nova Scotia Fencibles, many of whom were Catholics from the south of Ireland, settled along the projected road from Halifax to

Annapolis, where they were expected to flourish under the stewardship of Cork-born Captain William Ross.[33] However, only eighty six men remained in the settlement by 1818, and once government rations ran out, it was anticipated that few of the others would remain.[34] There was no question of further Irish being attracted to this site. Thus far, the funding had been quite phenomenal, more than £10,000 having been spent on rations alone. If just a fraction of this amount had been spent in assisting the impoverished Irish to settle near to the long-established Irish communities in the east, they and the province would have seen immediate benefits.[35]

Meanwhile, Lord Dalhousie, the lieutenant governor of Nova Scotia, braced himself for the next round of Irish arrivals from Newfoundland.

St. John's near collapse in 1815 following the economic depression at the ending of the Napoleonic Wars helped to stimulate the growing exodus to Halifax. Those arriving in 1817 included seventy-seven tradesmen from Dublin, who had gone to work in St. John's, but left because of the dire conditions. Forty-four of them arrived in Halifax in a distressed state.[36] In January 1817, Lord Dalhousie reported that "500 fine young men, chiefly Irish," who had lately arrived at Halifax, were "totally destitute of bread or means of subsistence; they are, I am told, the overflow of an immense Emigration to Newfoundland last summer."[37] He was informed later the same year by Michael Tobin and Samuel Cunard, both prominent Halifax merchants, that another Irish group from Newfoundland consisting of "about 300 Men, Women and Children,... most of whom landed amongst us in a destitute state, many of them being shipwrecked on their way here and had lost the Remains of what they may have saved from the fires of 7th and 21st November."[38]

After sending eighty-nine of them to different parts of the province, the authorities established a soup house in Halifax, which daily fed about five hundred people who would otherwise have starved. Soon after, the Nova Scotia Council made it known that the province no longer wished to receive this Irish overflow from Newfoundland.[39] Fortunately, providence stepped in and new passenger legislation was introduced to regulate the Newfoundland and Labrador trade.[40]

Shipping records reveal that while nearly one thousand Irish arrived in Halifax from Newfoundland in 1816 and 1817, they stopped arriving via this route immediately afterward, when new regulations became effective.[41] Nonetheless, with the downturn in employment in the Newfoundland fishery in 1820, Irish people continued to seek sanctuary in Nova Scotia, much to the annoyance of the authorities.[42] The tide turned in their favour, however, with the introduction of legislation in 1826 that exempted the Newfoundland trade from any kind of passenger regulation. Thus a second surge occurred ten years later. Yet again the Irish hopped on fishing vessels bound for St. John's, although their eventual destinations were to Halifax, Quebec, and other ports in the United States.[43] Under the cover of this legislation, at least five hundred Irish sailed to Halifax via St. John's between 1826 and 1830. This change allowed shipowners to pack more passengers into their holds, thus giving people brave enough to cross the Atlantic in substandard shipping via St. John's the option of cheaper fares.[44]

In many ways the Irish were locked into a humanitarian crisis. They faced starvation at home and loss of life at sea as they fled to escape their poverty. Survivors often came with terrible injuries, thus putting a further strain on Halifax's public purse. Sailing first to St. John's, followed by transfers to Halifax, exposed them to considerable dangers. With its fog, ice, and rocky coastlines, the Gulf of St. Lawrence was a perilous place to be at the best of times. Vessels were frequently battered in storms, particularly on their approach to Halifax. In late November/early December 1816, forty-nine Irish people were believed to have perished in the *Shamrock* during its crossing from St. John's to Halifax.[45] In the following year the *Consolation*, which meant to land its thirty Irish passengers at Halifax, was forced into Pope's Harbour while the *Lively* of Halifax, having lost both masts in a storm, was forced into Beaver Harbour.[46]

Of course, ships were also damaged in the middle of the Atlantic as happened in 1818 when fifty-one shipwrecked Irish immigrants, who had been rescued in the Azores, arrived in Halifax in the British schooner *Swift*.[47] When the *Lady Sherbrooke* sailed from Londonderry to Quebec with four hundred passengers in August 1831, the ship ran ashore in thick fog at Port aux Basques (Newfoundland) leaving only forty survivors: "There were reports of sailing through a great number of dead bodies in the area of the catastrophe by the master of a schooner."[48] Or, as was the case with the *Mermaid* of Dublin, sailing in July 1819 with seventy-three passengers aboard, the approach to Halifax was a vessel's ruination. The brig went aground at the very dangerous stretch of coastline along Cape Negro Island, but all were saved.[49] Although Atlantic crossings were potentially hazardous to everyone, shipwrecks were undoubtedly experienced far more by the impoverished southern Irish than by the Scots, English, and Ulster Irish. A particularly fine example of a good vessel used by the latter was the *Marcus Hill*, one of William McCorkell's first-class ships measuring seven hundred tons, which brought 250 Ulster Irish from Londonderry to Halifax in 1817.[50] Undoubtedly, the Ulster Irish, Scots, and English generally sailed to Nova Scotia in substantial vessels that were designed for the timber trade, while, in certain years, many of the southern Irish came in mere fishing vessels.

By 1831, the Nova Scotia authorities were becoming more receptive to having their population augmented by the Newfoundland Irish. The overflow from the island was now being regarded more favourably, since by that time, most people were arriving with adequate resources to become self-sufficient. The Nova Scotia council even went as far as saying that it regarded with approval "the emigrants who annually came from Newfoundland with the acquired means to enable them to distribute and form settlements without any expense or burden to the government or the Country."[51] However, the same could not be said of the people arriving directly from Ireland.

A deepening agricultural depression and a diminishing textile trade brought an ever-increasing number of impoverished Irish to Halifax, some suffering from smallpox, typhus, or cholera. When the *James* arrived from Waterford in September 1827 with 127 passengers aboard, "of the most wretched description, all of whom, as well as the whole crew ... labouring under typhus fever," it was reported that five had died at sea, while thirty-five had disembarked at St. John's, being "too ill to proceed."[52] Similarly, judging from the high death toll of the passengers who sailed in the *Cumberland* from Waterford two months earlier, typhus had taken its toll then as well.[53]

The New World had boundless charm for landless labourers and unemployed workers, but their arrival presented immediate challenges. After a decade of coping with the penniless and ill, the Nova Scotia legislature introduced a head tax of five shillings in 1832, payable by each overseas passenger, to raise funds for "the benefit of the poor emigrants arriving in the province."[54] While some immigrants endured great hardship to pay the tax, the scheme enabled the province to better contain diseases such as cholera and typhus, by using the money raised to build quarantine facilities at the port. Those people who wished to live in rural areas and eventually purchase their own farms headed for the large tracts of good land that were still to be found inland in the east of the province.

Meanwhile, with their intake of Loyalists and ex-soldiers in 1785, following the end of the American War of Independence, Antigonish and Guysborough Counties had acquired Irish communities, and because of this, both attracted later groups of Irish Catholics.[55] The Irish ex-soldiers who had served with the Nova Scotia Volunteers Regiment and received grants of land near Antigonish Harbour had clearly prospered. By 1787 they were reported to have significantly supplemented the Roman Catholic congregations in the region. With this head start, others followed.

After the severe economic downturn experienced by the Newfoundland fishery in 1815, a number of Irish families relocated to eastern Nova Scotia, choosing a location that they named Bantry, after a town in county Cork. Later abandoning it, they moved on to the Salmon River Lake region in Guysborough County, where they prospered. Founding Erinville, Ogden, and Rogerton as their principal settlements, they attracted other Irish colonizers who slowly progressed along the river frontages in the valley between Guysborough Intervale and St. Andrews.[56] Even today the area retains the name of Roman Valley in recognition of the Catholic affiliations of its early settlers. As was remembered by their descendents, "the land in these localities is fertile, and ere long they had flourishing farms and were in comfortable circumstances."[57]

The census of 1871 would reveal how people with Irish ancestry laid claim to much of Antigonish County and the northern half of Guysborough County (see Map 8). By 1871, the largest Irish concentrations were in the towns of Antigonish, Guysborough, and Manchester, the latter two being on the northeast side of Guysborough County. There were also substantial numbers at Meford near Manchester and farther north in Antigonish County at Lochaber, Ireland, and Cloverville.

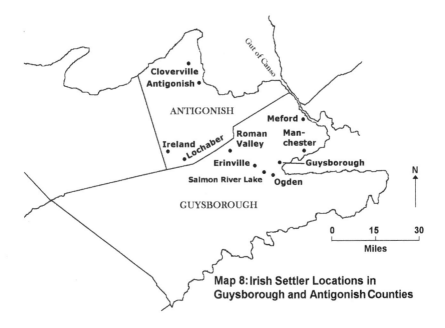

Map 8: Irish Settler Locations in Guysborough and Antigonish Counties

In the 1780s, Irish Catholics were also present in the town of Pictou in sufficient numbers to warrant a resident priest, and the same was true of Arichat and Sydney in Cape Breton. However, their principal destination was always going to be Halifax, while Cape Breton was often their second choice.

With its cod fishery and coal mines, Cape Breton Island offered well-paid employment to new arrivals anxious to make a start in a pioneering community without having to acquire new skills. Those with family or friends living in rural areas might have been more inclined to take up farming, assuming they could acquire land, while some might have become tradesmen and craftsmen in the burgeoning towns. The presence of Irish settlers along the Strait of Canso and the Western Shore in Inverness County, as revealed by the 1818 census, indicates that these were preferred locations. Port Hood, Mabou, and Judique had the occasional Irish merchant, tailor, and butcher, as well as a few Irish farmers.[58] The fishing stations along the east and south coasts of the island had also attracted Irish fishermen by 1818, with a substantial number being based at Louisbourg. With its good fishing opportunities, St. Peters near

Map 9: Irish Settler Locations in Cape Breton in 1871

Arichat in Richmond County was one of the earliest places of Irish settlement in the entire island (see Map 9).[59]

By the end of the eighteenth century, only around two thousand people lived on Cape Breton Island, half of whom were French-speaking Acadians. The rest were mainly Loyalist refugees from the United States.[60] It was still an undeveloped British colony. Cod fishing supported most of the island's economy, while farming operated at a subsistence level, with agricultural communities being dispersed over very large areas. There were no roads. No churches had been built. There was no effective local government. Nevertheless, Cape Breton attracted a great many Highland Scots, who became the dominant ethnic group; but it also had an appreciable number of Irish Catholics.

The fishing stations, which were concentrated on the south and east of the island, had been established in 1765 by merchants from the Channel Islands.[61] Just over one hundred years later, people of Irish descent would be a significant part of the population along the south coast, especially at Main-à-Dieu and Louisbourg (Cape Breton County) and at Arichat (Richmond County).[62] And in the mining villages, which began sprouting up at and near Sydney by the early nineteenth century, the Irish formed the second-largest ethnic group after the Scots.

The jobs on offer at the Sydney coal mines, which were being worked from at least 1807, were another obvious inducement to the Irish. Around fifty to one hundred men were employed by this time in the mines, but working under very unpleasant and austere conditions. Many were Irishmen who had previously worked in the Newfoundland fishery.[63] Bishop Plessis met some of them in 1815, on one of his visits to Nova Scotia and Cape Breton: "Most of these Catholics were Irish people, outcasts from their own country, who had made homes for themselves in Newfoundland and had come from there to the [Sydney] mine. Around it they housed their families in huts covered with the bark of trees and furnished with wooden fireplaces."[64] But many did not remain in mining.

After a few years employment as miners, some of the Irish became farmers, either in Cape Breton or in other locations, the most popular being the United States.[65] Waterford-born Michael Doyle is a typical example. Having arrived from Newfoundland in 1808, he worked at the mines for twenty years before going on to acquire land at Ingonish on the northeast side of the island.[66] James Fitzgerald took a similar route. He petitioned for a lot at Cape North on the north coast in 1819, having served "faithfully at the Coal Mines" for nearly ten years.[67]

Meanwhile, with the massive capital investment made by the British-based General Mining Association in Sydney's coalfield, production rose sharply from 1827, thus greatly increasing the size of the workforce and attracting even more Irish families to the area.[68] By 1871 both Sydney Mines and nearby Lingan Mines were major Irish strongholds. Yet for many, coal mining continued to be only a stepping stone on the way to owning a farm, though the process of acquiring a suitable plot was fraught with difficulty.[69]

Although plenty of Crown land was still available after 1820, some of it was of poor quality, the best having been snapped up by the first waves of settlers, many of whom were Highland Scots. Moreover, the British government had placed restrictions in the settlers' way in the hope of encouraging them to leave. Cape Breton's valuable coal mines were the reason. The government wished to have unfettered access to its coal reserves in order to supply the army units based in Halifax and Newfoundland. Additionally, it did not wish to have Britain's coal mines competing with Cape Breton mines or see Cape Breton's coal being exported to the United States. Thus, for reasons connected with coal, the government tried to stop all but Loyalists and fish merchants from acquiring freeholds on the island, a restriction that remained in force until 1817. In practice, though, immigrants took no notice of these legal restraints and simply slipped across into Cape Breton and squatted on the best land they could find.

After 1817 settlers could get freehold grants, and on very generous terms.[70] At last settlers were being welcomed. Those already on the island could acquire documentation to legitimize their holdings, while new arrivals could get land grants on the remaining available sites. Cape Breton's land grant records, which were produced retrospectively from 1817, once the legal restraints on land ownership were removed, reveal that many of the Irish seeking land had arrived from Newfoundland.[71] In all, about two hundred Irishmen petitioned for land grants between 1794 and 1839.

The Newfoundland Irish included men like Timothy Hogan from Limerick, who, having arrived in Cape Breton in 1796, became a school-master four years later. After living seven years in Newfoundland, Paul Downey from Kilkenny was working as a tailor in Port Hood in 1816. John Coady was granted twenty-five acres at Cheticamp on the northwest coast after living for two years in Newfoundland; John Costly from Kilkenny became a butcher in Port Hood after a brief time in Newfoundland; and James Fanning from Waterford tried his hand at farming in Port Hood and afterward worked as a weaver in Mabou. William Heffernan, who came to Cape Breton just a few months after arriving in Newfoundland, eventually became a farmer, living near Judique. Meanwhile, John Martin, having worked for five years in the Newfoundland fishery, was recorded in the 1818 census as a labourer in the Gut of Canso (now the Strait of Canso). These snippets of information indicate a wide dispersal of the Irish in farming communities across Cape Breton.

Significant Irish settlement clusters only developed in the mining and fishing regions of eastern Cape Breton, especially in those areas that offered good opportunities for farming. In 1829, Thomas Chandler Haliburton described "an old Irish settlement" between Sydney and Lingan [Mines] as an area where "the soil is fertile and well-timbered.... It is occupied chiefly by the Irish ... who give the name of Low Point to the whole settlement from the eastern side of Sydney harbour, round the coast to Lingan, the settlers of which are likewise principally Irish or their descendents ... the Irish settlement continues along the coast from Lingan to the small Boat Harbour of Glace Bay."[72] In addition to Lingan Mines and Sydney, the Irish were a significant part of the population at Margaree on the west coast, Ingonish and Main-à-Dieu on the east, and Arichat and St. Peters on the south coast.[73]

The settlement of Margaree by the Irish may have been stimulated by the Wexford-born Moses Doyle. Having taken part in the United Irishmen Rebellion of 1798 and been captured, he escaped from prison and shortly afterward moved to Cape Breton, where he worked for his uncle, a St. Peters merchant.[74] Following the British government's amnesty to those who had participated in the rebellion, he returned to Ireland in 1802–03, though he returned to Cape Breton in 1826 to claim an inheritance from his uncle's estate, part of which was a large grant of land at Margaree. Moses Doyle's description of the good land in Cape Breton in letters home would have helped to encourage followers from his native Wexford.[75]

The fairly orderly influx that occurred from Ireland and Newfoundland was rudely broken in 1847 when Halifax was deluged by the starving Irish.[76] The Great Potato Famine that struck Ireland that year was a catastrophe of immense proportions.[77] Thousands of distressed Irish headed for North America. Most of those who arrived in Halifax were reported to be "in the lowest depths of destitution — having neither food nor clothing."[78] Some had been struck down by fever and were wandering the streets, endangering the lives of Halifax residents.[79] One of the ships that arrived was the *Mary* from Cork. It had been meant to disembark its forty-six passengers at Boston, but had been turned away on the captain's refusal to give bonds for his pauper immigrants. Despite a mutiny among the passengers, the ship proceeded to Halifax. On May 31, *The Nova Scotian* exclaimed "Still They Come" and called for funds to be raised for the "sick and starving."

John Nowlan a resident of Weymouth, Nova Scotia, who had originated from county Wexford, described to his son, Patrick, the suffering he had witnessed first-hand: "The people, the young and the old, are dying as fast as they can bury them. The fever is raging here at such a rate that those in health in the morning, knows not but in the evening they may have taken the infection."[80] In total, around one thousand Irish entered Nova Scotia in 1847, with most sailing from Galway and Cork in the west of Ireland.

Leaving aside the horrors of 1847, the peopling of Nova Scotia by the Irish was predominantly brought about by the immigration that occurred in the 1820s and 1830s, most of it served by ports in the southeast and southwest of Ireland. The majority were Catholics, known far and wide for their poverty. There were no Irish proprietors or land company agents on hand to provide them with resources or to help them to organize their new communities in Nova Scotia. This is a story of ordinary people arriving singly or in small groups and taking one small step at a time.

The influx of Irish immigrants depended to a large extent on the fishing trade. The overflow from the Newfoundland fishery had brought many to the province and Nova Scotia's widespread fishing stations were a further incentive. Lieutenant governor Viscount Falkland went as far as claiming that Nova Scotia became home to so many poverty-stricken immigrants because of "the fisheries that are established all around the Coasts of Cape Breton and on the western shore of Nova Scotia which at once afford subsistence to those accustomed to similar pursuits in Europe." For this reason, "the greater number" of immigrants to Nova Scotia, who "frequently" possessed "no wealth but their labour, were in a different class from those who emigrate to New Brunswick or Canada."[81]

Celtic cross memorial in Halifax. The inscription reads: Dedicated to the original Irish settlers of 1749 and to the contributions of the Irish community to Halifax, to Nova Scotia and to Canada. Presented by the Charitable Irish Society of Halifax, established 1786, dedicated March 17, 2000.

Although a good many of the Irish had arrived via Newfoundland, they generally shared the same county origins as those arriving directly from Ireland, coming from Kilkenny, Waterford and Wexford, Tipperary, and Cork.[82]

While Nova Scotia had obvious appeal to the poor, it was less attractive to families with capital, who looked for the most advantageous economic locations in the hope of prospering as New World farmers. In 1831, an Irish soldier serving with the 34th Regiment told his father, William Keys, who was living in county Fermanagh, that having travelled through "the whole of Nova Scotia" and living in Cape Breton for twelve months, he found "nothing but a wilderness full of trees and stones and wild beasts.... There is scarcely a day passes but there are some accidents happening from drink, some going mad."[83] He clearly would not remain in the province following his discharge.

Nova Scotia was a mere taster for many, since the majority of Irish set their sights on New Brunswick. Its enormous timber trade and vast stretches of fertile land attracted waves of settlers from both the north and south of Ireland over a long period. In 1851 the Irish-born represented a staggering 71 percent of the total immigration to New Brunswick.

CHAPTER 5

New Brunswick's Irish and the Timber Trade

> They are all Irish, at least in this town [Saint John]. The brogue is not in higher perfection in Kilkenny.... I came through a whole tract of land peopled by Irish who came out not worth a shilling and now all own farms worth (according to the value of money in this country) from £1,000 to £3,000.
>
> The equality of everyone and their manner of life I like very much. There are no gentlemen; everyone is on an [equal] footing providing he works and wants nothing; every man is exactly what he can make [of] himself, or has made [of] himself by his industry."[1]

Lord Edward Fitzgerald, the Irish aristocrat and revolutionary who died in Ireland while resisting arrest for treason during the 1798 uprising for independence, wrote affectionately about the people he met in Saint John when based there ten years earlier. The accents seemed familiar because they were Irish. Edward, one of the many thousands of Loyalists who had arrived from the United States in 1784, and others like him, formed the initial core of New Brunswick's immigrant society. The city of Saint John, incorporated a year later, was founded almost exclusively by Loyalists, and within thirty years it would become the region's primary timber port.

Lord Edward's account of penniless immigrants who had been able to buy farms must have sounded like a dream come true. The egalitarian society that he described was an added bonus. The New World had no masters and no pecking order. Immigrants could be free-thinking individuals, seeking what was best for their families, rather than being subject to the dictates of landlords, bureaucrats, and factory owners, as was the case in Britain. But however attractive this set of advantages and opportunities may have sounded, New Brunswick had to wait until the opening up of the timber trade in the early nineteenth century before further waves of immigrants arrived at its shores. The large increase in tariffs on Baltic timber, first introduced during the Napoleonic Wars, gave North American timber a considerable cost advantage over traditional supplies from Europe.[2] The trade mushroomed, and by 1826, wood products accounted for 75 percent of the province's export revenues.[3] The growth in trade caused the volume of shipping between Ireland and the province to soar, bringing affordable and regular transport to immigrants. As trading links developed, they could simply purchase places on one of the many timber ships that regularly crossed the Atlantic.

Despite its promising Loyalist beginnings, the province struggled to retain its population. Most Loyalists had settled along the extensive river frontages of the Saint John and Kennebecasis valleys and in the Passamaquoddy Bay area at the southwestern corner of the province.[4] And yet, they failed to attract much in the way of followers, as had been hoped. On the contrary, many Loyalists were dissatisfied with their new locations and either returned to the United States or found better prospects in Upper Canada. To the dismay of local administrators, New Brunswick soon became a well-trodden gateway to the United States, not just for new arrivals from the British Isles seeking to avoid American immigration taxes, but also for its own disgruntled settlers. In 1806, New Brunswick's population was only thirty-five thousand, nearly half that of Nova Scotia and Upper Canada and a fraction of that of Lower Canada, which was almost seven times greater.[5] Good land was in shorter supply by the 1820s, and although the timber trade offered extensive employment opportunities, its appeal was limited, causing the province to experience a relatively high population turnover.

It had taken a severe economic depression, which followed the ending of the Napoleonic Wars in 1815, to kick-start New Brunswick's flow of British and Irish immigrants. The Irish who arrived starting in 1817 became widely scattered across the province, although their numbers cannot be quantified owing to the later loss of customs records.[6] The odd reference to particular groups, such as the seven thousand mainly Irish immigrants who arrived in 1819, suggests that the province's ports were inundated that year.[7] Given their wretched condition, emigrant societies were established at Fredericton, Saint John, and St. Andrews to provide needy arrivals with shelter and other necessities.[8] Some, like the one hundred passengers on board the *Commerce* of Workington, who had sailed from Belfast in 1822, only managed to reach Dublin. Fierce gales had not only damaged their ship, but also ruined their provisions. Unable to afford new supplies, they were stranded. Despite their "destitute condition," an appeal for help to the Marquis of Wellesley, Lord Lieutenant and General Governor of Ireland, to enable them to proceed to Saint John, went unheeded.[9]

It is impossible to determine precisely how many immigrants from the British Isles settled in New Brunswick. The available evidence indicates that the influx before 1817 was dominated by Scots[10] and after this by the Irish, who far outnumbered all other immigrant groups. The influx averaged around six to eight thousand immigrants a year between 1834 and 1847, although only a minority actually remained in the province, with most being in transit to the United States.[11] The major Irish influx occurred between 1817 and 1850, the timber trade providing the impetus and greatly influencing settlement choices. Quite simply, it drove New Brunswick's economic development. It built the towns of Saint John, Chatham, Newcastle, St. Andrews, and Fredericton, created employment for countless men, and encouraged the investment of capital in the province.

For the very poor, the timber trade provided the means to earn money to purchase land, although there were plenty of lumbermen who never became farmers. But, since fluctuations in Britain's economy caused huge variations in the demand for timber, the province had to cope with periods of economic stagnation. Nevertheless, the trade propelled New Brunswick's economic development during the first half of the nineteenth century and in doing so attracted a growing influx of Irish immigrants.[12] As Peter Fisher noted in his *History of New Brunswick* published in 1825, "the woods furnish a sort of simple manufactory for the inhabitants, from which after attending to their farms in the summer, they can draw returns during the winter for those supplies which are necessary for the comfort of their families."[13]

The 1851 census reveals that the Irish-born accounted for 71 percent of the total immigration from the British Isles to New Brunswick that year, with the Scottish-born representing only 15 percent and the English-born 10 percent.[14] At least 70 percent of the new arrivals in Carleton, Charlotte, Sunbury, Kings, Queens, and Saint John Counties (see Map 10) were Irishborn. In other words, the Irish had been drawn especially to the southwest of the province where Loyalists had made the first colonization advances. Irish Protestants predominated here, although the city of Saint John and its environs was the exception in attracting Catholics and Protestants more or less equally. Large concentrations of Irish Catholics also found frontages along the Miramichi River and its tributaries in the northeast. Twenty years later, people having Irish ancestry were mainly to be found in these same regions. They were prominent in southwestern New Brunswick, especially in Saint John County, where they represented 58 percent of the population, and in Northumberland County in the northeast, where they accounted for 40 percent (see Map 11).[15]

Shipping records indicate that until the 1830s the Irish immigrant stream came mainly from ports in Ulster in the north of the country. The source counties changed during the 1830s and 1840s when ports in the south and west of Ireland provided an ever larger proportion of the outflow. In the year of the Great Famine in 1847 the south and west accounted for 70 percent of the total immigration to New Brunswick from Ireland. The 1851 census reflects this shipping pattern in the sense that it shows that most of the province's Irish came from counties Donegal, Londonderry, Tyrone, Fermanagh, and Cork. People in the first four counties had ready access to the Ulster ports of Belfast and Londonderry, while people living in Cork had a major seaport on their

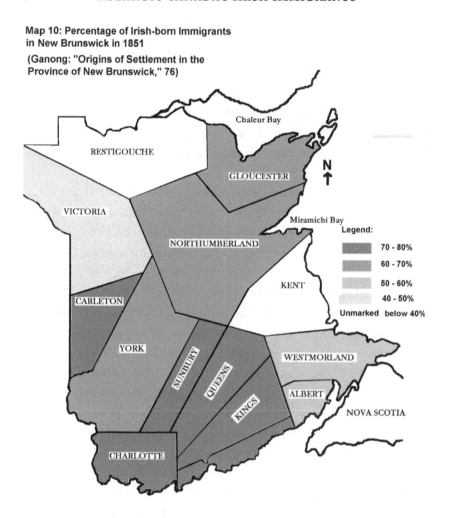

Map 10: Percentage of Irish-born Immigrants in New Brunswick in 1851

(Ganong: "Origins of Settlement in the Province of New Brunswick," 76)

doorstep. Before 1830 most Irish immigrants were Protestant, but the proportion of Catholics rose during the 1830s and 1840s. Detailed data for county Londonderry, taken from the Ordnance Survey Memoirs for Ireland, reveals that even during the 1830s it primarily lost Protestants to New Brunswick, the overwhelming proportion being Presbyterians.[16] The same source reveals that if the immigrants who came from county Antrim are typical, they often carried money with them, some bringing substantial sums.[17]

**Map 11: Percentage of New Brunswick's
Population Having Irish Ancestry in 1871**

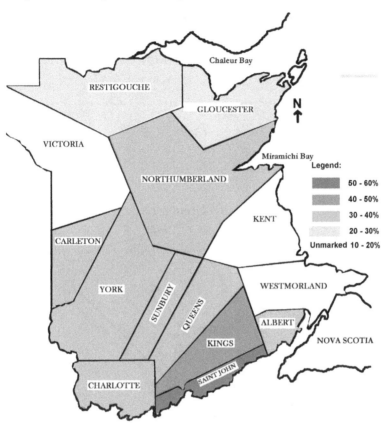

Charlotte County's timber trade, which had first been established by
Loyalists, quickly flourished, and by 1800 the county was the province's
leading timber producer.[18] Helping to achieve this outcome were men like
Peter Clinch, born in county Meath, who, having served as a lieutenant in
the Royal Fencibles American Regiment, became the founding father of
the town of St. George. However, the main influx of settlers from Ireland
began in 1817, with most originating from Ulster. For the people who travelled in the *Dorcas Savage* from Belfast in 1818, sailing conditions were

good: "No person had been afflicted [except with seasickness] during the passage" (see Table 4).[19] The attractiveness of the county to north of Ireland people is reflected in the continuing arrival of ships at St. Andrews from Belfast and the nearby ports of Portaferry and Strangford throughout the 1820s (Appendix I).[20] They selected sites along the county's seacoasts and riverbanks, becoming concentrated in the parishes of St. James, St. Andrews, St. George, and St. Stephen (see Map 12).

Map 12: Irish Settlements in South Western New Brunswick, 1851

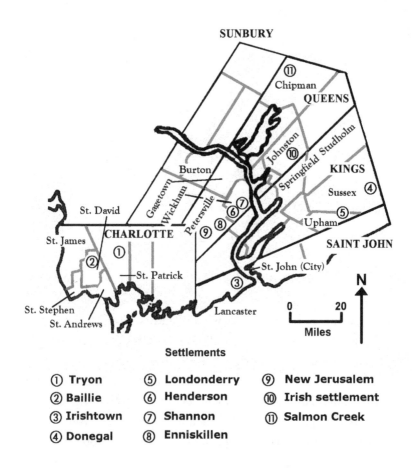

Settlements

① Tryon	⑤ Londonderry	⑨ New Jerusalem
② Baillie	⑥ Henderson	⑩ Irish settlement
③ Irishtown	⑦ Shannon	⑪ Salmon Creek
④ Donegal	⑧ Enniskillen	

Some of the Irish newcomers were very poor, especially the large number who arrived in 1817. The demands that they placed on the public purse caused considerable agitation, with the people of St. Andrews complaining the loudest. The townspeople had to support the feeble and infirm who remained in the area, while looking on askance as the able-bodied and independently minded took the first opportunity they could of going off to the United States.[21] Nevertheless, despite the loss of many people to the States, the growing flood of immigrants led to a doubling of the province's population between 1806 and 1824 (to just under 75,000) and by 1840 it had doubled again to just over 156,000.[22]

Henry Coulter, a Presbyterian from county Down, was certain that he had done the right thing in choosing to live in St. David Parish. Writing home in 1822, he proclaimed that "this country improves in my opinion every day. There is nothing but a small capital wanting to enable a man to farm successfully here and live happily. My brother [William] and I are getting land in the parish of St. David's [sic], one mile from the salt water; the land is excellent but in the woody state."[23] With positive feedback such as this, it is hardly surprising that there were many Irish followers, most of whom arrived between 1825 and 1835. The Baillie settlement[24] in St. James Parish was founded in 1828 by northern Irish immigrants, while the Tryon Settlement in St. Patrick Parish, laid out ten years later, housed Irish immigrants who had worked on the St. Andrews and Quebec Railway, which was operational in the 1830s.[25]

As forest clearance progressed, communities formed along the Passamaquoddy Bay and the lower St. Croix River. Thin lines of settlement also followed the St. Andrews to Saint John River Road and the middle stretches of the Magaguadavic River going northward. Population densities were particularly high in the three adjoining parishes of St. Andrews, St. David, and St. Stephen, on the west side of the county, but even here agriculture remained secondary to lumbering.[26] The town of St. Andrews, with its port in Passamaquoddy Bay, was second only to Saint John in population and economic importance.

Although much of the early trade was with the West Indies, some timber was being exported overseas. Being close to the American border, the county's merchants could easily circumvent trade restrictions and

TABLE 4

Partial Passenger List: Crossing of the *Dorcas Savage*, Captain Pollock, from Portaferry to St. Andrews, April 1818

[*Generations, Journal of the New Brunswick Genealogical Society* 36, no. 1 (Spring 2015): 66]

Rob Brown Johnson	James McHarg & family
John Wilson & family	Thomas Jones & family
Thomas Corhat	William Crangle
Matthew Downey	John Ramsey
Andrew Byers	Henry Murney
James Smyth	Eliza Mateer & family
John Dickson	Henry Seed
James Magee	James Graham & family
Leslie Coulter	Daniel Taggart
Pat McGrath	Andrew Cavanagh & family
Richard Polly and family	Hugh Taggart
John Seed	John Coates & family
Jno. Reynolds & family	John Hughes
Michael Hughes	John Cosbey & family
Samuel Shanks	Sam. Seeds & family
John Miskelly	

customs regulations and sell goods in the lucrative black markets that operated in the United States and the West Indies. They also enjoyed preferential trading privileges in the West Indies in the sale of their timber. But in 1821, when the tariff advantage of colonial timber was reduced, business confidence began to decline. Legislation, passed in 1823, allowing the West Indies to import American timber (or other foreign timber), was an even greater blow to local exporters.[27] The St. Andrews jail was said to be full of "the most respectable men," whose sad predicament was being blamed on the demise of Charlotte County's timber trade.[28] It recovered quickly with timber exports to Britain soaring ahead during the 1830s; but this was only a temporary respite. As logging progressed northward along the Northumberland Strait, Charlotte County lost its long-standing leadership in lumber production, and by the 1840s it was in the grip of a devastating economic depression.

The situation went from bad to worse. When the tariff on foreign timber was reduced in 1842, the local economy took another tumble.[29] A year earlier, "magistrates, merchants, shipowners, mill owners and other inhabitants of the parishes of St. Stephen, St. David, and St. James," who numbered 153, had complained that the proposed reduction "would give a decided advantage" to American timber over New Brunswick's. Being closer to the West Indies, American goods could be shipped there more cheaply. There were thirty-eight sawmills in St. Stephen producing "8,400 tons of shipping," which was taken on thirty-six vessels, "nearly all of which are calculated only for the West India trade." Charlotte County had more than one hundred sawmills and "the shipping amount[ed] to from 16,000 to 20,000 tons."[30] All of this was at risk, but their pleas went unanswered.

However, despite the downturn in its economic fortunes, Charlotte County attracted a second wave of Irish immigrants in the 1840s, most being Catholics. Since many sailed from Cork, a substantial proportion must have come from the south of Ireland. The majority headed for the town of St. Andrews, where they worked as railway and dock workers. Some also settled in the town of St. Stephen.[31] Meanwhile, the Scottish, English, and Irish families already resident in St. Andrews and St. Stephen moved out to escape the economic depression that bedevilled the area, thus increasing the proportion of Irish in these parishes.[32] By 1871, around 50 percent of the total population of St. Andrews and St. Stephen parishes had Irish ancestry, although the Irish were best represented in the largely Protestant St. Patrick Parish, where they made up 62 percent of the population.

Some of the earlier Ulster settlers had remained in the area despite the economic downturn in the 1840s, although life for many was a struggle. Writing to his brother in 1857, William Gamble from county Down reported how "the people here [St. George parish] in the winter are in the woods getting out lumber; one of the boys [his sons] has been employed at that this winter and I have been employed near home with one of the boys hauling with my own horse. The wages are from £3 10s to £4 10s per month but a good many are paid with what they call trade, that is provisions and clothing."[33] He hoped to establish his own farm, but that was easier said than done:

I have been employed burning lime ever since I came here [St. George parish] except what time I have off working on my own place.... I could not live by lime burning alone if I had not a small place of my own to raise a little on.... I have 25 acres of land part of it is cleared up and part not.... I am able to keep three cows and a horse and some calves and a few sheep. There is an agricultural society here; it was got up about four years ago; I am one of the members of it and last fall I received the most prizes of anyone in two parishes.... I cannot command much money but I can afford to live as well as the most of them that lives by working [has 12 children].[34]

In 1869, Malcolm Gamble, probably a relative, was still "away all winter in the woods about 50 miles from home working for the Master that I worked for last summer and I am hired with him again. I have not planted my potatoes yet but I will in a day or so."[35]

Although the fertile belt along the Saint John River Valley had accommodated much of the Loyalist influx to the province, its population centres grew very slowly. The future city of Saint John, at the mouth of the river, was little more than "a small English town" to the Methodist minister William Bennett, when he visited it in 1803.[36] However, by 1840, the town had twenty thousand residents, outstripping Halifax as the largest and most important city on the Atlantic seaboard. It dominated the business life of both New Brunswick and Nova Scotia.[37] And Irish immigrants flocked to the region in their thousands.

In 1851, the Irish-born of Saint John County represented an astounding 81 percent of the county's total immigrant population. Twenty years later, people with Irish ancestry accounted for 58 percent of the county's total population, far outnumbering other ethnic groups. Without a doubt, Saint John was the most Irish of the province's counties! As the city was a major port of entry and a centre for the timber trade, it offered exceptional employment opportunities and attracted many immigrants. Having begun life as a Protestant Loyalist city, Saint John acquired sufficient Irish Catholics by 1871 to give it a population that was equally divided between

Catholics and Protestants.[38] However, most of the Irish living in rural communities along the Saint John River Valley remained largely Protestant.[39] Thus, the county became home to an Irish population that was split by religion, with Catholics largely favouring the city and Protestants the valley hinterland. The Irish in Charlotte, Albert, Kings, Queens, Sunbury, York, and Carleton Counties were predominately Protestants (see Map 11).[40]

People of all backgrounds came from Ireland, although the majority were labourers and tradesmen.[41] Judging from the wage comparisons he related in a letter to his parents in Londonderry in 1819, Robert McClory was one of the many semi-skilled workers who had flocked to the area. Having failed to find employment in Cumberland County (Nova Scotia), where he first arrived, Robert "walked 120 miles through the woods, in some parts of which, having nine miles without a single hut and a narrow and rugged footpath," to reach Saint John. And yet, despite feeling that "the people in that part are generous and hospitable and anxious for strangers to settle in it," he judged wage rates to be low and soon left for Philadelphia.[42]

However, the legally trained Charles Devine from county Tyrone prospered in Saint John. Arriving with his wife and children in the 1830s, he became a prominent member of the city's early Catholic community.

James Ward, who hailed from Londonderry in 1834, found employment on a steamboat, but he was far from happy:

> Dear father, tho' I have no reason to complain since my arrival here, but one thing I must observe to you and for the information of all friends, that there is a long tedious winter here to what our countrymen at home is not used to, and that it takes great management to provide for the wet day. However, all who take the journey upon them endeavour to get through pretty fair. This country puts an Irishman to his wits, every man to his fancy. I will neither advise persons of my own or any other family to come out, or yet stop. One deviation I must suggest that I would feel happy that my cousin Mary Kelly would endeavour to get coming here, as I have every reason to believe she might do very well here.[43]

Charles Devine, his wife, Mary McCollough, and two of their children, circa 1850.

Prospects were probably better for the Irish Catholic fishermen and their families who settled along the coast to the south of the city of Saint John. The first group, who arrived in 1824, founded a community they named Irishtown (Lancaster Parish), situated near present-day Lorneville, within the city limits.[44] A much larger group of around two hundred Irish Catholics, who originated mainly from county Louth and included many people from Cooley Parish, arrived ten years later and settled nearby at Saint John's Lower Cove.[45] Many sought work in the harbour fishery. Attracting followers over the next decade, they turned this area of coastline into a county Louth enclave.[46]

With its fertile lands and plentiful river frontages, Kings County attracted many Irish who mainly settled in localities that had first been colonized by Loyalists in the mid 1780s. Most of these people had come from Ulster.[47] Visiting the area in 1851, the writer J.F.W. Johnston judged it to have acquired "the air of a civilized old settled region."[48] When he visited the town of Hampton, he was told how "good soils had rewarded those who found courage enough to clear them of trees and stones, and the beautiful landscape gave to a stranger's eye a double value to homes established, despite the obstacles in this portion of Kings County." According to local inhabitants "an industrious emigrant without capital will thrive even in this more stony part of their district."[49] While the Irish were widely scattered across the county, most were to be found in Sussex Parish. By 1871, 56 percent of its population had Irish ancestry.[50]

According to the historian W.F. Ganong, Sussex Parish was the most prosperous farming centre in the whole of New Brunswick.[51] And yet, the Reverend Christopher Atkinson was unimpressed with the area when he visited in 1844. Apparently it was "in a wilderness state or is again growing up with bushes, and in some instances has fallen into neglect, owing to the erection of saw mills which have called away the attention of the farmer from the more profitable and certain pursuits of agriculture."[52]

However, like many other contemporary commentators who thought timber production blighted the landscape, he failed to appreciate its importance to the local economy. Wide rivers and interconnecting tributaries were tailor-made for the transport of this commodity that brought welcome additional income to the area.

John and Ester Howe, who arrived in Springfield Parish from county Fermanagh in around 1819, were one of the many couples from Ulster who chose this location on the north side of the county.[53] Abraham Gesner noted that Irish and English immigrants living in Springfield Parish had arrived in the 1830s "without any means of subsistence." They had to live "in shanties among the trees and survive on the most humble fare.... By their industry they afterwards paid for their lots, cleared away the forest, made farms and now drive their wagons to the market at Saint John loaded with the surplus produce of their fields."[54]

The Reverend Daniel Welsh, a Scottish Presbyterian missionary who visited the area in 1829, described "a large settlement five miles back in the woods where there are about twenty Irish families who I visit occasionally."[55] No doubt, this was a north of Ireland community living in Springfield Parish. He also referred to another Irish community that had developed on the south side of the Hammond River, "extending six or seven miles back in the woods." This was almost certainly the Londonderry Settlement (Upham Parish), which was known to have been established by this time (see Map 12). According to the Reverend Atkinson, who visited the Londonderry settlement in 1844, "there are about forty families, who have to labour very hard to support themselves."[56] Meanwhile, Irish colonizers also founded the Donegal Settlement in about 1841 and the Long Settlement in around 1847, both in Sussex Parish, while Jordan Mountain (Studholm Parish) was yet another Irish immigrant farming community.[57]

The Irish were well-represented downriver in Gagetown's population in Queens County, a place that had once attracted Loyalists and, before that, settlers from New England.[58] One of the early arrivals included the Ulster-born Loyalist Patrick Robinson, who, having served with the Loyal American Regiment, settled with his wife Sally at nearby Cambridge Narrows.[59] As was the case in the rest of the Saint John River Valley, a striking characteristic of the growing Irish influx that followed the end of the Napoleonic Wars in 1815 was its Ulster credentials. Settlers from the north of Ireland, many named in the 1861 census as having originated from counties Donegal, Fermanagh, and Tyrone, spread their nets widely, forming their own communities across much of the county.

The settlements of Henderson (Wickham Parish)[60] and Salmon Creek (Chipman Parish)[61] were established around 1820 (see Map 12). New Jerusalem appeared in 1821, and the Irish Settlement (Johnston Parish), earlier called the Waterloo Settlement, emerged before 1824.[62] The McFarlane Settlement followed in 1825 and the Enniskillen Settlement (Petersville Parish) a year later.[63] The settlement of Shannon (Wickham Parish), which sprouted up in around 1829, was formed by immigrants from Shannon in county Clare in the south of Ireland as well as by settlers from Ulster.[64] Lawfield (Gagetown Parish) was founded in about 1840 by Michael Law, who arrived in the province in 1829.[65] But it was in Petersville Parish where the Irish really made their presence felt. In 1871, people of Irish ancestry accounted for 81 percent of the population!

New Jerusalem (Petersville Parish) seemed to be little more than a scattering of small clearings when Abraham Gesner visited it in 1847: "They [the clearings] bear a diminutive population to the extent of the wilderness lands around them."[66] Nevertheless, a vibrant community lived here as Alexander Machum's recollections of the settlement clearly show. Born in 1819, the year when his parents, Alexander Machum and Margaret Carson, arrived from Londonderry, he easily found a niche for himself in New Jerusalem once he left school. By the age of twenty, Alexander Jr. was a schoolteacher and later went on to run a general store and establish a farm.[67] His memoir, detailing events of his past, written in later life, provides a macabre but fascinating account of the causes of death in New Jerusalem during the 1840s. People were frozen to death, or died of scarlet fever and other illnesses with seeming regularity, indicating the precarious nature of pioneer life.[68] He also noted his enjoyment in attending the occasional Orange Lodge meeting in Gagetown, a social activity that brought him into contact with fellow Irish Protestants living in Queens County: "A more temperate, steady and respectable body of men is seldom seen."[69]

David Moore, a county Donegal man who arrived in New Brunswick with his wife Nancy Campbell in 1826, settled first in Saint John County but moved to New Jerusalem thirty years later. It was very much to his liking, as his letter to his brother in Donegal clearly indicates:[70]

> The part of the country where I have settled is different in some respects from what I have last mentioned. They do not grow large timber on this land. The timber that grows here is called hardwood, being of a hard nature, and best for firewood. Therefore this land where this hardwood grows is best for cultivation and most of the land in this settlement is equally as good as the land about Carndonagh [Ireland] when it is properly cleared and put under cultivation. There's one great benefit that the farmer enjoys here, that after he has once paid for his land, it is then a freehold forever. The freeholder pays no rent, no tithe, no taxes whatever, only a small tax yearly, for the support of the poor of each parish.[71]

Meanwhile, the Irish progression along the Saint John River Valley brought sizeable numbers of settlers to Burton Parish in Sunbury

**Map 13: Irish settlements in York and
Carleton Counties, New Brunswick, 1851.**

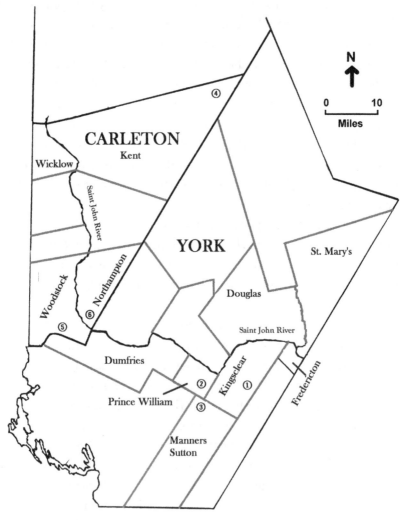

Settlements

① **Hanwell/Newmarket/Smithfield**
② **Magundy**
③ **Acton/Cork**
④ **Johnville**
⑤ **Irish settlement**
⑥ **Newburg**

The Irish Memorial in Fredericton, commemorating the city's earliest Roman Catholic parishioners, who were mostly Irish.

County;[72] but the Irish were much more widely dispersed in York County. The 1871 census indicates that about one-third of the York County Irish had headed for Fredericton, the province's capital, while the remaining two-thirds eventually settled in the rural parishes of Dumfries (later Canterbury), Prince William, Kingsclear, Douglas, and St. Marys (see Map 13).[73] As was the case generally in the southwest of the province, most of the Irish who settled in farming communities had originated from Ulster.[74]

Having arrived from county Armagh in 1816, Laurence Hughes settled in St. Marys Parish. Despite being situated fairly close to Fredericton, he was clearly dissatisfied with his prospects.[75] Nevertheless, twenty years went by before he felt he might return to Ireland. Meanwhile, his brother Thomas bombarded him with glowing accounts of life in Boston: "Lose no time in proceeding to Boston," where, if he "can get a little shop or store in a populous district, you would do well ... keep clear of whiskey if you can and be sure to give no credit."[76] And, later on, Laurence's brother-in-law, John Jackson, from county Monaghan, set out various reasons as to why Illinois and Minnesota offered the best farming opportunities, while Laurence's brother Edward wrote from Pennsylvania extolling the virtues of "a fine colony of settlers from [county] Carlow in Iowa," which he "intended to join."[77] Despite this hard sell from his family to relocate to the United States, Laurence remained in St. Marys Parish. Having taken this decision, he re-established contact with his brother Patrick. With the help of a local clergyman, he found him in Milltown (St. Stephen Parish in Charlotte County), where he was working in a sawmill for R.M. Todd. "Business here for a working man is very good. A person can always get work in the mills for pretty good wages." But it was his subsequent letter that explained why Patrick had gone missing: "I have given up liquor and I am a strong advocate of the Temperance cause. I have not taken anything for several years and I am in hopes I will never again.... With the help of the Almighty I will not."[78]

The proliferation of Irish communities in York County suggests that various groups had arrived from Ireland with the intention of settling together. This trend was especially noticeable in Kingsclear Parish, which, like St. Marys, was fairly close to Fredericton. The Hanwell Settlement, founded in 1825 and located along the Fredericton to St. Andrews Road, had been named after Thomas Baillie's place of birth in the London borough of Ealing.[79] A leading light in forming the London-based New Brunswick and Nova Scotia Land Company, Baillie had assisted the group to relocate to New Brunswick.[80]

When he visited Hanwell in 1851, J.F.W. Johnston described it as "Irish and less prosperous and extensive than Harvey," a settlement that had been founded in 1837 by English and Scottish settlers under the auspices of the New Brunswick and Nova Scotia Land Company.[81] Although the Newmarket Settlement and the Smithfield Settlement, both also in

A large boulder being drawn by a team of horses.

Kingsclear Parish, are reported to have been established by Ulster Irish immigrants in around 1839,[82] their place names suggest that they might have also attracted settlers from county Cork and Dublin respectively.[83] Protestant Irish immigrants, many from Donegal, Londonderry, and Tyrone, had also formed the Magundy Settlement in nearby Prince William Parish in 1822.[84]

The name of the Acton Settlement — also straddling the Fredericton to St. Andrews Road, but in Manners Sutton Parish just to the south of Kingsclear — almost certainly commemorates Acton in county Armagh, Ireland. Visiting it in 1851, six years after its formation, J.F.W. Johnston noted that it consisted of twenty Irish families: "The front lots are occupied by Cork men, Roman Catholics; the rear lots by Protestants." There was also the Cork settlement[85] "on a ridge to the right," a short distance from the Acton settlement, whose settlers he judged "to have not prospered as yet."[86]

However, Moses Perley, the province's emigration agent, presented a much rosier account ten years earlier when the Cork Settlement had made its first appearance as the "Teetotal settlement." Founded in 1842 by people from counties Cork and Kerry, the name was meant to reflect the temperance pledges made by the settlers, although they may not have been a requirement to receiving land grants.[87] As the acting commissioner, Perley had first-hand knowledge of their progress: "Where but two years ago stood a dense forest, there have been gathered by thirty-five settlers during the past autumn seven thousand two hundred and seventy-six bushels of Grain, Potatoes and Turnips." He estimated the total value of the Teetotal settlement's buildings and crops to be around £2,000 (see Table 5).[88]

Meanwhile, Carleton County,[89] in the Upper Saint John River Valley, became home to a large Irish Catholic community whose relocation arrangements had been masterminded by the Right Reverend John Sweeney, the Roman Catholic Bishop of Saint John. Named after him, the Johnville Settlement (Kent Parish) took shape in the second half of the nineteenth century (see Map 13).[90] This colonization scheme was Bishop Sweeney's answer to the ongoing spiral of poverty being endured by Irish immigrants in the province's towns and cities.[91] He commented how "hundreds of these hardworking, sober, honest men who have laboured and toiled about the city [Saint John] for ten, fifteen, twenty and even thirty years and who are no better off at the end of this period than they were commencing. Their conditions and prospect would have been very different had they gone into the country and settled on land."[92] His answer to their plight was to help them to go into the country.

Having persuaded the provincial government to release Crown land for his scheme, Bishop Sweeney appealed to Irish Catholics already residing in New Brunswick to grab the opportunity of acquiring land on easy terms. He also spread his net to the United States and other parts of Canada, especially Prince Edward Island, Nova Scotia, and Upper Canada. In the end, he acquired one-third of his recruits from the burgeoning city of Saint John and many of his other followers were probably urban dwellers. And to assist his followers in obtaining land grants he formed the Saint John Emigrants' Aid Society, which ultimately acquired thirty-six thousand acres of land on which the Johnville Settlement was established.[93]

TABLE 5

Irish Immigrants Residing at the Teetotal (Later Cork)
Settlement in New Brunswick, 1843
[PANB RS24: Journals of the House of Assembly, 1843, xcvi–xcvii]

Names	Acres Cleared	No. in Family	Estimated Value of Improvements £s
James Barrett	2	1	14
Daniel Donovan	7	1	44
Richard Davis	3	5	32
John Sullivan	3	1	14
Michael Sullivan	5	2	30
James Crane	5	3	35
James Cailey	4	1	25
Michael O'Brien	5	2	24
Cornelius Clancy	5	1	35
Cornelius McDonald	3	1	14
David Scanlin	3	4	27
Michael Crowley	5	2	31
Jeremiah Crowley	6	4	37
James Gorman	7	2	43
Owen Smith	5	1	31
Daniel O'Brien	4	1	33
John Mahoney	4	5	33
Dennis Riorden	5	2	31
John O'Brien	4	1	23
George Wynne	5	1	33
Miles O'Leary	4	0	8
Simon O'Leary	5	0	22
Michael Mahoney	5	4	31
Daniel Hurley	4	4	20
John Driscoll 1st	3	0	14
James Driscoll	5	1	35
Daniel Couglan	5	5	31
Jeremiah Donovan	3	1	14

Names	Acres Cleared	No. in Family	Estimated Value of Improvements £s
John Driscoll 2nd	5	3	31
John Barry	6	3	37
Edward Connor	5	4	31
John McCurdy	4	4	29
Daniel Sullivan	6	4	37
John Kingston	4	6	25
Timothy Daly 1st	5	4	35
John Couglan	5	4	35
John Russel	4	2	37
Timothy Daly 2nd	3	3	24
James Mahon	3	7	20
Henry Wynne	3	1	14
TOTALS	**177**	**101**	**1,119**

Father Thomas Connolly, the priest from Woodstock, was put in charge of the community, supervising the allocation of the lots and the location of the roads and bridges. Most of the original petitioners for land originated from Ulster — especially county Donegal. Hugh McCann and his wife Mary Jane Keleher are thought to have been the first Johnville settlers, arriving in the autumn of 1860, while the Boyds, Allisons, O'Keefes, Rileys, Sullivans, and others were said to have followed.[94] In his *History of Carleton County*, T.C.L. Ketchum noted that the McCanns came "with stout hearts and a year's provisions" and in the following year they "had fifty families for neighbours."[95]

John Maguire, editor of the *Cork Examiner* and an Irish member of the British Parliament, visited the settlement with Bishop Sweeney in 1862. As they approached, "the comfortable dwellings and substantial, and even spacious barns," opened up before them:

> Bounded on all sides by a wall of trees, which in one
> direction cover a range of mountains as beautiful in

their outline as those that are mirrored in the sweet waters of Killarney, an undulating plain of cleared land extends about two miles in length by a mile in breadth, dotted over with the most striking evidence of man's presence and the progress of civilization — comfortable dwellings, spacious barns.... Even to the eye of an Irish farmer, the vast plain before us would have presented a rough and rather unpromising aspect, for not two acres of the many hundred already cleared were yet free from the stumps of the great trees whose lofty branches had waved and moaned in the storms of ages.[96]

By this time Johnville had 160 houses and 600 residents. According to Maguire, most of the settlers had arrived without any capital "save that which comprises their health, their strength and their willingness to work." They earned enough money to get started by working for someone else, and when their provisions began to get low they resumed work and "thus they progressed from shanty to house … then came a barn, other buildings, additional stock, a yoke of oxen — and to independence, comfort and contentment."[97] During his visit, Bishop Sweeney said that he hoped that a tavern would never be built. Given that Carleton County already had a strong teetotalling tradition, his wish was complied with and no tavern was built in Johnville. Its first Catholic Church was constructed in 1864.

Long before Johnville came into existence, Carleton County had acquired many Loyalists, some having served in Loyalist regiments. Woodstock Parish had a strong Loyalist nucleus in 1791, but by 1837 its mainly Irish and English inhabitants were in an "almost unprecedented and unparalleled state of distress," driven to the alternative "of either digging their potatoes planted for seed, or starving."[98] Woodstock had acquired an Irish settlement near Richmond Corner in 1819,[99] while Newburg (Northampton Parish) at the southeast corner of the county was founded in 1830 by Irish immigrants who mostly originated from county Londonderry (see Map 13).[100] By 1871, most of Carleton County's Irish were concentrated in Kent and Wicklow Parishes[101] in the north of the county and in Woodstock and Richmond Parishes[102] in the south.

Meanwhile, as the focus of the timber trade gradually moved north-east to the Northumberland Strait, the counties of Northumberland, Gloucester, and Kent came to be exploited for their huge reserves.[103] When he visited in 1832, Joseph Bouchette found their thickly forested areas to be "the thinnest settled and the worst cultivated in the whole province. There is scarcely any collection of houses worthy of the name of a town in any of them."[104] There was a wealth of wood, but only mar-ginal amounts of farmland, and so settlements had spread as long, slen-der fingers along the coastline and riverbanks. Irish settlement patterns reflected the progress of the timber trade, with sites being cleared as timber-felling operations proceeded.

A few people from Ireland had been settling along the Miramichi River and its tributaries from the late eighteenth century, carving out small, scat-tered farms from the dense forests, but it was a slow process. Irish Loyalists settled in the area, but the main source of people from Ireland during this early stage were contracted labourers from counties Wexford and Cork. Employed as temporary workers by the Scottish businessmen who founded the region's timber operations, they eventually settled permanently, leav-ing the Chatham area with a small number of Irish Catholic communities (see Map 14).[105] In addition, their numbers were increased by like-minded Irish workers from Newfoundland who swapped their fishery jobs in St. John's for better-paid lumbering jobs in the Miramichi.

The pulling power of the Miramichi also extended to Prince Edward Island. Irish labourers living on the island saw great advantage in mov-ing to the region to benefit from its booming economy. After all, the Miramichi could be reached by simply crossing the Northumberland Strait (see Map 3). As late as 1832, Bouchette commented on the many "young men of steady habits who went from Prince Edward Island and other places to the Miramichi." They did so to earn money in the lumber camps, which they used to purchase land.[106] Bouchette might have been referring to men like Silvester Dooly from county Kilkenny. Having first found work in St. John's in 1826, he moved to Prince Edward Island five years later, but was dissatisfied. So he wrote to his cousin Valentine Gibbs, who lived in Gloucester County, asking for his advice on whether to relo-cate to the Miramichi region:

I am back and forth from there [St. John's] to this island
called Prince Edwards ever since the first winter I came to
this island. I happened to settle myself in this vicinity
called St. Peters, where I can see every day hundreds of my
fellow countrymen all around me, which was a great consolation to me being a poor youngster from Old Erin lately
… I hope you will let me know whether it would be better
for me to go over to you to that place [Miramichi] or settle
myself in this island or move to other climes [*sic*] I am
single as yet [and] don't like to settle on a farm.[107]

**Map 14: Irish Settlements in Northumberland,
Gloucester and Kent Counties, New Brunswick, 1851**

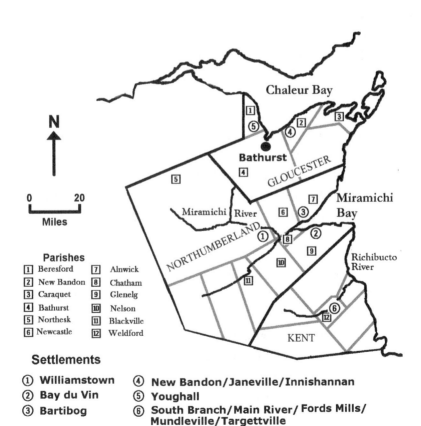

Parishes

[1]	Beresford	[7]	Alnwick
[2]	New Bandon	[8]	Chatham
[3]	Caraquet	[9]	Glenelg
[4]	Bathurst	[10]	Nelson
[5]	Northesk	[11]	Blackville
[6]	Newcastle	[12]	Weldford

Settlements

① **Williamstown**   ④ **New Bandon/Janeville/Innishannan**
② **Bay du Vin**   ⑤ **Youghall**
③ **Bartibog**   ⑥ **South Branch/Main River/ Fords Mills/
                          Mundleville/Targettville**

Like many other enterprising islanders, Silvester was considering whether to join the mounting army of Irish Catholics who were being enticed by the Miramichi's rapid economic expansion. In the end, he chose to settle in Chicago, where rates of pay were even better.[108]

Meanwhile, Irish Catholics continued to arrive in ever greater numbers, turning the lower Miramichi region into a major Irish Catholic enclave. They came from many parts of Ireland, but the greatest number of the pre-1851 arrivals originated from county Cork.[109] Most settled near the present-day town of Newcastle, opposite Chatham, near the junction of the northwest and southwest branches of the Miramichi, thus placing them at the region's economic hub and principal centres of trade.[110] Having been settled principally by Scots before 1785, Newcastle and Chatham were already well-developed by 1816 when the Irish first began to arrive in substantial numbers. Although they were more numerous in Saint John County, the Irish eventually had a commanding presence along the lower stretches of the Miramichi River. They brought their Roman Catholic religion and Gaelic language to the area, thus setting themselves apart culturally from the rest of the local population. By 1871 they were mainly to be found in Nelson, Newcastle, and Chatham Parishes (see Map 14). They were particularly dominant in Nelson Parish, where they represented 69 percent of the population.

Life was a struggle for the early arrivals. Having sailed with about 150 passengers from Cork to Chaleur Bay in 1822, Mary Ann Harley's first challenge was to get herself from Pokeshaw, on Chaleur Bay, to Newcastle:

> My brother expected me and was there [at Pokeshaw] waiting for me. We had to walk 75 miles to get to his home. There were no roads no conveyances of any kind not even a path. It was a trackless forest, in which not one tree had been cut. We made our way by the aid of a compass over windfalls and across brooks to Newcastle. We were three nights on the road and we had to sleep in the woods without any shelter. On the

fourth night we got to Newcastle and here we found a
very small settlement.[111]

Despite the privations of pioneer life, business was booming and the
region looked set to prosper when tragedy struck in 1825. On October
7–8, vast tracts of forest were burned. The fire destroyed six thousand
square miles of forest, causing devastation as far south as Fredericton
and killing 160 people. The prosperous town of Newcastle, with its 269
houses and nearly one thousand inhabitants, was almost completely
destroyed, and only six of the seventy buildings at nearby Douglastown
escaped the fire. The scale of the disaster was overwhelming:

> More than one hundred miles of the shores of Miramichi
> are laid waste … from one to two hundred people have
> perished within immediate observation, and thrice that
> number are miserably burnt or otherwise wounded....
> The loss of property is incalculable, for the fire born upon
> the wings of a hurricane, rushed upon the wretched
> inhabitants with such inconceivable rapidity that the
> preservation of their lives could be their only care.
>
> The hurricane raged with such dreadful violence that
> large bodies of timber on fire, as also trees from the
> forest and parts of the flaming houses and stores were
> carried to the rivers with amazing velocity … to occa-
> sion large quantities of salmon and other fish to resort
> to land; hundreds of which were scattered on the shores
> of the north and west branches.[112]

The Irish journalist Robert Cooney noted that "but a few hours had
elapsed, and hundreds were hurled from comparative affluence to utter
destitution."[113] In the wake of the fire, hundreds of people were forced to
seek new homes. And yet, despite the high death toll and harm done to
the region's economy, recovery was swift.

Barnaby River (Nelson Parish) was settled after the Great Miramichi
Fire of 1825 by displaced Irish immigrants living in the Miramichi who

had come originally from county Longford, most having been employed by the Gilmour and Rankin establishment.[114] Visiting Blackville Parish to the southwest of Nelson in 1847, Abraham Gesner noticed "several flourishing new clearings, occupied chiefly by Irish immigrants."[115] He also observed forty Irish families who were living along the Bartibog River in Alnwick Parish at the northeast end of the county.[116] John McCarthy, who left Cork in 1815 and settled at a farm in Bartibog, was one of its earliest Irish arrivals.[117] Meanwhile, another Irish community at Bay du Vin (Glenelg Parish) attracted the eye of Johnston when he visited in 1851. It consisted of "about a dozen Irish families who have a school and Catholic Chapel."[118]

However, poverty and distress often travelled with the Irish, causing fundraising concerns for the inhabitants of the major port cities and towns, and in some cases general unrest. Sometimes violence flared up. In the summer of 1822 it had been necessary to send troops of the 74th Regiment to Newcastle to deal with marauding gangs of recently arrived Irishmen who were wandering about seizing and destroying property and burning houses and barns.[119] Even after arresting the rioters, the troops had to fight their way into the jail to restore order among those they had locked up. The local authorities failed to cope and in the end it became necessary to station troops at Chatham and Newcastle from 1822 to 1830, "for the purpose of quelling the numerous riots and disturbances among the lower order of Irish Emigrants."[120]

Also, some Irish were clearly not enamoured by the demands of the timber trade. At the Miramichi's Hibernian Society St. Patrick's Day dinner in 1824, several glasses were raised to the timber trade, but there were also laments over the loss of so many Irish labourers from the area. They knew nothing of "that powerful engine of improvement, the axe," when they arrived, and some soon left.[121] This tendency of the Irish to up sticks, together with anti-Catholic bigotry, led Lieutenant Governor Sir Archibald Campbell to proclaim in 1832 that they should be discouraged from coming to New Brunswick. While they might have excellent qualities, their "naturally wandering disposition, added to the ties, associations and inducements, which lead them to the States — have hitherto rendered the great body of Irish emigration to this quarter, not only useless but extremely burdensome to the Province, and worse than a dead loss to the British Empire."[122]

Needless to say, the Irish continued to arrive in ever greater numbers. Although the majority were Catholic, a small number of Irish Protestants from West Cork arrived in Northesk Parish in the 1820s. Here they founded Williamstown about six miles west of Wilson's Point. It was located at the upper end of the Miramichi River, some distance away from the coast, since the river frontage plots had already been taken (see Map 14).

When he visited Northesk in 1832, Robert Cooney noted that "on the west side [of the Miramichi River] about four miles from the entrance there is a neat little Baptist Church, in the rear of which is Williamstown, a new but thriving settlement, established and owned by Irish Methodists. Eight miles higher up, the Roman Catholics have lately erected the frame of a large chapel."[123] In fact, both Protestants and Catholics from West Cork had come to live in the area, and their religious differences often created friction. Their general situation was not helped by the prevalence of poor, rocky soil and the volatile nature of the timber trade. Nevertheless, many of the original Methodist settlers remained, including Robert, Joseph, and Sarah Tweedy from county Leitrim; Benjamin, Jonathan, and Margaret Hosford from county Cork; and Ann, Arthur, John, Margaret, and Robert McLean, also from county Leitrim. Similarly, the Catholic Fitzgeralds and Harrigans and many others acquired one-hundred-acre lots at Williamstown, but religion and their Gaelic and English language differences set the two groups apart until the demise of the settlement in the early twentieth century.[124]

Because the timber trade was a boom and bust industry, pioneer life in Northumberland County was particularly problematic. There were frequent bankruptcies. Isolation was another problem. Lieutenant Governor Sir Howard Douglas described the "Miramichi Basin" in 1825 as consisting of "scattered houses, hamlets and commercial establishments, with many souls distant from each other."[125] He felt that the people should "be more located in one town," and recommended that more population growth should be encouraged in Chatham.[126] Writer Peter Fisher considered the Miramichi settlements to be unworthy of mention, "the improvement of the country being neglected for lumbering."[127] And when he visited the region in 1832, Joseph Bouchette was surprised to see so few outward signs of the wealth being created at Chatham and Newcastle by their burgeoning timber trade. "There is nothing that can accord with the expectation that would naturally be formed from the immense resources of the country."[128] He thought that lumbering had been pursued to the detriment of farming, not a view shared by the settlers, who welcomed the jobs it produced.

The early arrivals engaged in logging operations both for employment and as a means of clearing land for settlement. As is to be expected, the areas which produced the most timber initially also attracted the most settlers.[129] Even after they had established their farms, many settlers continued to work in lumber camps and, without their earnings they could not have survived. Some made no attempt to farm, simply moving to the towns and cities to find labouring and tradesmen's jobs. There were also some Irish who did more than just cope. John Harley and George Burchill, both from county Cork, became major shipbuilders and timber merchants. Harley, who arrived in the Miramichi in 1822, established a shipyard that produced sixty-two vessels, mostly large barques and full-rigged ships for the British market.[130] Arriving at roughly the same time as Harley, George Burchill became the business manager of Joseph Russell's shipyard on Beaubears Island. Together, Harley and Burchill purchased the yard and went on to construct ocean-going vessels and like most Maritime shipbuilders were also large-scale timber merchants.[131]

Meanwhile, the timber trade also brought the Irish to Gloucester County, with many of them settling in New Bandon and Bathurst parishes on the south side of Chaleur Bay (see Map 14). A few Loyalists had arrived in the 1780s to exploit the fishing, but large-scale colonization only began in the late 1820s when the timber trade reached Restigouche, some five years after the Miramichi's timber industry had begun its explosive growth.[132] Outnumbered by the large indigenous Acadian population, the Irish were never going to be the county's dominant immigrant group; but they were the largest non-French ethnic group and by 1871 represented 20 percent of the county's population.

Irish settlers escaping the Miramichi Fire of 1825 founded Belledune (Beresford Parish) and were joined by compatriots from Tipperary.[133] Visiting it in 1847, Abraham Gesner noted that "there are some good farms.... The settlers are chiefly Roman Catholics who have a Chapel and the occasional services of a Missionary." Writing in 1855, Alexander Munro described the banks of the Pokemouche River (Caraquet Parish) as having good soil. "This tract is well farmed by people principally from Ireland."[134] However, it was in New Bandon Parish where the Irish made their greatest strides.

Founded by seventy families from Bandon in Cork in 1816–19, New Bandon became the county's most impressive Irish community. Francis and Margaret Ellis were first on the scene, but they moved to Ohio nearly twenty years later. However, additional members of the Ellis family, such as sixty-year-old Edward Ellis, who arrived in 1819 with ten of his thirteen children, remained, as did many others. New Bandon clearly prospered as evidenced by the two satellite settlements of Innishannon and Janeville that sprouted next to it.[135] Thirty-six heads of household had petitioned for land together, stating that "having been neighbours in Ireland, the land of their birth, they wanted to continue as neighbours in this country," despite having had to cope with many privations and difficulties since their arrival.[136] By 1871, the Irish in New Bandon, many from county Cork, outnumbered all ethnic groups, including the Acadians.[137]

According to Robert Cooney, New Bandon was "a flourishing settlement" in 1832: "The soil is good and the people have by unremitting industry, good management and an exclusive attention to agriculture, succeeded in raising themselves from comparative poverty to a respectable proprietorship of land and cattle. Some of them have 50 acres under cultivation ..."[138] In contrast, J.F.W. Johnston was highly disapproving when he visited twenty years later. Although he marvelled at the good crops of oats and potatoes, he thought that the settlers "were for the most part miserably clothed, keeping wretched houses, have much dirt about themselves and their holdings, nasty-looking pigs running about the doors of their dwellings and their land and fences for the most part in an untidy condition. It is 'Ould Ireland' over again transplanted here, little altered from its home appearance and fashions."[139] He might have also mentioned that the

William Ellis with his wife and family, photographed at their farmhouse in Youghall, near Bathurst, circa 1901. The man with the beard fourth from the left is Dr. Ellis. His wife, Martha (Moorhead) Ellis, is sitting beside him on the right. Next to her on the right is their son Robert, who became a medical doctor.

entire region was in a state of decline, owing to the continuing downturn in the timber trade. By 1850 times were tough everywhere.

Meanwhile, Bathurst, particularly the town, proved popular with the Irish. Having first settled in New Bandon in 1824 and moved on to Janeville nine years later, the Cork-born Robert Eddy and his wife,

Jane Morgan, were living in Bathurst in 1837.[140] Similarly, members of the Ellis family moved from New Bandon to Youghall (named after Youghal in county Cork), just to the west of the town of Bathurst, soon after it was founded by Protestant Irish and Scottish settlers in around 1830.[141] William Ellis, described as "one of the pioneers of Gloucester county," was born in Youghall in 1841. Educated at McGill University, he was said to have "belonged to that school of old country doctors whose role often goes far beyond the mere curing of physical illness and becomes that of a wise counsellor and friend of every family in the district."[142]

Bathurst grew rapidly, and by the mid-nineteenth century it had become a substantial lumbering and shipbuilding centre with a population of more than five hundred people.[143] One of its leading lights was the young John Meahan, who had came from county Tyrone with his parents in the 1830s.[144] Establishing a major shipbuilding enterprise, he built some of the county's largest ships, including the *Herald* (1,200 tons) and the *Patrician* (1,214 tons), launched in 1855 and 1860 respectively.[145] His brother James later joined him in running the family business. However, while some entrepreneurs made good, Bathurst was in a state of decline by the mid-nineteenth century. William Smith grumbled to Daniel McGruar, a friend living in Newcastle (Miramichi), that "the codfish aristocracy of Bathurst" was getting its clothes "made by women," leaving his tailoring business with insufficient work.[146]

Having arrived in Bathurst from county Clare in the early 1820s, John Browne found plenty of work as a carpenter and joiner, but thirty years later he was frequently unemployed or was working for low wages:

> Trade of every description has disappeared altogether from the merchant establishment to the lumberers' camp, nothing doing; in former years in this place at this season [July] a person could scarcely get into a store to transact a little business, [with] horses, sleds and men from the lumber camps coming for supplies, but now there is no such bustle at all, only two or three little parties lumbering.[147]

The timber trade was suffering from the combined effects of a declining shipbuilding industry and Britain's decision to remove the protective tariffs that had initially given British North American timber such a price advantage over Baltic timber. Joseph Cunard's shipbuilding firm in Bathurst "suspended business" in 1848, "throwing from five to six hundred persons out of employment ... many of them with large families." In the following year, John Browne declared that "our province and the adjoining provinces are in a state of bankruptcy, no trade, no money and no employment."[148]

As was the case elsewhere in the province, the rapid growth in the Richibucto region's timber production, that began in 1818–19, provided the stimulus for Irish immigration to Kent County. The Irish mainly settled among the Acadians along the Richibucto River and its tributaries, forming separate farming/lumbering communities at South Branch (of the St. Nicholas River), Fords Mills, Main River, Mundleville, Girvan, and Targettville, all in Weldford Parish (see Map 14).[149] Fords Mills was an Irish immigrant mill village established before 1832, while the Girvan community was probably part of the old Irish settlement established along the Coal Branch of the Richibucto River, which was mentioned by J.F.K. Johnston.[150] William Martin's list, compiled in 1831, of the families "of Irish descent known to have lived along the Richibucto River" certainly confirms a strong Irish presence in Weldford Parish.[151] Originating from Bandon, county Cork, Martin had settled at Main River, arriving before 1824 and, for at least some of the time, he was employed as a carpenter. A notable arrival in the 1850s was Henry O'Leary, a Catholic from county Cork, who became a successful merchant. Establishing several lobster- and salmon-canning plants in Richibucto, he exported salmon mainly to France and Britain and lobsters to Britain and the United States. His commercial interests also extended to lumbering and shipbuilding.[152]

By 1818 the Irish had also established themselves along the Shepody Road in Albert County, a prime site in the Chignecto Bay region near to the border with Nova Scotia (see Map 15).[153] Founding the New Ireland Settlement in Harvey Parish,[154] their lumbering and farming community drew Irish people both from their homeland as well as from other areas of the Maritimes, especially the city of Saint John and parts of Nova

Map 15: Irish Settlements in Albert and Westmorland Counties, New Brunswick, 1851

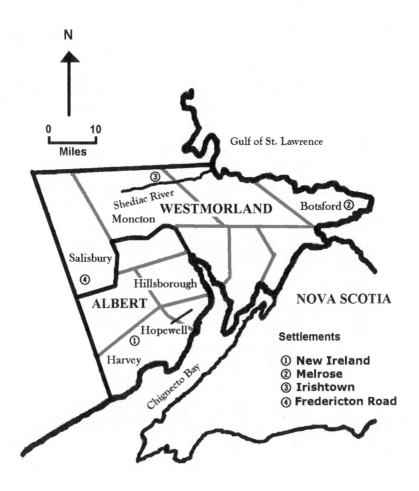

Scotia and Prince Edward Island.[155] Originating from both the north and south of Ireland, they clearly came in substantial numbers. By 1871, Irish colonizers extended their territory to the east, becoming well represented in Hillsborough and Hopewell Parishes.

The New Ireland settlement flourished despite having relatively poor soil. Visiting it in 1851, J.F.W. Johnston commented that the residents "do not appear so prosperous therefore as many other settlements we have seen."[156] But it did prosper, mainly due to its timber production. It had sixty-eight families and a Catholic church in place with a resident priest by 1866, and the area's steadily growing population would soon create a need for an even bigger church, which was built in 1887.[157] The Baptist cause found favour with the Irish in nearby Hillsborough and Hopewell Parishes, becoming the dominant Protestant religion by 1871.[158] However, the population declined soon after this, and by 1920 most families had left.

With its fertile marshlands, the Petitcodiac River region in Westmorland County had been long settled by the time that Irish colonizers began arriving after 1815. Some of Alexander MacNutt's Ulster colonizers, who came to the area in the 1760s, chose it in preference to the sites in Colchester County, Nova Scotia, where they were meant to settle.[159] However, this site in Salisbury Parish on the western side of the county was bypassed by later Ulster colonists, who were far more inclined to head for Saint John or Quebec City in the 1820s and '30s, these being the principal timber trade ports. And yet, the largest Irish community in the entire county was formed at Melrose in the Tormentine Peninsula on the eastern side (see Map 15). The catalyst was the New Brunswick government's decision to build a colonization road through the peninsula and offer free land grants to settlers along its route. The east–west road did its job in encouraging the pioneering Irish, who flocked to the area. Many Catholics from the south of Ireland as well as Irish Catholics already settled in Nova Scotia and Prince Edward Island responded.[160]

John Savage from Cork was one of the many Irishmen to submit a claim to the authorities for land. Plots of about two hundred acres were on offer:

> Having emigrated to this country in the year 1822 in order to look out for a small tract of land to settle upon, I am induced from a desire to live near to my brother, to apply to you, Sir for a quantity of Emigrant Land containing two hundred acres situated at Tormentine, once located by a Michael Houlahan but surrendered to me. I have chopped down three acres on the same and God willing intend to go on improving it as I have a family of five boys.[161]

Despite having an interior location and relatively poor land, the settlement prospered. Markets were some distance away and most people had to supplement their farming incomes by working as labourers or finding jobs in Moncton. Yet, being part of a close-knit Irish community and having the opportunity to acquire land was a powerful enough incentive to overcome these drawbacks.[162]

Westmorland County also acquired an Irishtown, which was located along the Shediac River in Moncton Parish.[163] First settled in 1812 by John and William Woods, who were brothers, and Walter Crowley, it attracted followers in 1812 and 1816. Growing rapidly, it mainly attracted settlers from the south of Ireland.[164] In 1855 Alexander Munro described it as "one of several thriving settlements in this part of the country."[165] By 1871, it had around fifty families. A third Irish community, the Fredericton Road Settlement in Salisbury Parish, was formed in about 1843 along a projected colonization road from Moncton to Fredericton.[166]

The amazing advances made by the Irish in the great wildernesses of New Brunswick speak volumes for their courage and enterprise. Once initial footholds had been created, the first settlers communicated their benefits to friends and family back in Ireland and elsewhere in the region. Chain migration fuelled by personal recommendation, and little else, propelled the Irish to this one area. The prospect of settling side by side with others who shared their culture and values while enjoying the economic benefits of the region's booming timber trade was an unbeatable combination. Yet, despite these positive developments, most of the Irish who arrived at ports in New Brunswick after 1840 left immediately for the United States. Administrators agonized over solutions to halt the drift, but because Upper Canada and the United States were viewed far more favourably by most British and Irish arrivals, there was little they could do.

While the timber trade was also the bedrock of the Prince Edward Island economy, it had a thriving fishing industry that attracted many Irish settlers, both from the surrounding area as well as from Ireland. More than ten thousand Irish settled on the island in the nineteenth century and in 1850 they comprised a quarter of its population.

CHAPTER 6

Prince Edward Island's
Irish Communities

Prince Edward Island formed early cross-roads between Newfoundland and New Brunswick, and the origins of its settlers were among the most mixed of any Irish Community in Canada. Two thirds of Ireland's counties were represented on the island, though the largest group was from Monaghan.[1]

Situated opposite New Brunswick and Nova Scotia and within easy reach of Newfoundland, Prince Edward Island occupies a strategic location in the Gulf of St. Lawrence. Shipping routes, used to transport goods, also served Irish fishery workers in Newfoundland who moved to Prince Edward Island starting in the late eighteenth century to take up farming or find better-paid jobs. They were Catholics who had mainly originated from counties Wexford, Waterford, Carlow, Kilkenny, and Tipperary in southeast Ireland. Later on, many of the Irish who had settled on the island, driven by similar motives of self-betterment, hopped on vessels that regularly crossed to the Miramichi region of New Brunswick. Thus, the island effectively became a crossroads for Irish people who either arrived from Newfoundland or went on to New Brunswick to benefit from its timber trade.

Those of the Newfoundland Irish who settled on the island became the catalysts for further immigration. Letters home to family and friends, extolling the better life to be had, no doubt helped to fuel the influx to the island from southeast Ireland. Between 1817 and 1840, at least 1,850 Irish sailed to the island from this one region, mostly from the port of Waterford. However, the Irish immigrant stream changed direction in the mid 1830s. The rise in departures for Charlottetown from Belfast, together with the drop in departures from Waterford, indicate that people began coming from Ulster in the north. Shipping data reveals that about four thousand mainly Irish Catholics sailed to the island from Belfast between 1830 and 1850, with many originating from county Monaghan.[2] Overall, the island acquired around ten thousand Irish immigrants between 1767 and 1850, accounting for around 25 percent of the island's population.[3] However, given that there had also been an influx of Irish workers from Newfoundland, which went largely unrecorded, the actual proportion of the islanders who were Irish-born was probably even higher.

A prerequisite to the arrival of Irish immigrants had been the founding of the British North American timber trade. It not only brought cheap transport and steady winter employment for settlers, it forged regular shipping routes between Ireland and North America that had not previously existed. This in turn created opportunities for colonizers. As the search for timber supplies moved along the Northumberland Strait in the late eighteenth century, so too came the advance of Irish settlers to Prince Edward Island, Cape Breton, eastern Nova Scotia, and the Miramichi region of New Brunswick. Timber was the sole reason why ships left in such numbers from Irish ports, and without them the early Irish exodus to the eastern Maritimes could not have happened.

Although Prince Edward Island had good land and a thriving timber trade, it was saddled with a semi-feudal landlord regime that made it unattractive to immigrants and this retarded its economic growth. Having sold off the island's land in a lottery held in 1767, its townships fell under the control of wealthy landowners who were expected to rent their holdings to ordinary settlers, the latter being the ones who would

Painting of the Charlottetown waterfront, circa 1849.

clear the land. The reality was somewhat different. Settlers faced a murky and haphazard world of land dealers and absentee landlords who effectively held power but felt little or no sense of responsibility for the economic well-being of the island. There was little rhyme or reason to the way settlements developed. The island's inhabitants were left vulnerable to the uncertainties and economic disadvantages of leasehold tenure for the best part of one hundred years.[4] Little wonder, then, that few immigrants wanted to settle on the island.

Predictably, the island's population grew slowly. In the late 1770s it had only 1,300 inhabitants of European origin and forty-nine of the sixty-seven townships had no settlers at all.[5] While a large number of Catholic Scottish Highlanders arrived in the 1770s and 1790s, they were a far cry from the government's preferred English-speaking, Church of England stereotype.[6] With the end of the Napoleonic Wars in 1815 and the arrival of the timber trade to facilitate immigrant travel across the Atlantic, the island's population experienced modest growth, reaching just over twenty-three thousand in 1827.[7] However, this was primarily an intake of Scots. They were the dominant ethnic group at this stage, outnumbering the Irish and English. As a result, when the Irish first began arriving in appreciable numbers in the 1830s they found that the best land and the best locations had gone to the Scots. This placed them at a considerable disadvantage, but, despite this, the island's attraction for the Irish grew. By the 1840s, as hundreds of Ulster immigrants streamed onto the island, the Irish overtook the Scots numerically. Thus, while Scots dominated the British influx to the island during the late eighteenth and early nineteenth centuries, the Irish did so in later decades.[8]

In addition to having a dysfunctional land holding system, Prince Edward Island's overtly Protestant society was another stumbling block for Catholics. Even though they comprised 45 percent of its population, the island's governing class was solidly Protestant. This meant that Catholics had to contend with widespread prejudice and discrimination wherever they went. They were not even legally permitted to hold land until the 1780s, nor could they be counted as settlers in terms of fulfilling proprietor settlement obligations.[9] Officials and ministers in London were not best pleased with their presence on the island. But they could rant and rave all they liked about the characteristics of the ideal immigrant. In the end, the choice of person was not theirs. It was self-selection, determined by the immigrants themselves. Thousands of Scottish and Irish Catholics chose to settle on Prince Edward Island, partly for economic reasons, but also because of its beauty and splendid coastline. They could cope well with the privations of pioneering, but endless, dreary forests would have been much harder to bear. The island gave them a semblance of a home away from home, particularly when they were joined by others who shared their cultural roots.

In 1797, some thirty years after the lottery, the island could claim only 4,400 inhabitants and by the end of the century twenty-three townships still remained completely uninhabited.[10]

Given the large intake of poor Scottish Highlanders with limited farming skills, the island's agriculture was slow to develop. After visiting in 1803, Edward Walsh blamed the Scots for the dismal appearance of the island's landscape: "By far the greater number of farmers on the island are Scotch Highlanders, ignorant, indolent and selfish in the extreme, who have no idea of agriculture and who are content to clear away some wood in a slovenly manner, in order to breed cattle, from which they derive their sole sustenance."[11] He clearly had little sympathy for the hard-pressed pioneer who had to cut the trees in vast forests while enduring hordes of mosquitoes and "cold weather, the ground being covered with snow nearly four months in the year."[12] John McGregor, who visited the island in 1828, formed a similar impression — except he blamed the Irish:

> The Irish peasant may be easily distinguishable by his brogue, his confidence, readiness of reply, seeming happiness, although often describing his situation as worse than it is. The Irish emigrants are more anxious in general to gain a temporary advantage, by working sometime for others, than by beginning immediately on a piece of land for themselves; and this, by procuring the means, leads them too frequently into the habit of drinking, a vice to which a great number of English and Scotch become also unfortunately addicted.[13]

So Prince Edward Island had its critics. Father James De Calonne, a priest from France, based in Charlottetown in 1799, was highly disapproving of the town's Scottish and Irish inhabitants: "All drunkards to an incredible excess, as well as supremely ignorant." He went on. "The greater number of the Irish we have here bring with them nothing but vices because they are the very dregs of Ireland and Newfoundland. They came to this place, not because they emigrate, but because they have been expelled from their own country."[14] Of course, these comments are absurd. However, the expulsion claim may reflect strong anti-British feelings in both Ireland and Newfoundland following the Irish rebellion a year earlier.[15]

An anonymous observer who visited Charlottetown in 1808 noted that it had had fewer than 150 houses, which were "small and wretchedly built," although he begrudgingly added that "some of the streets were well laid out."[16] However, by 1812 the town was being admired for its "wide streets, elegant private residences and imposing public buildings." According to Bishop Plessis, it had acquired "an air of importance."[17]

Although it was yet to acquire its first Catholic church, Charlottetown at the time had an Anglican church, a new courthouse, and barracks for the soldiers. Arriving in 1823, Father Alexander Thomas Fitzgerald, an Irish Dominican friar who had served in Newfoundland, was equally approving and was happy to preside over a mission "made up principally of emigrants from Ireland and Newfoundland.[18]

As is obvious from Father Fitzgerald's remarks, the Newfoundland Irish were a significant part of the island's Irish population. Coming often singly or in small groups, they sought locations that best suited them according to whether they wanted to fish, take up a trade, or eventually run a farm. This meant that they became widely scattered. When John White moved to the island in 1822 with his wife and six children, after having lived in St. John's for fifteen years, he obtained a land grant of one hundred acres at Lot 17, a Loyalist area of Prince County.[19] Francis Barry, whose father originated from county Waterford, moved in 1812 from Newfoundland to Egmont Bay (Lot 15), an Acadian stronghold. When he moved from Newfoundland to St. Peters Harbour (Lot 41) in 1830, Gerald Barry, probably a relative, would have joined Catholic Highlanders.[20] Having emigrated first to Newfoundland, the Wexford-born Edward Redmond, lived amongst Scots at Cardigan Bridge (Lot 52) from 1842.[21] And so it went on.

Similarly, Irish people who had settled in other parts of the Maritimes simply took the option that worked best for them irrespective of who their neighbours would be. After first settling in Nova Scotia in 1817, the Donegal-born Reverend John Crawford joined English and Scottish communities at Port Hill (Lot 13).[22] William Dillon, who had initially emigrated to Halifax from county Tipperary in 1835, later moved to Kildare Capes (Lot 3), another Acadian stronghold.[23] James Leonard, born in county Queens, who had emigrated to the Miramichi, sought land in the Charlottetown area when he moved in around 1825.[24] This dispersed settlement pattern was a typical feature of Irish immigration to Prince Edward Island. The one exception was the great influx from the north of Ireland that began in 1830. The largest single group unquestionably originated from county Monaghan. Over three thousand of them arrived between 1830 and 1848 and together they stamped a strong Irish identity on the island.[25]

Meanwhile, Prince Edward Island landowners fretted over the province's inability to attract sufficient farmers with adequate capital to purchase their land. In 1817 the "owners of one half of Prince Edward Island" launched a land scheme, whose purpose was to sell land on the island to potential settlers as well as speculators.[26] An advertisement appearing in the *Belfast Newsletter* in 1818 announced the departure of the *John* (Captain George Campbell) of Prince Edward Island, which was to sail from Donegal in the spring of the following year. The ad stated that "the owners of the *John* will let or sell to passengers by her, excellent land for a trifling consideration."[27] With William Marquis, the Dublin shipping agent, acting as their representative, they clearly hoped to lease or sell large quantities of land. The *John* did sail from Belfast to the island, arriving before May 30, 1819, but no passengers were recorded.[28] The scheme flopped. In 1830 the situation was little changed. In a newspaper advertisement the owners of the "fine new brig *Charlotte Kerr*," due to sail from Belfast to Nova Scotia and Prince Edward Island, announced that they had "large tracts of cleared land to dispose of, and will assist respectable farmers, inclined to locate there."[29] However, people did not leave Belfast for the island in appreciable numbers until 1835. And in the end, it was not clever marketing that persuaded them to this, but the organizational talents of a Glasgow priest.[30]

The Irish suffered from many disadvantages. They were poor, barely able to scrape together the funds to pay for their fares, and, being Catholics, were treated like second-class citizens. Many of them had little experience of managing a farm and therefore needed time to learn the required skills and accumulate sufficient capital to purchase stock and equipment. And, unlike Scottish Highlanders, who had men like the fabulously wealthy Lord Selkirk to finance and organize the relocation of their communities, they were largely self-reliant. Nor did they have the good fortune to benefit from the shipbuilding ventures of English entrepreneurs who brought much needed capital and jobs to the island.[31] Their one stroke of luck was the help given to them by Father John MacDonald. Taking pity on the many poor Irish people who were living in Glasgow during his time as a priest there in the 1830s, he organized their departures to the island. Mainly originating from the north, especially county

Map 16: Predominant Ethnic Groups in P.E.I. Townships, 1881

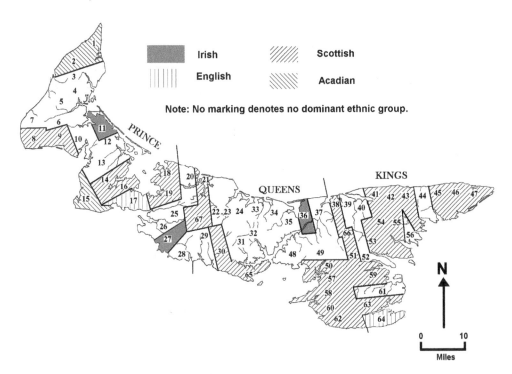

Monaghan, the Glasgow Irish relocated to central Queens County and along the boundaries between Queens and Prince Counties and Queens and Kings Counties, these being the areas where they could most easily find sufficient land to form their communities (see Map 16).

Looking back to the early stages of colonization, the Irish took some time to build up a presence on the island. Only forty-five Irish families lived there in 1798, mostly in and around Charlottetown, the rest being scattered across Prince and Queens Counties.[32] In 1848 the Irish were principally to be found in the interior areas of Queens County and in western Prince County (see Map 16).[33] And by 1881, one half of the island's Irish lived in Queens County, while the remainder was split between Prince and Kings Counties. One of the earliest Irish communities to form was in Tignish (Lot 1) in Prince County (see Map 17). Edward Reilly and his brother Michael are believed to have been its first Irish inhabitants.[34]

Map 17: Irish Settlements in Prince County, P.E.I., 1881

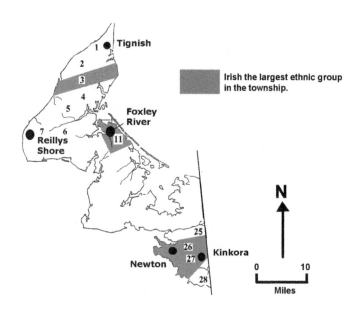

Initially founded by Acadian families in 1799, Tignish acquired its Irish settlers from New Brunswick in 1811. Having come from lumbering and fishing encampments on Chaleur Bay, they chose the nearest place on the island, settling at the northeastern tip of Prince County (see Map 2). Irish farmers and fishermen built their dwellings in an outer circle around the mainly Acadian Tignish village, thus spreading themselves along the coast at a place they named Waterford and at Skinners Pond, Nail Pond, Christopher Cross, Norway, North Cape, and Seacow Pond. A few of them also settled at Kildare Capes (Lots 2 and 3).[35] Genealogical sources indicate that most of the Tignish Irish had originated from the southern counties of Kerry, Waterford, Cork, Louth, Tipperary, Kilkenny, and Wexford, and that they mainly arrived between 1811 and 1839.[36]

It was similar story with Lot 7, lying to the south of Tignish. In the early 1820s it, too, attracted Irish families wishing to take up fishing and farming, most of them originating from counties Wexford, Laois (Queens), and Kerry. Some of the men had worked in the Newfoundland fishery beforehand, while others had previously worked in Joseph Pope's shipyard in Bedeque or had found jobs at Charlottetown, Tryon, and perhaps Kerrytown (Lot 20).[37] Once again the Irish lived side by side with the Acadians and this time conferred the name Reillys Shore on their locality.[38] They established communities at Burton, Cape Wolfe, and Glengarry in Lot 7 and beyond this at Campbellton in Lot 4. It was a daunting undertaking. Schoolteacher James Fitzgerald described the place as "the thicket of a forest and the haunt of wild beasts."[39] There were no roads. "The only way was by wood-paths, zigzagged and crooked, from tree to tree, knee-deep in mud and mire; or round the shores creeping along the brow of the cliffs, eighty or one hundred feet above the surfy beach and attended with no small danger to life and limb."[40]

Unusually, the earliest Irish families to arrive at Lot 11, on the opposite coastline, included Protestants. This was one of the few occasions when the island's feudal land regime actually worked to the advantage of the Irish, but only after a considerable wait. Lot 11 was acquired in the 1767 lottery by General Hunt Walsh, an Irish Protestant landowner who lived in county Laois (formerly Queens); but he did not set foot on the island nor did he seek tenants.[41] After his death in 1795 the land remained in the hands of his heirs for another sixty years. The turning point came when Sir E.H. Walsh, an Irishman from county Offaly (formerly Kings), decided to lease Lot 11 to Irish tenants. He chose John Large as his agent, knowing that he would be a good spokesman. Large is believed to have arrived unintentionally at New London (Lot 21) from Dublin in 1817 and soon sent favourable reports of life on Prince Edward Island to his contacts in Ireland.[42] Mainly Catholics from the southeast of Ireland, but also some Protestants from counties Laois and Offaly, responded, and under Large's supervision they founded a thriving Irish community at Foxley River in 1823.[43] Twenty-nine families had settled by 1833 and the population more than tripled by 1861.[44] Predictably, some people objected to tenancies, and despite this being an ongoing irritant, they were unable to buy farmland at reasonable prices until 1856.[45]

St. Brigid's Roman Catholic Church, Foxley River (Lot 11).

The 1830 influx of Monaghan settlers to the MacDonald estate at Fort Augustus (Lot 36) in Queens County was undoubtedly one of the high points of this immigration saga. Having begun life as a strongly Scottish enclave in the 1770s, Fort Augustus was now a place where Scots and Irish shared a common location. This was no ordinary influx. An island-born priest by the name of John MacDonald, who later moved to Glasgow, was the catalyst behind this extraordinary movement of people. Having inherited Fort Augustus from his father, John MacDonald of Glenaladale,[46] he made its land available to the poor Irish people who formed a good part of his Glasgow congregation.[47] They had fled from periodic crop failures and the catastrophic decline of the linen industry in Ireland only to find that their plight was little better in Glasgow, where they endured poor wages, poor job prospects, and poor housing. Father MacDonald offered them a way out, and the response to his plan was overwhelming.[48] Such were the numbers coming forward that two other locations, apart from Fort Augustus, had to be found for them, these being Kelly's Cross (Lot 29) and Kinkora (Lot 27).

When the first group of 236 settlers left Greenock for Charlottetown in the *Corsair* in the spring of 1830,[49] the *Glasgow Chronicle* noted that "they are by no means the poorest of our Catholic population; as all of them have taken away a considerable amount of money."[50]

Whether this was true or not, they benefitted from Father MacDonald's well-organized scheme, which enabled them to settle as a group and perpetuate their religious and social customs in the New World. MacDonald accompanied them in the *Corsair* and on arrival headed for his mother's house at Tracadie, near Fort Augustus. Once settled, he combined the duties of landlord and priest on his Fort Augustus estate for several years.[51] Meanwhile, the many settlers on board the *Corsair* who originated from Donagh Parish in county Monaghan had an additional source of help. Their parish priest, the Reverend Patrick Moynagh, had been offering encouragement while raising funds on their behalf and organizing their departure and relocation to Fort Augustus.[52] The Monaghan settlers went initially to Lot 36, but eventually occupied land at Lot 35 to the west and Lot 49 to the south. By 1881, all three townships would have large Irish populations (see Map 18).[53]

Monaghan settlers created yet another large imprint on the landscape to the southwest of Fort Augustus when they founded Kelly's Cross (Lot 29) during the 1830s.[54] One-hundred-acre farms were rented on reasonable terms, while Father James Duffy, who had previously served Catholic congregations in Newfoundland and Nova Scotia, travelled to Kelly's

St. Patrick's Roman Catholic Church, Fort Augustus (Lot 36).

Cross to join them. Over the following two years he provided comfort and support to the new arrivals.[55] It was only a matter of time before Irish family groups spread eastward to Emyvale (Lot 30), a place with a Monaghan name, and Lot 65, both areas having large Scottish populations. Meanwhile, Hope River (Lot 22), just to the north, attracted Irish colonizers from counties Wexford and Kerry, although some went to other parts of North America before choosing it. For instance, the Cullen family, who first settled in Quebec, moved to Prince Edward Island two years later in 1830 "after hearing that it resembled Ireland."[56] Lot 20, with its Irishtown and Kerrytown (later renamed Clinton) also has an Irish footprint, with most of its Irish settlers originating from county Kerry directly or coming via Newfoundland.[57]

The Kinkora district (Lots 26 and 27), named after Kincora in county Clare in the south of Ireland, was the third Monaghan cluster to form, with most of the settlers arriving in the 1840s.[58] Straddling the Prince/ Queens County line, the Irish community here eventually extended its

Map 18: Irish Settlements in Queens County, P.E.I.,1881

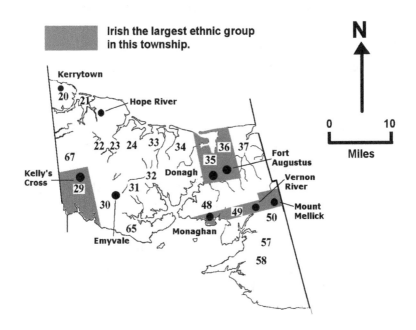

territory to include Lots 26, 27, and 29 (see Maps 17 and 18). Following their arrival in the Kinkora district, Monaghan settlers headed for the village of Kinkora itself, and formed new communities at Maple Plains, Shamrock, Emerald, South Freetown, Newton, and Middleton.[59] The many hundreds who sailed from Belfast to Charlottetown in the *Rose Bank*, the *Margaret Pollock*, and the *Lady Constable* accepted leaseholds on Horatio Mann's land in Lot 27, whose agent, Joseph Pope, offered liberal terms.[60] Most were the former tenants of Lord Rossmore (Henry Westenra) in county Monaghan, and possibly some others came from the Bishop estate in county Armagh, which was being administered by twelve Protestant clergymen. They settled within easy reach of the Loyalist town of Bedeque, thus ensuring access to good employment opportunities until they found their feet as farmers. And another wave of settlers came in the following year:

In 1841 some seven hundred [Irish] came from the counties of Armagh and Monaghan in a vessel called the "Consbrook." These landed in Charlottetown and from there some went to Fort Augustus [Lot 36] and DeSable [Lot 29] in Queens County, but others came to Sea Cow Head [Lot 1] and fifty of them settled in what was then known as Southwest, afterwards as Somerset and latterly as Kinkora [Lot 27].[61]

The Irish population of Kinkora grew steadily, and by 1872 St. Malachy's, its Catholic church, needed to be enlarged. That year, a chancel, vestry, tower, and spire were added. Father Albert E. Burke, who was based at Alberton (Lot 4), evidently visited the place and was much impressed:

There are few prettier mission churches in Prince Edward Island than St. Malachy's of Kinkora, and few more prosperous settlements than that which has sprung up on the level acres of Township Twenty Seven. Well cultivated farms and tasteful homes are the portion of the sons of those industrious and law-abiding emigrants of the "forties." Good roads intersect their settlement, good bridges span its streams, the branch line of railway to Cape Traverse runs through the village and everything points to prosperity and progress for Kinkora.[62]

When it came to Kings County, on the east side of the island, Irish luck ran out. Most of the productive farming tracts had long since been occupied by Scots before they made an appearance, and the land that was left was often swampy, rocky, and thickly wooded. Another factor was the stranglehold that major landowners such as Sir Samuel Cunard and Robert Bruce Stewart had over the area. Their shipbuilding and lumbering interests guided their every move with little priority being given to the use of their extensive holdings in encouraging settlers. The result was a sporadic appearance of the Irish who formed communities more by happenstance than by any preconceived plan.

Irish settler memorial at Charlottetown, Prince Edward Island.

The only areas to acquire a significant number of Irish were Morell (Lot 39) and Baldwin Road (Lot 51). The latter attracted Irish settlers who had relocated themselves from Fort Augustus. They, in turn, were joined in 1841 by other Irish immigrants who found "a dense forest, but by steady work it soon became a thriving settlement."[63] Lot 51 was also an extension of the Irish communities that had sprouted at Vernon River and Mount Mellick in Lot 49.[64]

Meanwhile, Lord James Townshend's attempt to bring Irish colonizers to his estate at Bay Fortune (Lot 56) in 1811 ended in failure.[65] Nevertheless, the Irish did make strides in a substantial area. Becoming clustered on either side of the Queens/Kings boundary line by 1881, they became the largest ethnic group in the Fort Augustus, Morell, Vernon River, and Baldwin Road areas (see Maps 18 and 19).

Map 19: Irish Settlements in Kings County, P.E.I.,1881

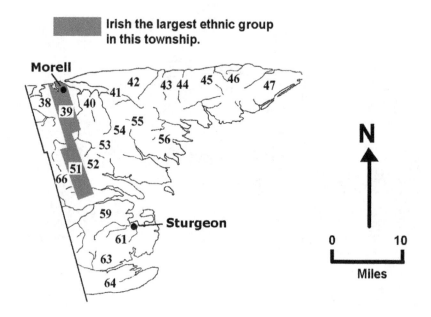

The Limerick-born William Creed, who arrived at Lower Montague (Lot 59) in 1767, gave his name to Creed's Point, having established the area's first general store. However, despite his successful ventures as a merchant and timber supplier, he did not attract any followers.[66] Meanwhile, Sturgeon (Lot 61) acquired people from the southeast of Ireland in the 1820s and with the opening of St. Mary's Road it received some of the Monaghan settlers, who arrived in the 1840s.[67] This being a remote location, it was a case of attempting to farm land that was only "something better than very bad."[68]

The last word should go to the writer John Maguire. When he visited the so-called Monaghan Settlement in Lot 48, just south of Fort Augustus, in 1866, accompanied by Daniel Brennan,[69] he found settlers who had long since passed the log cabin stage and "were occupying substantial and commodious frame houses." Although it had a Monaghan name, evidence from death notices indicates that its Irish inhabitants had originated from many parts of Ireland, not just Monaghan. Maguire was told that "they had not a sixpence in their pockets when they landed," but since then "had brought up their families with care and in respectability, could drive to church on Sunday in a well-appointed wagon, with a good horse, or a pair of good horses and probably had what they would call 'a little money' laid by in the bank."[70] His extensive tour of the area revealed a well-organized and prosperous community:

> As a rule ... I did not see a single habitation that was not decent in appearance or that did not evince an air of neatness and comfort. All were constructed of timber; but they were well-glazed, well-roofed and kept as white and clean as lime or paint could render them. We must have seen hundreds of farm houses in our ten hours' tour....
>
> Those Irish emigrants who landed in Prince Edward Island forty, thirty, or twenty years since, had to go into the forest and fight their way rood by rood, acre by acre, and win their daily bread by ceaseless labour, until field was added to field, and the encircling forest was driven back by the resistless force of human energy.... In no one proof of progress or evidence of solid and substantial comfort were the Irish settlers behind their Scotch or English or native-born neighbours. Their land was in good condition, there was as great activity in clearing, their cattle were as numerous and valuable, their hay and their potatoes were as good and as abundant; there was not even the suspicion of inferiority in any respect whatsoever, whether of capacity or in success.[71]

Despite this ringing endorsement, conditions for the settlers had been fraught with anxiety. A principal grievance was the leasehold system, and there were later complaints from the settlers about Father MacDonald's alleged condescending attitudes; a friend had become a foe. While he clung on to Old World practices and values, they embraced the egalitarian principles of the New World. This meant that they had a passionate desire to own their land, but Father MacDonald was still steeped in the greater glories of leasehold tenure. They thought that he talked down to them, treating them as inferior, while he appeared hurt and confused. Antagonisms between the two became so great that MacDonald had to go. He could no longer combine being a landlord with being a priest. He left the island in 1845 and spent his later life in the south of England.[72]

But the anguish being caused by the land question would not go away. In 1847 an election contested between Irish Catholics and Scottish Presbyterians at Belfast (Lot 57) led to a bloody battle that resulted in three deaths.[73] Although sectarian prejudice fanned the flames, the real issue was land, not religion. Settlement was being impeded by the preponderance of tenancies, and tenants became ever more vocal about their grievances. They resented the elitist landlords who ran the island's affairs to suit themselves, caring little for the ordinary residents or economic development. This long-running battle was only resolved in 1873 when the island entered the Canadian confederation. Then and only then was the leasehold system finally abolished.

Following the dramatic collapse of the island's shipbuilding industry in the 1870s (with the arrival of steamships), its Scottish and Irish inhabitants began to leave in droves. With its better land, climate, and employment opportunities, Upper Canada beckoned, as did many parts of the United States. As a consequence, the Irish proportion of the population on Prince Edward Island declined. Having been 25 percent of the total island population in 1881, the Irish only represented 19 percent of it by 1951.[74]

Bleak economic prospects in Ireland led people with a sense of adventure, enterprise, and the ability to finance their sea crossings to seek the better economic prospects that the island offered. As is clear from the undoubted success of Irish colonizers, this story had a happy ending for most people. And yet, no issue provokes more passion than the circumstances surrounding the Great Irish Famine, which struck with such force between 1845 and 1850.

Although Charlottetown's inhabitants were largely spared the daily arrivals of dead and dying Irish passengers during this period, the impact of one ship's arrival was huge. People watched in fear and dismay in April 1847 as 444 disease-ridden and destitute Irish immigrants disembarked from the *Lady Constable* at Charlottetown.[75] Political bungling turned tragedy into scandal. The authorities appeared to lose sight of the sorry state of the passengers as squabbling broke out over who was responsible for their care. It became a cause célèbre that was extensively reported on in local newspapers. After much bitter debate, it was decided to put the sick passengers into the newly opened Lunatic Asylum, after moving its inmates to other accommodations.

Meanwhile, Charlottetown residents could read many heart-rending accounts of similar processions of the sick and the dying who were arriving daily at ports in New Brunswick from Ireland. These so-called coffin ships did regrettably claim the lives of many Irish immigrants during the famine years, when unprecedented numbers came to North America. However, it should be remembered that most of the Irish who settled in Atlantic Canada arrived before the famine struck. Nevertheless, it is a story that must be told.

CHAPTER 7

❧

Emigration During the Great Irish Famine

The vast majority of Canada's Irish arrived before the Famine and not as exiles.[1]

The Great Famine that struck Ireland in the mid 1840s, one of the greatest human catastrophes of modern times, requires its own chapter.[2] Caused principally by successive failures of the potato crop,[3] it claimed one million Irish lives while precipitating the relocation of a further two million people to North America.[4] A collapsing economy and scarcity of food had created a sense of panic by 1847. The desire to escape possible starvation and destitution fuelled an exceptionally large exodus. Many were in a wretched condition on arrival, having contracted infectious diseases during the sea crossing. In some cases people died on the sea crossing or soon after arriving. Understandably, this aspect has attracted considerable attention. Just over two thousand people perished while travelling to Saint John, New Brunswick, representing one in seven of the total arrivals. Distressing issues concerning the dead and dying at this time have received major prominence, but unfortunately this focus has created the false impression that all Irish immigration was a consequence of the famine.

The famine lasted three to four years, but Irish immigration to Canada actually began a hundred years before this tragedy struck. This means that most Canadians with Irish ancestry can trace their geographical origins back to pre-famine times, and this was especially true in Atlantic Canada.[5] In New Brunswick, the famine Irish represented less than a quarter of the earlier arrivals.[6] In fact, by 1871 the Irish were Canada's largest immigrant group. But they did not see themselves as exiles. Most were labourers, tradesmen, and farmers who had actually paid their own way, doing so even during the famine years. The growing number of paupers from the south and west of Ireland who came in 1847–1848, when the famine was at its height, had been financially assisted by landlords and poor law guardians. They, too, had positive motives for leaving. They were fleeing extreme poverty. Because of the imbalance between the size of the population and the food supply, normal economic life in parts of Ireland was unsustainable. People knew from family and friends already living in North America that a better life was possible. Many had long pleaded for the funds to emigrate. With death staring them in the face, the offer of help to fund their relocation would have been grabbed with both hands. Staying put was not a realistic option.

Irish arrivals peaked in 1847 with the landing of around 17,000 in Saint John and approximately triple that number in Quebec City. (This compared with around 2,000 in 1844, 6,000 in 1845, and 9,000 in 1846.)[7] That same year, a total of 2,115 Irish people died, either during the crossing or while in quarantine or in hospital later. It is likely that some deaths went unrecorded, and for this reason Moses Perley, the New Brunswick emigration agent, estimated the total to be 2,400 — representing around 14 percent of those who set sail for the province.[8]

By today's standards this was an appalling and unacceptable death toll, but back then it was sadly inevitable. Almost all of the deaths were due to disease and malnourishment, the two often working hand in hand. The primitive state of medical knowledge at the time meant that contagious diseases such as typhus and dysentery could neither be prevented nor cured by outside intervention. Disease swept rapidly through the confines of a ship's hold and once people fell ill the outcome depended much more on chance than on any preventive measures that might have been taken. Ference McGowan, who sailed in the *Aeolus* from Sligo to Saint John in May 1847, escaped death by sheer luck:

> They are coming here and dying in Dozens there is not a vessel comes here [Saint John] but the fever is on Board.... Let none of you attempt to come here this season as there are so many here and the Fever is in every House almost. It is a good place for young people but there are enough at present until next summer.[9]

Most of the Irish who came to New Brunswick during the famine years (1845–50) headed for Saint John. A good half of them were on their way to the United States. The explosive growth in immigrant arrivals in 1847 caught New Brunswick officials by surprise, despite the fact that the possible starvation faced by people in Ireland was being reported widely in newspapers. Moses Perley fretted over the dilapidated state of the quarantine station at Partridge Island, but nothing was done until the arrival of sick immigrants forced the city to act. A hastily appointed medical board claimed that "the difficulties came upon us like a thunderbolt," and because disease was so prevalent, "a sufficient number of nurses and attendants could not be obtained at any price."[10]

The province's unpreparedness for the sudden deluge of needy and diseased immigrants at its ports caused tempers to fray, and criticisms were lashed out, often unfairly, at Irish landlords. They were accused of callously shipping off weak and aged tenants on their estates to rid themselves of the financial burden of caring for them. Little distinction was made between their infirm and helpless tenants and those able-bodied people who became that way as a result of having caught typhus or dysentery during the crossing. The concerns felt by local officials are understandable, but the extent of landlord culpability in the case of the New Brunswick arrivals was somewhat exaggerated. Mortality rates fell sharply after 1847, although outbreaks on occasional voyages claimed the lives of Irish immigrants in the following year. Once adequate facilities were put in place by the New Brunswick government, the sense of

Partridge Island and the Harbour of St. John, 1844. The Irish were quarantined at Partridge Island, where more than a thousand eventually died. Lithograph by Mary G Hall taken from *View of British America Drawn from Nature, & on Stone by Mrs. Hall,* Saint John, New Brunswick, 1835.

panic and outrage subsided. By 1848 the situation at the ports was a great deal calmer. Irish immigration to Canada decreased substantially in 1850, and five years later it slowed to a relative trickle as the United States increasingly gained in popularity as a destination.[11]

The fallout from the famine years continued to evoke strong passions on both sides of the Atlantic. The authorities, incensed by the large influx of paupers at the New Brunswick ports, directed their fury at Irish landlords. The problem was that while New Brunswick desperately needed healthy and strong working men, so did Ireland. With the passing of the 1838 Poor Law (Ireland) Act, landlords were for the first time required to fund financial relief for their tenants.[12] This was the catalyst that caused so many to fund emigration assistance schemes. By making one-off payments, they could reduce their poor rate payments while at the same time give their tenants an escape route to a better life. It made no sense for them just to send their fit and able-bodied tenants, since their principal objective was to free themselves from the burden of paying poor rate assessments. Meanwhile, the British government offered little financial help at the time, leaving the provinces to pick up the bill for the care of the needy Irish who landed at their ports.

When Sir Robert Gore-Booth organized the departure of tenants on his Sligo estate, he had his personal physician check each one for signs of disease and only allowed the healthy ones to travel. Some five hundred people sailed in the *Aeolus* of Greenock to Saint John in May 1847. However, no one could stop the inevitable. Even though there were no symptoms at the outset of a voyage, disease spread like wildfire once one or two people became ill. Coming down with the "sickness," John Mullawny, travelling with his sisters Mary and Margaret, said his last farewells, not expecting to survive the voyage.[13] Enduring a fierce storm, others expected "a watery grave." In all, twenty-six passengers died during the first week of the voyage and another seven were dead on arrival.[14] Nevertheless, the passengers thanked Gore-Booth "for the good store of provisions" that had been provided.[15] The captain, Michael Driscoll, boasted that the *Aeolus* "could not be classed among the dirty old emigrant-hired vessels" and with "the good diet, the superior medicine and the supplying of clean bed clothes," which had been made available, passengers had been well served.[16]

This same stoic attitude in the face of death was demonstrated by the 137 people who travelled to Saint John in the *Thorny Close* from Donegal. "When death spread his devouring shaft amongst us and carried away six children and one woman by the name of Mrs. Magwood," the passengers were exceedingly grateful to Captain James Horan for his care and consideration.[17]

Unfortunately, death at sea became an increasingly common occurrence. The *Midas* of Galway arrived in May with 163 passengers, some being from Robert D'Arcy's Galway estate, with ten having died during the crossing.[18] The *Aldebaran* landed soon after from Sligo with 418 passengers, 36 having died en route and another 105 who were ill on arrival. More than 80 died later in quarantine (see Appendix II).

However, some crossings were exemplary. Moses Perley heaped praise on Captain Anderson for the good health of the 337 passengers who arrived in the *Lady Bagot* from Waterford in July, some of whom had gone to destinations in Nova Scotia and Prince Edward Island. He attributed their good state to Anderson's excellent stewardship, as did the passengers who conveyed their "thankfulness and gratitude" in a letter to a local newspaper.[19]

But in the following month there were more shocking death tolls. Stricken with fever, 33 of the 338 passengers who had sailed in the *British Merchant* from Cork in August perished during the crossing; about 50 were ill on landing and another 56 subsequently died.[20] However, it was the arrival that same month of the *Yeoman* of Greenock with 504 Gore-Booth tenants, and the *Lady Sale* of Greenock the following month with 412 people from both Gore-Booth's and Lord Palmerston's estates, both in county Sligo, that attracted the greatest condemnation from officials. The issue was not the death toll, which was below average, but the decrepit state of the arrivals. Moses Perley stated that he had never seen "such abject misery, destitution and helplessness," and he later accused landlords of "exporting and shovelling out the helpless and infirm," whom he feared would remain a permanent charge on the province.[21]

Lord Palmerston, the British Foreign Secretary, caused further indignation when he sent 128 of his Sligo tenants to Shippigan (Gloucester County) in August and another 77 in November, both groups sailing in the *Eliza Liddell*.[22] The authorities at Shippigan, in the northeast of the province, had never before received such large numbers of diseased and distressed people, and they felt they were unable to cope. The arrivals were in a wretched state despite Palmerston's agents' claim that they had been inspected before travel by a doctor and anyone showing symptoms of disease had been removed. When the second group arrived there was near hysteria. John Doran, the county emigration agent, only let the passengers disembark after destroying their clothes and bedding and ordering them to wash in salt water.[23] And when Moses Perley learned of their plight, he repeated his earlier accusation that landlords like Palmerston were callously clearing out their destitute tenants knowing that they would be a burden to others. The Saint John Council waded in as well, expressing its regret that one of Her Majesty's ministers "should have exposed such a numerous and distressed portion of his tenantry to the severity and privations of a New Brunswick winter, unprovided as they are with the common means of support, with broken-down constitutions and nearly all in almost a state of nudity."[24]

Further rebukes followed after the *Aeolus* arrived at Saint John in November with 428 of Lord Palmerston's tenants, long after the quarantine station had closed for the year. A local newspaper commented that "we have rarely, if ever, witnessed a more sickening and heart rending spectacle, as these unfortunate people were carted through the principal streets in the city, towards the county alms house. Some of them were almost denuded of clothing, and they appeared from their extreme prostration to be in the last stage of disease."[25] The health officer, Dr. William S. Harding, was shocked by the appearance of the *Aeolus* passengers and said no verbal description could do justice to the scene. In his view "ninety-nine of every hundred will have to be supported by charity."[26] Forty of the children were orphans and had to be placed in the Emigrant Orphan Asylum.[27] Many of the sick and needy adults were housed in the local almshouse. Later on, the captain and owners of the *Aeolus* agreed to pay the Saint John authorities £250 for their upkeep.[28]

However, even with these frequent occurrences of illness, officials were also able to welcome perfectly healthy immigrants. Forty-four of Mr. Folliott's tenants from county Sligo, who arrived in the *Triumph* of Halifax at the same time as the *Aeolus*, were reported to be in good condition and Moses Perley hailed the *Cushla Machree* from Galway, which had carried 337 passengers "of the humblest class from the wilds of Connemara," as a shining example of a well-managed ship. The master had provided a clean, well-ventilated vessel and all of the passengers were healthy.[29]

Tempers flared in St. Andrews in April of the following year, however, with the arrival of the *Star* from New Ross. The 383 people from the Earl of Fitzwilliam's Wicklow estate arrived in a destitute state.[30] This was the case despite Fitzwilliam's obvious concern for his tenants' welfare. The ship's provisions were said to be exemplary, and he had instructed his agent, William Graves, to keep a close eye on their sea crossing. He was to obtain "a report from the medical attendant of the *Star* of the state of health of her passengers," both before sailing and upon her arrival.[31] But mere observation could not stop the inevitable. Nine people died on the crossing, another eleven had to be quarantined on arrival, and a further one hundred had to be assisted in St. Andrews with public funds.[32]

Saint John Almshouse, circa 1860. Opened in 1842, the almshouse provided a hospital for the care of the sick. Because of unexpected demand for its facilities, an immigrant hospital was built nearby in 1847.

Meanwhile the arrival of the *Elizabeth Grimmer* at St. Andrews from Londonderry in June with 229 passengers brought a large group of Ulster people to the area. Eight had died on the crossing while eight were placed in quarantine.[33]

The Wicklow group were meant to benefit from Fitzwilliam's influence over the St. Andrews and Quebec Railway Company,[34] of which he was a major shareholder. It was hoped that most of the men would be offered labouring jobs. However, ill health made many unsuitable for heavy physical work, at least in the short term. As a result, the Wicklow arrivals were abandoned by the company, leaving the local authority to pick up the tab for the £500 relief payments that had to be made on their behalf.[35] As was the case with the other landlord-assisted groups from county Sligo, this appeared to be yet another instance where the province was being used as a receptacle for Ireland's poor and unwanted. However, the main culprit was disease. Many of the people who had boarded ship in a healthy state became frail and infirm during the crossing. Whether a person succumbed to illness and recovered from it was beyond anyone's control. It was certainly not the landlords' fault. Landlords Gore-Booth,

Moses Perley, who was the New Brunswick emigration agent from 1843 to 1858. A very conscientious and energetic man, Perley supervised the arrival of passengers and dealt with any infringements of the regulations swiftly and thoroughly.

Palmerston, and Fitzwilliam had each provided their tenants with abundant provisions and good ships and had made every effort to screen each and every one of them for illness before their departure.[36] With the best will in the world, there was little more that they could have done.

The arrivals from Irish workhouses also attracted controversy. The people who stepped off the *Susan* at St. Andrews in May 1849 had come principally from county Kerry. Because they had friends in the United States who were going to pay for their onward passages, officials were relatively unconcerned by the fact that nearly all of the *Susan*'s 109 passengers would require short-term financial support.[37] But the "eighty paupers" who arrived at St. Andrews in November 1850 from a Cork workhouse were a cause for concern. Twenty-seven were ill on arrival and the rest appeared listless. Moses Perley complained of the "annoyance, vexation and trouble I have had with them. The greater part are the worst emigrants that ever came here.[38] They are helpless, idle, ignorant and dissipated, without the desire or pride to help themselves." It was expected that the immigrants would be mainly young, but Perley's examination of their details revealed that their ages had been incorrectly stated on paper. Hugh Conder was 41 not 27, Eliza Magner was 50 not 30 and Thomas Leary was 76 not 50, and so on.[39]

Understandably, provincial authorities remained uneasy about the sudden arrival of so many Irish paupers and alarmed that many would become permanent charges on the local parish. Their fears were understandable given that, at the time, Atlantic Canada was suffering from a severe economic depression caused by a decline in the timber trade. This meant that there was a diminishing pool of labouring work on offer. The Irish had to compete with local residents for fewer jobs, thus creating a labour surplus that drove down wages. Those of the Irish who found jobs often sent money back to Ireland to help others to leave or used it to fund their transport to the United States. Meanwhile, many local people had to support themselves on lower wages while finding the money to feed and shelter those of the Irish who needed help. These economic pressures, together with growing religious tensions caused by the sudden arrival of large numbers of Catholics, created a difficult climate for all concerned. Nevertheless, Catherine Bradley, formerly one of Gore-Booth's Sligo tenants, told her uncle John about her "good situation.... I do feel most happy and content here, so much so that I almost forget old Ireland for a time.... I have seen little of the country but understand that farmers from the Old Country do well here, and soon get on very comfortable and respectable."[40]

Where to settle was the priority for the able-bodied Irish, although some felt dispirited by the circumstances that confronted them. Bryan Clancy, another Gore-Booth tenant, "often wished to be home again. Bad and all as we were, we often wished we never seen Saint John."[41] Owen and Honor Henigan, also from the Gore-Booth estate, warned their son that "miserable Saint John is almost as bad as Ireland."[42]

Many of the Gore-Booth tenants who settled in New Brunswick let it be known that they intended to eventually move on to Boston, New York, or other urban centres in the United States. They were attracted by considerably higher pay and better employment opportunities there. Evidence from the 1851 census, revealing that a great many Sligo people settled in the city of Saint John, supports the presumption that some were leaving the option open of moving south.

The province's intake of Sligo people during the famine years would have come principally from the Gore-Booth and Palmerston estates. While most settled in Saint John, a substantial number chose rural locations in Charlotte and Kings Counties. In most cases they opted for parishes where Sligo people had been residing for up to twenty years (see Table 6).[43] However, with the arrival of Palmerston's tenants at the northern port of Shippigan in 1847, it was clearly intended that some Sligo people would also seek locations in northern New Brunswick. According to John Doran, the county emigration agent, this is precisely what they did. They settled in Richibucto (Kent County), Tabusintac (Northumberland County), Pokemouche, New Bandon, and Bathurst (Gloucester County).[44] He later reported that they were mainly to be found along the south side of Chaleur Bay between Bathurst and Shippigan and from there along the Gulf coast down to Tabusintac (see Map 14). Doran went on to say that they "are comfortably settled for the winter, enjoying the blessings of good health."[45]

These locations, although not revealed in the 1851 census owing to a loss of records, indicate that Sligo 1847 arrivals had cast their nets widely in the northeast of the province.

The Fitzwilliam tenants from county Wicklow were quite different in that they had one overwhelming preference, and that was to settle near St. Andrews in Charlotte County. Having been sent out to work on the St. Andrews and Quebec Railway, they did not want to move on, despite being advised to do so by the railway company once they terminated their employment.

Having been abandoned by the company, they were in a dreadful state, with many suffering from near starvation.[46] In desperation, they petitioned Lieutenant Governor Edward Wicker in March 1849 for each family to be given fifty acres of land along the Woodstock and Oakly Road, as well as money to help them while they became established. However, this request was refused, as were previous ones. In the end they defied local officials, who were urging them to move to the United States, and somehow managed to support themselves and put down roots in this, their chosen area. In 1851 some 60 percent of the former Fitzwilliam tenants were still residing in the St. Andrews district, a fact borne out by the census taken that year (see Table 7).[47]

TABLE 6

New Brunswick Locations of Ninety-Four Sligo Settlers in 1851
[Census of 1851]

Parish/Ward	County	Number	Religion
St. James	Charlotte	9	Anglican
St. David	Charlotte	5	Anglican
St. Patrick	Charlotte	2	Anglican
Pennfield	Charlotte	3	n/k
St. Andrews	Charlotte	1	RC
Studholm	Kings	4	RC
Westfield	Kings	1	RC
Norton	Kings	9	mixed
Saint John/Kings	Saint John	40	RC
Saint John/Dukes/Queens	Saint John	13	RC
Saint John/Sydney	Saint John	1	RC
Woodstock	Carleton	1	RC
Fredericton	York	5	RC

Although nearly all of the Wicklow settlers came during the famine years, people from the adjoining county Wexford (back in Ireland) had been arriving in St. Andrews since the 1820s. Possibly this explains the district's appeal to Wicklow people. The railway offered good employment opportunities and, once they acquired their land, people who were near neighbours back in Ireland were on hand to familiarize them with tree felling procedures and New World farming methods.

Around 2,400 Irish immigrants were assisted in getting to New Brunswick in 1847, most coming from the Gore-Booth estate in county Sligo. However, they account for only about 13 percent of the total number of New Brunswick's Irish arrivals, which was around 18,000.[48] Although immigration in the famine years was largely a flight from poverty, it is well to recognize that most Irish actually organized their own transport and paid their own fares. While considerable attention has been paid to the hardships suffered by the landlord-assisted Irish

TABLE 7

New Brunswick Locations of Seventy-Seven County Wicklow Settlers in 1851
[Census of 1851]

Parish/Ward	County	Number	Religion
St. Andrews	Charlotte	56	RC
Northesk	Northumberland	4	RC
Saint John Dukes/Queens	Saint John	14	RC
Saint John/Kings	Saint John	2	RC
Simonds	Saint John	1	RC

who came during the famine period, those who came unaided, who
were in the majority, have been widely ignored. Little information on
Irish settlement choices is available, even for the well-documented
landlord-assisted groups. However, their geographical origins in
Ireland can at least be inferred from the shipping data, which reveals
a sudden surge of arrivals from the south and west of Ireland between
1845 and 1848.

Although the scale of the exodus and the suffering caused by disease-
ridden voyages were unprecedented, the emigration process followed a
familiar pattern in the sense that people left from nearby seaports and
sought locations in New Brunswick where they could find work or be
close to friendly faces. The principal difference was that after 1840 an
increasing proportion of Irish immigrants were Catholics and many
more were coming from the south and west of Ireland. Before 1840,
most had left from ports in Ulster. While the Irish continued to leave
from the Ulster ports in slightly greater numbers after 1840, there was
an explosive increase in the number departing from Cork, Galway, and
Sligo between 1845 and 1848 (see Map 1). This indicates that the western
half of Ireland was the prime supplier of immigrants to New Brunswick
during the famine years (see Table 8). Some 70 percent left from ports in
the south and west of Ireland during this period.[49]

The 1851 census reveals that a large proportion of the Irish who came from counties Cork, Kerry, and Limerick in the south of Ireland and counties Sligo and Galway in the west, headed for Saint John, where they constituted an increasing portion of the urban labour force. In stark contrast were those who came from counties in Ulster. They became widely dispersed in the Saint John River Valley, especially in Carleton, Kings, Sunbury, York, and Charlotte Counties, while a substantial number also settled in the city of Saint John. People from the south and west probably left in great haste. They were less likely to have community ties with any part of New Brunswick, since relatively few people from the south and west had come to the province before 1840. In such circumstances, Saint John would have seemed to be an ideal location. It offered employment and it was also a well-recognized staging post for the United States. On the other hand, people from Ulster had established early footholds across the entire province. Thus they were able to join family and friends who had long since preceded them, although in the frenetic atmosphere of the famine years this was probably easier said than done.

TABLE 8

Irish Immigrant Arrivals at Maritime Ports During the Famine Years (1845–50)
[Newspaper shipping reports, provincial administrative and customs records]

Year	Londonderry, Belfast, and Other Ulster Ports	Waterford, Wexford, and Other Southeast Ports	Cork and Other Southern Ports	Galway, Sligo, and Other Ports in the West
1845	269	nil	2,236	2,617
1846	1,776	276	5,112	963
1847	3,652	571	4,559	4,848
1848	1,072	96	2,072	372
1849	339	nil	631	nil
1850	405	nil	417	nil

Meanwhile, ports in Nova Scotia, Prince Edward Island, and Newfoundland received relatively few Irish during the famine period. More Irish than usual arrived at Halifax in 1847, but they amounted to only around 1,255, just 7 percent of the Saint John total.[50] As ever, newspaper columnists concentrated on the paupers and survivors of shipwrecks who had to be found places in Halifax's almshouses and hospitals. The arrival of diseased, poorly dressed Irish caused considerable public alarm, particularly as many were living rough on the streets of Halifax. As was the case in New Brunswick, Nova Scotia's port officials were completely unprepared for the scale of human misery with which they had to deal.[51]

Most of the Irish arrivals at Halifax had sailed from Waterford in the southeast. This is despite the fact that the main exodus from Ireland at this time was coming from the south and west.[52] This represents a reaffirmation of the province's traditional links with those Irish from the southeast of Ireland who had relocated to its shores from Newfoundland, doing so beginning in the eighteenth century.[53] Having worked in the Newfoundland fishery, they had used their wages to fund the costs of moving to eastern Nova Scotia, with many selecting the city of Halifax and its environs. The Irish who sailed from Waterford in 1847 no doubt hoped to be given a helping hand by Halifax's long-standing Irish community. They were largely Catholics and they were decidedly impoverished. Describing themselves as "poor working class people," sixty one of them petitioned Sir John Harvey, the lieutenant governor of Nova Scotia, for help in finding jobs: "The best part of this body of labourers [has] never done one day's work since we landed in this country."[54] No help was provided.

These poor Irish never stood a chance. Harvey had issued a statement to the British press in the spring of 1847 making it very clear that paupers were not welcome in Nova Scotia and Cape Breton. He emphasized that the building of a railway between Halifax and Quebec would not generate jobs as had been claimed:

> This province [Nova Scotia] is in no respect prepared for
> the reception of poor people…, the landing, under pres-
> ent circumstances, of even a small number in the colony,

suffering as it is under the scarcity produced by the failure in the potato and grain crops in the last two seasons,
would be seriously injurious to the province itself; while
those resorting to it in the expectation of ameliorating
their condition would be grievously disappointed.[55]

Harvey warned that there was "no demand for unskilled labour in any
part of the province" and as a consequence "extreme privation and misery" would come to those foolish enough to come to the province. His
intervention had an immediate impact in that Irish people ceased sailing
from Waterford to Halifax in the early summer.

The reaction in Prince Edward Island was similar. Although relatively
few Irish came, the ones who did arrive excited considerable alarm. The
appearance in Charlottetown in April 1847 of the *Lady Constable* with
444 poor Irish, some sick and dying, caused near hysteria. Charlottetown
lacked the resources, personnel, and facilities to deal with a humanitarian crisis on this scale. In the end, those needing care had to be placed
in a hastily vacated Lunatic Asylum and the dead were simply buried in
rough board coffins in anonymous graves.[56]

It seems that most of the Irish who arrived on the island had originated from county Monaghan in the north of Ireland. Around seven
hundred Monaghan people are believed to have come in 1847, and some
almost certainly had sailed in the *Lady Constable* from Liverpool.[57] Their
arrival supplemented the already high numbers of people from this one
Ulster county who had come to live on the island.[58] Tombstone data
and death notices in newspapers, although incomplete, reveal that most
ended their days in Kings County on the east side of the island, in or
close to those areas that had been settled by other Monaghan people.

Newfoundland was the least affected by the famine, with St. John's
experiencing only a modest increase in immigrant arrivals between 1845
and 1850.[59] A significant increase in the number of passenger ship arrivals
from Waterford in 1847 suggests that more people than normal may have
sought to join family and friends who had already settled in the province
(see Table 9).[60] They, like those before them, would have originated from
southeastern counties such as Wexford, Waterford, and Tipperary.

TABLE 9

Ships Carrying Passengers from Waterford to Halifax, Saint John (NB), and St. John's (NFLD) 1845–50
[*Waterford Mail, Waterford Chronicle*. Tommy Deegan, "A List of Passengers Ships from Waterford Port to America and Canada, 1845–1850." In *DECIES Journal of the Waterford Historical and Archaeological Society* 51 (1995): 49–55.]

	Departure Date	Ship	Captain	Destination
1845	April 11	*Margaret Parker*	Reddy	St. John's
	20	*Eliza*	Bellord	Saint John
	20	*Velocity*	McGrath	ditto
	28	*John*	McGrath	ditto
	August 19	*Ratchford*	Flavin	St. John's
	September 23	*Michael A. Fleming*	Fitzgerald	ditto
1846	April 7	*Lady Mary Fox*	Dalton	St. John's
	8	*Margaret Parker*	Culliton	ditto
	15	*Velocity*	McGrath	Saint John
	18	*Rose Macroom*	Power	ditto
	25	*Ratchford*	Flavin	St. John's
1847	April 12	*Bolivar*	White	St. John's
	12	*Friends*	Byrne	ditto
	22	*Eliza*	Cheasty	Halifax
	23	*Rose Macroon*	Power	St. John's
	30	*Grace Darling*	McLea	ditto
	30	*Velocity*	McGrath	ditto
	May 31	*Lady Bagot*	Anderson	Saint John
	August 5	*Michael A. Fleming*	Walsh	St. John's
1849	April 7	*Laurel*	Maher	St. John's
	July 12	*Laurel*	Potts	ditto
	August 17	*Velocity*	White	ditto
1850	April 16	*Sophia*	Bellord	Halifax
	August 22	*Sophia*	Bellord	Saint John

The Great Irish Famine left a trail of desperation and anguish for both the immigrants who flooded Atlantic Canada's ports and the officials who had to cope with their medical and accommodation needs. It also fuelled growing religious tensions in the towns and cities of New Brunswick and Newfoundland, as well as in Halifax — where the greatest concentrations of Irish were to be found.

The situation was particularly fraught in the Saint John River Valley, which had the greatest concentration of Irish in the Maritimes. Whereas Irish Protestants had been dominant in the region before 1830, they suddenly found themselves being surrounded by ever-increasing numbers of Irish Catholics during the famine years. Fearing a Catholic takeover, Irish Protestants turned to the Orange Order to defend their interests. With each Irish feast day, especially the anniversary of the Battle of the Boyne in 1690, they extolled symbols of perceived Protestant supremacy, thus sparking major disturbances in Fredericton and Saint John.

Alexander Machum, a visiting schoolteacher and farmer from New Jerusalem (Kings County) witnessed the great Saint John riot of July 12, 1849. Marching Orangemen confronted local Catholics while celebrating King William of Orange's victory over the Catholic King James II, with predictable results. Hundreds were injured, although, according to Machum, few of those injured were Protestants. At least thirty "Papists" were killed.[61]

Prince Edward Island and Newfoundland experienced similar problems. A by-election held in Belfast, Prince Edward Island, resulted in a riot in which hundreds of men did battle, while a Conception Bay by-election in 1840 caused rioting at nearby Carbonear, where seven people were shot, a magistrate had his skull fractured, and a hundred soldiers from St. John's were required to restore order.[62]

Although immigration was a logical response to the Great Irish Famine, it attracted considerable negative publicity. The loudest accusers were the provincial officials, who berated landlords for sending out their poor and bedraggled tenants in such numbers. The fact is that their tenants had been living in a wretched state of poverty and were probably enduring near-starvation already. It was an unsustainable situation all round. Tenants had good reason to be thankful for the generous backing they received with their emigration expenses. It is ludicrous to argue that it was only the landlords who benefited from these arrangements. Passionate rhetoric is all very well, but it does not address the real issues.

Landlords used emigration to restructure their estates into more viable units and to give their tenants the opportunity of finding a decent livelihood in the provinces. They assumed that the provinces would welcome their labour. However, the provincial authorities were so preoccupied by the short-term costs of caring for the sick and needy that they seemed to regard the great influx of Irish solely as a burden. In fact, they were the province's future colonists and deserved better treatment than they received. The irony is that the authorities were as guilty as the landlords in putting what they regarded as the province's interests first. In the short term, most people lost. In the long term, most people gained.

The memory of the famine-stricken Irish who found a new life in Atlantic Canada looms large over the overall emigration saga, even though they represent only a fraction of the total. The terrible imagery of the so-called coffin ships also continues to shock and horrify. That deaths occurred during the sea crossings is indisputable. But high death rates and isolated worst-case examples of dreadful crossings do not tell the complete story. As will be demonstrated in the following chapter, the shipping services that were used by the Irish were generally of the highest standard.

CHAPTER 8

Sea Crossings

The Irish emigrant, before he comes out, knows not what it is to lie on a bed. If you put him in a bed and give him pork and flour, you make the man sick; but when a man comes to Newfoundland he gets no more than his breadth and length upon the deck of a ship and he has no provisions but a few herrings, and he comes out a healthy man and he has no doctor.[1]

John Uniacke, the attorney general of Nova Scotia, described the cheap and cheerful mode of transport used by poor Irish immigrants when crossing the Atlantic. In his evidence to the U.K. Emigration Select Committee, which sat in 1826–27, he explained how they could sail at a low-cost rate to Halifax by landing first at St. John's, Newfoundland. Because Newfoundland shipowners were exempted from passenger legislation, stipulating the space allocations and food that had to be provided during a sea crossing, they charged cheaper fares. No one checked to see if there was a physician and medicine chest on board or whether "so much pork and so much meat and so much bread" had been provided. It was effectively a do-it-yourself arrangement. An immigrant arrived with a large chest, which acts "as his bed, and his provisions are in it: he has his potatoes and his oatmeal and he has a little pot of butter and two or three dozen eggs and in this kind of way he lays up a supply of provisions which he subsists upon; then he earns a little money in the fishery, and in that way he is enabled to pay for his second passage to Nova Scotia."[2]

Nearly one quarter of the ships that arrived in Halifax between 1816 and 1838 had taken the St. John's detour (see Appendix I). However, unlike the example cited by Uniacke, these immigrants had not required a spell in the Newfoundland fishery to pay for their onward voyage to Halifax. They remained on the ship once it reached St. John's and had its cargo offloaded, then waited for the second leg of the voyage to begin. However, there were some drawbacks to taking this route. There was no redress if the conditions on board were unsatisfactory. And the crossing from St. John's to Halifax was very hazardous — a treacherous body of water known for its rocky ledges, sandbanks, icebergs, stony coastline, and dense fog. Before lighthouses came into use in the 1830s, there was a significant risk of being shipwrecked. Also, a substantial portion of the Irish who came via Newfoundland between 1816 and 1818 arrived in October and November — the worst possible time to travel or begin a new life as an immigrant. This suggests an air of panic among desperately poor people seeking an affordable route.

Crossing the Atlantic to Nova Scotia via Newfoundland was almost a sign of desperation and poverty. However, this route was used by very few Irish immigrants, and most came to North America on the coattails of the timber trade. They hopped on the ships that regularly left Ireland to collect timber cargoes at Halifax, Saint John, Charlottetown, and other Maritime ports. The timber trade revolutionized transatlantic shipping and brought the chance for affordable crossings to most people.

With the introduction of tariffs on European timber in 1811, North American timber had suddenly become the cheaper alternative.[3] By 1815, ships that were built to carry timber and to withstand the heavy storms and severe conditions found in the North Atlantic plied regularly between the British Isles and North America. With their arrival came passenger legislation to ensure minimum standards of comfort and safety, although in the early days these were not always enforceable.

The timber trade determined the quality and frequency of the shipping services on offer to passengers, and without it the main influx of Irish settlers could not have happened.[4]

It was essentially a simple two-way process. Timber was loaded into the ship's hold one way and immigrants were accommodated in the same hold the other way. Because there was a huge shipping capacity, seeking a relatively small number of people, shippers usually competed with one another, both on the cost of fares and also on the quality of the service they offered. The service may have been very basic by modern-day standards, but it was affordable and regular. Of course, this is far removed from many popular depictions of immigrant sea crossings, which concentrate on squalid conditions and high death tolls.

The so-called coffin ships did regrettably claim the lives of many Irish immigrants, especially during the famine years between 1846 and 1850 when unprecedented numbers arrived in the Maritime provinces. The deaths and suffering are indisputable. Disease spreads rapidly when people are crowded together, and the hold of a ship was the worst place to be in such circumstances. Try as they might, ship captains and physicians could not control the spread of disease; nor did they have the medicines or medical knowledge to cure people once they were infected. Any vessel could be a potential coffin ship in the sense that a high fever and an inability to eat could be a death sentence.

Horror stories about Irish suffering during sea crossings, which are usually based on one or two lurid case studies, frequently appear in print. However, they are totally misleading. Factual evidence taken from shipping sources and newspaper accounts reveals that the Irish generally sailed in decent-quality ships. While it was certainly pretty awful travelling in the hold of a sailing ship, the service offered was usually the best available at the time. People had to face the discomforts of being cooped up for several weeks and the misery of being blown about in stormy seas; but this was how transatlantic shipping services operated.

The accommodation in a ship's steerage was certainly very basic. Temporary wooden planking was hammered over crossbeams and temporary sleeping berths were constructed along each side of a hold. There were the added problems of not being able to eat because of sea sickness

FOR PICTOU AND PORT WALLACE, NOVA SCOTIA,

The fine new Brig

CHARLOTTE KERR,

Of Port Wallace,

ABRAHAM PYTCHE, Commander,

To Sail on the 1st April.

The *Charlotte Kerr* presents a most favourable opportunity for passengers bound to Halifax or Prince Edward's Island, now one of the most thriving Settlements in British America.

The Messrs. KERR, owners of the brig, have large tracts of cleared land to dispose of, and will assist respectable farmers inclined to locate there. The *Charlotte Kerr* will be *single* birthed, and otherwise comfortably fitted up, and well supplied with fuel and water.

Rates of Passage, and further particulars, may be had by applying to Captain PYTCHE on board, or at the Counting House of Mr. HENRY JOY HOLMES, Ritchie's-Quay; or to

JOHN HIRAM SHAW, Broker,

Belfast, 22d Feb. 1830.   7, Chichester-Quay.

Who has the fine new Ship *WILLIAM BOOTH*, Capt. BARKLAY, for St. Johns', New Brunswick; and a first class Sur for Quebec, both to sail on the fist of April.   149

Advertisement for the crossing of the *Charlotte Kerr* from Belfast to ports in Nova Scotia in the *Belfast Newsletter,* February 23, 1830.

and of coping with smelly and foul-tasting drinking water. There were no portholes, nor any means of ventilation beyond the hatches. Moreover, in stormy seas the hatches had to be kept battened down to stop water from pouring into the hold. Sometimes the hatches could be kept down for days at a time. The stench and squalor would have been almost unbearable. But this was unavoidable, even in the best-run ships.

Beginning in the late 1820s there had been a gradual move toward larger and roomier ships, although the only stipulation before 1842 was that ships were to have a floor-to-ceiling height of five and a half feet

THE LARGEST SHIP IN THIS HARBOUR.

DIRECT from CORK, for ST. JOHN'S, NEW BRUNSWICK, to Sail about the 26th of APRIL, the splended First Class Fast Sailing Ship, MARY CAROLINE, 736 Tons Register, 1400 Tons Burthen, JAMES BREWER, Commander.

This splendid Ship, the largest that ever sailed from Cork to St. John's, New Brunswick with Passengers, will be elegantly fitted up for the accommodation of Cabin and Steerage Passengers, being upwards of eight feet high between Decks, she will be well supplied with Water and Fuel, and the Captain and Crew will pay every attention to the Passengers during the voyage. Immediate application is necessary to JOHN M'AULIFFE, Ship Agent, Merchant's Quay, Cork.

April 11, 1842.

The *Mary Caroline*'s spacious accommodation for passengers wishing to travel from Cork to Saint John is highlighted in this advertisement in the *Cork Examiner*, March 2, 1842.

between decks.[5] With the passing of the 1842 Passenger Act, shipowners had to provide passengers with a minimum height between decks of six feet. This minimum figure increased to seven feet in 1855.[6] However, in reality, many immigrants crossed the Atlantic in much roomier conditions than the minimum legal limit. When the seven-hundred-ton *Marcus Hill* of Londonderry sailed to Halifax in 1817, it offered its 250 passengers seven feet between decks. Built specifically for the combined timber and passenger trade by William McCorkell, founder of the shipping line named after him, it was one of the finest ships of the time.[7] Another example was the 711-ton *Clyde* sailing from Cork in 1842 whose floor-to-ceiling space in the steerage was between eight and nine feet, at a time when the legal limit was six feet.[8]

While immigrants sought the best accommodation they could afford, they were at the mercy of the weather when it came to the actual crossings. Without accurate charts or other navigational aids, it was difficult at the best of times for ship captains to judge where they were and especially their proximity to dangerous shorelines. This was a time when captains shouted out their latitude and longitude to each other when

their ships passed at sea, simply to get their bearings. A constant threat
was the weather. Ferocious storms could blow vessels off course, leaving them to founder on sandy ridges or rocks, as frequently happened
along Nova Scotia's notorious western and southern coasts. Sailing from
Londonderry in 1819, the *Consolation* struck a rock at Green Island, off
the southern coast of Cape Breton — now a lighthouse site — and was
smashed to smithereens. Nevertheless, the passengers and crew totalling
144 survived and eventually reached Halifax.[9]

Even in the 1830s, after rudimentary lighthouses had been introduced,
ships could still be smashed to pieces, as happened to the *Lerwick* of Saint
John at Gull Rock near Digby.[10] Remarkably, the crew and 150 passengers were saved. And two years later, when the *Jane*, carrying eighty-six
passengers from Dublin to St. Andrews, went aground near Shelburne, it,
too, ended up a wreck, but all lives were saved.[11] And in 1839, two local
schooners rescued the *Aide-de-Camp*'s passengers when the vessel was
wrecked near Friar Island to the east of Halifax. Having left Londonderry
for Saint John, it had been driven ashore in a thick fog. All but fifteen of the
vessel's 306 passengers survived.[12] Passengers on board the *Dispatch*, which
sailed from Londonderry for Quebec, were less fortunate. It struck rocks at
Cape Ray near Port aux Basques along the south coast of Newfoundland
and quickly sank, with the loss of around sixty passengers. The survivors
managed to swim to a huge rock, where they remained for five days, surviving on food that happened to float past from the sunken ship:

> Finally, on the fifth day, a fisherman noticed an empty
> boat floating nearby and went to investigate. Then he
> discovered the stranded passengers and came to their
> assistance as soon as possible. He brought his fishing
> boat as close to the huge rock as was safe. He tied a
> long rope around his dog's neck and sent the dog to the
> rock. One by one, the survivors were tied securely by
> the rope and were pulled and helped to the fisherman's
> boat. Each man who left the rock carried two children.
> Finally, the rescue was complete. Of the three hundred
> passengers who had sailed from Ireland with such high

hopes, only sixty were saved. Some had died of starvation and shock while on the rock, and some had been washed into the sea by heavy waves.[13]

Sailing from Limerick for Quebec with 251 passengers and a crew of sixteen, the *James* hit heavy gales in the Grand Banks of Newfoundland. The storm "carried away the studdingsail (an additional sail used only in good weather) and jib-boom (wooden support), mainsail and foresail," causing the vessel to fill up with water. The pumps were activated but failed to work:

> They set about pumping the ship, but were not long engaged before the pumps were found to be choked with the passengers' potatoes, which, from the rotten description of the bags in which they were kept, went adrift about the hold, filling the pump wells and preventing the possibility of working the pumps, which were hoisted on deck and a great quantity of potatoes brought away with them.[14]

The passengers and crew tried to remove the rising water by baling it out with buckets, but when Henry Morgan, one of the passengers, broke three fingers in trying to do this, the attempt was abandoned. When the water reached between the decks it was time to abandon ship. The captain ordered the lifeboats to be lowered, but by the time the *Margaret* of Newcastle reached them there were only eleven survivors. A staggering 254 people lost their lives to the stormy sea.[15]

A captain's reputation and expertise were crucial to the success of a crossing, and countless accolades to named individuals have been written by grateful passengers. Captain James Strang was thanked "for his gentlemanly and human conduct" during the crossing of the *Ann* from Londonderry to Saint John in 1832, while praise was heaped on Captain Samuel Garrison for his "correct and gentlemanly deportment" during the crossing of the *Duncan*, also from Londonderry.[16] Nathaniel Kinney, in charge of the *Niger* of Saint John, was thanked by his Cork passengers in 1837 for his help "to those who were attacked by sickness," while passengers sailing in the *Redwing* from Galway under Thomas York's captaincy were similarly grateful for the help given to the sick. "In stormy weather he was ever at his post."[17] And so it went on. These tributes are but a small sample of the total.

Although a tiny minority, there certainly were some dreadful captains. The 260 passengers who were bound for Saint John in the *Duncan* from Dublin in 1831 realized to their horror that they were running short of food and that their drunken captain was incapable of dealing with the situation. Mercifully, the vessel was near Sydney, Cape Breton, enabling the passengers to attract the attention of the captain of the *Acadia*, whose vessel sailed close to theirs. Having been at sea for forty-two days, they were exceedingly grateful to be given fish, water, and other provisions. They explained that their captain "had been for several days in a state of intoxication, and did not know where the vessel was and that they intended next day to put her in charge of the mate and make for the next port."[18] That having been achieved, the passengers survived their ordeal, with two hundred disembarking at Halifax and sixty at Saint John.

Thomas Burnett, in charge of the *Nelson* of Whitby, which sailed from Killala (county Sligo) in 1831, was another incompetent captain. He was fined by the police magistrate in Saint John for "illegal overloading of passengers" and with not supplying sufficient provisions and water. Sixteen of the passengers had died during the crossing and many others were sick.[19]

Apart from observing the legal requirements for food and space, captains could do little to provide their passengers with comfortable accommodation. This was a time when immigrants were treated as just another commodity. Creature comforts had little priority. When John Cooke, one of Londonderry's principal shipping agents, made arrangements for the *Prudence* of Londonderry to take 170 passengers to Saint John in 1837 he informed a colleague in Saint John that he was sending "30 barrels of pork, 12 bales of bacon, 55 2/3rds passengers and some watch glasses which you ordered for Mr. Burns."[20] The passengers were the third item in his list!

It would not be until the steamship era, beginning in the 1850s, that custom-built accommodation would become available for passengers. Until then, passenger needs had a low priority, with shipping services

FOR ST. ANDREW'S, NEW BRUNSWICK,

The fine fast-sailing British-built copper-fastened Snow,

PORTAFERRY,

Burthen 500 Tons,

J. POLLOCK, Commander,

Will Sail from PORTAFERRY for ST. ANDREW'S first fair wind after SUNDAY the 28th March.

The letters from the many Passengers that have crossed the Atlantic by this conveyance will best testify the comfort and accommodation afforded them. As the Subscriber will go out in the Vessel himself, persons wishing to go to America in the *Portaferry,* may rely on his pursuing that line of conduct which has procured for him so many friends in the Passenger trade during the last Fifteen Years. The Births will be most comfortably fitted up, and abundance of Fuel and Water provided.—Apply to

J. POLLOCK,

PORTAFERRY, 22d February, 1830.   (164

Advertisement for the *Portaferry*'s crossing from Portaferry (near Belfast) to St. Andrews, New Brunswick from the *Belfast Newsletter,* February 26, 1830.

being haphazardly run and primarily geared to the stowage requirements of the timber trade. However, for people who could not afford the greater privacy and comforts of a cabin, a berth in the steerage was their only practical means of crossing the Atlantic.

Although passengers faced many discomforts, conditions significantly improved in the 1820s with the arrival of the so-called regular traders.[21] The Irish ones plied between ports in Ireland and Atlantic Canada, often twice a year, and frequently under the same captain. They carried goods, mail, and passengers westward to Halifax, Saint John, St. Andrews, and Charlottetown and timber eastward to Ireland. They marked a new era in passenger travel. They varied in size from the 135-ton *Britannia* of Sligo and the 313-ton *Albion* of Cork (which sailed regularly to Saint John),

TABLE 10

Frequent Passenger Carriers: Passengers Carried and Ship Quality

J: Saint John   H: Halifax
A: St. Andrews   C: Charlottetown

Vessel	Captain(s)	Year Built	Place Built	Lloyd's Code	Dep. Yrs	Dep. Port	Arr. Port	Crossings/ psgrs
Albion of Cork (bk, 313 tns)	Errington/ Tardiff	1834	N.S.	A1	1841–52	Cork	J	7/833
Bache McEver of Cork (bg, 229 tns)	several	1840	N.S.	AE1	1844–48	Cork	J	5/582
Britannia of Sligo (bg, 133 tns)	Potts	1801	N.S.	E1	1830–38	Sligo	J	4/324
British Queen (bk, 300 tns)	Bell	n/k		n/k	1837–49	Cork& Derry	J	6/605
Coxon of North Shields (sw, 278 tns)	Morgan	1843	Sunderland	A1	1845–46	Cork	J	4/376
Dealy of Bantry (bg, 245 tns)	Sterrat	1839	Saint John	A1	1841–48	Bantry (Co. Cork)	J	7/718
Dorcas Savage of Belfast (bg, 205 tns)	Pollock	1799	Workington	E1	1818–34	Portaferry	A	10/377
Eagle of Waterford (bg, 205 tns)	Buchanan/ Edwards	1819	Greenock	AE1	1836–44	Waterford	H	5/510
Elizabeth (s, 770 tns) [owned by J. Cooke]	several	1836	N.B.	A1	1857–63	Derry	J	7/504

Vessel	Captain(s)	Year Built	Place Built	Lloyd's Code	Dep. Yrs	Dep. Port	Arr. Port	Crossings/ psgrs
Hibernia of Kinsale (s, 193 tns)	Feneron	n/k	n/k	n/k	1832–38	Kinsale	J	3/228
Isadore (sw, 144 tns)	n/k	1836	N.B.	AE1	1837–45	Kinsale/ Cork	J	4/185
James Bailie of St. Andrews (s, 281 tns)	n/k	1810	Belfast	E1	1825–28	Belfast	A	5/348
Leviathan of Cork (bg, 216 tns)	Roycroft	1840	P.E.I.	AE1	1845–48	Baltimore	J	4/354
Londonderry (bk, 299 tns)	Hattrick	1837	Saint John	n/k	1837–51	Derry	J	13/1538
Martha (sw, 254 tns)	Linn	1841	Sunderland	A1	1842–46	Cork	J	5/470
Mary Ann (bk, 405 tns) [owned by J. Cooke]	n/k	n/k	n/k	n/k	1852–59	Derry	J	10/1545
Mary of Cork (bg, 180 tns)	Dunbar	1837	P.E.I.	E1	1846–50	Cork	J	5/434
Midas of Galway (bg, 255 tns)	Still	1838	N.B.	AE1	1842–47	Galway	J	5/624
Molly Moore of Waterford (bg, 161 tns)	n/k	1832	N.S.	A1	1833–36	Waterford	H	4/249
Pallas of Cork (bk, 316 tns)	Hall	1826	N.B.	E1	1830–49	Cork	J	9/1514

Vessel	Captain(s)	Year Built	Place Built	Lloyd's Code	Dep. Yrs	Dep. Port	Arr. Port	Crossings/ psgrs
Pandora (147 tns)	n/k	1829	P.E.I.	E1	1829–42	Waterford	H&C	11/419
Pons Aeli of Cork (bk, 315 tns)	several	1824	Gat'shd	AE1	1834–46	Cork	J	5/646
Portaferry of St. Andrews (bg, 283 tns)	several	1820	Workington	A1	1823–30	Portaferry	A	12/981
Thomas Hanford of Cork (sw, 228 tns)	Herbert	1824	N.B.	AE1	1833–46	Cork	J	6/521
Zephyr of Sligo (bg, 161 tns)	McDonnell	1832	N.B.	AE1	1833–34	Sligo	J	3/278

the 147-ton *Pandora* (plying between Waterford and Charlottetown), the 205-ton *Eagle* of Waterford (to Halifax), and the 770-ton *Elizabeth*, crossing between Londonderry and Saint John (see Table 10).

The 205-ton *Dorcas Savage* of Belfast, the 281-ton *James Bailie*, and the 283-ton *Portaferry* were the earliest, offering regular services to St. Andrews starting in the 1820s, while the *Londonderry* did the longest continuous stint, taking passengers from Londonderry to Saint John in most years between 1837 and 1851. Owned by John Cooke, it had been built specifically for the passenger trade. In 1838 he wrote that he had "a new ship called the *Londonderry*, burthen 229 tons, just arrived on her first voyage from Saint John where she was built under the inspection of the present master (Samuel Hattrick) for myself and is a remarkably strong and well-built ship."[22] Cooke also owned the 481-ton *Envoy*, which sailed from Londonderry to Saint John between 1842 and 1847, the 525-ton *John Clarke*, sailing in 1847, the 405-ton *Mary Ann*, sailing between 1852 and 1859, and the 770- ton *Elizabeth*, sailing between 1857 and 1863 (see Appendix III).[23] One of the foremost shipping agents in the north of Ireland and owner of many ships, Cooke established himself as a major player in the combined timber and passenger trade.

Regular traders could offer captains like Robert Hall, who, having made frequent crossings, were familiar with the ice flows and heavy gales that bedevilled the North Atlantic route. He regularly took charge of the 316-ton *Pallas* of Cork, which sailed either to Saint John or St. Andrews between 1830 and 1847.

Having captained the 380-ton *Protector* of Londonderry from 1830 to 1834, John Bell took charge of the 300-ton *British Queen*, which sailed from both Cork and Londonderry between 1837 and 1849, while Samuel Hattrick generally captained the *Londonderry*, which sailed most years from Londonderry to Saint John between 1837 and 1851. James Pollock also regularly commanded ships leaving from Portaferry near Belfast, being in charge of the 550-ton *Caroline* in 1817, the 205-ton *Dorcas Savage* of Belfast between 1818 and 1822, and the 283-ton *Portaferry* of St. Andrews between 1823 and 1825, each time taking his passengers to St. Andrews.

Similarly, Captain Sterrat regularly captained the 245-ton *Dealy* of Bantry, which took Cork people to Saint John between 1841 and 1848. And then there was Captain Kirkpatrick, who was in charge of the *Caroline*, which regularly sailed with passengers from Ballyshannon (county Donegal) to Saint John between 1841 and 1847.

The provision of a well-constructed ship was also very important. Convincing proof that immigrants were offered a good service is to be found in the *Lloyd's Shipping Register*. This source, dating back to the late eighteenth century, records the overall quality of individual ships.[24] As major insurers, Lloyd's of London needed reliable shipping intelligence, which it procured through the use of paid agents in the main ports in Britain and abroad. Vessels were inspected by Lloyd's surveyors and assigned a code according to the quality of their construction and maintenance.[25] These codes were then used by insurers and shipowners to determine levels of risk and freight rates.[26] An "A" rating represented the top standard, while an "AE" ranking was slightly below the best. It was assigned when a ship's age and place of construction placed it just below the top ranking.[27] An "E" designation meant that a vessel was second class, although it was perfectly seaworthy, having only minor defects.[28]

As can be seen from the codes that were assigned to some of the regular traders identified in this study, Irish immigrants fared particularly well (see Table 10). They indicate that the vessels that plied regularly between ports in Ireland and ports in Atlantic Canada generally had a top ranking. Fifteen of the twenty five vessels listed had "A" or "AE" ranking, while six were second class. Codes for the remaining four could not be found.[29]

The standards of service relating to space allocations and food were enforced by legislation first introduced in 1803. The Passenger Act of that year gave passengers an entitlement to far more space than was the case before, but this led to a sudden rise in fares. As a consequence, transatlantic travel became unaffordable to all but the very few. Continuing pressure from shipowners led to a relaxation of these space requirements and new legislation was passed in 1817.[30] Nevertheless, fares remained high. In 1818, a typical steerage crossing to the Maritimes cost immigrants £7.7s if they supplied their own food and £10.10s if food was supplied by the shipowner. By the 1820s basic steerage fares were as low as £3.10s. And yet, this represented a considerable outlay for the average farm labourer or servant, who often had to rely on the financial help given by friends and relatives already settled.

When three hundred destitute Irish arrived at St. Andrews in the *William Henry* from Dublin in 1827, without sufficient provisions or water, leaving thirty-nine of them to be cared for by the parish, there was uproar. Concerns over the growing number of destitute arrivals in Nova Scotia and New Brunswick led to further space restrictions being introduced in legislation and passed in 1828.[31] The secretary of the New Brunswick Agricultural and Emigrant Societies claimed that such people were "being deluded from their homes by false but specious statements of brokers and ship masters," whose sole object was to fleece them. The lieutenant governor retorted that more fundraising was needed locally to deal with the problem.[32] This enlightened thinking led to the introduction of a 5 shilling per passenger immigrant tax in 1832, which funded the building of the quarantine centre and other facilities needed to care for the sick and destitute.[33] By this time the average steerage fare was £2 to £2.10s (double this if the shipper provided food), while ten years later fares were roughly the same.[34] In fact, the relatively low fares to Saint John and the Miramichi were seized upon by the Nova Scotia and New Brunswick Land Company as one of the many advantages that New Brunswick offered to potential immigrants.[35]

Of course, overcrowding and poor sanitary conditions were facts of life at this time. Enduring such hardships on board a ship was nothing new. And disease was always a major concern. The captain and crew were meant to follow a strict daily routine for cleaning the ship and provide what assistance they could to anyone who fell ill, but in practice this did not always happen. When the *James* arrived from Waterford at Halifax in 1827 with more than one hundred passengers, all suffering from typhus fever, Lieutenant Governor Sir James Kempt announced that their plight had been caused "solely by their scanty nourishment during the voyage, by the crowded and filthy state of the ship and by want of medical assistance."[36]

That same year, more lives were lost during the sailing of the *Cumberland*, also from Waterford. Four years later the *Charity* of Saint John and *Hibernia* of Kinsale both arrived at Saint John with Cork passengers suffering from smallpox. Both captains were charged for infringements under the Passenger Act.

Captain Risk of the *Charity* was fined £30 for "leaving the vessel without just cause" and Captain John Driscoll of the *Hibernia* £50 for "a breach of the fifteenth section of the Quarantine Law in landing passengers infected with smallpox."[37] Captain Risk had falsely accused his passengers of being "in a state of mutiny," but when Alderman Sandall went on board he found them to be "in a quiet and orderly state."[38] Risk's false claim that the passengers were refusing to cooperate with the quarantine procedures was uncovered by a courageous local official.

While Charlottetown's quarantine arrangements were largely improvised, Halifax had specially built quarantine facilities in place by 1834, with buildings having been constructed with money raised from the five shilling head tax. Cholera made a brief but deadly visit to Halifax in 1834, and 284 people died.[39] But even when the disease was checked relatively quickly, as in this case, ports could not relax their vigilance. Such diseases travelled with the immigrants and therefore stringent quarantine arrangements had to be in place. The reports of vessels arriving in Arichat, Cape Breton, and

Dr. William Stenning Harding, brother of George, the chief physician at Partridge Island. Dr. Harding was called over to work at the quarantine station in the summer of 1847 after the death of Dr. James Collins. By the end of the summer a total of eight doctors worked on the island.

in Prince Edward Island with immigrants suffering from cholera galvanized the Newfoundland government into action. Between 1832 and 1834 it established quarantine facilities at Kelly's Island and Harbour Grace in and along Conception Bay, some considerable distance west of St. John's.[40]

Although New Brunswick also levied the same head tax on immigrants, the province did not construct a quarantine centre until the great influx of 1847 when seventeen thousand Irish immigrants arrived at Saint John. A quarantine station was then hastily built at Partridge Island, a short distance from the city.[41]

The hoisting of yellow flags by vessels on their approach to Partridge Island was a frequent occurrence in 1847. If disease was aboard, captains were required to raise a yellow flag, this being the official signal that alerted the Custom House to send a physician out to board the ship. If disease was confirmed, the ship was fumigated and placed in quarantine

Dr. John Vondy, born circa 1820 in Miramichi, died at the age of twenty-seven while treating Irish immigrants during the height of the Famine in 1847. They had been among the 467 people who sailed in the *Looshtauk* from Dublin and were on their way to Quebec. After two weeks out at sea, most of the crew and some of the passengers had died from typhus. The captain managed to sail the vessel to the Miramichi. He requested medical assistance in Chatham, but was refused by the available doctors until Dr. Vondy offered his services. He soon fell ill and died, while the ship's captain and many of the passengers also died in hospital. Upon hearing of his death, the shops in Saint John were closed and all business was suspended throughout the day.

for up to forty days. Apart from the human misery involved, this was a highly undesirable state of affairs for shipowners and captains, since such a prolonged delay lost them considerable money. However, because of the strict enforcement procedures, captains could not circumvent the regulations. The heavy fines payable ensured their cooperation.

Once released, the sick and dying were cared for in the Saint John Alms House Infirmary and, because of the high demand for beds, in another hospital that was built close to it. In peak periods during 1847, when almost seven hundred Irish immigrants were being treated at any one time, the accommodation was hopelessly inadequate.[42] George J. Harding, the resident physician at the infirmary, was so overwhelmed by work that he was authorized to hire his brother, Dr. William S. Harding, and the twenty-three-year-old Dr. James Collins, who hailed from county Cork.[43]

Like Dr. John Vondy, who died in 1847 treating sick arrivals from Dublin at the Miramichi hospital, Dr. James Collins also paid with his life for his heroism. In that one year alone, a total of 601 people died on Partridge Island. They were mainly Irish immigrants, but the victims also included mariners and one doctor.[44]

Conditions on Partridge Island were particularly horrible in the summer of 1847. Some days, more than five thousand sick people required attention, and there were occasions when all the doctors and nurses were sick and the dying had to be left on the ground in the graveyard. The soil on the island was so "thin in many places that the bodies were little more than covered with earth, and after a heavy rain, portions of the clothing could be seen protruding."[45]

Cholera visited Saint John again in 1854 when 319 passengers sailing in the *Blanche* from Liverpool were detained at Partridge Island. Thirty-five people died in all, with eight being among fifty-seven German immigrants who had embarked at Liverpool.[46]

Typhoid also visited Charlottetown in 1847. Twenty-five of the 444 passengers, probably all Irish, who sailed in the *Lady Constable* from Liverpool had contracted the disease and were admitted to a makeshift hospital, where eight did not survive.[47]

With the increasing demand for passages across the Atlantic between 1846 and 1850, some captains occasionally packed more than the legal limit of passengers into their vessels, though they faced heavy fines for so doing. Moses Perley, New Brunswick's beady-eyed emigration agent, was assiduous in prosecuting captains and shipping firms for infringements under the passenger and quarantine regulations. Captains who allowed overcrowding or failed to supply sufficient provisions had their knuckles rapped publically by him, thus ensuring that misdemeanours were kept to a minimum. If charged, they had to face a magistrate's court hearing at Saint John and, if found guilty, a steep fine. Meanwhile, their vessel lay idle while they awaited the proceedings. Their reputation would be in tatters. Perley was the person who distressed passengers spoke to on arrival. He heard their complaints and regularly made recommendations on how passenger regulations could be improved. He was their champion.

Perley took action against several captains in 1846. James Cooper was fined for not providing his 224 passengers with sufficient food and water during the *Renewal's* crossing from Berehaven (county Cork), while Captain Richard Power, in command of the *Racer* of Waterford with 181 passengers, was fined £5 for having an overcrowded ship, with the amount having been reduced because he "had done everything in his power for the safety and comfort of the passengers after the fever broke out."[48] Captain Austin Yorke, captain of the *Linden* of London, which sailed from Galway, was charged with issuing insufficient water and provisions under the terms of the Passenger Act, but his fine was reduced because he had replaced his brother at short notice and had not overseen the supplies being loaded. Nevertheless, he was fined £20 to serve "as a sufficient warning for the future."[49] Meanwhile, Patrick Beegan, captain of the *Bloomfield*, which sailed from Galway, was fined £50 for failing to supply adequate provisions, his vessel having been driven on shore in a gale, leaving his seventy-four passengers "in a destitute and starving state."[50]

These infringements were minor when compared with the misdeeds of Alexander McNaughton, captain of the *Danube*, a 110-ton brig that carried sixty-one passengers from Donegal in 1846. He was a fined a total of £105 for having an overcrowded ship and failing to supply adequate food and water. Evidence was provided that the brig had only a single deck and yet "temporary beams were put across the vessel, supported at the ends by strips of wood, running fore and aft, and spiked to the ceiling." This practice was illegal at the time. The Mate stated that "the [water] casks were leaky and unseaworthy, and three of them were so bad that Captain McNaughton sent them on shore to James McDonagh, the agent for the vessel at Donegal, who sent them onboard again, saying there were no others to be got, and the vessel must not be detained. The day after the vessel sailed, the passengers were put on short allowance of water and restricted to two quarts only a day."[51]

By this time Perley was becoming increasingly concerned that unsuitable vessels were being used to carry passengers. North of England colliers (vessels carrying coal in bulk), although sturdily built and well-equipped to withstand mountainous seas, required the installation of temporary decking to accommodate passengers. Temporary decking made a vessel less stable and it could also adversely affect air quality and ventilation for passengers. It was for this reason that a passenger deck was legally required to form part of the permanent structure of a vessel. Thus, colliers should not have been used to carry passengers.[52] Perley spoke out against this practice and recommended that the regulations be amended to exclude them.[53] For the same reason, he took a dim view

TABLE 11

Selected Vessels Carrying Two Hundred or More Passengers, 1817–46

A: St. Andrews   J: Saint John
C: Charlottetown   M: Miramichi
H: Halifax   P: Pictou

Vessel	Captain(s)	Year Built	Place Built	Lloyd's Code	Dep. Yrs	Dep. Port	Arr. Port	No. of Psgrs
Adelphi (bg, 337 tns)	Irvin	n/k	n/k	E1	1831	Cork	H	241
Argyle (bk, 307 tns)	Buchanan	1824	Quebec	A1	1831	Waterford	H	225
Benjamin Shaw (bg, 283 tns)	n/k	1806	n/k	E1	1830	Waterford	P	300
Betsy Heron of North Shields (sw, 250 tns)	Storey, James	1832	North Shields	A1	1834	Belfast	J	219
Bolivar of Waterford (bk, 355 tns)	n/k	1826	P.E.I.	E1	1841	Waterford	M	235
Brunswick of London (bk, 571 tns)	Walker	1791	London	AE1	1817	Derry	H	231
Champion of Whitby (bk, 364 tns)	Galilee	1789	Whitby	E1	1837	Cork	J	223
Cherub (bg, 232 tns)	Selkirk, J.	1823	Maryport	A1	1827	Waterford	H	200
Chieftain (325 tns)	Legate	1826	Montreal	AE1	1843	Belfast	C	208
Consbrook (423 tns) (two crossings)	Pollock, J.	1827	N.B.	A1	1836, 1839	Belfast	C	616
Corsair (bg, 273 tns)	Hamilton	1823	N.B.	E	1830	Grnk	C	207

Vessel	Captain(s)	Year Built	Place Built	Lloyd's Code	Dep. Yrs	Dep. Port	Arr. Port	No. of Psgrs
Cupid of Londonderry (bg, 247 tns)	Stephenson, Samuel	1830	N.S.	A1	1834	Newry	J	208
Dominica of Cork (bk, 381 tns)	n/k	1808	Whitby	AE1	1845	Cork	J	232
Eliza Ann of Cork (bg, 324 tns)	Watson, Earnest	1828	N.B.	AE1	1842	Cork	A	226
Ellergill (bk, 369 tns)	Hale, William	1814	Hull	AE1	1833	Derry	J	321
Envoy of Londonderry (bk, 481 tns) (two crossings) [owned by J. Cooke]	Haffney/ Hattrick	n/k	n/k	n/k	1842, 1846	Derry	J	614
Halifax Packet (s, 272 tns)	Clark, John	1804	U.S.A.	E1	1818	Derry	J	213
Hannah of Maryport (bg, 287 tns)	Byram, Ralph	1826	N.B.	AE1	1834	Cork	J	278
Independence of Kinsale (s, 326 tns)	Griffith, George	1827	Kinsale	A1	1834	Kinsale	J	237
John Francis of Cork (s, 362 tns) [two crossings]	Kent, John/ Deaves, H	1827	Montreal	AE1	1842, 1846	Cork	J	429
John & Mary of Galway (bk, 297 tns)	Wright	1787	Whitby	E1	1842	Galway	J	212
Linden of London (bk, 297 tns)	Yorke	1845	N.S.	A1	1846	Galway	J	220

Vessel	Captain(s)	Year Built	Place Built	Lloyd's Code	Dep. Yrs	Dep. Port	Arr. Port	No. of Psgrs
Londonderry (bk, 299 tns) [owned by J. Cooke]	Hattrick, L.	1838	N.B.	n/k	1842	Derry	J	211
Lord Sandon of Cork (bk, 407 tns) (two crossings)	Feneran, George	1839	Richibucto	A1	1841, 1842	Kinsale	J	442
Marcus Hill (s, 700 tns) [McCorkell line]	White	1811	Quebec	n/k	1817	Derry	H	250
Margaret Pollock (917 tns) [Pollock & Gilmour]	Pye, John	1840	n/k	n/k	1841	Belfast	C	685
Mars (s, 306 tns)	Frier	n/k	n/k	E1	1820	Belfast	J	210
Mersey (s, 620 tns)	Mather	1837	N.B.	A1	1837	Derry	J	500
Nestor (s, 387 tns)	n/k	1812	Whitby	E1	1823	Belfast	A	294
Pallas of Cork (bk, 316 tns)	Hall, Robert	1826	N.B.	E1	1842	Cork	A	200
Perseus of Hull (bk, 363 tns)	Bruce, G.	1799	Stockton	E1	1834	Derry	J	294
Pons Aeli of Cork (bk, 315 tns) [two crossings]	Havelock, G/ Wright, H.	1824	Gateshead	AE1	1834, 1842	Cork	J	454
Recovery of Dublin (bk, 329 tns)	Moore, Lawrence	1826	N.S.	E1	1846	Galway	J	245
Robert Burns of Liverpool (bg, 296 tns)	Messenger, J.	1827	Aberdeen	A2	1834	Derry	J	243

Vessel	Captain(s)	Year Built	Place Built	Lloyd's Code	Dep. Yrs	Dep. Port	Arr. Port	No. of Psgrs
Robert Watt of St. Joseph Andrews (bk, 491 tns)	Dallimore, Joseph	1835	St. Andrews	A1	1837	Cork	J	288
Rose Bank (308 tns)	Liget	1825	North Scotland	AE1	1840	Belfast	C	208
Thomas Gelston	n/k	1812	St. Andrews	E2	1842	Belfast	C	280
Venus of Liverpool (bk, 388 tns)	Butters, J.	1787	Bristol	E	1837	Cork	J	232
William Henry (bg, 312 tns)	n/k	1817	N.B.	A1	1827	Dublin	A	300

of the similarly illegal practice of installing temporary decking in schooners and brigs. He brought thirteen prosecutions against captains, whose vessels included the 185-ton *Charles* of Youghall, carrying 106 passengers, the *Jane* of Cork, a 109-ton schooner with 68 passengers, the *David*, a 139-ton schooner with 91 passengers, the 105-ton *Caledonia* of Cork with 69 passengers, the 114-ton *Blanche* with 73 passengers, the 127-ton *Sally* of Cork with 96 passengers, and the 130-ton *Kingston* of Cork with 68 passengers (see Appendix II). In each case, the captains found themselves answerable to Moses Perley when they reached Saint John.

However, Perley also found much good practice in 1846–1847. The 525 passengers who sailed in the *John Clarke* said they owed their "preservation from sickness" to Captain Robert Disbrow's kindness and attention.[54] Perley praised Captain Hyacinth Duffy for his "able management of the ship *Chieftain* of Galway in her crippled condition in

Notice in May 1847 of the sailing of the *Lady Caroline* of Newry to Saint John. The ship arrived in July with 105 passengers.

1846."[55] Captain Laidler, in charge of the *Envoy* of Londonderry with 276 passengers in 1847, was commended for his kindness "particularly to those of us who were sick" and for the great care he had taken "to prevent any infectious disease in the vessel by enforcing cleanliness and order" (although there was one death and one person was quarantined).[56] The eighty-three passengers who travelled in the *Caroline* of Liverpool from Limerick that year expressed "their unbounded gratitude" to Mr. H. Thompson, the ship's owner, who gave free passage to those of them "having no means of paying for it. He had the kindness also to remain with them on board the vessel until she got to the entrance of the River Shannon, which is 60 miles from Limerick, and at the parting gave orders to have every attention paid them during the voyage. He also sent on board provisions of the best quality for their use, which was given to them regularly."[57]

These accolades are at odds with the generally negative commentaries of Irish ship crossings. However, as is clear from the Lloyd's shipping codes, the Irish were not only treated well by their captains, but they also generally sailed in good-quality vessels. Table 11 provides codes for the larger ships that operated before the Great Irish Famine struck in the mid 1840s. Because many only made a single crossing, there is insufficient data to readily identify their rankings. However, codes have been identified for forty-one of the larger ships that took two hundred or more passengers in a single crossing.[58] Seventy percent had a first-class ranking and the rest were second class. As can be seen, the vessels used by the county Monaghan settlers, who sailed from Belfast to Charlottetown between 1830 and 1848, were mainly top quality. The *Consbrook* was "A1," the *Rose Bank*, *Moriana*, and *Lady Anne* of Newcastle were ranked as "AE1," while the *Margaret Pollock*, built by Pollock and Gilmour, was also at the top end of the available shipping.[59] Together they brought more than two thousand Irish immigrants to Prince Edward Island.

With the onset of the famine period beginning in 1846, Saint John and other Atlantic ports experienced a sudden increase in Irish arrivals. Remarkably, the quality of shipping actually improved at this busy and frantic time. Where codes can be identified, they show that the vessels that arrived with Irish immigrants between 1846 and 1850 were of outstanding quality (see Table 12). Around 80 percent of the fifty-six

TABLE 12

Selected Vessels Carrying Fifty or More Passengers, 1846–50

A: St. Andrews   J: Saint John
H: Halifax   Ω: Denotes disease on board.

Vessel	Captain(s)	Year Built	Place Built	Lloyd's Code	Dep. Yrs	Dep. Port	Arr. Port	No. of psgrs
Ω *Aeolus* of Greenock (two crossings) [owned by Gore-Booth]	Driscoll, Michael	1846	N.S.	n/a	1847	Sligo	J	928
Alarm (bg, 201 tns)	Leonard, J.	1838	P.E.I.	AE1	1846	Cork	J	119
Albion (255 tns)	Daly	1841	N.S.	A1	1849	Cork	J	169
Ω *Amazon* (bk, 357 tns)	Hayes	1838	N.S.	AE1	1847	Liverpool	J	262
Ann Wise (sw, 231 tns)	Ellwood, Thomas	1827	Workington	AE1	1846	Sligo	J	122
Ω *Bache McEver* of Cork (bg, 229 tns) (three crossings)	Betty, J.	1840	N.S.	AE1	1846–48	Cork	A & J	396
Barbara of Galway (bk, 418 tns)	Mackay	1846	Halifax, N.S.	A1	1847	Galway	H	296
Ω *British Merchant* (bk, 334 tns)	Sanderson	1847	Jersey	A1	1847	Cork	J	328

Vessel	Captain(s)	Year Built	Place Built	Lloyd's Code	Dep. Yrs	Dep. Port	Arr. Port	No. of psgrs
Ω *Charles* of Youghall (bg, 185 tns) (two crossings)	McCarthy, Hanlon	1840	P.E.I.	AE1	1846, 1848	Youghall	J	201
Ω *Chieftain* of Galway (s, 490 tns)	McDonough, William	1845	Cape Breton	A1	1847	Galway	J	344
Coxon of North Shields (sw, 278 tns)	Morgan	1843	Sunderland	A1	1846	Cork	J	192
Eliza of Youghall (bg, 123 tns)	McCarthy	1828	N.S.	AE1	1847	Youghall	J	70
Ellen and Margaret of Cork (bg, 157 tns)	Joams, D.	1842	N.B.	AE1	1846	Cork	J	95
Enterprise of Kinsale (bg, 127 tns)	Leonard, J.	1842	N.S.	AE1	1847	Kinsale	J	60
Ω *Envoy* of Londonderry (bk, 481 tns) (two crossings) [owned by J. Cooke]	Hattrick/ Laidler	n/k	n/k	n/k	1846	Derry	J	574
Garland of Cork (bg, 208 tns) (two crossings)	Robertson, J.	1843	N.B.	A1	1846	Berehaven	J	281

Vessel	Captain(s)	Year Built	Place Built	Lloyd's Code	Dep. Yrs	Dep. Port	Arr. Port	No. of psgrs
Goliath of Liverpool (s, 900 tns)	Slater, C.	1840	Quebec	AE1	1849	Liverpool	J	51
Ω *Governor Douglas* of Cork (bk, 434 tns)	Clark	1826	Miramichi	AE1	1847	Baltimore	J	261
Hannah of Maryport (bg, 287 tns)	Shaw	1826	N.B.	AE1	1847	Sligo	J	211
James Redden of Dumfries (sw, 218 tns)	n/k	1841	P.E.I.	AE1	1850	Derry	J	92
John Clarke [owned by J. Cooke]	Disbrow, Robert	n/k	n/k	n/k	1847	Derry	J	525
John Francis of Cork (s, 362 tns) (two crossings)	Deaves, H.	1827	Montreal	AE1	1846, 1848	Cork	J	396
Lady Sale of Greenock (s, 675 tns)	Anderson	1843	N.B.	A1	1847	Sligo	J	412
Leviathan of Cork (bg, 216 tns) (two crossings)	Roycroft	1840	P.E.I.	AE1	1846, 1847	Baltimore	J	260
Ω *Linden* of London (bk, 297 tns) (three crossings)	Yorke, Austin	1845	N.S.	A1	1846–48	Galway	J	581

Vessel	Captain(s)	Year Built	Place Built	Lloyd's Code	Dep. Yrs	Dep. Port	Arr. Port	No. of psgrs
Ω *Londonderry* (bk, 299 tns) (five crossings) [owned by J. Cooke]	Boyle/ Hattrick	1838	N.B.	n/k	1847– 50	Derry	J	831
Ω *Lord Maidstone* of Liverpool (bk, 568 tns)	Sheridan	1840	Pictou, N.S.	AE1	1848	Derry	J	332
Malvina of Baltimore (bk, 249 tns)	Chantley	1846	P.E.I.	A1	1847	Baltimore	J	183
Marchioness of Clydesdale (s, 565 tns) [owned by J. Cooke]	Ferguson	n/k	n/k	n/k	1847	Derry	J	386
Martha (sw, 254 tns)	Linn, John	1841	Sunderland	A1	1846	Cork	J	153
Mary Harrington of Ardrossan (bk, 411 tns)	Montgomery	1844	Pictou, N.S.	A1	1847	Donegal	J	135
Ω *Mary* of Cork (bg, 180 tns)	Dunbar, J.	1837	P.E.I.	E1	1846,	Cork	J	251
Midas of Galway (bg, 255 tns) (two crossings)	Still, J.	1838	N.B.	AE1	1846, 1847	Galway	A & J	220
Mountaineer (bk, 490 tns)	Carey	1809	Whitby	AE1	1847	Cork	H	279

Vessel	Captain(s)	Year Built	Place Built	Lloyd's Code	Dep. Yrs	Dep. Port	Arr. Port	No. of psgrs
Ω *Pallas* of Cork (bk, 316 tns) (three crossings)	Hall/Harvey	1826	N.B.	E1	1846–49	Cork	J	594
Ω *Pero* of Cork (bg, 225 tns) (two crossings)	Meredith	1823	Sunderland	AE1	1846, 1847	Cork	A & J	291
Ω *Portland* of Liverpool (bk, 542 tns) [owned by J. Cooke]	Stalker	1834	N.B.	AE1	1847	Derry	J	338
Princess Royal of Cork (bk, 186 tns) (three crossings)	Callaghan/Driscoll	1840	N.S.	AE1	1846–48	Cork/Limerick	J	379
Ω *Progress* of Londonderry (sw, 201 tns) [owned by J. Cooke]	Fagen, P.	1840	Dundee	AE1	1847	Derry	J	138
Recovery of Dublin (bk, 329 tns)	Moore, Lawrence	1826	N.S.	E1	1846	Galway	J	245
Redwing (bk, 238 tns)	Bell	1840	Shields	AE1	1847	Galway	H	140
Regina of Cork (bg, 223 tns)	Reynolds	1845	P.E.I.	A1	1846	Baltimore	J	142
Ω *Royal Mint* of Liverpool (bk, 310 tns)	Williams	1837	Sunderland	AE1	1847	Liverpool	J	166

Vessel	Captain(s)	Year Built	Place Built	Lloyd's Code	Dep. Yrs	Dep. Port	Arr. Port	No. of psgrs
Saint Lawrence of Cork (bk, 221 tns) (two crossings)	Bullin, J.	1841	P.E.I.	AE1	1846, 1847	Baltimore/ Cork	J	293
Sea Bird of Newry (bg, 492 tns)	Rae, J.	1846	P.E.I.	A1	1847	Newry	J	346
Ω *Sir Charles Napier* of Liverpool (s, 714 tns) [owned by J. Cooke]	Sear	n/k	n/k	n/k	1847	Derry	J	434
Sir James McDonnell of Dublin (bg, 225 tns) (two crossings)	Dunn, L.	1841	P.E.I.	AE1	1846, 1847	Tralee, Dublin	J	291
Susan of Cork (bk, 168 tns)	Griffith	1814	Ayr	AE1	1849	Cork	A	109
Thomas Hanford of Cork (sw, 228 tns)	Herbert	1824	N.B.	AE1	1846	Cork	J	150
Ω *Thorney Close* of Sunderland (sw, 249 tns)	Horan, James	1840	Sunderland	A1	1847	Donegal	J	137
Ω *Trafalgar* of Maryport (bg, 198 tns)	Younghusband	1807	Workington	AE1	1847	Cork	J	127

Vessel	Captain(s)	Year Built	Place Built	Lloyd's Code	Dep. Yrs	Dep. Port	Arr. Port	No. of psgrs
Triumph of Halifax (bg, 176 tns) (three crossings)	Raycroft	1846	N.S.	A1	1846–48	Berehaven/ Limerick	J	259
Ω *Ward Chipman* of Liverpool (bk, 740 tns)	Bilton	1840	N.B.	AE1	1847	Cork	J	505
Ω *Waterford* of Harrington (bg, 296 tns)	Robinson	1841	N.S.	A1	1849	Limerick	J	152
Woodland Castle of Cork (bk, 168 tns)	Williams	1802	Yarmouth	E1	1846	Cork	J	116
Ω *Yeoman* of Greenock (s, 840 tns)	Purdon, J.	1845	N.S.	A1	1847	Sligo	J	504

vessels whose Lloyd's shipping codes have been identified were top ranking. Forty-six were first class ("A" or "AE"), four were second class, and six had reputable builders. The 673-ton *Lady Sale* of Greenock, carrying 412 tenants from the Gore-Booth and Palmerston estates in county Sligo to Saint John was "A1," as was the 176-ton *Triumph* of Halifax, which carried nearly 300 people in three crossings from ports in the southwest of Ireland. The 229-ton *Bache McEver* of Cork, carrying 273 passengers, the 185-ton *Charles* of Youghall, with 201 passengers, and the 225-ton *Sir James McDonnell* of Dublin, with 391 passengers, were "AE1" vessels, each making two crossings between 1846 and 1848. The 299-ton *Londonderry*, carrying a total of 900 immigrants between 1847 and 1850, was one of John Cooke's top ships.

There is no reason to believe that the vessels whose codes or builders could not be determined were any different. There can be no finer endorsement of Irish shipping than this! And yet the term "coffin ship" is bandied about and no one challenges its use. The data left behind by the hard-nosed mercantile community reveals that the Irish generally sailed in good ships. There was a high death toll at sea, but this was due to disease and not to failings in the quality of the shipping service.

The most serious problem facing captains and officials in 1847 was the control of disease. Moses Perley raged against the Irish landlords who he claimed were sending their sick and destitute tenants to New Brunswick. The problem was that while they may have been destitute, they were probably fit at the time of sailing. Most would have picked up deadly diseases such as typhus and smallpox just before or during the embarkation process. Diet deficiencies, overcrowding, and poor ventilation contributed to the spread of disease once the crossing was underway, but the cause of their ailment probably was the fever that they would have caught from others while waiting to board the ship.[60] Good-quality ships did not necessarily offer a better chance of survival where disease was concerned. Many of the top-ranked vessels that brought the Irish to New Brunswick during the famine period arrived with sick and dying passengers (see Table 12). Conversely, when breaches of the regulations occurred, and where unsuitable vessels were used, immigrants might arrive in a perfectly healthy state.

Infectious diseases lurked in public places. The risk of catching deadly bacteria and viruses was ever-present, but it was highest at busy ports such as Liverpool, Londonderry, and Cork, where over 30 percent of the vessels arrived with disease on board during the period between 1846 and 1850. There were no illness reports for vessels sailing from Waterford and only two Limerick crossings out of a total of twelve experienced illness. Fever appeared also to be raging at Sligo, where a third of all crossings during this period reported disease on board. Although the *Aeolus* of Greenock was a well-built ship owned by Sir Robert Gore-Booth, the Sligo tenants of this same man experienced an appalling disease-ridden crossing with many deaths. Accolades were addressed to Captain Michael Driscoll for his excellent stewardship. There was a surgeon on board and the best possible provisions were available. And yet, this crossing claimed many lives. If Gore-Booth's tenants had sailed from one of the smaller ports, their survival chances would have been considerably greater. In the end, the small brigs and schooners offering a basic service were a better bet, but people had no way of realizing this at the time. If the spread of disease had been better understood, the misery and deaths associated with the Irish Famine period could have been greatly reduced.

The lasting effect of the famine period has been to distort the immigration saga. Contrary to popular belief, 1847 was not the year when the Irish first came to Atlantic Canada. The fact is that most people's Irish family links with the Atlantic Canada date back to a time well before this. In fact, most of the Irish who landed at Saint John during the famine years were in transit to the United States. Like them, those Irish who remained in the Maritimes had reason to thank their lucky stars that they had survived. Many offered tributes to the good captains who helped them cope with their ordeals and some probably remembered the kindly soul at the pier who questioned them on their arrival. The last word must go to him — Moses Perley — who used his public office to ensure that the best possible standards were maintained for passengers. Having a legal background, he was well-placed to identify infringements of the passenger legislation and ensure that captains and shipowners who were guilty of malpractices, were prosecuted in court.

The Irish who settled in New Brunswick, Nova Scotia, and Prince Edward Island in the first half of the nineteenth century rarely experienced disease during their crossings. In most years the mortality on board ship and in quarantine was less than 1 percent. Although many would have felt apprehensive about crossing the Atlantic, they expected to arrive safely. And apart from the famine period, most people did. On reaching their destinations they faced the daunting task of adjusting to a new life in their adopted country. In many respects, this was even more challenging than the sea crossing.

CHAPTER 9

❧

The Irish in Atlantic Canada

The Fourth Annual Picnic will be held on Tuesday, August 4, on the beautiful grounds situate[d] on Partridge Island.... Valuable Prizes will be given for Archery, Races, Foot, Sack, and Hurdle, Jumping, Throwing the Hammer, and for the best Irish Jig and Reel! A Greased Pig will enliven the proceedings of the evening. The Pig will appear punctually at 5.30 o'clock ...[1]

The aforementioned picnic, held in the 1860s on Partridge Island, located at the mouth of Saint John Harbour, was being hosted by the Irish Friendly Society. The island, which came to be known as "Canada's Emerald Isle," was an appropriate venue, given that many tens of thousands of Irish immigrants had earlier passed this way.[2] The now derelict quarantine station, which had once witnessed harrowing scenes of suffering, offered a graphic reminder of the death toll experienced during the famine years; but the Irish connection with Partridge Island runs deeper than this. Events such as this picnic commemorate an Irish past and an Irish self-belief that underpins their immigration story.

The St. Mary's Brass Band, which played in Halifax on St. Patrick's Day 1892.

Irish Catholics brought their St. Patrick's Societies with them to Atlantic Canada, while Irish Protestants brought their Orange Order, both groups sharing a long history of mutual mistrust. St. Patrick's Day parades, which celebrate Ireland's patron saint, keep alive the memory of an Irish homeland, but they evoke a distant past that has largely been lost. Only symbols of the actual culture that the early settlers brought with them still survive.

Having acquired its Gaelic-speaking Irish settlers earliest, Newfoundland was the most successful of the provinces in retaining the Irish language and Irish traditions. Hurling, an ancient Irish field sport, was played regularly in St. John's in the 1780s.[3] This was also a time when Irish-speaking interpreters were needed to translate proceedings in the Newfoundland courts.[4] The concentration of settlers from southeastern Ireland brought to the island a distinctive and widely spoken Irish language, but by the early twentieth century it had all but disappeared. Odd words such as *scrob* (scratch) *sleveen* (rascal) and *streel* (a slovenly person) survive today, and Irish accents are still detectable in many parts of the province, but the language itself has vanished.

Irish Gaelic never stood a chance in the rest of Atlantic Canada. The substantial Gaelic-speaking Irish communities that formed in Cape Breton and the Miramichi region of New Brunswick were swamped numerically by their Highland neighbours. Many thousands of Highlanders had come to settle in Prince Edward Island, Cape Breton, and the Miramichi starting in the late eighteenth century, giving their language and customs plenty of time to take hold.[5] Arriving much later, mainly in the 1830s and 1840s, the Irish and their culture had far less impact. Although the 1901 census for New Brunswick reveals a scattering of people who listed Irish as their mother tongue, they represent a tiny minority.[6] The language that they brought with them was absorbed in a melting pot having many ingredients. Music, which has no language barriers, was even more susceptible to this process of assimilation. For instance, the folksong traditions of the Miramichi region represent a blend of musical influences, reflecting the cultural roots of its Irish, Scottish, and Acadian population. Thanks to Lord Beaverbrook's initiative in 1958, "lumber and river songs" dating back to the eighteenth and nineteenth centuries have been saved and continue to be played annually at the Miramichi Folksong Festival.[7] Even in Newfoundland, where Irish culture had a stronger foundation, the music of the early settlers has almost completely disappeared. What survives is Irish-sounding music, designed to appeal to popular tastes.[8]

Michael Whelan, a poet of Irish descent who grew up in a remote part of the Miramichi, just to the north of Blackville, in the latter part of the nineteenth century, dedicated his life to recording what was once New Brunswick's pioneer life in verse and song.[9] He peddled his books from door to door to supplement his income as a schoolteacher and later as a lumber firm bookkeeper, but few people took any interest in his work and he died a pauper's death in 1937.[10] Described as "an old drunk who fell down in the snow bank and froze his eyeball," he was also remembered as "one of the kindest and gentlest of people."[11] Forty years after his death, Whelan's poetry was revived. At a dedication ceremony, Father Robert Grattan, the parish priest, stated that Whelan "had to die in order to live on in the hearts of posterity." Describing him as a man "who captured the pulse of the pioneers," he spoke for many in wishing to acknowledge Whelan's contribution in preserving local history by recording the region's early folklore.[12]

In the 1860s, concern was being expressed in the cities that authentic Irish music was fast disappearing. In a lecture held at this time in Saint John on Irish music and song, a Mr. Brown warned that the Irish music of the 1860s was not being given its "true expression." The fear among musicians of "being too Irish" was driving change.[13] A similar view was expressed by Smith O'Brien in the *Saint John Morning Freeman* as he pleaded for the revival of "a thoroughly Irish literature."[14] As was happening elsewhere in the region, Irish culture in all of its forms was being popularized to suit modern tastes. As this happened, its origins were being lost to future generations.

Strangely enough, the Orange Order made the deepest impression of any Irish group in Atlantic Canada, but not in a cultural sense.[15] Presenting itself as a bastion of British values and the Protestant faith, it reached out to English, Scottish, and Irish males. It became a social organization whose members espoused what it meant to be of British origin, Protestant, and Canadian. In Prince Edward Island, its membership was mainly Scottish and English.[16] Similarly, membership in Nova Scotia's Orange Lodges was greatest in mining and industrial districts such as Pictou, Truro, north Sydney, and Cumberland County, where a shared Protestant faith brought men together.[17] Most surprising of all was the Orange Order's outstanding success in Newfoundland. This was a province that had attracted few Irish Protestant settlers.[18] And yet the Orange Order found considerable support outside the principal population centres — especially along Conception, Trinity, and Bonavista Bays on the eastern coast. The Orange Lodge Hall that was built in Bonavista in 1907 was said to be "the most remarkable in the Orange world" and the largest in North America.[19]

However, the Orange Order parades celebrating the victory of the Protestant King William over the Catholic King James II at the Battle of the Boyne in 1690 did occasionally provoke riotous behaviour across the Atlantic region. Following the arrival of large numbers of Irish Catholics during the 1840s, the Saint John River Valley of New Brunswick became a trouble spot. Already-established Protestants felt threatened by what

Orangemen's Parade, Harbour Grace, Newfoundland, circa 1900–1930s. Orangemen's parades commemorated the Protestant William of Orange's victory over the Catholic James II at a battle fought across the River Boyne in Ireland in 1690.

they perceived to be a Catholic takeover of their territory. Membership in the Orange Order rocketed, and triumphant parades, extolling perceived Protestant supremacy, became increasingly irksome to Catholics. The area was a cauldron of unrest:

> In 1846 the Glorious Twelfth [of August] was marked by major confrontations in every urban centre in the St. John River Valley. At Woodstock and Fredericton there were processions, riots, beatings and killings as the native populations cowered in their homes and gave up the streets to the Irishmen. In Saint John, again, the mayor called out the troops, although they were not required to act.[20]

James Sproul of Saint John, New Brunswick, shown here wearing a Mason uniform, circa 1905–11. A successful builder and contractor, Sproul was a prominent member of the city's Irish Protestant community and attained the highest rank in the Orange Order.

Between 1841 and 1849, Orange parades sparked off major distur-bances in Woodstock, Fredericton, and Saint John, with order being restored only through the use of militia or British troops.[21] The violence reached its peak in the great Saint John riot of 1849, when hundreds of Orangemen marched through Catholic strongholds in the city. At least a dozen died, although both sides jealously guarded details about their dead and wounded. The Orangemen claimed victory, having "marched through the very heart" of Saint John's Catholic districts, tearing down a memorial arch and emerging more or less intact. After the melee the Orangemen then marched, completely unopposed, up and down the streets of Saint John for nearly five hours.[22]

A double standard that prevented Catholics from participating in the machinery of government ensured that only they, and not Protestants, would be found guilty of rioting. Even on the rare occasions when Orangemen stood trial, such as happened after the 1849 riot, partisan juries expeditiously exonerated them.[23] Irish Catholics were excluded from virtually all roles of governance or representation in the province. In fact, they were "rebuffed, isolated and repressed in a systematic fashion by both legal and extra-legal forces."[24]

Despite the overt discrimination suffered by Catholics in the Atlantic Canada, it was still a far better place to be than Ireland. When the Irish aristocrat Edward Fitzgerald first experienced life in Saint John in 1788, he was struck by the "equality of everyone," even then. "Everyone is on an [equal] footing providing he works ... every man is exactly what he can make [of] himself, or has made of himself by his industry."[25] Ireland was light years away from anything like this. It was still a feudal society run by an elite for their benefit only. Ordinary people had no prospect of self-advancement. They were essentially nonentities in their own country. Although they suffered many disadvantages, the Irish Catholics who came to live in Atlantic Canada could at least see their way to enjoying the benefits of a fairer society some day. They had a partially opened door to push at, whereas in Ireland there was an impenetrable barrier. Anti-Catholic discrimination, rigidly enforced by legislation, was their lot there, and there was nothing they could do to influence change; whereas Canada had ladders of opportunity that they could climb.

The prospect of living in a more liberal society was one of the factors that drew well-to-do merchant Patrick Gallagher to Saint John. A Catholic born in Donegal, he established a lumber business that was clearly prospering by the 1830s. Wishing his son Francis to join him, he held out the prospect of the better life that Saint John offered: "If you bring what little means you could with you in goods and go into business ... you may depend that before three years you will find yourself happier than ever you would be in Lurgabreck [Count Donegal]; it is true you will not have so fine a house ... and so many other things [but] you will have peace of mind."[26]

In other words, along with the prospect of economic self-betterment, Irish people were also being attracted by Canada's more egalitarian society. It was one of the pull factors that prompted them to emigrate. In a speech given in 1841, the chairman of Fredericton's St. Patrick's Society recalled the days when Irish people arrived, having been "crushed by a narrow-minded and cruel oppression" in their homeland; but in New Brunswick they found a land "conceived in liberty.... They possess many virtues which we call our own. Our national characteristic, hospitality, will hereby be recognized as a prominent feature in the Colonial character."[27]

When he visited Saint John in the 1860s, John Maguire was struck both by the strong prejudice against Irish Catholics and by the great strides that some of them had made in overcoming this obstacle:

> The prejudice which they had to encounter was nei-
> ther latent nor slumbering — it was open and active. It
> met the Catholic Irishman in every rank of life and in
> every branch of industry.... And yet, while labour, rude
> or skilled, is the lot of the majority of the Irish in Saint
> John, and throughout the province generally, a consid-
> erable portion are to be found in every department of
> business, and enjoy as merchants, traders and manufac-
> turers, the highest position which character and wealth
> can secure to their possessor.[28]

The paucity of Irish Catholics among the professional classes, which Maguire noted, had created a problem for Patrick Gallagher. Writing to a business colleague in Manchester (England), he asked for help in finding "a young man of some means, a Catholic who would join me and take an active part and who would purchase the goods; then we could make it pay well. I could get persons here to join me but they are not of that class that I would wish to have anything to do with."[29]

The extreme poverty of many of the Irish Catholics who arrived in Halifax just after 1815 had left an indelible mark. The sheer size of the Catholic influx may have also made people uneasy. From that moment on, public opinion grew wary about their poverty-stricken state and dependence on public funds. Abraham Gesner approved of the low rates of pay being offered to Irish labourers in New Brunswick. He felt that their inexperience of Canadian farming methods reduced the value of their labour, although he neglected to point out that the same was true for the Scots and English:

> Many [Irish] have suffered severely by holding out for
> higher wages on their first arrival. I have seen hundreds
> of Irish labourers, whose families were starving, stand
> idle on the streets of Saint John, from week to week,
> rather than work for less than sixpence an hour; and
> when any individual would engage for a less sum, he was
> immediately caught and beaten by his companions.[30]

According to Gesner, they lacked "sobriety, industry and a resolute spirit of enterprise," qualities that, according to him, the English, Lowland Scots, and Germans had in abundance.[31] There were many other opinion formers like Gesner who held deep-rooted prejudices against the Irish.

However, even worse than their alleged reputation for being unreliable workers was the Irish tendency to drink excessively. Author William Adams believed that the Irish needed to face up to the fact that drunkenness was "their chief vice." And their best weapon in overcoming this blight on their good name was, he argued, to pledge their total abstinence from drink.[32] Pledging abstinence was as good as the best letter of recommendation that anyone might write on their behalf. It promised upward social mobility and it is a route that many, like Laurence Hughes's nephew, took. After moving to Fredericton, Laurence received a letter from him asking for help in paying for his travel costs to go from his present location in Philadelphia to join an uncle in Cambria County, Pennsylvania. In the letter, he was careful to state that he has not had "any kind of liquor. I am pledged for the last twelve years and I am going on my twentieth year now."[33]

By the same token, an inability to overcome a drink problem not only spelled economic ruin; it also reinforced the Irish reputation for excessive drinking. Juliana Horatia Ewing, an English officer's wife, living in Fredericton in the 1860s, found to her dismay that "an Irish lady named Sarah," whom she employed as a housemaid, had "a taste for the bottle." Wracked with guilt over the need to dismiss her, Juliana came face to face with local anti-Irish prejudice and its association with drink.[34] She hoped that a chat with the local priest would save Sarah's job prospects, but there was nothing he could do. In the end, people had to reform their ways or go under. In this social climate the temperance movement blossomed.

Saint John had a temperance movement in the 1840s, which later evolved into Saint Malachi's Total Abstinence Relief Society, while Charlottetown had its St. Dunstan's Total Abstinence Society.[35] Newfoundland's various temperance societies and their abstinence society successors also appeared by this time, as did equivalent groups in Nova Scotia.[36] They formed bands, held concerts and parades on St. Patrick's Day, and also sponsored teas, picnics, and other social gatherings.[37] In 1842, St. Patrick's Day was celebrated in Chatham, New Brunswick, by "a Roman Catholic Tee-total Procession ... which paraded through several streets in the town, crossed the ice to Douglas town, through which they passed, as well as Newcastle, and again crossed the ice to Nelson, where an address was presented in St. Patrick's Chapel.... About 1,800 persons walked in the ranks ... and the evening was spent in Temperance style at the Amateur Band Room, which was tastefully decorated for the purpose."[38]

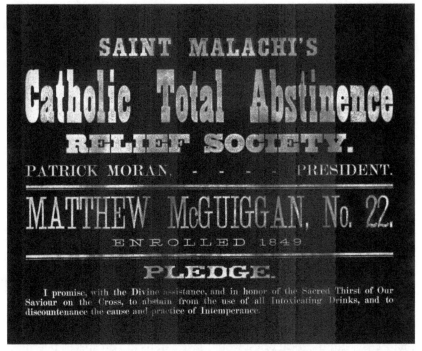

A pledge form for Saint Malachi's Catholic Total Abstinence Relief Society of Saint John, New Brunswick, 1849. This was one of many local groups that had been founded by Bishop John Sweeney, who sought to improve the material and spiritual life of the people in the city.

Lawrence O'Connor Doyle (1804–64). A lawyer and politician, he was the son of a Roman Catholic merchant in Halifax. He was an ardent member of the Charitable Irish Society of Halifax and was the first president of the St. Patrick's Temperance Society of Halifax.

Some of the Catholic Irishmen who achieved success in Atlantic Canada went on to serve in government, where they sought social reforms for the benefit of their local communities. One of the earliest was the Cork-born Richard John Uniacke, the Nova Scotia solicitor general between 1781 and 1797, who was the leading light behind the foundation of Halifax's Charitable Irish Society, the first of its kind in the region.[39] Other benevolent groups include the Benevolent Irish Society of Charlottetown, founded in 1825, which held charitable, cultural, and social activities, the highlight being an annual church parade and banquet on St. Patrick's Day, and the Irish Friendly Society, formed by Saint John's business community in the 1850s to provide social and scholarly opportunities for young men.[40]

Meanwhile, Laurence O'Connor Doyle, a lawyer and politician and son of a Roman Catholic merchant in Halifax, took up the cause of more representative government when serving as a member of the Nova Scotia Assembly between 1832 and 1855. Henry O'Leary, another county

The Hon. Timothy Warren Anglin, circa 1861–66. Born in county Cork, he immigrated to Saint John in 1849. That year he published the first issue of the Weekly Freeman, a newspaper that spoke out on behalf of Irish Catholics. He was a member of the Legislative Assembly from 1861.

Cork man, became active in politics after establishing his highly successful lobster and salmon canning plants in New Brunswick and Prince Edward Island. As a member of the New Brunswick House of Assembly for Kent County during the 1870s, he pressed for Catholics to be given better educational opportunities.[41]

The cause of social reform and responsible government also lay behind Edward Whelan's political and journalistic career in Prince Edward Island.[42] A Catholic, born in county Mayo, he served in the House of Assembly from 1846 to 1867, during which time he battled to rid the island of its pernicious leasehold-based land tenure regime, which denied ordinary settlers the means to own land.[43]

Timothy Warren Anglin, an influential Irish-born journalist and politician, dedicated himself to defending Irish Catholics in Saint John through his newspaper, the *Saint John Weekly Freeman*, fighting for them against accusations that they were useless drunkards and encouraging them to better themselves.

However, the social reforming ambitions of many of these Catholic journalists, politicians, and businessmen went well beyond the Atlantic region. Not content with helping to bring representative government and other social reforms to Atlantic Canada, they also wanted to see them take root in their homeland. Michael Dunne, from county Laois, who organized the St. Patrick's Day teetotal parade in Chatham in 1842, was the founder of the Miramichi Repeal Association, part of a popular movement which sought self-government for Ireland under the British Crown.[44] Laurence Doyle lent his support in Nova Scotia to this cause, while Halifax became a major focus for the repeal movement, having 383 members by 1843.[45]

Doom-mongers, seeking to make political capital out of their story, have sold the Irish short, preferring to present them as helpless exiles with little aspiration or ability to control their own lives. On the contrary, through their toughness, courage, and incredible resilience they triumphed in Atlantic Canada. They overcame huge obstacles and seized their opportunities. Set free from the oppressive constraints that held them back in their homeland, they prospered. As they made the transition from Irish immigrant to Canadian citizen they helped to shape the egalitarian and prospering society that was being formed around them.

As the *Armagh Guardian* pointed out to its readers in 1895, Irish colonists in Nova Scotia, New Brunswick, and Prince Edward Island "are to be found in the front rank of the professions of agriculture and of industrial enterprise."[46] They steadily rose through the ranks of civic society, grasping the levers of power as they prospered. In the best traditions of Canadian pioneer history, the Irish took advantage of the opportunities presented by their new home to carve out a better life for themselves and their children.

EXPLANATORY NOTES FOR
APPENDICES I TO III

Vessel name:

The vessel name often includes the port at which the vessel is registered. The vessel type and tonnage, where known, appears after the vessel name.

Vessel type:

Brig (bg) is a two-masted vessel with square rigging on both masts.

Barque (bk) is a three-masted vessel, square-rigged on the fore and main masts and for-and-aft rigged on the third aftermost mast.

Ship (s) is a three-masted vessel, square-rigged on all three masts.

Schooner (sr) has fore-and-aft sails on two or more masts. They were largely used in the coasting trade and for fishing, their advantage being that they required a smaller crew than the square-rigged vessels of comparable size.

Snow (sw) is rigged as a brig with square sails on both masts but with a small triangular sail-mast stepped immediately toward the stern of the main mast.

Tonnage:

The tonnage was a standard measure used to determine customs dues and navigation fees. Because it was a calculated figure, tonnage did not necessarily convey actual carrying capacity. Before 1836, the formula used to calculate tonnage was based only on breadth and length, but after 1836 it incorporated the vessel's depth as well.

Month:

Unless otherwise stated, the month shown is the vessel's arrival month; but where the month is followed by (d) it refers to the departure month.

Passenger Lists:

Appendix II, listing ship crossings from Ireland to New Brunswick, refers to 138 passenger lists. Ninety-four have been taken from the customs data printed in *Passengers to New Brunswick: Customs House Records — 1833, 34, 37, and 38*. These are indicated by NBGS.

Apart from those appearing as tables in this book, the remainder have been taken from the following sources:

> www.sligoheritage.com
> www.olivetree.com
> www.theshipslist.com
> www.archives.gnb.ca/irish/databases en.html (Irish Portal)
> Mitchell, *Irish Passenger Lists, 1847–71*
> Rees, *Surplus People: From Wicklow to Canada*, 131–37

APPENDIX I

❦

Ship Crossings from Ireland to Nova Scotia, 1816–1850

The following table lists the year, month of sailing, and number of passengers carried by each ship identified as having left Ireland for Nova Scotia between 1816 and 1850. It provides details of 165 sea crossings, involving a total of 15,067 Irish passengers, showing the different Irish ports from which they embarked and their arrival ports in Nova Scotia. However, because of gaps in the customs and shipping records, the list is incomplete, signifying that the actual number of Irish immigrants was somewhat greater.

Most of the Irish disembarked at Halifax. Around one thousand Irish did the voyage in two stages, stopping first at St. John's, Newfoundland, before continuing on to Halifax.

Ship crossing data has been obtained from the following documentary sources:

J.S. Martell, *Immigration to and Emigration from Nova Scotia, 1815–1838. (*Halifax: PANS 1942).
Susan Longley, Morse, "Immigration to Nova Scotia 1839–51."
(Halifax, NS: Dalhousie University, unpublished M.A. 1946).

George MacLaren, *The Pictou Book: Stories of Our Past.* (New
  Glasgow, NS: Hector Pub. Co., 1954.)
Terrence Punch, "Ships from Ireland to Nova Scotia, 1765–1850," *An
  Nasc* 13 (Spring 2001): 3–10.
The *Acadian Recorder.*

See "Explanatory Notes" on page 217 for an explanation of the shipping terms used in this listing.

For details of the quality of the ships that brought the Irish to Nova
Scotia, see Tables 10, 11, and 12.

Year	Month	Vessel	Master	Departure Port	Arrival Port	Passenger Numbers
1816	11	*Hibernia* (bg, 183 tns)	Walmsley	Cork	Halifax	105

Farmers and mechanics with their families.

Year	Month	Vessel	Master	Departure Port	Arrival Port	Passenger Numbers
1816	12	*Industry and Susan* (sr)	n/k	Ireland	Halifax	150

Via St. John's, Newfoundland.

Year	Month	Vessel	Master	Departure Port	Arrival Port	Passenger Numbers
1816	12	*William and Jane* (sr)	Graham	Ireland	Halifax	51

Called at St. John's, Newfoundland.

Year	Month	Vessel	Master	Departure Port	Arrival Port	Passenger Numbers
1817	01	*Consolation* (sr)	Marvin	Ireland	Pope's Harbour	30

Via St. John's, Newfoundland.

Mainly mechanics. Vessel bound for Halifax but forced into Pope's Harbour as a result of a storm.

Year	Month	Vessel	Master	Departure Port	Arrival Port	Passenger Numbers
1817	01	*Isabella* (sr)	Walten	Ireland	Halifax	55

Via St. John's, Newfoundland.

Year	Month	Vessel	Master	Departure Port	Arrival Port	Passenger Numbers
1817	02	*Lively* of Halifax (sr)	Davis	Ireland	Beaver Harbour	20

Vessel lost both masts and was forced into Beaver Harbour by a storm. One passenger was killed and several injured.

Year	Month	Vessel	Master	Departure Port	Arrival Port	Passenger Numbers
1817	07	*Angelique* (sr)	Beauchamps	Ireland	Halifax	30

Via St. John's, Newfoundland.

Year	Month	Vessel	Master	Departure Port	Arrival Port	Passenger Numbers
1817	07	*Brunswick* of London (bk, 571 tns)	Walker	Londonderry	Halifax	231
1817	07	*Halifax Packet* (s, 185 tns)	Craige	Londonderry	Halifax	171

Year	Month	Vessel	Master	Departure Port	Arrival Port	Passenger Numbers
1817	07	*Kitty*	Duggan	Ireland	Halifax	44

In 1815, seventy-seven Dublin tradesmen had sailed to St. John's, Newfoundland, in the *Concord*. Two years later, forty-four were said to be in a distressed state. They sailed to Halifax in the *Kitty*. See Punch, *Erin's Sons*, Volume 1, page 70 for the names of the Dublin tradesmen.

Year	Month	Vessel	Master	Departure Port	Arrival Port	Passenger Numbers
1817	08	*Critic* (sr)	Jeffreys	Ireland	Halifax	36

Via St. John's NF.

Year	Month	Vessel	Master	Departure Port	Arrival Port	Passenger Numbers
1817	08	*Marcus Hill* (s, 700 tns)	White	Londonderry	Halifax	250

McCorkill Line of Londonderry. Seven feet between decks.

Year	Month	Vessel	Master	Departure Port	Arrival Port	Passenger Numbers
1817	09	*Amelia*	Johnston	Coleraine	Halifax	84
1817	09	*Hibernia* (bg)	Simpson	Londonderry	Halifax	17
1817	09	*Mary* (bg)	Kay	Dublin	Halifax	88
1817	10	*Union* (sr)	Good	Dublin	Halifax	65

Via St. John's, Newfoundland.

Year	Month	Vessel	Master	Departure Port	Arrival Port	Passenger Numbers
1817	11	*Angelique* (sr)	Beauchamps	Ireland	Halifax	50

Cabin passengers: Mr. and Mrs. John Stayner. Steerage passengers mostly labourers.

Year	Month	Vessel	Master	Departure Port	Arrival Port	Passenger Numbers
1817	11	*Elizabeth* (sr)	Walker	Ireland	Halifax	28

Via St. John's, Newfoundland.

Year	Month	Vessel	Master	Departure Port	Arrival Port	Passenger Numbers
1817	11	*Sisters*	Allen	Ireland	Halifax	46

Via Newfoundland.

Year	Month	Vessel	Master	Departure Port	Arrival Port	Passenger Numbers
1817	12	*Comet* (bg)	Bell	Cork	Halifax	30
1818	06	*Alexander Buchanan*	Clements, Thomas	Londonderry	Cape Sable	200

Vessel wrecked on Cape Sable Island. All saved.

Year	Month	Vessel	Master	Departure Port	Arrival Port	Passenger Numbers
1818	06	*Fame*	Owens	Waterford	Halifax	103
1818	06	*Industry*	Burns	Newry	Halifax	157

Fifty-five passengers went on to Philadelphia.

Year	Month	Vessel	Master	Departure Port	Arrival Port	Passenger Numbers
1818	07	*Four Brothers* (bg)	n/k	Waterford	Halifax	50
1818	09	*Clyde* (bg, 134 tns)	Greig	Dublin	Halifax	85
1818	10	*Fame* (bg)	Hardy	Belfast	Cole Harbour	114

Vessel went ashore at Cole Harbour. Passengers and crew saved.

Year	Month	Vessel	Master	Departure Port	Arrival Port	Passenger Numbers
1818	10	*Marinhull* (bg)	Eckerman	Ireland	Halifax	22

Via Burin, NF.

Year	Month	Vessel	Master	Departure Port	Arrival Port	Passenger Numbers
1818	10	*Martha* (bg, 198 tns)	Kennedy	Newry	Halifax	84
1818	n/k	*Swift*	n/k	Ireland	Halifax	51

On board were Irish immigrants who had been shipwrecked in the Azores.

Year	Month	Vessel	Master	Departure Port	Arrival Port	Passenger Numbers
1819	06	*Enterprise*	n/k	Dublin	Halifax	103
1819	06	*Halifax Packet* (s, 185 tns)	Buchanan	Londonderry	Halifax	113
1819	06	*Johns* (bg)	Stobo	Kinsale	Halifax	130
1819	06	*Sir John Cameron* (bg, 268 tns)	Lilly	Waterford	Halifax	112

Year	Month	Vessel	Master	Departure Port	Arrival Port	Passenger Numbers
1819	07	*Frances-Ann* (bg)	Holmes	Londonderry	Halifax	120
1819	07	*Mary* (sr)	Sutton	Ireland	Halifax	n/k

Via St. John's, Newfoundland.

| 1819 | 07 | *Mermaid* of Dublin (bg) | n/k | Dublin | Halifax | 73 |

Vessel went aground on Cape Negro Island, Nova Scotia. Passengers and crew all saved.

1819	09	*Chatty* (bg, 170 tns)	Gilbert	Dublin	Halifax	113
1820	05	*Rubicon* (s, 304 tns)	n/k	Waterford	Halifax	150
1820	06	*Oliphant* (bg, 250 tns)	Christie, Richard	Belfast	Halifax	43
1820	09	*Frances and Lucy* (bg)	Collins	Londonderry	Halifax	n/k
1821	05	*Amicus* (bg)	Norton	Cork	Halifax	102

Cabin passengers: Mr. and Mrs. Lawler and family, Mr. Manning, Mr. Taylor, and ninety-eight steerage passengers.

| 1821 | 05 | *Rob Roy* (bg, 241 tns) | Kenn, William | Belfast | Halifax | 141 |

Cabin passengers: Major Hull (62nd Regiment), Mr. Scott, and 139 steerage passengers.

| 1824 | 07 | *Brothers* (sr) | McHarron | Ireland | Halifax | 9 |

Via St. John's, Newfoundland. Cabin passengers: W.B. Thomas, Esq., Lieutenant Tilden, R.A., Mr. W. Lawson Jr., Mr. Goutea and family, Mrs. Barry, Mrs. Doner. Three in the steerage.

Year	Month	Vessel	Master	Departure Port	Arrival Port	Passenger Numbers
1824	09	*Elizabeth of New Brunswick*	Kay	Sligo	Barrington	112

Vessel was bound for Saint John, New Brunswick, but hit a ledge near Cape Sable Island and was towed to Barrington.

Year	Month	Vessel	Master	Departure Port	Arrival Port	Passenger Numbers
1825	06	*Brothers* (sr)	McHarron	Ireland	Halifax	18

Cabin passengers: Mr. Spillard, Mr. Clare, plus sixteen steerage passengers.

Year	Month	Vessel	Master	Departure Port	Arrival Port	Passenger Numbers
1825	07	*Resolution* (bg)	Flinn	Dublin	Halifax	34

Year	Month	Vessel	Master	Departure Port	Arrival Port	Passenger Numbers
1826	05	*Rubicon* (s, 304 tns)	Armstrong	Waterford	Halifax	150

Year	Month	Vessel	Master	Departure Port	Arrival Port	Passenger Numbers
1826	06	*Maria* (bg)	Bibbin	Cork	Halifax	29

Cabin passengers: Captain Patterson, Mr. Kennedy, plus twenty-seven in the steerage.

Year	Month	Vessel	Master	Departure Port	Arrival Port	Passenger Numbers
1826	06	*Thomas* (bg)	Moffet	Waterford	Halifax	91

Year	Month	Vessel	Master	Departure Port	Arrival Port	Passenger Numbers
1826	06	*Two Brothers* and the *Mary*	n/k	Dublin	Halifax	140

They were survivors of the *Nassau*, which was wrecked at Sable Island on the way to Quebec. All were Irish. Seven dead. Ninety-five of the survivors were transferred to the *Two Brothers* and the remainder were taken by the schooner *Mary*.

Year	Month	Vessel	Master	Departure Port	Arrival Port	Passenger Numbers
1826	07	*Albion* (bg)	Whitten	Cork	Halifax	47

Year	Month	Vessel	Master	Departure Port	Arrival Port	Passenger Numbers
1826	07	*Hopewell* (bg, 300 tns)	Berkeley	Belfast	Pictou	50

Year	Month	Vessel	Master	Departure Port	Arrival Port	Passenger Numbers
1826	07	*Nancy* (bg)	Stokes	Dublin	Halifax	116

Year	Month	Vessel	Master	Departure Port	Arrival Port	Passenger Numbers
1826	10	*Mary* (sr)	Blamey	Ireland	Halifax	31

Via St. John's, Newfoundland.

Year	Month	Vessel	Master	Departure Port	Arrival Port	Passenger Numbers
1826	11	*Admiral Lake* (bg)	Davis	Ireland	Halifax	>14

Via St. John's, Newfoundland. Cabin passengers: Mr. Gilmour and family plus thirteen in the steerage.

| 1826 | 11 | *Caledonia* (bg) | Henley | Ireland | Liverpool NS | 86 |

Via St. John's, Newfoundland. Cabin passengers: Captain John Pridham, Mr. Thomas Dellor, plus eighty-four in the steerage.

| 1826 | 11 | *William Hunter* (sr) | McHarron | Ireland | Halifax | 54 |

Via St. John's, Newfoundland. Cabin passenger: Mr. John Carty plus fifty-three in the steerage.

| 1827 | 05 | *Liberty* (bk, 258 tns) | Cooper | Waterford | Halifax | 127 |

| 1827 | 06 | *Bolivar* (s, 357 tns) | Hearl | Waterford | Halifax | 350 |

| 1827 | 06 | *Cherub* (bg, 232 tns) | Selkirk, J. | Waterford | Halifax | 200 |

| 1827 | 06 | *Letitia* | n/k | Dublin | Halifax | 200 |

Passengers included some troops.

| 1827 | 07 | *Cumberland* (s) | Eswoner | Waterford | Halifax | 350 |

Several passengers died from disease during the voyage or shortly after arriving in Halifax. Partially reconstructed passenger list in Punch, *Erin's Sons*, vol. 1, 97–99.

| 1827 | 09 | *Forte* (bg) | Morris | Ireland | Halifax | n/k |

Via St. John's, Newfoundland. Cabin passenger: Colonel R.E. Nicholas and forty masons (with their families) to work on the Shubenacadie Canal.

| 1827 | 09 | *James* | n/k | Waterford | Halifax | 160 |

Via St. John's, Newfoundland. The passengers were very poor and suffering from typhus. Five died at sea. Thirty-five left behind in Newfoundland because they were too ill to proceed to Halifax.

Year	Month	Vessel	Master	Departure Port	Arrival Port	Passenger Numbers
1827	09	*Rode*	n/k	Ireland	Halifax	206
1828	05	*Saltern's Rock* (bg)	Taylor	Cork	Halifax	80
1828	06	*Dale* (bg, 158 tns)	McNeil, J.	Dublin	Halifax	100

Boarded by the Health Officer and ordered to come to anchor under the guns of the fort until the necessary bonds were given.

Year	Month	Vessel	Master	Departure Port	Arrival Port	Passenger Numbers
1828	09	*Henry Arnot* (bg)	Siene	Ireland	Halifax	223

Part of a large Irish group who were sailing to Brazil. Some also arrived at Saint John, NB.

Year	Month	Vessel	Master	Departure Port	Arrival Port	Passenger Numbers
1829	05	*Marchioness of Donegal* (s)	n/k	Belfast	Pictou	42
1829	12	*Gleaner* (bg)	Daley	Ireland	Halifax	n/k

Via St. John's, Newfoundland.

Year	Month	Vessel	Master	Departure Port	Arrival Port	Passenger Numbers
1830	05	*Benjamin Shaw* (bg, 283 tns)	n/k	Waterford	Pictou	300
1830	05	*Bittern* (bg)	Wick	Ireland	Pictou	n/k
1830	06	*Kelton*	n/k	Cork	Halifax	195

Twelve died on voyage.

Year	Month	Vessel	Master	Departure Port	Arrival Port	Passenger Numbers
1830	06	*Solon* (bg, 273 tns)	n/k	Waterford	Halifax	150
1830	07	*Amity* (s)	Gray	Dublin	Halifax	n/k

One of three vessels (*Endymion, Amity, Asia*) carrying part of the 8th Regiment from Dublin to Halifax.

Year	Month	Vessel	Master	Departure Port	Arrival Port	Passenger Numbers
1830	07	*Asia*	n/k	Dublin	Halifax	n/k

One of three vessels (*Endymion, Amity, Asia*) carrying part of the 8th Regiment from Dublin to Halifax.

| 1830 | 07 | *Charlotte Kerr* (bg, 129 tns) | Pyche, Abraham | Belfast | Pugwash | n/k |

New brig.

| 1830 | 07 | *Endymion* (bg) | Smith | Dublin | Halifax | n/k |

One of three vessels (*Endymion, Amity, Asia*) carrying part of the 8th Regiment from Dublin to Halifax.

1830	08	*John and Mary*	n/k	Belfast	Halifax	35
1831	05	*Adelphi* (bg, 337 tns)	Irvin	Cork	Halifax	241
1831	05	*Argyle* (bk, 307 tns)	Buchanan	Waterford	Halifax	225
1831	05	*Don* (bg, 200 tns)	Anderson	Waterford	Halifax	135
1831	05	*Pandora* (bg, 147 tns)	n/k	Waterford	Pictou	130
1831	06	*Archibald* (bg)	Wilson	Belfast	Halifax	31
1831	06	*Aurora* (bg, 126 tns)	Cock	Waterford	Halifax	101
1831	06	*Charlotte Kerr* (bg, 129 tns)	Pyche, Abraham	Sligo	Halifax	93

Year	Month	Vessel	Master	Departure Port	Arrival Port	Passenger Numbers
1831	06	*Hibernia* (bg)	n/k	Kinsale	Halifax	200

Fifty of two hundred passengers left at Halifax. The remainder may have gone on to Saint John, New Brunswick.

Year	Month	Vessel	Master	Departure Port	Arrival Port	Passenger Numbers
1831	06	*Powels* (sr)	n/k	Ireland	Sydney, NS	n/k

| 1831 | 07 | *Adelaide* | n/k | Galway | Annapolis, NS | 60 |

| 1831 | 07 | *Carleton* (sr) | n/k | Ireland | Halifax | 4 |

Via St. John's, Newfoundland.

| 1831 | 08 | *Duncan* | n/k | Dublin | Halifax | 260 |

Drunk captain. Mate was put in charge by passengers. Two hundred passengers disembarked at Halifax and sixty went on to Saint John, New Brunswick.

| 1831 | 08 | *Success* (sr) | n/k | Ireland | Halifax | n/k |

Via St. John's, Newfoundland.

| 1831 | 08 | *William Hannington* (bk) | n/k | Limerick | Pictou | 115 |

Via Saint John, New Brunswick. Vessel sailed with an inadequate supply of drinking water. Had left Limerick with 133 passengers.

| 1831 | 10 | *Marinhull* (bg) | Eckerman | Ireland | Halifax | 22 |

Via Newfoundland.

| 1832 | 04 | *Pallas* (bk, 316 tns) | n/k | Cork | Halifax | 120 |

Passengers quarantined at Halifax. Many went on to Saint John, New Brunswick, but some passengers may have disembarked at Halifax.

| 1832 | 05 | *Betock* (bg, 450 tns) | n/k | Waterford | Halifax | 126 |

Year	Month	Vessel	Master	Departure Port	Arrival Port	Passenger Numbers
1832	05	*Wellington* (bg)	n/k	Cork	Halifax	128
1832	06	*Friends* (bg)	n/k	Waterford	Halifax	181
1832	06	*Jane*	n/k	Cork	Halifax	101
1832	06	*Jane* (bg, 142 tns)	n/k	Waterford	Halifax	111
1832	08	*John & Mary* (bg)	n/k	Belfast	Wallace	68
1832	08	*Minstrel* (bk)	n/k	Cork	Halifax	145
1832	12	*Betsy and Nancy* (sr)	n/k	Ireland	Halifax	14

Via St. John's, Newfoundland.

Year	Month	Vessel	Master	Departure Port	Arrival Port	Passenger Numbers
1833	05	*St. Catherine* (bg)	Hume	Waterford	Halifax	138
1833	06	*Dolphin* (sr)	Mahoney	Ireland	Halifax	10

Via St. John's, Newfoundland.

Year	Month	Vessel	Master	Departure Port	Arrival Port	Passenger Numbers
1833	06	*Rambler* (sr)	Morrisey	Ireland	Halifax	14

Via St. John's, Newfoundland.

Year	Month	Vessel	Master	Departure Port	Arrival Port	Passenger Numbers
1833	06	*Sea Horse* of Saint John (bg, 173 tns)	Roberts	Dublin	Halifax	70
1833	06	*Sydney* (sr)	Cullerton	Ireland	Halifax	30

Via St. John's, Newfoundland.

Year	Month	Vessel	Master	Departure Port	Arrival Port	Passenger Numbers
1833	06	*Union* (bg)	n/k	Cork	Halifax	30

Year	Month	Vessel	Master	Departure Port	Arrival Port	Passenger Numbers
1833	07	*Latona* (bg)	n/k	Dublin	Pugwash	176
1833	08	*Creole* (bg)	Pecktort	Ireland	Halifax	n/k

Via St. John's, Newfoundland.

Year	Month	Vessel	Master	Departure Port	Arrival Port	Passenger Numbers
1833	08	*Molly Moore* of Waterford (bg, 161 tns)	n/k	Waterford	Pictou	38
1833	08	*William* (bg)	Griffin	Cork	Halifax	80

Initially bound for St. John's, Newfoundland. Sickness broke out on the voyage and nine passengers died. Vessel called at Halifax for assistance.

Year	Month	Vessel	Master	Departure Port	Arrival Port	Passenger Numbers
1834	05	*Brunswick* of London (bk, 571 tns)	Blake, H.	Cork	Halifax	n/k

Vessel carried four companies of the 83rd Regiment under the command of Major P. Crofton.

Year	Month	Vessel	Master	Departure Port	Arrival Port	Passenger Numbers
1834	05	*Ceres* of Sligo (bk, 218 tns)	Barret, T.	Sligo	Halifax	172

Bound for Saint John, New Brunswick, but forty-seven passengers disembarked at Halifax.

Year	Month	Vessel	Master	Departure Port	Arrival Port	Passenger Numbers
1834	05	*Henrietta* of Liverpool NS (sw., 128 tns)	Kennedy, D.	Ireland	Halifax	30

Via St. John's, Newfoundland.

Year	Month	Vessel	Master	Departure Port	Arrival Port	Passenger Numbers
1834	05	*King* (br)	n/k	Waterford	Halifax	159
1834	05	*Molly Moore* of Waterford (bg, 161 tns)	n/k	Waterford	Halifax	119

Vessel proceeded to Pictou where fourteen passengers disembarked.

Year	Month	Vessel	Master	Departure Port	Arrival Port	Passenger Numbers
1834	06	*Eden* (bg)	Powell	Cork	Halifax	181

Bound for Chaleur Bay.

Year	Month	Vessel	Master	Departure Port	Arrival Port	Passenger Numbers
1834	06	*Jane* (bg, 142 tns)	Burke	Waterford	Halifax	108
1834	08	*Molly Moore* of Waterford (bg, 161 tns)	n/k	Waterford	Pictou	14

Via St. John's, Newfoundland.

Year	Month	Vessel	Master	Departure Port	Arrival Port	Passenger Numbers
1835	06	*Timandra* of Saint John (sw, 232 tns)	n/k	Waterford	Halifax	66
1835	10	*Cordelia* (bg)	Lane	Ireland	Halifax	38

Via St. John's, Newfoundland. Cabin passengers: Sir John C. Brown, Mrs. Brown, Miss Tobin, Messrs Lang, Power, and Quin, Miss Walsh, Miss O'Connell (Messrs Williamson and McKeller for Boston) and twenty-eight in the steerage.

Year	Month	Vessel	Master	Departure Port	Arrival Port	Passenger Numbers
1836	05	*Bob Logic* of Liverpool (bg, 123 tns)	Errington	Cork	Halifax	86
1836	05	*Eagle* of Waterford (bg, 205 tns)	Buchanan	Waterford	Halifax	109
1836	05	*Lancaster*	n/k	Dublin	Halifax	77

Bound for New York. Vessel had been set on fire by the captain. The passengers saved it and the vessel landed at Halifax.

Year	Month	Vessel	Master	Departure Port	Arrival Port	Passenger Numbers
1836	06	*Elizabeth* of Cork (sr, 145 tns)	Keller, W.	Cork	Halifax	75
1836	06	*Maria* (bg)	Lewis	Ireland	Halifax	67

Via Sable Island.

Year	Month	Vessel	Master	Departure Port	Arrival Port	Passenger Numbers
1836	06	*Michael Wallace* of Cork (sr, 104 tns)	Darby	Sable Island	Halifax	17
1836	06	*Molly Moore* of Waterford (bg, 161 tns)	McGrath	Waterford	Halifax	78
1836	07	*Water Witch* (sr)	Clark	Ireland	Halifax	94

Mr. Emerson, Mrs. Cote and family, Miss Trae, Mr. and Mrs. Quinn and child, Mr. Ryan, and steerage passengers.

Year	Month	Vessel	Master	Departure Port	Arrival Port	Passenger Numbers
1837	05	*Don* (bg)	Toole	Waterford	Halifax	112
1837	05	*Lord John Russell* (bk)	n/k	Waterford	Halifax	181
1837	05	*Royalist* (bg)	n/k	Londonderry	Sydney, NS	136

Probably carried Irish miners and their families.

Year	Month	Vessel	Master	Departure Port	Arrival Port	Passenger Numbers
1837	06	*Eagle* of Waterford (bg, 205 tns)	Buchanan	Waterford	Halifax	106
1837	06	*Emily* (sr)	Crowell	Ireland	Halifax	16

Via St. John's. Cabin passengers: Captain Orr and Lieutenant Kelsall of the 83rd Regiment, plus fourteen steerage passengers.

Year	Month	Vessel	Master	Departure Port	Arrival Port	Passenger Numbers
1837	08	*Clitus* (bg, 191 tns)	Howie	Cork	Halifax	108
1837	n/k	*Belsay Castle* (sw, 203 tns)	n/k	Belfast	Sydney, NS	136

Year	Month	Vessel	Master	Departure Port	Arrival Port	Passenger Numbers
1837	n/k	*Lady Ann* (bg)	n/k	Belfast	Pictou	36
1838	06	*Jane* (bg)	n/k	Cork	Halifax	59

Vessel abandoned near Shelburne. Passengers travelled in the *Zephyr* to Halifax.

Year	Month	Vessel	Master	Departure Port	Arrival Port	Passenger Numbers
1838	06	*Margaret* (sr)	Conrad	Ireland	Halifax	6

Via St. John's, Newfoundland.

Year	Month	Vessel	Master	Departure Port	Arrival Port	Passenger Numbers
1838	06	*Pictou* (bg)	Clark	Ireland	Halifax	14

Via St. John's, Newfoundland. Mrs. Languish and two children, Mrs. Morris, Mr. Brine, Mr. White and son, plus seven steerage passengers.

Year	Month	Vessel	Master	Departure Port	Arrival Port	Passenger Numbers
1838	08	*Granville* (bk)	Darby	Sligo	Halifax	29
1838	08	*Pictou* (bg)	n/k	Ireland	Halifax	7

Via St. John's, Newfoundland. Mr. Green, Mr. Byers, Dr. McKee, Miss Clark, and three in the steerage.

Year	Month	Vessel	Master	Departure Port	Arrival Port	Passenger Numbers
1838	09	*Jane*	Doane	Ireland	Halifax	6
1838	10	*Hebe* (bg)	Percy	Ireland	Halifax	9

Via St. John's, Newfoundland.

Year	Month	Vessel	Master	Departure Port	Arrival Port	Passenger Numbers
1838	10	*Pictou*	Clark	Ireland	Halifax	11

Via St. John's, Newfoundland. Messrs. Runley and Manning plus nine steerage passengers.

Year	Month	Vessel	Master	Departure Port	Arrival Port	Passenger Numbers
1840	06	*Carricks*	n/k	West Point, Ireland	Sydney	32
1841	06	*Pandora* (bg, 147 tns)	Doyle	Limerick	Halifax	33
1842	05	*Eagle* of Waterford (bg, 205 tns)	Edwards, Samuel	Waterford	Halifax	123

Year	Month	Vessel	Master	Departure Port	Arrival Port	Passenger Numbers
1842	06	*John*	McGrath	Waterford	Halifax	91
1842	06	*Pandora* (bg, 147 tns)	Doyle	Waterford	Halifax	40
1842	06	*Pons Aeli* (bk)	Wright	Cork	Saint John, NB	117

Bound for Saint John, New Brunswick. Vessel had insufficient provisions and water. Called in at Halifax to replenish its supplies.

Year	Month	Vessel	Master	Departure Port	Arrival Port	Passenger Numbers
1843	05	*Eagle* of Waterford (bg, 205 tns)	Edwards, Samuel	Waterford	Halifax	

Thirty of the passengers were children. The *Halifax Morning Herald* described the passengers when they disembarked as "a fine robust, healthy-looking set of people" (May 29, 1843). Twelve passengers wrote a letter thanking the captain for his many kindnesses (names shown in Punch, *Erin's Sons*, vol. 1, 141).

Year	Month	Vessel	Master	Departure Port	Arrival Port	Passenger Numbers
1844	05	*Eagle* of Waterford (bg, 205 tns)	Edwards, Samuel	Waterford	Halifax	114
1845	07	*Catherine* (bk)	Daley	Cork	Halifax	108
1847		*Mayflower* (bg)	n/k	Limerick	Pictou	39

Smallpox aboard.

Year	Month	Vessel	Master	Departure Port	Arrival Port	Passenger Numbers
1847	05	*Barbara* of Galway (bk, 418 tns)	Mackay	Galway	Halifax	296
1847	05	*Leila* (bg)	n/k	Galway	Halifax	160

Year	Month	Vessel	Master	Departure Port	Arrival Port	Passenger Numbers
1847	05	*Mary* (bg)	Wyman	Cork	Halifax	46

Passenger list: www.theshipslist.com. Intended destination was Boston but passengers in such a destitute state that authorities would not allow them to land unless captain paid a bond for their care. He refused and despite the passengers' protests the vessel sailed to Halifax where the passengers disembarked.

Year	Month	Vessel	Master	Departure Port	Arrival Port	Passenger Numbers
1847	05	*Mountaineer* (bk, 490 tns)	Carey	Cork	Halifax	279
1847	06	*Eliza* (bg)	n/k	Waterford	Halifax	96
1847	06	*Redwing* (bk, 238 tns)	Bell	Galway	Halifax	140
1850	95	*Sophia* (bg)	Bellamy	Waterford	Halifax	80

APPENDIX II

Ship Crossings from Ireland to New Brunswick, 1799–1867

The table below lists the year, month of sailing, and number of passengers carried by each ship identified as having left Ireland for New Brunswick between 1799 and 1867. It provides details of 780 sea crossings, involving a total of 67,560 Irish passengers, showing the different Irish ports from which they embarked and their arrival ports in New Brunswick.

Because most of New Brunswick's Customs Records were lost in a fire in 1877, ship crossing details are difficult to find. Apart from the detailed data that survives for 1833–34 and 1838, the rest of the information has been obtained by piecing together material from many documentary sources, including:

> New Brunswick Genealogical Society, *Passengers to New Brunswick: Custom House Records — 1833, 34, 37 & 38.*
> Elizabeth Cushing et al., *A Chronicle of Irish Emigration to Saint John, New Brunswick 1847.*
> Daniel F. Johnson, *Irish Emigrants and their Vessels, Port of Saint John NB 1841–1849.*
> Provincial Archives of New Brunswick ("Irish Portal" website)
> *New Brunswick Courier*

Because Saint John was used as a port of transit to the United States, arrival numbers do not necessarily relate to people who actually settled in New Brunswick.

See "Explanatory Notes" on pages 217–18 for an explanation of the shipping terms used in this listing.

For details of the quality of the ships that brought the Irish to Nova Scotia, see Tables 10, 11, and 12.

Year	Month	Vessel	Master	Departure Port	Arrival Port	Passenger Numbers
1799	n/k	Energy	n/k	Londonderry	Saint John	n/k
1816	03(d)	Thomas Gelston (s, 800 tns)	Strachen, Alex	Belfast	St. Andrews	n/k
1817	03(d)	Caroline (s, 550 tns)	Pollock, James	Portaferry (County Down)	St. Andrews	n/k
1817	03(d)	Union (bg, 300 tns)	Armstrong, Matthew	Belfast	St. Andrews	n/k

Passengers wrote letter of appreciation to Captain Armstrong.

Year	Month	Vessel	Master	Departure Port	Arrival Port	Passenger Numbers
1817	06(d)	Jesse (bg)	Lyon, William	Belfast	St. Andrews	n/k
1818	03(d)	Halifax Packet (s, 272 tns)	Clark, John	Londonderry	Saint John	213
1818	04(d)	Sarah & Eliza (bg, 240 tns)	Mortimer, Francis	Portaferry (County Down)	Saint John	n/k
1818	06	Dorcas Savage of Belfast (bg, 350 tns)	Pollock, James	Portaferry (County Down)	St. Andrews	150

The *Belfast Newsletter* of July 1818 printed a letter of appreciation to Captain Pollock from the passengers. See Table 4 for the list of names.

Year	Month	Vessel	Master	Departure Port	Arrival Port	Passenger Numbers
1818	06(d)	Fame (bg, 350 tns)	Holton, Henry	Belfast	St. Andrews	n/k
1818	08(d)	Ganges (bg)	Martin, Alexander	Belfast	St. Andrews	n/k
1818	n/k	Bartley of Londonderry (bg, 138 tns)	n/k	Londonderry	Saint John	130

Year	Month	Vessel	Master	Departure Port	Arrival Port	Passenger Numbers
1818	n/k	*Draper*	n/k	Londonderry	Saint John	114
1818	n/k	*Ganges* (bg, 209 tns)	n/k	Belfast	Saint John	43
1818	n/k	*George*	n/k	Belfast	Saint John	90
1818	n/k	*Neptune*	n/k	Belfast	Saint John	n/k
1819	05(d)	*Amelia* (s, 600 tns)	Storey, John	Belfast	St. Andrews	n/k
1819	06(d)	*Rodie* (s, 600 tns)	Reid, Thomas	Belfast	St. Andrews	n/k
1819	07(d)	*Ann* (400 tns)	Mason, James	Belfast	St. Andrews	n/k
1819	07(d)	*Edward Downes* (s, 500 tns)	Russell, Arthur	Belfast	St. Andrews	n/k
1819	08(d)	*Thomas Gelston* (s, 800 tns)	Strachmand	Portaferry (County Down)	St. Andrews	n/k
1819	08(d)	*William Wise* (bg, 500 tns)	Winder, James W.	Belfast	St. Andrews	n/k
1819	09(d)	*Nancy* of Dumfries (bg, 500 tns)	Kirk, Joseph	Belfast	St. Andrews	n/k
1820	03(d)	*Clyde* (bg, 500 tns)	Morrison	Belfast	Saint John	n/k
1820	03(d)	*Dorcas Savage* of Belfast (bg, 205 tns)	Pollock, James	Portaferry (County Down)	St. Andrews	n/k

Year	Month	Vessel	Master	Departure Port	Arrival Port	Passenger Numbers
1820	03(d)	Dykes (bg, 500 tns)	Graves, George	Belfast	St. Andrews	n/k
1820	04	Eclipse (bg)	Hannah, James	Belfast	St. Andrews	n/k
1820	04(d)	Dorcas Savage of Belfast (bg, 205 tns)	Pollock, James	Portaferry	St. Andrews	n/k
1820	05	Clyde (bg, 500 tns)	Morrison	Belfast	Saint John	n/k
1820	05(d)	Nancy of Dumfries (bg, 350 tns)	Kirk, Joseph	Belfast	St. Andrews	n/k
1820	05(d)	Vittoria	Bowman, William	Belfast	St. Andrews	n/k
1820	07(d)	Edward Downes (s, 500 tns)	Russell, Arthur	Belfast	Saint John	n/k
1820	08(d)	Fame (bg)	Hardy, James	Belfast	Saint John	n/k
1820	08(d)	Mars (s, 306 tns)	Frier	Belfast	Saint John	210

Vessel was a prize.

Year	Month	Vessel	Master	Departure Port	Arrival Port	Passenger Numbers
1821	03(d)	Dorcas Savage of Belfast (bg, 205 tns)	Pollock, James	Belfast	St. Andrews	n/k

Following and autumn voyage by the Dorcas Savage, the Saint Andrews Herald, October 23, 1821 printed a letter of appreciation to Captain Pollock from some of the passengers, stating that "our minds are deeply impressed with a sense of your attention to us all during this autumn voyage; permit us to assure you of our lasting gratitude."

Year	Month	Vessel	Master	Departure Port	Arrival Port	Passenger Numbers
1821	04	Ann (s)	Cuthbert	Belfast	St. Andrews	n/k

Year	Month	Vessel	Master	Departure Port	Arrival Port	Passenger Numbers
1821	04(d)	*Hope* of Workington (bg, 350 tns)	Simpson, George	Belfast	St. Andrews	n/k
1821	04 (d)	*Integrity* (bg, 350 tns)	Wilson, Jeremiah	Strangford (County Down)	St. Andrews	n/k
1821	04(d)	*Nancy* of Dumfries (350 tns)	Kirk, Joseph	Belfast	St. Andrews	n/k
1821	08(d)	*Alexander* (bg, 400 tns)	Booth, James	Belfast	Saint John	n/k
1822	03(d)	*Dorcas Savage* of Belfast (bg, 205 tns)	Pollock, James	Portaferry (County Down)	St. Andrews	n/k
1822	04(d)	*Alexander* of Aberdeen	Booth	Belfast	Saint John	n/k
1822	04(d)	*Union* (bg, 300 tns)	Armstrong, Matthew	Belfast	St. Andrews	n/k
1822	05 (d)	*Edward Downes* (s, 500 tns)	Russell, Arthur	Belfast	St. Andrews	n/k
1822	05(d)	*Robert Quaile* (s, 750 tns)	Murray	Belfast	Saint John	n/k
1822	05(d)	*Thomas Gelston* (s, 800 tns)	Strachan, Alex	Belfast	St. Andrews	n/k
1822	07	*Baron Ardrossan* (bg)	Johnson	Belfast	St. Andrews	n/k
1822	07	*Hibernia* of Belfast	Porter, William	Belfast	St. Andrews	n/k

Year	Month	Vessel	Master	Departure Port	Arrival Port	Passenger Numbers
1822	07	*Xenophon* of London (bg, 700 tns)	Eyly	Belfast	Saint John	n/k
1822	07(d)	*Juno* of Aberdeen (bg)	Henderson, John	Belfast	Saint John	n/k
1822	09(d)	*Alexander* (bg)	Booth, James	Belfast	Saint John	n/k
1823	05	*Portaferry* of St. Andrews (bg, 283 tns)	Pollock, James	Portaferry (County Down)	St. Andrews	157
1823	06	*Collins* (bg, 226 tns)	Attridge	Belfast	St. Andrews	189
1823	06	*Nestor* (s, 387 tns)	n/k	Belfast	St. Andrews	294
1823	08	*Ardent* (bg)	n/k	Londonderry	Saint John	n/k

Passengers expressed their gratitude to Joseph Thornton, mate of *Ardent*, "during the late tedious and dangerous passage from Londonderry."

Year	Month	Vessel	Master	Departure Port	Arrival Port	Passenger Numbers
1823	08	*Plantagenet*	n/k	Belfast	St. Andrews	180
1823	09	*Francis*	n/k	Belfast	St. Andrews	144
1823	09	*Portaferry* of St. Andrews (bg, 283 tns)	n/k	Strangford (County Down)	St. Andrews	32
1823	10	*Beaver*	n/k	Dublin	St. Andrews	17
1823	10	*Indian Chief* (bg, 177 tns)	Wright, J.	Belfast	St. Andrews	87

Year	Month	Vessel	Master	Departure Port	Arrival Port	Passenger Numbers
1824	04	*Dorcas Savage* of Belfast (bg, 205 tns)	n/k	Portaferry (County Down)	St. Andrews	15
1824	04	*Portaferry* of St. Andrews (bg, 283 tns)	n/k	Portaferry (County Down)	St. Andrews	89
1824	06	*Albuera* (sw, 177 tns)	n/k	Belfast	St. Andrews	24
1824	06	*Heart of Oak*	n/k	Limerick	St. Andrews	90
1824	09	*Dorcas Savage* of Belfast (bg, 205 tns)	n/k	Portaferry (County Down)	St. Andrews	6
1824	09	*Portaferry* of St. Andrews (bg, 283 tns)	n/k	Portaferry (County Down)	St. Andrews	20
1825	05	*Dorcas Savage* of Belfast (bg, 205 tns)	n/k	Belfast	St. Andrews	17
1825	05	*Portaferry* of St. Andrews (bg, 283 tns)	Pollock, James	Portaferry (County Down)	St. Andrews	152
1825	07	*Hylton* (bg)	Hudson, R.	Cork	Saint John	120

Called at Halifax for supplies.

Year	Month	Vessel	Master	Departure Port	Arrival Port	Passenger Numbers
1825	07	*James Bailie* of St. Andrews (s, 281 tns)	Murray, J.	Belfast	St. Andrews	57
1825	08	*Dorcas Savage* of Belfast (bg, 205 tns)	n/k	Strangford (County Down)	St. Andrews	17

Year	Month	Vessel	Master	Departure Port	Arrival Port	Passenger Numbers
1825	10	*Portaferry* of St. Andrews (bg, 283 tns)	n/k	Portaferry (County Down)	St. Andrews	32
1826	05	*Portaferry* of St. Andrews (bg, 283 tns)	n/k	Portaferry (County Down)	St. Andrews	139
1826	05	*Williams*	n/k	Belfast	St. Andrews	116
1826	08	*Cossack*	n/k	Belfast	St. Andrews	147
1826	09	*Portaferry* of St. Andrews (bg, 283 tns)	n/k	Portaferry (County Down)	St. Andrews	110
1827	05	*Hibernia* (bg, 288 tns)	n/k	Strangford (County Down)	St. Andrews	120
1827	05	*James Bailie* of St. Andrews (s, 281 tns)	n/k	Belfast	St. Andrews	170
1827	05	*Trafalgar*	n/k	Dublin	St. Andrews	110
1827	06	*William Henry* (bg, 312 tns)	n/k	Dublin	St. Andrews	300

Arrived with insufficient water and provisions. There were two deaths on the voyage. Thirty-nine passengers to be cared for by the parish. The arrivals were described as being mainly "beggars."

Year	Month	Vessel	Master	Departure Port	Arrival Port	Passenger Numbers
1827	09	*Hibernia*	n/k	Strangford (County Down)	St. Andrews	27

Year	Month	Vessel	Master	Departure Port	Arrival Port	Passenger Numbers
1827	09	*James Bailie* of St. Andrews (s, 281 tns)	n/k	Belfast	St. Andrews	55
1827	09	*Portaferry* of St. Andrews (bg, 283 tns)	n/k	Strangford (County Down)	St. Andrews	30
1828	05	*Hibernia* (bg, 288 tns)	n/k	Strangford (County Down)	St. Andrews	130
1828	05	*James Bailie* of St. Andrews (s, 281 tns)	n/k	Belfast	St. Andrews	50
1828	09	*James Bailie* of St. Andrews (s, 281 tns)	n/k	Belfast	St. Andrews	16
1829	05	*Portaferry* of St. Andrews (bg, 283 tns)	n/k	Strangford (County Down)	St. Andrews	93
1829	06	*Henry Carse*	n/k	Belfast	St. Andrews	172
1829	07	*Margaret*	n/k	Cork	St. Andrews	58
1829	09	*Portaferry* of St. Andrews (bg, 283 tns)	n/k	Strangford (County Down)	St. Andrews	24
1829	10	*William & George*	n/k	Londonderry	St. Andrews	20
1830	06	*Emma Foller*	n/k	Belfast	St. Andrews	150

Year	Month	Vessel	Master	Departure Port	Arrival Port	Passenger Numbers
1830	06	*Portaferry* of St. Andrews (bg, 283 tns)	n/k	Portaferry (County Down)	St. Andrews	103
1830	11	*Dunlop*	n/k	Belfast	St. Andrews	23
1830	11	*Emma Foller*	n/k	Belfast	St. Andrews	28
1830s	n/k	*Ann & Mary* of Cork (s, 157 tns)	Lloyd, Thomas	Cork	Saint John	50
Passenger list: NBGS.						
1830	n/k	*Breeze* (157 tns)	Robinson, William	n/k	Saint John	115
Passenger list: NBGS.						
1830s	n/k	*Britannia* of Sligo (bg, 135 tns)	Potts, Joseph	Sligo	Saint John	105
Passenger list: NBGS.						
1830s	n/k	*Dan O'Connell* of Londonderry (bg, 122 tns)	Warnock, John	Londonderry	Saint John	99
Passenger list: NBGS.						
1830s	n/k	*Jane* of Cork (sr, 109 tns)	Williams, Benjamin	Galway	Saint John	58
Passenger list: NBGS.						
1830s	n/k	*Pallas* of Cork (bk, 316 tns)	Hall, Robert	Cork	Saint John	133
Passenger list: NBGS.						

Year	Month	Vessel	Master	Departure Port	Arrival Port	Passenger Numbers
1830s	n/k	*Protector* of Londonderry (bk, 380 tns)	Bell, John	Londonderry	Saint John	325

Passenger list: NBGS.

Year	Month	Vessel	Master	Departure Port	Arrival Port	Passenger Numbers
1830s	n/k	*Thetis* of Troon	Hamilton, Robert	n/k	Bathurst NB	69

Passenger list: PANB Irish Portal.

Year	Month	Vessel	Master	Departure Port	Arrival Port	Passenger Numbers
1830s	n/k	*Mary* of Saint John (s, 558 tns)	n/k	Newry (County Armagh)	Saint John	30

Passenger list: NBGS.

Year	Month	Vessel	Master	Departure Port	Arrival Port	Passenger Numbers
1830s	n/k	*Matilda* (bg)	Stafford, Patrick	Cork	Saint John	163

Passenger list: NBGS.

Year	Month	Vessel	Master	Departure Port	Arrival Port	Passenger Numbers
1831	05	*Billow* (bg)	Elder	Newry (County Armagh)	Saint John	n/k

Vessel arrived with fever on board and landed at Partridge Island. The captain was fined for breaking the Passenger Act.

Year	Month	Vessel	Master	Departure Port	Arrival Port	Passenger Numbers
1831	05	*Charity* of Saint John (bg, 208 tns)	Risk, Samuel	Kinsale	Saint John	n/k

Vessel arrived with smallpox on board and landed at Partridge Island. The passengers were in a state of mutiny. The captain was fined for leaving the vessel without cause and not complying with the terms of the Passenger Act.

Year	Month	Vessel	Master	Departure Port	Arrival Port	Passenger Numbers
1831	05	*President*	M'Caskey	n/k	Saint John	n/k

Master was fined £20 for breaking the terms of the Passenger Act.

Year	Month	Vessel	Master	Departure Port	Arrival Port	Passenger Numbers
1831	09 (d)	*Eleanor Gordon*	Turner, John E.	Londonderry	Saint John	56

Passenger list: NBGS.

Year	Month	Vessel	Master	Departure Port	Arrival Port	Passenger Numbers
1832	05	*Hibernia* of Kinsale (s, 193 tns)	Driscoll, John	Kinsale (County Cork)	Saint John	85

Passengers were infected with smallpox. The captain was fined for breaching the quarantine laws. Passenger list: NBGS.

Year	Month	Vessel	Master	Departure Port	Arrival Port	Passenger Numbers
1832	06	*Ann* (bg)	Strang, James	Londonderry	Saint John	n/k

Passengers expressed their thanks to the captain "for his gentlemanly and humane conduct" toward them during the voyage.

Year	Month	Vessel	Master	Departure Port	Arrival Port	Passenger Numbers
1832	06	*Duncan* of Saint John (bg)	Garrison, Samuel	Londonderry	Saint John	n/k

Passengers recorded their gratitude to the captain and the mate, Mr. Marshall, for his "kindness and attention during the voyage" and also commended his "parental treatment of all the passengers" together with his "skill as a seaman."

Year	Month	Vessel	Master	Departure Port	Arrival Port	Passenger Numbers
1832	06	*Waterloo* (bg)	n/k	Belfast	Saint John	n/k

One death on the voyage. The captain had placed passengers in the coal hole and the provisions were inadequate. He later absconded.

Year	Month	Vessel	Master	Departure Port	Arrival Port	Passenger Numbers
1833	01	*Symmetry* of Londonderry (bg, 337 tns)	Dall, Alexander	Londonderry	Saint John	40

Passenger list: NBGS.

Year	Month	Vessel	Master	Departure Port	Arrival Port	Passenger Numbers
1833	03 (d)	*Ward* (311 tns)	Hare, Charles	Limerick	Saint John	74

Passenger list: NBGS.

Year	Month	Vessel	Master	Departure Port	Arrival Port	Passenger Numbers
1833	04	*Independence* of Kinsale (s, 326 tns)	Griffith, George	Kinsale (County Cork)	Saint John	61

Passenger list: NBGS.

Year	Month	Vessel	Master	Departure Port	Arrival Port	Passenger Numbers
1833	04	*Ugioni* of St. Andrews (bg)	Young, John	Belfast	Saint John	184

Passenger list: NBGS.

Year	Month	Vessel	Master	Departure Port	Arrival Port	Passenger Numbers
1833	04 (d)	*Billow* of Saint John (bg, 200 tns)	Warnock, John	Londonderry	Saint John	109

Passenger list: NBGS.

Year	Month	Vessel	Master	Departure Port	Arrival Port	Passenger Numbers
1833	04 (d)	*Dorcas Savage* of Belfast (bg, 205 tns)	Lemon, John	Belfast	Saint John	151

Passenger list: NBGS.

Year	Month	Vessel	Master	Departure Port	Arrival Port	Passenger Numbers
1833	04(d)	*John & Mary*	Robson, Mark	Belfast	Saint John & St. Andrews	n/k

Year	Month	Vessel	Master	Departure Port	Arrival Port	Passenger Numbers
1833	04 (d)	*Madewaska* of Campbelltown (bg, 270 tns)	McMurchy, Daniel	Londonderry	Saint John	179

Passenger list: NBGS.

Year	Month	Vessel	Master	Departure Port	Arrival Port	Passenger Numbers
1833	04 (d)	*Neptune* of Dysart (bg, 227 tns)	Brown, James	Newry (County Armagh)	Saint John	70

Passenger list: NBGS.

Year	Month	Vessel	Master	Departure Port	Arrival Port	Passenger Numbers
1833	04 (d)	*Salus* of Sunderland (bg, 250 tns)	Laing, James	Londonderry	Saint John	176

Passenger list: NBGS.

Year	Month	Vessel	Master	Departure Port	Arrival Port	Passenger Numbers
1833	04 (d)	*Trial* of Londonderry (bg, 145 tns)	Moore, Thomas	Londonderry	Saint John	101

Passenger list: NBGS.

Year	Month	Vessel	Master	Departure Port	Arrival Port	Passenger Numbers
1833	04 (d)	*Zephyr* of Sligo (bg, 161 tns)	McDonnell, Hugh	Sligo	Saint John	89

Passenger list: NBGS.

Year	Month	Vessel	Master	Departure Port	Arrival Port	Passenger Numbers
1833	05(d)	*Bartley* of Londonderry (bg, 138 tns)	Webber, Thomas	Londonderry	Saint John	111

Passenger list: NBGS.

Year	Month	Vessel	Master	Departure Port	Arrival Port	Passenger Numbers
1833	05 (d)	*Susan Jane* of Portaferry (95 tns)	Hughes, Thomas	Sligo	Saint John	53

Anthony Doughtery, a sawyer, is reported to have leapt overboard during the crossing. Passenger list: NBGS.

Year	Month	Vessel	Master	Departure Port	Arrival Port	Passenger Numbers
1833	06	*Active* of Newcastle (s, 352 tns)	Robson, Jasper	Londonderry	Saint John	274

Passenger list: NBGS.

Year	Month	Vessel	Master	Departure Port	Arrival Port	Passenger Numbers
1833	06	*Elizabeth*	n/k	Galway	Saint John	96

Passenger list: NBGS.

Year	Month	Vessel	Master	Departure Port	Arrival Port	Passenger Numbers
1833	06	*Ellergill* (bk, 369 tns)	Hale, William	Londonderry	Saint John	321

Passenger list: NBGS.

Year	Month	Vessel	Master	Departure Port	Arrival Port	Passenger Numbers
1833	06	*John and Mary* of Newcastle	Robson, Mark	Belfast	Saint John	148

Passenger list: NBGS.

Year	Month	Vessel	Master	Departure Port	Arrival Port	Passenger Numbers
1833	06	*Sea Horse* of Saint John (bg, 173 tns)	Roberts, T.	Dublin	Saint John	59

Passenger list: NBGS.

Year	Month	Vessel	Master	Departure Port	Arrival Port	Passenger Numbers
1833	06	*Thomas Hanford* of Cork (sw, 228 tns)	Dunbar, John	Cork	Saint John	158

Twelve passengers died on the crossing (not included in Passenger Numbers). Passenger list: NBGS.

Year	Month	Vessel	Master	Departure Port	Arrival Port	Passenger Numbers
1833	06 (d)	*Edward Reid* of Londonderry (bk, 333 tns)	Forrest, C.	Londonderry	Saint John	120

Passenger list: NBGS.

1833	06 (d)	*Eweretta* of Hull (bk, 352 tns)	Skinner, George	Londonderry	Saint John	42

Passenger list: NBGS.

1833	06 (d)	*Forth* (s)	Ure, James	n/k	Saint John	80

Passenger list: NBGS.

1833	07	*Leslie Gault* of Londonderry (bg, 245 tns)	Hughes, John	Londonderry	Saint John	70

Passenger list: NBGS.

1833	07 (d)	*Providence* of Cork (s, 212 tns)	Fox, Thomas	Cork	Saint John	32

Passenger list: NBGS.

1833	07 (d)	*Reward* of Cork (bg, 108 tns)	Jones, James	Cork	Saint John	83

Passenger list: NBGS.

1833	08	*Silistria* (bg, 131 tns)	Cole, Thomas	Belfast	Saint John	66

Passenger list: NBGS.

1833	08	*William* of Fishguard (s, 134 tns)	Griffiths, Daniel	Cork	Saint John	80

Passenger list: NBGS.

Year	Month	Vessel	Master	Departure Port	Arrival Port	Passenger Numbers
1833	08	*William* of Saint John (bg, 138 tns)	Bennett, William	Cork	Saint John	14
Passenger list: NBGS.						
1833	08 (d)	*Quintin Leitch* (s)	MacKay, Adam	Warrenpoint (County Down)	Saint John	10
Passenger list: NBGS.						
1833	08 (d)	*Zephyr* of Sligo (bg, 161 tns)	McDonnell, Hugh	Sligo	Saint John	71
Passenger list: NBGS.						
1833	09	*Billow* of Saint John (bg, 200 tns)	Warnock, John	Londonderry	Saint John	39
Passenger list: NBGS.						
1833	09	*Charity* of Saint John (bg, 208 tns)	Risk, Samuel	Cork	Saint John	68
Passenger list: NBGS.						
1833	11	*Sarah* of Belfast (sr, 121 tns)	McAuly, Neil	Belfast	Saint John	40
Passenger list: NBGS.						
1834	03 (d)	*Independence* of Kinsale (s, 326 tns)	Griffith, George	Kinsale (County Cork)	Saint John	237
Passenger list: NBGS.						
1834	04 (d)	*Lady Douglas* of Wexford (bg, 126 tns)	Pierce, John	New Ross (County Wexford)	Saint John	27
Passenger list: NBGS.						

Year	Month	Vessel	Master	Departure Port	Arrival Port	Passenger Numbers
1834	04 (d)	*Levant Star* of Liverpool (147 tns)	Lloyd, Thomas	Cork	Saint John	89
Passenger list: NBGS.						
1834	04 (d)	*Sea Horse* of Saint John (bg, 173 tns)	Newton, James	Galway	Saint John	129
Passenger list: NBGS.						
1834	04 (d)	*William* of Saint John (bg, 138 tns)	Lawton, William	Londonderry	Saint John	77
Passenger list: NBGS.						
1834	05	*Charity* of Saint John (bg, 208 tns)	Risk, Samuel	Kinsale (County Cork)	Saint John	152
Passenger list: NBGS.						
1834	05	*Edwin* of Saint John (bg, 206 tns)	Carr, G.	Dublin	Saint John	160
Passenger list: NBGS.						
1834	05	*Hannah* of Maryport (bg, 287 tns)	Byram, Ralph	Cork	Saint John	278
Passenger list: NBGS.						
1834	05	*Neptune* of Dysart (bg, 227 tns)	Brown, James	Newry (County Armagh)	Saint John	119
Passenger list: NBGS.						
1834	05	*Pons Aeli* of Cork (bk, 315 tns)	Havelock, George	Cork	Saint John	246
Passenger list: NBGS.						

Year	Month	Vessel	Master	Departure Port	Arrival Port	Passenger Numbers
1834	05 (d)	*Ambassador* of Saint John (bg, 196 tns)	Vaughan, Thomas	Londonderry	Saint John	178

Passenger list: NBGS.

1834	05 (d)	*Betsy Heron* of North Shields (sw, 250 tns)	Storey, James	Belfast	Saint John	219

Passenger list: NBGS.

1834	05 (d)	*Cupid* of Londonderry (bg, 247 tns)	Stephenson, Samuel	Newry (County Armagh)	Saint John	208

Passenger list: NBGS.

1834	05 (d)	*Eleanor* of Londonderry (bg)	Hegarty, John	Londonderry	Saint John	74

Passenger list: NBGS.

1834	05 (d)	*Nancy* of Londonderry (sr, 111 tns)	McCaskey, J.N.	Londonderry	Saint John	95

Passenger list: NBGS.

1834	05 (d)	*Sarah* of Belfast (sr, 121 tns)	McIntyre, Peter	Belfast	Saint John	98

Passenger list: NBGS.

1834	06	*Ceres* (bk)	Henry, James	Sligo	Saint John	31

Vessel called at Halifax.
Passenger list: NBGS.

1834	06	*Dorothy* (bg)	Lamb, Thomas	Sligo	Saint John	172

Vessel was quarantined at Partridge Island.
Passenger list: NBGS.

1834	06	*Highlander* of Liverpool (bg, 241 tns)	Gardner, James	n/k	Saint John	200

Year	Month	Vessel	Master	Departure Port	Arrival Port	Passenger Numbers
1834	06	*Leslie Gault* of Londonderry (bg, 245 tns)	Hughes, John	Londonderry	Saint John	140

Passenger list: NBGS.

Year	Month	Vessel	Master	Departure Port	Arrival Port	Passenger Numbers
1834	06	*Perseus* of Hull (bk, 363 tns)	Bruce, G.	Londonderry	Saint John	294

Passenger list: NBGS.

Year	Month	Vessel	Master	Departure Port	Arrival Port	Passenger Numbers
1834	06	*Trafalgar* of Maryport (bg, 198 tns)	Christopherson, Louther	Galway	Saint John	162

Passenger list: NBGS.

Year	Month	Vessel	Master	Departure Port	Arrival Port	Passenger Numbers
1834	06 (d)	*Maria* of Halifax NS (bg)	Wylie, Robert	Cork	Saint John	75

Captain thanked for his "generous and humane conduct."
Passenger list: NBGS.

Year	Month	Vessel	Master	Departure Port	Arrival Port	Passenger Numbers
1834	06 (d)	*Ranger* of Peterhead (sr, 153 tns)	Anderson, Andrew	Londonderry	Saint John	114

Passenger list: NBGS.

Year	Month	Vessel	Master	Departure Port	Arrival Port	Passenger Numbers
1834	06 (d)	*Robert Burns* of Liverpool (bg, 296 tns)	Messenger, J.	Londonderry	Saint John	243

Passenger list: NBGS.

Year	Month	Vessel	Master	Departure Port	Arrival Port	Passenger Numbers
1834	06 (d)	*Zephyr* of Sligo (bg, 161 tns)	McDonnell, William	Sligo	Saint John	118

Passenger list: NBGS.

Year	Month	Vessel	Master	Departure Port	Arrival Port	Passenger Numbers
1834	07	*Dorcas Savage* of Belfast (bg, 205 tns)	Milligan, Hugh	Belfast	Saint John	171

Passenger list: NBGS.

Year	Month	Vessel	Master	Departure Port	Arrival Port	Passenger Numbers
1834	07	*Nicholson* (bg)	Bowes, Daniel	Sligo	Saint John	182
Passenger list: NBGS.						
1834	08	*Britannia* of Sligo (bg, 135 tns)	Potts, Joseph	Sligo	Saint John	101
Passenger list: NBGS.						
1834	08 (d)	*Cupid* of Londonderry (bg, 247 tns)	Stephenson, Samuel	Newry (County Armagh)	Saint John	18
Passenger list: NBGS.						
1834	08 (d)	*Leslie Gault* of Londonderry (bg, 245 tns)	Hughes, John	Londonderry	Saint John	24
Passenger list: NBGS.						
1834	09	*William* of Saint John (bg, 138 tns)	Lawton, William	Londonderry	Saint John	21
Passenger list: NBGS.						
1834	09 (d)	*Protector* of Londonderry (bk, 380 tns)	Bell, John	Londonderry	Saint John	30
Passenger list: NBGS.						
1834	10	*Ceres* (bk)	Dempsey	Sligo	Saint John	9
Passenger list: NBGS.						
1834	10	*Minerva* (s)	Banks, John	Cork	Saint John	33
Passengers had sailed in the *Independence* from Cork. It was shipwrecked at Cape Sable, Nova Scotia, and the passengers were transferred to the *Minerva*. Passenger list: NBGS.						
1835	07	*Morning Star*	n/k	Belfast	St. Andrews	32

Year	Month	Vessel	Master	Departure Port	Arrival Port	Passenger Numbers
1836	04(d)	*Charity*	n/k	Londonderry	Saint John	n/k
1836	06	*Charlotte* of Newport (bg)	Parsons, J.	n/k	Saint John	89

Passenger list: NBGS.

1836	07(d)	*Enterprise* (s, 660 tns)	McCready	Warrenpoint (County Down)	Saint John	n/k
1836	08(d)	*Spruce*	Whiteburn	Londonderry	Saint John	n/k
1837	05	*Hope* (bk)	Douthwaite	Cork	Saint John	238
1837	05	*Mersey* (s, 620 tns)	Mather	Londonderry	Saint John	500
1837	05	*Niger* of Saint John (bg)	Kinney, Nathaniel	Cork	Saint John	n/k

Passengers expressed their gratitude to the captain for "his unremitting attention to each and every one" of them and particularly to those who were attacked by sickness.

1837	05	*Royal William*	Driscoll, Michael	Cork	Saint John	n/k

Passengers recorded their grateful thanks to the captain for "his kindness, attention and humanity to his passengers during a trying and tedious passage."

1837	05	*Samuel Freeman* (bg)	Phelan	Ballyshannon (County Donegal)	Saint John	62
1837	05	*Venus* of Liverpool (bk, 388 tns)	Butters, J.	Cork	Saint John	232
1837	05(d)	*James Lemon*	White	Belfast	Saint John	n/k

Year	Month	Vessel	Master	Departure Port	Arrival Port	Passenger Numbers
1837	06	*Ann & Mary* of Waterford (sr, 157 tns)	Bellord	Waterford	Saint John	83
1837	06	*Bell* of Whitehaven (bg, 175 tns)	Campbell	Sligo	Saint John	115
1837	06	*Bob Logic*	Hall	Cork	Saint John	72
1837	06	*Britannia* of Sligo (bg, 135 tns)	Price	Sligo	Saint John	76
1837	06	*Campion* of Whitby (bk, 364 tns)	Galillee	Cork	Saint John	223
1837	06	*Charlotte*	n/k	Donegal	Saint John	n/k

Passenger list: NBGS.

Year	Month	Vessel	Master	Departure Port	Arrival Port	Passenger Numbers
1837	06	*Douglas* (sr)	Douglas	Limerick	Saint John	165
1837	06	*Edward Reid* of Londonderry (bk, 333 tns)	Wiley	Londonderry	Saint John	198
1837	06	*Elizabeth*	Hall	Ballyshannon (County Donegal)	Saint John	111
1837	06	*Elizabeth & Sarah* of Cork (bg, 107 tns)	Pierce	Cork	Saint John	51
1837	06	*Henry* (bg)	Elliott	Cork	Saint John	70
1837	06	*Hibernia* of Kinsale (s, 193 tns)	Feneron, George	Kinsale (County Cork)	Saint John	112

Year	Month	Vessel	Master	Departure Port	Arrival Port	Passenger Numbers
1837	06	*Isadore* (sw, 144 tns)	Pitt	Kinsale (County Cork)	Saint John	78
1837	06	*James Sayre*	Nickerson	Cork	Saint John	82
1837	06	*Jane* of Cork (sr, 109 tns)	Price	Cork	Saint John	54
1837	06	*Kingston* of Cork (bg, 130 tns)	Sterrat	Bantry (County Cork)	Saint John	76
1837	06	*Pomona*	Stevens	Dublin	Saint John	204
1837	06	*Prudence* of Londonderry (s, 281 tns)	Dall	Londonderry	Saint John	170
1837	06	*Spruce* of Belfast (bg, 143 tns)	Campbell	Belfast	Saint John	94
1837	06	*Susan Jane* of Donegal (bg, 95 tns)	Hughes, Thomas	Donegal	Saint John	49
1837	06	*Townshend* (bg)	Abbot	Cork	Saint John	140
1837	06	*Trafalgar* of Maryport (bg, 198 tns)	Christopherson, Louther	Galway	Saint John	125
1837	07	*Robert Watt* of St. Andrews (bk, 491 tns)	Dallimore, Joseph	Cork	Saint John	288

Passenger list: NBGS.

Year	Month	Vessel	Master	Departure Port	Arrival Port	Passenger Numbers
1837	10	*British Queen* (bk, 300 tns)	Bell	Londonderry	Saint John	44
1837	n/k	*Londonderry* (bk, 299 tns)	n/k	Londonderry	Saint John	92

Passenger list: Olive Tree website.

1837	n/k	*Susan*	n/k	Berehaven (County Cork)	Saint John	n/k
1838		*Hibernia* of Kinsale (s, 193 tns)	Feneron, George	Cork	Saint John	31

Passenger list: NBGS.

1838		*Prudence* of Londonderry (s, 281 tns)	Phillips, Robert	Londonderry	Saint John	180

Passenger list: NBGS.

1838	04 (d)	*Maria Brooke* of Sligo	Hughes, Thomas	Donegal	Saint John	65

Passenger list: NBGS.

1838	05	*Leslie Gault* of Londonderry (bg, 245 tns)	Mitchell, William	Londonderry	Saint John	29

Passenger list: NBGS.

1838	05	*Pallas* of Cork (bk, 316 tns)	Hall, Robert	Cork	St. Andrews	95

Passenger list: NBGS.

1838	05 (d)	*Mary Caroline* (s)	Stickany, Samuel	Cork	Saint John	17

Passenger list: NBGS.

Year	Month	Vessel	Master	Departure Port	Arrival Port	Passenger Numbers
1838	06	*Harmony* of Strangford (bg, 179 tns)	Baillie, John	Strangford (County Down)	Saint John	16
Passenger list: NBGS.						
1838	06	*Susan* (bk)	Neil, Thomas	Londonderry	Saint John	125
Passenger list: NBGS.						
1838	06	*Susan Jane* of Donegal (bg, 95 tns)	Hughes, Thomas	Ballyshannon (County Donegal)	Saint John	38
Passenger list: NBGS.						
1838	07	*Camilla* of Belfast (bg, 153 tns)	Briars, James	Belfast	Saint John	57
Passenger list: NBGS.						
1838	08	*Britannia* of Sligo (bg, 135 tns)	Pyne, Patrick	Sligo	Saint John	42
Passenger list: NBGS.						
1838	08	*Condor* of Yarmouth NS (bg, 188 tns)	Robbin, Lemuel	Londonderry	Saint John	57
Passenger list: NBGS.						
1838	10	*Caronge* (bk)	Willams, David	Londonderry	Saint John	19
Passenger list: NBGS.						
1839	05(d)	*Camilla* of Belfast (bg, 153 tns)	Byers, James	Belfast	Saint John	n/k

Year	Month	Vessel	Master	Departure Port	Arrival Port	Passenger Numbers
1839	07	*Josph P. Dobree* of Belfast (bg)	Hayes, John	Londonderry	Saint John	n//k

The *Belfast Newsletter* of September 3, 1839, stated: "The emigrant passengers, on board the brig *Joseph P. Dobree*, of Belfast, from Londonderry, have, by subscription, presented to Captain John Hayes (nephew to Mr. Halloway Hayes, of this town) a handsome silver snuff box, as a farewell and grateful remembrance, for his most humane and attentive conduct to them on the passage from Ireland to New Brunswick, in that vessel."

Year	Month	Vessel	Master	Departure Port	Arrival Port	Passenger Numbers
1840	04(d)	*Zephyr* (bg)	McAuley, J.	Belfast	Saint John	n/k
1840	07	*Currywell* (bg)	n/k	Belfast	Saint John	n/k
1840	07	*Sir Allen McNab* (bg)	Press	Londonderry	Saint John	n/k
1840	09	*Edward Reid* of Londonderry (bk, 333 tns)	Williams	Londonderry	Saint John	104

Vessel went ashore in dense fog near Musquash, on its approach to Saint John. Passengers and crew saved.

Year	Month	Vessel	Master	Departure Port	Arrival Port	Passenger Numbers
1841	05	*Albion* of Cork (bk, 313 tns)	Errington, Wm.	Cork	Saint John	185

One death on the voyage.

Year	Month	Vessel	Master	Departure Port	Arrival Port	Passenger Numbers
1841	05	*Aldebaran* (bk, 521 tns)	n/k	Sligo	Saint John	418

Quarantined on arrival.

Year	Month	Vessel	Master	Departure Port	Arrival Port	Passenger Numbers
1841	05	*Annie* (sc, 180 tns)	n/k	Limerick	Miramichi	97
1841	05	*Bolivar* of Waterford (bk, 355 tns)	n/k	Waterford	Miramichi	235
1841	05	*Brothers* of Newry (bk, 504 tns)	Daniel, James	Newry (County Armagh)	Saint John	65

Year	Month	Vessel	Master	Departure Port	Arrival Port	Passenger Numbers
1841	05	*Caroline*	Kirkpatrick	Ballyshannon	Saint John	n/k
1841	05	*Dealy* of Bantry (bg, 245 tns)	Smith	Bantry (County Cork)	Saint John	137
1841	05	*Dove* (195 tns)	n/k	Waterford	Miramichi	66
1841	05	*Eagle* of Waterford (bg, 205 tns)	n/k	Waterford	Miramichi	51
1841	05	*Friends* (242 tns)	McLean, Alexander	Westport (County Mayo)	Saint John	139
1841	05	*Globe* (205 tns)	Parker, James	Belfast	Saint John	81
1841	05	*Gratitude* of Newcastle (sw, 256 tns)	Forrest, T.	Cork	Saint John	153
1841	05	*Isadore* (sw, 144 tns)	Dunbar, John	Kinsale (County Cork)	Saint John	75

One death on the voyage.

Year	Month	Vessel	Master	Departure Port	Arrival Port	Passenger Numbers
1841	05	*John Wesley* of Cork (sr, 166 tns)	Davis, David	Cork	Saint John	91
1841	05	*Kathleen*	Mills, Robert	Limerick	Saint John	n/k
1841	05	*Lord Sandon* of Cork (bk, 407 tns)	Feneron, George	Kinsale (County Cork)	Saint John	218

One death on the voyage.

Year	Month	Vessel	Master	Departure Port	Arrival Port	Passenger Numbers
1841	05	*Louisa*	Davies	Cork	Saint John	210

Year	Month	Vessel	Master	Departure Port	Arrival Port	Passenger Numbers
1841	05	*Montreal Packet*	Stewart	Dublin	Saint John	n/k
1841	05	*Pallas* of Cork (bk, 316 tns)	Hall, Robert	n/k	Saint John	185

Two deaths on the voyage.

Year	Month	Vessel	Master	Departure Port	Arrival Port	Passenger Numbers
1841	05	*Prudence* of Londonderry (s, 281 tns)	Bridon, Christopher	Londonderry	Saint John	63
1841	05	*Rowena* (314 tns)	Williams, R.	Cork	Saint John	191

One death on the voyage.

Year	Month	Vessel	Master	Departure Port	Arrival Port	Passenger Numbers
1841	05	*Voluna* (600 tns)	Fovey	Londonderry [Greenock]	Saint John	16
1841	05	*Wilkinson*	Banks	Belfast	Saint John	61
1841	06	*Agnes*	Muir	Sligo	Saint John	n/k
1841	06	*Amazon*	Fife	Cork	Saint John	n/k
1841	06	*Carrywell* of Belfast	Buchanan	Ballyshannon (County Donegal)	Saint John	n/k
1841	06	*Cherub*	Dougan	Londonderry	Saint John	160
1841	06	*Comet* (222 tns)	Gilpin, Robert	Cork	Saint John	n/k
1841	06	*Elizabeth*	Sinclair	Londonderry [Liverpool]	Saint John	n/k
1841	06	*Emerald*	Sharp	Kinsale (County Cork)	Saint John	n/k

Year	Month	Vessel	Master	Departure Port	Arrival Port	Passenger Numbers
1841	06	*Glengarry*	Hill	Londonderry [Liverpool]	Saint John	n/k
1841	06	*Harmony* of Strangford (bg, 179 tns)	Baillie, John	Dublin	Saint John	85
1841	06	*Industry*	Allison	Cork	Saint John	n/k
1841	06	*Jane*	Rose	Limerick	Saint John	n/k
1841	06	*Kangaroo* of Cork (bk, 151 tns)	Prosser, T.	Cork	Saint John	95
1841	06	*Larch*	McAdam	Cork	Saint John	n/k
1841	06	*Lawrence Finestal* (201 tns)	n/k	Waterford	Miramichi	52
1841	06	*Leila* of Galway (sw, 269 tns)	McDonagh, John	Galway	Saint John	n/k
1841	06	*Londonderry* (bk, 299 tns)	McDonald	Londonderry	Saint John	185
1841	06	*Maria*	Doran	Londonderry	Saint John	n/k
1841	06	*Mary*	Nichols	Baltimore (County Cork)	Saint John	n/k
1841	06	*Mary Campbell* (415 tns)	Simons, James	Londonderry	Saint John	n/k
1841	06	*Pons Aeli* of Cork (bk, 315 tns)	Carroll	Cork	Saint John	n/k

Year	Month	Vessel	Master	Departure Port	Arrival Port	Passenger Numbers
1841	06	Prince Albert	Jouett	Dublin	Saint John	n/k
1841	06	Queen (275 tns)	Gaymer, J.	Cork	Bathurst, NB	14
1841	06	Sarah	Way	Sligo	Saint John	n/k
1841	06	Thomas Hanford of Cork (sw, 228 tns)	McGrath	Cork	Saint John	150
1841	06	Thyayrin	Cowlie	Londonderry	Saint John	n/k
1841	07	Albert	Keith	Greenock	Saint John	n/k
1841	07	Edwin	Davis	Sligo	Saint John	n/k
1841	07	Jane Duffus	McDonald	Donegal	Saint John	n/k
1841	07	Sarah Jane	Muir	Donegal	Saint John	n/k
1841	08	George	Power	Cork	Saint John	n/k
1841	08	Minerva	Harrison	Belfast	Saint John	n/k
1841	08	Trusty	McCarthy	Belfast	Saint John	n/k
1841	09	Caroline	Kirkpatrick	Ballyshannon (County Donegal)	Saint John	n/k
1841	09	Dealy of Bantry (bg, 245 tns)	Sterrat, M.	Bantry (County Cork)	Saint John	n/k
1841	09	Kentville	Hughes	Donegal	Saint John	n/k

Year	Month	Vessel	Master	Departure Port	Arrival Port	Passenger Numbers
1841	09	*Londonderry* (bk, 299 tns)	Hattrick	Londonderry	Saint John	n/k
1842	04	*Lord Sandon* of Cork (bk, 407 tns)	Feneron, George	Kinsale (County Cork)	Saint John	224
1842	04	*Midas* of Galway (bg, 255 tns)	Moore, Thomas	Galway	Saint John	133
1842	05	*Albion* of Cork (bk, 313 tns)	Errington, Wm.	Cork	Saint John	n/k
1842	05	*Andover* of Liverpool (bk, 291 tns)	Buckley	Cork	Saint John	178
1842	05	*Bolivar* of Waterford (bk, 355 tns)	Locke, H.J.	Waterford	Miramichi	149
1842	05	*British Queen* (bk, 300 tns)	Irvine, A.	Cork	Saint John	197
1842	05	*Clyde* (711 tns)	Pentreath, Edwin	Cork	Saint John	219
1842	05	*Dealy* of Bantry (bg, 245 tns)	Linn	Bantry (County Cork)	Saint John	137
1842	05	*Envoy* of Londonderry (bk, 481 tns)	Haffney, Francis	Londonderry	Saint John	316
1842	05	*John Francis* of Cork (s, 362 tns)	Kent, John	Cork	Saint John	215

Year	Month	Vessel	Master	Departure Port	Arrival Port	Passenger Numbers
1842	05	*John & Mary* of Galway (bk, 297 tns)	Wright	Galway	Saint John	212
1842	05	Londonderry (bk, 299 tns)	Hattrick, L.	Londonderry	Saint John	211
1842	05	*Martha Ann* (191 tns)	Feran, Thomas	Cork	Saint John	134

One death on the voyage.

Year	Month	Vessel	Master	Departure Port	Arrival Port	Passenger Numbers
1842	05	*Medina* of Waterford (bk, 378 tns)	Buchannan, Neil	Dungannon (County Tyrone)	Miramichi	79
1842	05	*Pallas* of Cork (bk, 316 tns)	Hall, Robert	Cork	St. Andrews	200
1842	05	*Perthshire* (846 tns)	Risk, S.	Greenock	Saint John	36
1842	05	*Portland* of Liverpool (722 tns)	Robinson	Liverpool	Saint John	19
1842	05	*Promise* (362 tns)	Rickford, R.	Newry (County Armagh)	Saint John	122

The *Newry Telegraph* of April 19, 1842, reported that the *Agnes and Ann*, the *Promise*, and the *Gratitude*, sailed for Saint John "with their full complement of passengers. These ships, and the *St. Martins*, which sailed on the 30th, have taken to Canada about 1,800 of the population."

Year	Month	Vessel	Master	Departure Port	Arrival Port	Passenger Numbers
1842	05	*Scotland*	Johnston	Greenock	Saint John	n/k
1842	05	*Westmoreland* of Saint John (bg, 280 tns)	Walker, M.G.	Cork	Saint John	177
1842	06	*Agnes*	Evans	Sligo	Saint John	n/k

Year	Month	Vessel	Master	Departure Port	Arrival Port	Passenger Numbers
1842	06	*Albion* (255 tns)	Meredith, Thomas	Baltimore (County Cork)	Saint John	153
1842	06	*Argyle* (307 tns)	Power, Robert	Cork	Saint John	193

One death on the voyage.

Year	Month	Vessel	Master	Departure Port	Arrival Port	Passenger Numbers
1842	06	*Ariel* (sr, 168 tns)	Stuart, John	Limerick	Miramichi	87
1842	06	*Caroline*	Kirkpatrick	Ballyshannon (County Donegal)	Saint John	n/k
1842	06	*Carrywell* of Belfast	Buchanan	Belfast	Saint John	n/k
1842	06	*Cordelia* of Belfast (bg, 179 tns)	McMillan, John	Belfast	Saint John	76
1842	06	*Creole* (bk, 455 tns)	Clark, James	Londonderry	Saint John	214
1842	06	*Dykes*	Harrison	Sligo	Saint John	n/k
1842	06	*Eliza*	Evans, Evan	New Ross (County Wexford)	Miramichi	20
1842	06	*Eliza Ann* of Cork (bg, 324 tns)	Watson, Earnest	Cork	St. Andrews	226
1842	06	*Elizabeth Grimmer* (331 tns)	Frye, C.I.	Liverpool	Saint John	194

Two deaths on the voyage.

Year	Month	Vessel	Master	Departure Port	Arrival Port	Passenger Numbers
1842	06	*Jessie*	Felix (Fittock)	Limerick	Saint John	n/k
1842	06	*John*	McGraw	Waterford	Saint John	n/k
1842	06	*John Wesley* of Cork (sr, 166 tns)	Davies, David	Cork	Saint John	109
1842	06	*Kingston* of Cork (bg, 130 tns)	Small	Cork	Saint John	n/k
1842	06	*Lady Douglas*	Serin	Drogheda (County Meath)	Saint John	n/k
1842	06	*Lady Milton* (636 tns)	Sinnott, John	Londonderry	Saint John	366
1842	06	*Lavinia*	Evans	Tralee (County Kerry)	Saint John	n/k
1842	06	*Leila* of Galway (sw, 269 tns)	McDonagh, John	Galway	Saint John	179
1842	06	*Maria*	Doran	Londonderry	Saint John	n/k
1842	06	*Martha* (sw, 254 tns)	Linn, John	Cork	Saint John	151
1842	06	*Mary*	Garde, Wm.	Cork	Saint John	n/k
1842	06	*Mary Caroline* (s)	Brewer	Liverpool	Saint John	n/k
1842	06	*Odessa*	Vaughan	Londonderry	Saint John	n/k

Year	Month	Vessel	Master	Departure Port	Arrival Port	Passenger Numbers
1842	06	*Silksworth* (sw, 291 tns)	Meldrum	Cork	Saint John	n/k
1842	06	*South Esk*	Nisbet	Liverpool	Saint John	n/k
1842	06	*Thomas*	Edmonton	Sligo	Saint John	n/k
1842	06	*Thomas Hanford* of Cork (sw, 228 tns)	Herbert	Cork	Saint John	n/k
1842	07	*Clifton*	Bisson	Cork	Saint John	n/k
1842	07	*Comet* (222 tns)	Gilpin, Robert	Dublin	Saint John	59
1842	07	*Defiance*	Kitton	Cork	Saint John	n/k
1842	07	*Friendship*	Nichol	Londonderry	Saint John	n/k
1842	07	*Jessie*	Duncan	Limerick	Saint John	n/k
1842	07	*Lord Sidmouth* (595 tns)	Bryan, Samuel	[Glasgow]	Saint John	35
1842	07	*Pons Aeli* of Cork (bk, 315 tns)	Wright, H.	Cork	Saint John	208

The vessel called at Halifax to replenish its provisions and water supply.

Year	Month	Vessel	Master	Departure Port	Arrival Port	Passenger Numbers
1842	07	*Susan Jane*	Strong	Sligo	Saint John	n/k
1842	07	*Trial* of Dublin (bg, 168 tns)	Bell, H.	Dublin	Saint John	99
1842	08	*Aisthorp*	Warwick	Sligo	Saint John	n/k

Year	Month	Vessel	Master	Departure Port	Arrival Port	Passenger Numbers
1842	08	*Britannia*	Coulthart	Cork	Saint John	n/k
1842	08	*Samuel*	Fleming	Liverpool	Saint John	n/k
1842	08	*Symmetry*	Bryon	Liverpool	Saint John	n/k
1842	09	*Indemnity*	Williamson	Cork	Saint John	n/k
1842	09	*Londonderry* (bk, 299 tns)	Hattrick, L.	Londonderry	Saint John	n/k
1842	09	*Midas* of Galway (bg, 255 tns)	Vaughan	Galway	Saint John	133
1842	09	*Plutus* of St. Andrews (331 tns)	Aymar, John	Belfast	St. Andrews	13
1842	10	*Mabel*	Nicholson	Liverpool	Saint John	n/k
1842	10	*Portland* of Liverpool (722 tns)	Robinson	Liverpool	Saint John	19
1843	05	*Louisa*	n/k	Cork	Saint John	n/k
1843	05	*Sally*	Ditchburn	Belfast	Saint John	n/k
1843	06	*Don*	O'Brien	Waterford	Saint John	n/k
1843	07	*Martha* (sw, 254 tns)	Linn, John	Cork	Saint John	n/k
1843	07	*Sir Charles Napier* of Liverpool (s, 714 tns)	Griffin	Liverpool	St. Andrews	83

Year	Month	Vessel	Master	Departure Port	Arrival Port	Passenger Numbers
1843	07	*Thomas Naylor*	Gale	Cork	Saint John	n/k
1843	07	*Victory*	Gloucester	Youghall (County Cork)	Saint John	n/k
1843	09	*Pandora* (147 tns)	Doyle, Richard	Waterford	Miramichi	4
1844	05	*Coxon* of North Shields (sw, 278 tns)	Morgan	Cork	Saint John	n/k
1844	05	*John Francis* of Cork (s, 362 tns)	Deaves, H.	Cork	Saint John	n/k
1844	05	*Martha* (sw, 254 tns)	Linn, John	Cork	Saint John	n/k
1844	05	*Nero*	Ellis	Limerick	Saint John	n/k
1844	05	*Pallas* of Cork (bk, 316 tns)	Hall, Robert	Cork	Saint John	138
1844	05	*Thomas Hanford* of Cork (sw, 228 tns)	Herbert	Cork	Saint John	n/k
1844	06	*Asia* (bk, 164 tns)	Hannah, James	Londonderry	Saint John	n/k

Captain fined for not supplying sufficient water for passengers.

Year	Month	Vessel	Master	Departure Port	Arrival Port	Passenger Numbers
1844	06	*British Queen*	Card	Dingle	Saint John	n/k
1844	06	*Clio*	Kelly	Cork	Saint John	n/k

Year	Month	Vessel	Master	Departure Port	Arrival Port	Passenger Numbers
1844	06	*Envoy* of Londonderry (bk, 481 tns)	Mason	Londonderry	Saint John	n/k
1844	06	*Fellowship*	Armstrong	Londonderry	Saint John	126
1844	06	*Isadore* (sw, 144 tns)	n/k	Cork	Saint John	n/k
1844	06	*Mars*	Flagg	Liverpool	Saint John	n/k
1844	06	*Normandy*	Smales	Stockton	Saint John	n/k
1844	06	*Pearl*	Ross	Liverpool	Saint John	n/k
1844	06	*Redwing* (bg)	York, Thomas	Galway	Saint John	n/k

Captain thanked by passengers for "his kindness, attention, and humanity."

Year	Month	Vessel	Master	Departure Port	Arrival Port	Passenger Numbers
1844	06	*Rose*	Kelley	Belfast	Saint John	n/k
1844	06	*Wanderer*	Raycroft	Baltimore (County Cork)	Saint John	n/k
1844	06	*Woodstock*	Taber	Liverpool	Saint John	n/k
1844	07	*Bache McEver* of Cork (bg, 229 tns)	Clancy, John	Cork	St. Andrews	49
1844	07	*Blanche* (114 tns)	White	Donegal	Saint John	n/k
1844	07	*Caroline*	Kirkpatrick	Ballyshannon (County Donegal)	Saint John	n/k
1844	07	*Kitty*	Rex	Cork	Saint John	n/k

Year	Month	Vessel	Master	Departure Port	Arrival Port	Passenger Numbers
1844	07	*Thorney Close* of Sunderland (sw, 249 tns)	Forland, Samuel	Donegal	Saint John	102
1844	09	*Sovereign*	n/k	Newry (County Armagh)	Saint John	n/k
1844	10	*Londonderry* (bk, 299 tns)	Hattrick, Samuel	Londonderry	Saint John	57
1844	10	*Midas* of Galway (bg, 225 tns)	Oliver	Galway	Saint John	n/k
1845	01	*Clyde*	n/k	Liverpool	Saint John	n/k
1845	05	*Albion* of Cork (bk, 313 tns)	Tardiff	Cork	Saint John	n/k
1845	05	*Coxon* of North Shields (sw, 278 tns)	Morgan	Cork	Saint John	n/k
1845	05	*Eliza Ann* of Cork (324 tns)	Clarke	Cork	Saint John	182
1845	05	*Governor Douglas* of Cork (bk, 434 tns)	Hyde	Baltimore (County Cork)	Saint John	n/k
1845	05	*Isadore* (sw, 144 tns)	Walsh	Cork	Saint John	32
1845	05	*John Wesley* of Cork (sr, 166 tns)	Davis, David	Cork	Saint John	n/k

Year	Month	Vessel	Master	Departure Port	Arrival Port	Passenger Numbers
1845	05	*Leviathan* of Cork (bg, 216 tns)	Roycroft	Baltimore (County Cork)	Saint John	n/k
1845	05	*Londonderry* (bk, 299 tns)	Hattrick	Londonderry	Saint John	n/k
1845	05	*Ocean* (bk)	Power	Cork	Saint John	193
1845	05	*Pons Aeli* of Cork (bk, 315 tns)	Mock	Cork	Saint John	192
1845	05	*Redwing* (bg)	York, Thomas	Galway	Saint John	n/k
1845	05	*Rose Macroom* (bg)	Powers	n/k	Saint John	n/k
1845	05	*Saint Lawrence* of Cork (bk, 221 tns)	Robinson	Cork	Saint John	157
1845	05	*Sophia*	Ballard	Waterford	Saint John	n/k
1845	05	*Venelia*	Frink	Londonderry	Saint John	n/k
1845	06	*Albion* of Cork (bk, 313 tns)	n/k	Cork	Saint John	155
1845	06	*Ann*	White	Donegal	Saint John	n/k
1845	06	*Bache McEver* of Cork (bg, 229 tns)	Slack	Cork	Saint John	137
1845	06	*Britannia*	Coulthart	Liverpool	Saint John	112

Year	Month	Vessel	Master	Departure Port	Arrival Port	Passenger Numbers
1845	06	*Brothers*	Rowell	Cork	Saint John	n/k
1845	06	*Caroline*	Lovett	Londonderry	Saint John	n/k
1845	06	*Caroline*	Kirkpatrick	Ballyshannon (County Donegal)	Saint John	n/k
1845	06	*Champlain* of Cork (bk, 300 tns)	Peneten	Cork	Saint John	165
1845	06	*Coxon* of North Shields (sw, 278 tns)	n/k	Cork	Saint John	184
1845	06	*Creole* (bk, 455 tns)	Clark, James	Londonderry	Saint John	269
1845	06	*Cygnet*	Hughes	Sligo	Saint John	n/k
1845	06	*Dominica* of Cork (bk, 381 tns)	n/k	Cork	Saint John	232
1845	06	*Henry Pottinger*	Keohan	Cork	Saint John	91
1845	06	*Lady Mary Fox* of Waterford (bg, 299 tns)	Dalton	Cork	Saint John	118
1845	06	*Lord Fitzgerald* (sr)	York	Galway	Saint John	n/k
1845	06	*Martha* (sw, 254 tns)	MacKay, John	Cork	Saint John	166
1845	06	*New Zealand*	Mackie, P.R.	Londonderry	Saint John	n/k

Year	Month	Vessel	Master	Departure Port	Arrival Port	Passenger Numbers
1845	06	*Pallas* of Cork (bk, 316 tns)	Hall, Robert	Cork	Saint John	169
1845	06	*Sarah*	Fletcher	Cork	Saint John	n/k
1845	06	*Thorney Close* of Sunderland (sw, 249 tns)	Horan, James	Donegal	Saint John	n/k
1845	06	*Velocity* of Waterford (bg, 166 tns)	McGrath	Waterford	Saint John	n/k
1845	06	*Warrior* of Drogheda (bk, 221 tns)	Tiernan	Drogheda (County Meath)	Saint John	n/k
1845	07	*Agnes*	Dougherty	Sligo	Saint John	n/k
1845	07	*Eliza Gills*	n/k	Galway	Saint John	n/k
1845	07	*Harriet* (bg)	Wallace	Londonderry	Saint John	n/k
1845	07	*Jane*	Casey	Cork	Saint John	n/k
1845	07	*Mary* of Cork	Dunbar, J.	Cork	Saint John	n/k
1845	07	*Time*	Driscoll	Cork	Saint John	n/k
1845	07	*Wakefield*	n/k	Newry (County Armagh)	Saint John	n/k
1845	08	*Ann*	McFee	Limerick	Saint John	n/k
1845	08	*Hornet* of Limerick (sr, 139 tns)	Hedigan, Michael	Limerick	Saint John	n/k

Year	Month	Vessel	Master	Departure Port	Arrival Port	Passenger Numbers
1845	08	*Thomas Hanford* of Cork (sw, 228 tns)	Gourley, J.	Cork	Saint John	63
1845	08	*Woodland Castle* of Cork (bg, 168 tns)	Williams	Cork	Saint John	n/k
1845	09	*Dealy* of Bantry (bg, 245 tns)	Sterrat	Bantry (County Cork)	Saint John	n/k
1845	n/k	*Atlas*	n/k	Cork	Saint John	n/k
1845	n/k	*Sun*	n/k	Donegal	Saint John	n/k
1846	05	*Alarm* (bg, 201 tns)	Leonard, J.	Cork	Saint John	119
1846	05	*Albion* of Cork (bk, 313 tns)	Tardiff	Cork	Saint John	160
1846	05	*Brothers* of Newry (bk, 504 tns)	Nowell	Bantry (County Cork)	Saint John	116
1846	05	*Coxon* of North Shields (sw, 278 tns)	Morgan	Cork	Saint John	192
1846	05	*Creole* (bk, 455 tns)	Kirk, James	Londonderry	Saint John	254
1846	05	*Dealy* of Bantry (bg, 245 tns)	Sterrat	Bantry (County Cork)	Saint John	152
1846	05	*Envoy* of Londonderry (bk, 481 tns)	Hattrick	Londonderry	Saint John	298

Year	Month	Vessel	Master	Departure Port	Arrival Port	Passenger Numbers
1846	05	*George Ramsay*	Farrell	Kinsale (County Cork)	Saint John	n/k
1846	05	*Hornet* of Limerick (sr, 139 tns)	Hedigan, Michael	Limerick	Saint John	32
1846	05	*Lady Napier* (bg)	Stowe	Westport (County Mayo)	Saint John	93
1846	05	*Leviathan* of Cork (bg, 216 tns)	Roycroft	Baltimore (County Cork)	Saint John	133
1846	05	*Mary* of Cork (bg, 180 tns)	Dunbar, J.	Cork	Saint John	121
1846	05	*Pallas* of Cork (bk, 316 tns)	Hall, Robert	Cork	Saint John	189
1846	05	*Princess* (bk)	Vaughan	Cork	Saint John	313
1846	05	*Richard N Parker* of Cork (bg, 170 tns)	Power	Cork	Saint John	93

All passengers landed at Partridge Island.

Year	Month	Vessel	Master	Departure Port	Arrival Port	Passenger Numbers
1846	05	*Rose Macroom* (bg)	Power	Waterford	Saint John	35
1846	05	*Saint Lawrence* of Cork (bk, 221 tns)	Bullin, J.	Baltimore (County Cork)	Saint John	160
1846	05	*Sir James McDonnell* of Dublin (bg, 225 tns)	Dunn, L.	Tralee (County Kerry)	Saint John	135

Year	Month	Vessel	Master	Departure Port	Arrival Port	Passenger Numbers
1846	05	*Thomas Hanford* of Cork (sw, 228 tns)	Herbert	Cork	Saint John	150
1846	05	*Triumph* of Halifax (bg, 176 tns)	Raycroft	Berehaven (County Cork)	Saint John	112
1846	05	*Velocity* of Waterford (bg, 166 tns)	McGrath	Waterford	Saint John	n/k
1846	05	*Victoria* of Galway (bk, 248 tns)	Price, T.	Galway	Saint John	79
1846	05	*Warrior* of Drogheda (bk, 221 tns)	Tiernan	Drogheda (County Meath)	Saint John	68
1846	06	*Aerial* (bg)	n/k	Cork	St. Andrews	179
1846	06	*Alanby*	n/k	Cork	Saint John	n/k
1846	06	*Alexander* (bg)	Weightman, William	Londonderry	Saint John	148

Captain was fined for not providing sufficient water on the voyage.

Year	Month	Vessel	Master	Departure Port	Arrival Port	Passenger Numbers
1846	06	*Ann Wise* (sw, 231 tns)	Ellwood, Thomas	Sligo	Saint John	122

Captain fined for not providing sufficient provisions for passengers.

Year	Month	Vessel	Master	Departure Port	Arrival Port	Passenger Numbers
1846	06	*Aulaby* (sr)	Driscoll	Cork	Saint John	73
1846	06	*Bache McEver* of Cork (bg, 229 tns)	n/k	Cork	St. Andrews	137

Year	Month	Vessel	Master	Departure Port	Arrival Port	Passenger Numbers
1846	06	British Queen	n/k	Newry (County Armagh)	Saint John	n/k
1846	06	Charles of Youghall (bg, 185 tns)	McCarthy	Youghall (County Cork)	Saint John	106
1846	06	Charlotte	Fowles	Ballyshannon (County Donegal)	Saint John	51
1846	06	Coronation (bk)	n/k	Liverpool	Saint John	27
1846	06	Ellen & Margaret of Cork (bg, 157 tns)	Joams, D.	Cork	Saint John	95
1846	06	Fogan-Bealach (sr)	Broughall	Dublin	Saint John	173
1846	06	Garland of Cork (bg, 208 tns)	Robertson, J.	Berehaven (County Cork)	Saint John	146
1846	06	Harriet (bg)	Wallace	Londonderry	Saint John	154
1846	06	Jane of Cork (sr, 109 tns)	Casey	Cork	Saint John	68
1846	06	John Begg of Galway (bg, 149 tns)	MacKay, G.	Galway	Saint John	35
1846	06	John Francis of Cork (s, 362 tns)	Deaves, H.	Cork	Saint John	214

Year	Month	Vessel	Master	Departure Port	Arrival Port	Passenger Numbers
1846	06	*Linden* of London (bk, 297 tns)	Yorke	Galway	Saint John	220
1846	06	*Lord Fitzgerald* (sr)	York	Galway	Saint John	74
1846	06	*Lord Glenelg* (bk)	Martin	Cork	Saint John	234
1846	06	*Margaret Thompson* (bk)	Lacey	Donegal	Saint John	162
1846	06	*Martha* (sw, 254 tns)	Linn, John	Cork	Saint John	153
1846	06	*Midas* of Galway (bg, 255 tns)	Still, J.	Galway	St. Andrews	57
1846	06	*Moy* of Limerick (sr, 144 tns)	O'Grady	Limerick	Saint John	33
1846	06	*Ocean*	n/k	Cork	Saint John	224
1846	06	*Pero* of Cork (bg, 225 tns)	n/k	Cork	St. Andrews	141

Vessel quarantined owing to smallpox on board.

Year	Month	Vessel	Master	Departure Port	Arrival Port	Passenger Numbers
1846	06	*Pons Aeli* of Cork (bk, 315 tns)	n/k	Berehaven (County Cork)	Saint John	n/k
1846	06	*Princess Royal* of Cork (bk, 186 tns)	Callaghan	Cork	Saint John	134

Year	Month	Vessel	Master	Departure Port	Arrival Port	Passenger Numbers
1846	06	*Racer* of Waterford (bg)	Power, Richard	Dingle (County Kerry)	Saint John	181

All passengers landed at Partridge Island. Captain fined for overcrowding.

Year	Month	Vessel	Master	Departure Port	Arrival Port	Passenger Numbers
1846	06	*Recovery* (bg)	Flinn, Matthew	Sligo	Saint John	n/k

Captain fined for not supplying sufficient water to passengers.

Year	Month	Vessel	Master	Departure Port	Arrival Port	Passenger Numbers
1846	06	*Recovery* of Dublin (bk, 329 tns)	Moore, Lawrence	Galway	Saint John	245

Captain fined for overcrowding. Fine was reduced as captain "had been very kind to passengers during the voyage."

Year	Month	Vessel	Master	Departure Port	Arrival Port	Passenger Numbers
1846	06	*Regina* of Cork (bg, 223 tns)	Reynolds	Baltimore (County Cork)	Saint John	142

Year	Month	Vessel	Master	Departure Port	Arrival Port	Passenger Numbers
1846	06	*Renewal* (bk)	Cooper, James	Berehaven (County Cork)	Saint John	224

Captain fined for not supplying sufficient provisions to passengers and for overcrowding.

Year	Month	Vessel	Master	Departure Port	Arrival Port	Passenger Numbers
1846	06	*Sophia*	n/k	Waterford	Saint John	n/k
1846	06	*Themis* of Waterford (bg, 178 tns)	Dobbin	Bantry (County Cork)	Saint John	98
1846	06	*Victoria* (bg)	Wheton	Youghall (County Cork)	Saint John	31
1846	06	*Virgilia* (bk)	Cormack	Londonderry	Saint John	178
1846	06	*Volant* (bk)	n/k	Londonderry	St. Andrews	24
1846	06	*Warner*	n/k	Drogheda (County Meath)	Saint John	n/k

Year	Month	Vessel	Master	Departure Port	Arrival Port	Passenger Numbers
1846	06	*Wellington* (bg)	Carey	Galway	Saint John	55
1846	06	*Woodland Castle* of Cork (bg, 168 tns)	Williams	Cork	Saint John	116
1846	07	*Blanche* (114 tns)	Falconbridge	Donegal	Saint John	n/k
1846	07	*Bristol*	Brinton	Londonderry	Saint John	n/k
1846	07	*Burman* (bg)	Cann, James	Sligo	Saint John	76

Captain was fined for not having sufficient provisions and for irregularities during the voyage.

1846	07	*Danube* of Belfast (bg, 110 tns)	McNaughton, Alexander	Donegal	Saint John	61

Captain was fined £105 for overcrowding, inadequate provisions, and insufficient medicines.

1846	07	*Elizabeth* (sr)	Young	Cork	Saint John	34
1846	07	*Harry King* (bg)	n/k	Cork	Saint John	74
1846	07	*Mary Campbell* (415 tns)	Berger	Londonderry	Saint John	251
1846	08	*Brothers* of Newry (bk, 504 tns)	n/k	Newry (County Armagh)	Saint John	42
1846	08	*Caroline*	Kirkpatrick	Ballyshannon (County Donegal)	Saint John	n/k
1846	08	*Chieftan* of Galway (s, 490 tns)	Duffy, Hyacinth	Galway	Saint John	n/k

Captain commended for kind treatment of passengers.

Year	Month	Vessel	Master	Departure Port	Arrival Port	Passenger Numbers
1846	08	*Emerald*	n/k	Liverpool	Saint John	n/k
1846	08	*Emigrant*	n/k	Liverpool	Saint John	n/k
1846	08	*Oregon*	n/k	Liverpool	Saint John	n/k
1846	08	*Pearl* of Saint John (bk, 398 tns)	Rowles, T.	Londonderry	Saint John	60
1846	09	*Renewal* (bk)	Cooper, James	Berehaven (County Cork)	Saint John	n/k
1846	n/k	*Cynthia Ann*	n/k	Drogheda (County Meath)	Saint John	n/k
1846	n/k	*Duke of Wellington* (bk)	n/k	London	Saint John	42
1846	n/k	*Emulous*	n/k	Newry (County Armagh)	Saint John	n/k
1847	05	*Aeolus* of Greenock (s, 817 tns)	Driscoll, Michael	Sligo	Saint John	500

Tenants of Sir Robert Gore-Booth (Lissadell estate) who owned the *Aeolus* of Greenock. Eight passengers were dead on arrival and twenty-two were admitted into quarantine. It had been a stormy crossing. Passengers wrote a letter of appreciation to Captain Driscoll for his kind treatment. In August many were still being housed in the Poor House, Alms House, and Infirmary. Passenger list: Sligo Heritage website.

Year	Month	Vessel	Master	Departure Port	Arrival Port	Passenger Numbers
1847	05	*Aldebaran* (bk, 521 tns)	Barres	Sligo	Saint John	418

There were thirty-six deaths during the voyage. One hundred and five were sick on arrival. Passengers complained about bad quality of provisions and water.

Year	Month	Vessel	Master	Departure Port	Arrival Port	Passenger Numbers
1847	05	*Amazon* (bk, 357 tns)	Hayes	Liverpool	Saint John	262

There were two deaths on the voyage. Thirty-four were admitted to quarantine station on arrival.

| 1847 | 05 | *Caledonia* of Liverpool (bg, 597 tns) | McAlley | Liverpool | Saint John | 30 |

| 1847 | 05 | *David* (sr, 139 tns) | Yorke, A. | Galway | Saint John | n/k |

Vessel arrived via Halifax.

| 1847 | 05 | *Dealy* of Bantry (bg, 245 tns) | Sterrat | Bantry (County Cork) | Saint John | 169 |

| 1847 | 05 | *Inconstant* (bg, 185 tns) | n/k | Cork | Saint John | 114 |

There were three deaths on the voyage. On arrival, nine passengers were admitted to quarantine.

| 1847 | 05 | *Marchioness of Clydesdale* (s, 565 tns) | Ferguson | Londonderry | Saint John | 386 |

Captain commended for his "kind treatment" and "the creditable state of the Vessel." Passenger list: Olive Tree website.

| 1847 | 05 | *Mary Harrington* of Ardrossan (bk, 411 tns) | Montgomery | Donegal | Saint John | 135 |

| 1847 | 05 | *Mary* of Cork (bg, 180 tns) | Dunbar, J. | Cork | Saint John | 130 |

There were twelve deaths on the voyage. Thirty-two passengers were admitted into quarantine.

| 1847 | 05 | *Midas* of Galway (bg, 255 tns) | Still, J. | Galway | Saint John | 163 |

There were ten deaths on the voyage.

Year	Month	Vessel	Master	Departure Port	Arrival Port	Passenger Numbers
1847	05	*Ocean* (bg, 122 tns)	n/k	Baltimore (County Cork)	Saint John	89
1847	05	*Orbit*	n/k	Glasgow	Saint John	26
1847	05	*Pallas* of Cork (bk, 316 tns)	Hall, Robert	Cork	Saint John	204

There was one death on the voyage. Thirty-one passengers were admitted into quarantine.

Year	Month	Vessel	Master	Departure Port	Arrival Port	Passenger Numbers
1847	05	*Princess Royal* of Cork (bk, 186 tns)	Driscoll	Limerick	Saint John	129
1847	05	*Sea Bird* of Newry (bg, 492 tns)	Rae, J.	Newry (County Armagh)	Saint John	346
1847	05	*Shakespeare* of Liverpool (bk, 525 tns)	Henderson	Liverpool	Saint John	29
1847	05	*Sir Charles Napier* of Liverpool (s, 714 tns)	Sear	Londonderry	Saint John	434

There were two deaths on the voyage. Six admitted into quarantine. Passenger list: Olive Tree website.

Year	Month	Vessel	Master	Departure Port	Arrival Port	Passenger Numbers
1847	05	*Thorney Close* of Sunderland (sw, 249 tns)	Horan, James	Donegal	Saint John	137

There were six deaths on the voyage. The passengers thanked Captain Horan for "his kind and prompt attention to us during the time we were sea-sick." (*New Brunswick Courier*, July 19, 1847.)

Year	Month	Vessel	Master	Departure Port	Arrival Port	Passenger Numbers
1847	06	*Aeneas* of Cork (175 tns)	n/k	Cork	Saint John	62

Year	Month	Vessel	Master	Departure Port	Arrival Port	Passenger Numbers
1847	06	*Eliza* (158 tns)	Cheasty	Waterford	Saint John	28

Vessel called at Halifax.

Year	Month	Vessel	Master	Departure Port	Arrival Port	Passenger Numbers
1847	06	*Eliza Ann*	Wallace	Galway	Saint John	65
1847	06	*Elizabeth Grimmer* (331 tns)	Grant	Londonderry	St. Andrews	229

Eight died on the voyage and eight were admitted to quarantine station.

Year	Month	Vessel	Master	Departure Port	Arrival Port	Passenger Numbers
1847	06	*Ella* (130 tns)	Small	Cork	Saint John	26

Passengers admitted to quarantine station.

Year	Month	Vessel	Master	Departure Port	Arrival Port	Passenger Numbers
1847	06	*Enterprise* of Kinsale (bg, 127 tns)	Leonard, J.	Kinsale (County Cork)	Saint John	60
1847	06	*Friends* of Waterford (bg, 128 tns)	Byrnes, G.	Waterford	Saint John	n/k

Vessel called at St. John's, Newfoundland.

Year	Month	Vessel	Master	Departure Port	Arrival Port	Passenger Numbers
1847	06	*Garland* of Cork (bg, 208 tns)	Small, J.	Cork	Saint John	135
1847	06	*Gem*	Murray	Galway	Saint John	123
1847	06	*Governor Douglas* of Cork (bk, 434 tns)	Clark	Baltimore (County Cork)	Saint John	261

Twenty-six passengers and five crew sick on arrival.

Year	Month	Vessel	Master	Departure Port	Arrival Port	Passenger Numbers
1847	06	*Gowrie*	Perkins	Cork	Saint John	71

Four deaths on the voyage. Passengers were reported as being "in a sickly and miserable state" in quarantine.

Year	Month	Vessel	Master	Departure Port	Arrival Port	Passenger Numbers
1847	06	*Helen Anna*	Leonard	Galway	Saint John	n/k
1847	06	*John Clarke*	Disbrow, Robert	Londonderry	Saint John	525

Passenger list: Olive Tree website. Captain Disbrow was commended by Moses Perley, the immigration agent.

Year	Month	Vessel	Master	Departure Port	Arrival Port	Passenger Numbers
1847	06	*Linden* of London (bk, 297 tns)	Yorke, Austin	Galway	Saint John	189

Captain fined for not providing sufficient provisions to the passengers.

Year	Month	Vessel	Master	Departure Port	Arrival Port	Passenger Numbers
1847	06	*Malvina* of Baltimore (bk, 249 tns)	Chantley	Baltimore (County Cork)	Saint John	183
1847	06	*Margaret Elizabeth* of Youghall (sr, 142 tns)	Stainstreet	Youghall (County Cork)	Saint John	n/k
1847	06	*Mary Dunbar*	n/k	Cork	Saint John	n/k
1847	06	*Mary Murray*	n/k	Cork	Saint John	n/k
1847	06	*Nancy*	n/k	Killala (County Sligo)	Saint John	106
1847	06	*Perseverance*	Callaghan	Cork	Saint John	123
1847	06	*Progress* of Londonderry (sw, 201 tns)	Fagen, P.	Londonderry	Saint John	138

Five deaths on the voyage. Passenger list: Olive Tree website.

Year	Month	Vessel	Master	Departure Port	Arrival Port	Passenger Numbers
1847	06	*Rose*	n/k	Cork	Saint John	56
1847	07	*Abeona* (bg)	Attridge	Cork	Saint John	73

One death in quarantine.

Year	Month	Vessel	Master	Departure Port	Arrival Port	Passenger Numbers
1847	07	*Ambassadress* (s, 846 tns)	Bannerman	Liverpool	Saint John	498

There were nineteen deaths on the voyage: sixteen adults and three children.

| 1847 | 07 | *Bache McEver* of Cork (bg, 229 tns) | Betty, J. | Cork | Saint John | 136 |

Eleven passengers died in quarantine. There were two cases of smallpox.

| 1847 | 07 | *Blanche* (114 tns) | Green | Donegal | Saint John | 73 |

| 1847 | 07 | *British Queen* (bk, 300 tns) | Bell | Londonderry | Saint John | 123 |

| 1847 | 07 | *Caledonia* of Cork (bg, 105 tns) | Parker, T. | Cork | Saint John | 69 |

| 1847 | 07 | *Caroline* | Kirkpatrick | Ballyshannon (County Donegal) | Saint John | 84 |

| 1847 | 07 | *Chieftain* of Galway (s, 490 tns) | McDonough, William | Galway | Saint John | 344 |

There were thirteen deaths on the voyage.

| 1847 | 07 | *Eliza* of Youghall (bg, 123 tns) | McCarthy | Youghall (County Cork) | Saint John | 70 |
| 1847 | 07 | *Hannah* of Maryport (bg, 287 tns) | Shaw | Sligo | Saint John | 211 |

| 1847 | 07 | *James* | n/k | Cork | Saint John | 156 |

Year	Month	Vessel	Master	Departure Port	Arrival Port	Passenger Numbers
1847	07	*Kingston* of Cork (bg, 130 tns)	Matson, B.	Cork	Saint John	68
1847	07	*Lady Bagot* (bk)	Anderson	Waterford	Saint John	337

Captain commended for "kindness and attention to passengers."

Year	Month	Vessel	Master	Departure Port	Arrival Port	Passenger Numbers
1847	07	*Lady Caroline*	Maloney	Newry (County Armagh)	Saint John	105
1847	07	*Magnes*	Scammell	Galway	Saint John	131

Vessel was driven on shore at Partridge Island. There were ten deaths on the voyage; four died in quarantine. Thirty passengers and two crew members were very ill in quarantine at the end of July.

Year	Month	Vessel	Master	Departure Port	Arrival Port	Passenger Numbers
1847	07	*Mary* of Cork (bg, 180 tns)	Sutton, W.	Cork	Saint John	87
1847	07	*Portland* of Liverpool (bk, 542 tns)	Stalker	Londonderry	Saint John	338

There were four deaths on the voyage.

Year	Month	Vessel	Master	Departure Port	Arrival Port	Passenger Numbers
1847	07	*Royal Mint* of Liverpool (bk, 310 tns)	Williams	Liverpool	Saint John	166

There were nineteen deaths on the voyage.

Year	Month	Vessel	Master	Departure Port	Arrival Port	Passenger Numbers
1847	07	*Ruby*	Ellingwood	Sligo	Saint John	105
1847	07	*Sally* of Cork (sr, 127 tns)	Twohig, J.	Cork	Saint John	96

There were seven deaths in quarantine.

Year	Month	Vessel	Master	Departure Port	Arrival Port	Passenger Numbers
1847	07	*Seraph* (bg)	Mather	Cork	Saint John	114

Vessel arrived at Boston. Because of the sick state of the passengers the captain was required to provide a bond to ensure that the passengers would not be chargeable on public funds. The captain refused and came to Saint John instead. There were three deaths on the voyage and forty-five sick in quarantine.

| 1847 | 07 | *Susan* | n/k | Berehaven (County Cork) | Saint John | 68 |

There were three deaths on the voyage and eighteen passengers were ill in quarantine.

| 1847 | 07 | *Susan Ann* of Brixham (bg, 98 tns) | Fox, S. jnr. | Castletownbere (County Cork) | Saint John | 59 |

| 1847 | 07 | *Trafalgar* of Maryport (bg, 198 tns) | Younghusband | Cork | Saint John | 127 |

There was one death in quarantine.

| 1847 | 07 | *Very Rev. Theobold Matthew* | Yorke | Galway | Saint John | n/k |

| 1847 | 07 | *Ward Chipman* of Liverpool (bk, 740 tns) | Bilton | Cork | Saint John | 505 |

There were twenty-three deaths on the voyage and five in quarantine.

| 1847 | 08 | *Adeline* of Cork (101 tns) | Neil | Cork | Saint John | 61 |

| 1847 | 08 | *Alice* | n/k | Galway | Saint John | 125 |

There was one death in quarantine.

| 1847 | 08 | *Bethel* | Mosher | Galway | Saint John | 128 |

| 1847 | 08 | *Bloomfield* (bg) | Beegan, Patrick | Galway | Saint John | 74 |

Vessel was driven on shore in gale and passengers found to be in a destitute and starving state. Captain Beegan fined £50 for failing to supply sufficient water and provisions.

Year	Month	Vessel	Master	Departure Port	Arrival Port	Passenger Numbers
1847	08	*British Merchant* (bk, 334 tns)	Sanderson	Cork	Saint John	338

There were forty-five deaths on the voyage and five in quarantine.

Year	Month	Vessel	Master	Departure Port	Arrival Port	Passenger Numbers
1847	08	*Cushla*	Machree, Thomas	Galway	Saint John	337

Passengers came from Connemara.

Year	Month	Vessel	Master	Departure Port	Arrival Port	Passenger Numbers
1847	08	*Eliza Liddell* (sw, 261 tns)	n/k	Sligo	Shippigan, NB	128

Passengers arrived with fever and disease. Seventy-seven passengers were tenants from Lord Palmerston's estate in Sligo. Others came from the local workhouse.
Passenger List: PANB Irish Portal website.

Year	Month	Vessel	Master	Departure Port	Arrival Port	Passenger Numbers
1847	08	*Envoy* of Londonderry (bk, 481 tns)	Laidler	Londonderry	Saint John	276

There was one death on the voyage and one death in quarantine. Letter of appreciation from passengers to Captain Laidler and his first mate Mr. Gibson for their attention to cleanliness and order to prevent infections. Vessel owned by J & J Cooke of Londonderry.
Passenger list: Olive Tree website.

Year	Month	Vessel	Master	Departure Port	Arrival Port	Passenger Numbers
1847	08	*Glory*	n/k	Cork	Saint John	n/k

Year	Month	Vessel	Master	Departure Port	Arrival Port	Passenger Numbers
1847	08	*Jane* of Saint John (s)	McLean	Limerick	Saint John	98

There were two deaths in quarantine. Letter of appreciation from passengers to master and crew for their kindness and courtesy.

Year	Month	Vessel	Master	Departure Port	Arrival Port	Passenger Numbers
1847	08	*John S. DeWolfe*	Reed	Killala (County Sligo)	Saint John	362

There were four deaths in quarantine.

Year	Month	Vessel	Master	Departure Port	Arrival Port	Passenger Numbers
1847	08	*Leviathan* of Cork (bg, 216 tns)	Roycroft	Baltimore (County Cork)	Saint John	127

Year	Month	Vessel	Master	Departure Port	Arrival Port	Passenger Numbers
1847	08	*Londonderry* (bk, 299 tns)	n/k	Londonderry	Saint John	182

Passenger list: Olive Tree website.

| 1847 | 08 | *Midas* of Galway (bg, 255 tns) | Still, J. | Galway | Saint John | 138 |

Thirty-six passengers from Robert D'Arcy's estate.

| 1847 | 08 | *Sea* | Hubert | Liverpool | Saint John | 243 |

There was one death in quarantine.

| 1847 | 08 | *Sir James McDonnell* of Dublin (bg, 225 tns) | Dunn, L. | Dublin | Saint John | 156 |

| 1847 | 08 | *Warrior* of Drogheda (bk, 221 tns) | Tiernan | Belfast | Saint John | 95 |

| 1847 | 08 | *Yeoman* of Greenock (s, 840 tns) | Purdon, J. | Sligo | Saint John | 504 |

Tenants from Gore-Booth estate. There were four deaths in quarantine.

| 1847 | 09 | *John* | Knox | Waterford | Saint John | 50 |

| 1847 | 09 | *Lady Dunblain* of Sligo (bg, 113 tns) | Brown | Killybegs (County Donegal) | Saint John | 50 |

| 1847 | 09 | *Lady Sale* of Greenock (s, 673 tns) | Anderson | Sligo | Saint John | 412 |

One hundred and fifty passengers from Robert Gore-Booth estate, two hundred from Lord Palmerston estate. Sixty-two passengers were former tenants of other landowners. There were twenty-one deaths on the voyage.

Year	Month	Vessel	Master	Departure Port	Arrival Port	Passenger Numbers
1847	09	*Lord Fitzgerald* (sr)	York	Galway	Saint John	78
1847	09	*Pekin* of Ardrossan (bg, 288 tns)	Harvey, T.	Sligo	Saint John	72
1847	09	*Pero* of Cork (bg, 225 tns)	Meredith	Cork	Saint John	150

There were twenty-one deaths on the voyage.

Year	Month	Vessel	Master	Departure Port	Arrival Port	Passenger Numbers
1847	09	*Saint Lawrence* of Cork (bk, 221 tns)	Bullin, J.	Cork	Saint John	133
1847	10	*Caroline* of Liverpool (bg, 225 tns)	Honey, Thomas	Limerick	Saint John	83

Vessel owned by Mr. H. Thomson, who remained on board vessel until entrance of River Shannon. Fulsome letter of thanks and praise from passengers for his many kindnesses.

Year	Month	Vessel	Master	Departure Port	Arrival Port	Passenger Numbers
1847	10	*David* (sr, 139 tns)	Yorke, A.	Galway	Saint John	91
1847	10	*James* (bk)	Cochran	Limerick	Saint John	129
1847	11	*Aeolus* of Greenock (s, 817 tns)	Driscoll, Michael	Sligo	Saint John	428

Lord Palmerston's former tenants.

Year	Month	Vessel	Master	Departure Port	Arrival Port	Passenger Numbers
1847	11	*Eliza Liddell* (sw, 261 tns)	n/k	Sligo	Shippigan, NB	77

All healthy.

Year	Month	Vessel	Master	Departure Port	Arrival Port	Passenger Numbers
1847	11	*Fanny* (bk)	Quinn	Londonderry	Saint John	225

Year	Month	Vessel	Master	Departure Port	Arrival Port	Passenger Numbers
1847	11	*Triumph* of Halifax (bg, 176 tns)	O'Brine, P.	Sligo	Saint John	44

Mostly from the estate of M. Folliott, M.P. for Sligo.

1848	04	*Lockwoods* (s, 776 tns)	Errington	Cork	Saint John	298

Judging from a customs official pronouncement that the arrivals were "of a superior class to the emigrants from the south of Ireland who have heretofore landed at this port," the passengers were relatively affluent. No sickness or deaths on the voyage.

1848	04	*Londonderry* (bk, 299 tns)	Boyle, George	Londonderry	Saint John	181

There were ten deaths on the voyage. Passenger list: Olive Tree website.

1848	05	*Bache McEver* of Cork (bg, 229 tns)	n/k	Cork	Saint John	123
1848	05	*British Queen* (bk, 300 tns)	Bell	Londonderry	Saint John	122
1848	05	*Charles* of Youghall (bg, 185 tns)	Hanlon	Youghall (County Cork)	Saint John	95

Seven very ill passengers were sent to Partridge Island.

1848	05	*Clara*	Allan	Donegal	Saint John	91
1848	05	*Exchange*	Hewson	Sligo	Saint John	59
1848	05	*Frederick*	n/k	n/k	Saint John	n/k
1848	05	*John Francis* of Cork (bk 362 tns)	Deaves, H.	Cork	Saint John	182

Year	Month	Vessel	Master	Departure Port	Arrival Port	Passenger Numbers
1848	05	*Leviathan* of Cork (bg, 216 tns)	McDowall	Skibbereen (County Cork)	Saint John	94
1848	05	*Lord Sandon* of Cork (bk, 407 tns)	O'Brien	Kinsale (County Cork)	Saint John	167
1848	05	*McDonnell* (bk)	McDonnell, Hugh	Cork	Saint John	220
1848	05	*Redwing* (bg)	Isbister	Galway	Saint John	141

There were three deaths on the voyage.

Year	Month	Vessel	Master	Departure Port	Arrival Port	Passenger Numbers
1848	05	*Star* (s, 727 tns)	Baldwin	New Ross (County Wexford)	St. Andrews	383

Passengers were Earl Fitzwilliam's tenants. Reconstructed passenger list: Rees, *Surplus People: from Wicklow to Canada*, 131–37.

Year	Month	Vessel	Master	Departure Port	Arrival Port	Passenger Numbers
1848	05	*Triumph* of Halifax (bg, 176 tns)	Dudley	Limerick	Saint John	103
1848	06	*Adeline*	Cann	Waterford	Saint John	96
1848	06	*Commerce*	n/k	Galway	Saint John	n/k
1848	06	*Dealy* of Bantry (bg, 245 tns)	Dee	Bantry (County Cork)	Saint John	123

There were four deaths on the voyage. Seven passengers with smallpox and five with fever on arrival.

Year	Month	Vessel	Master	Departure Port	Arrival Port	Passenger Numbers
1848	06	*Grace Darling*	Hanratty	Newry (County Armagh)	Saint John	n/k

Year	Month	Vessel	Master	Departure Port	Arrival Port	Passenger Numbers
1848	06	*Linden* of London (bk, 297 tns)	York	Galway	Saint John	172

One person with smallpox and six with fever on arrival.

Year	Month	Vessel	Master	Departure Port	Arrival Port	Passenger Numbers
1848	06	*Lord Maidstone* of Liverpool (bk, 568 tns)	Sheridan	Londonderry	Saint John	332

There were six deaths on the voyage.

Year	Month	Vessel	Master	Departure Port	Arrival Port	Passenger Numbers
1848	06	*McDonald* (s)	McDonald	Cork	Saint John	220
1848	06	*Springhill* (bk, 348 tns)	Gunn, W.	Donegal	Saint John	103

Captain, second mate, and twelve passengers ill with fever. All passengers landed at Partridge Island.

Year	Month	Vessel	Master	Departure Port	Arrival Port	Passenger Numbers
1848	07	*Agnes Jermyn* (sr, 90 tns)	Hart, Andrew	Limerick	Saint John	78

Fourteen cabin passengers, sixty-four steerage.

Year	Month	Vessel	Master	Departure Port	Arrival Port	Passenger Numbers
1848	07	*Blanche* (114 tns)	Green	Donegal	Saint John	67
1848	07	*Concord* (sr)	Bowler, Thomas	Limerick	Saint John	77
1848	07	*Hornet* of Limerick (sr, 139 tns)	Hedigan, Michael	Limerick	Saint John	86
1848	07	*Princess Royal* of Cork (bk, 186 tns)	Driscoll	Cork	Saint John	116
1848	08	*Aeneas* of Cork (175 tns)	Cushman	Berehaven (County Cork)	Saint John	n/k
1848	08	*British Queen* (bk, 300 tns)	Bell	Londonderry	Saint John	32

Year	Month	Vessel	Master	Departure Port	Arrival Port	Passenger Numbers
1848	08	*Lady Lilford* (bg)	Hughan	Limerick	Saint John	90
1848	08	*Londonderry* (bk, 299 tns)	Boyle, George	Londonderry	Saint John	144

Passenger list: Olive Tree website.

Year	Month	Vessel	Master	Departure Port	Arrival Port	Passenger Numbers
1848	09	*William Kerry*	n/k	n/k	Saint John	n/k
1848	10	*Margaret*	n/k	New Ross (County Wexford)	Saint John	n/k
1848	12	*Anglo Saxon*	n/k	n/k	Saint John	n/k
1848	n/k	*Jonathan Hawkes*	n/k	n/k	Saint John	n/k
1848	n/k	*Steven Heath*	n/k	n/k	Saint John	n/k
1848	n/k	*Themis*	Leighton, W.	n/k	Saint John	n/k
1848	n/k	*Ward Chipman* of Liverpool ("Spring") (bk, 740 tns)	n/k	n/k	Saint John	n/k
1849	05	*Albion* (255 tns)	Daly	Cork	Saint John	169
1849	05	*British Queen* (bk, 300 tns)	Bell	Londonderry	Saint John	87

Passenger list: Olive Tree website.

Year	Month	Vessel	Master	Departure Port	Arrival Port	Passenger Numbers
1849	05	*Goliath* of Liverpool (s, 900 tns)	Slater, C.	Liverpool	Saint John	51

Year	Month	Vessel	Master	Departure Port	Arrival Port	Passenger Numbers
1849	05	*John*	n/k	Westport (County Mayo)	Saint John	98
1849	05	*Londonderry* (bk, 299 tns)	Hattrick	Londonderry	Saint John	154

Passenger list: Olive Tree website.

Year	Month	Vessel	Master	Departure Port	Arrival Port	Passenger Numbers
1849	05	*Pallas* of Cork (bk, 316 tns)	Harvey, Robert	Cork	Saint John	201
1849	05	*Susan* of Cork (bk, 168 tns)	Griffith, Owen	Cork	St. Andrews	109

Passenger list: PANB Irish Portal website.

Year	Month	Vessel	Master	Departure Port	Arrival Port	Passenger Numbers
1849	05	*Waterford* of Harrington (bg, 296 tns)	Robinson	Limerick	Saint John	152

There were thirteen deaths on the voyage.

Year	Month	Vessel	Master	Departure Port	Arrival Port	Passenger Numbers
1849	06	*Coronation*	n/k	Liverpool	Saint John	n/k
1849	06	*Governor Douglas* of Cork (bk, 434 tns)	Locke	Westport (County Mayo)	Saint John	n/k
1849	06	*Nancy*	Brough	Westport (County Mayo)	Saint John	n/k
1849	06	*Sophia*	n/k	Waterford	Saint John	n/k
1849	07	*Ann Hall*	n/k	Liverpool	Saint John	n/k
1849	07	*Eliza Edward*	Walker	Tralee (County Kerry)	Saint John	n/k
1849	07	*Sarah*	Cook	Londonderry	Saint John	n/k

Year	Month	Vessel	Master	Departure Port	Arrival Port	Passenger Numbers
1849	07	*Whitehaven*	n/k	Sligo	Saint John	n/k
1849	08	*Charlotte*	n/k	Donegal	Saint John	n/k
1849	08	*Granville*	Brown	Ballina (County Westmeath)	Saint John	n/k
1849	08	*Ruby*	Cook	Westport (County Mayo)	Saint John	n/k
1849	08	*Standard*	Crosby	Limerick	Saint John	n/k
1849	09	*Velocity* of Waterford (bg, 166 tns)	n/k	Waterford	Saint John	n/k
1849	10	*Unicorn*	n/k	Liverpool	Saint John	n/k
1849	n/k	*Alexander Stewart*	Williams	Cork	Saint John	n/k
1849	n/k	*Blanche* (114 tns)	Green	Donegal	Saint John	n/k
1849	n/k	*Eliza*	Couran	Sligo	Saint John	n/k
1849	n/k	*Hibernia* of Kinsale (s, 193 tns)	Codd	Wexford	Saint John	n/k
1849	n/k	*Jane*	Shea	Berehaven (County Cork)	Saint John	n/k
1849	n/k	*Ocean*	Guest	Berehaven (County Cork)	Saint John	n/k

Year	Month	Vessel	Master	Departure Port	Arrival Port	Passenger Numbers
1849	n/k	*Rover*	Allen	Baltimore (County Cork)	Saint John	n/k
1849	n/k	*Aeneas* of Cork (175 tns)	Cardigan	Berehaven (County Cork)	Saint John	n/k
1850	05	*Abby* (sr, 159 tns)	Irvine, D.	Limerick	Saint John	79
1850	05	*Albion* of Cork (bk, 313 tns)	n/k	Cork	Saint John	163
1850	05	*John S. DeWolf* (s)	Roberts, Thomas	Liverpool	Saint John	n/k

Cabin passengers thanked the captain for his "very great attention and kindness."

Year	Month	Vessel	Master	Departure Port	Arrival Port	Passenger Numbers
1850	05	*Kingston* of Cork (bg, 130 tns)	n/k	Cork	Saint John	79
1850	05	*Londonderry* (bk, 299 tns)	n/k	Londonderry	Saint John	170

Passenger list: Olive Tree website.

Year	Month	Vessel	Master	Departure Port	Arrival Port	Passenger Numbers
1850	05	*Mary* of Cork (bg, 180 tns)	n/k	Cork	Saint John	96
1850	11	*Susan*	n/k	Cork	St. Andrews	80

Passenger list: Ships List website.

Year	Month	Vessel	Master	Departure Port	Arrival Port	Passenger Numbers
1850	n/k	*Eagle*	n/k	Londonderry	Saint John	143

Passenger list: Olive Tree website.

Year	Month	Vessel	Master	Departure Port	Arrival Port	Passenger Numbers
1850	n/k	*James Redden* of Dumfries (sw, 218 tns)	n/k	Londonderry	Saint John	92

Passenger list: Olive Tree website.

Year	Month	Vessel	Master	Departure Port	Arrival Port	Passenger Numbers
1851	04	*Onyx* (bk)	n/k	Glasgow	Saint John	12

Passengers came from Ireland.

Year	Month	Vessel	Master	Departure Port	Arrival Port	Passenger Numbers
1851	04	*Speed* (s, 1,009 tns)	n/k	Liverpool	Saint John	218
1851	04	*St. Lawrence* (bk)	n/k	Cork	Saint John	121
1851	05	*Barbara* (s, 325 tns)	Haggarty	Londonderry	Saint John	162

Passenger list: Olive Tree website.

Year	Month	Vessel	Master	Departure Port	Arrival Port	Passenger Numbers
1851	05	*Charles* (bg, 170 tns)	Kines	Youghall (County Cork)	Saint John	105
1851	05	*Field Marshall*	Gore	Cork	Saint John	191
1851	05	*Londonderry* (bk, 299 tns)	n/k	Londonderry	Saint John	162

Passenger list: Olive Tree website.

Year	Month	Vessel	Master	Departure Port	Arrival Port	Passenger Numbers
1851	05	*Pamona* (s, 845 tns)	Cronk	Liverpool	Saint John	286
1851	05	*Perseverance* (597 tns)	Morris	Cork	Saint John	302
1851	05	*Susan* (bk, 168 tns)	n/k	Cork	Saint John	91
1852	05	*Albion* of Cork (bk, 313 tns)	Daly	Cork	Saint John	170

Some passengers with smallpox and quarantined.

Year	Month	Vessel	Master	Departure Port	Arrival Port	Passenger Numbers
1852	05	*Industry* (bk, 487 tns)	Keat	Dublin	Saint John	122

Passengers were said to be "of the better class." Some had smallpox and were quarantined.

Year	Month	Vessel	Master	Departure Port	Arrival Port	Passenger Numbers
1852	05	*Mary* (bg, 180 tns)	Howell	Cork	Saint John	88
1852	05	*Ocean* (bg, 122 tns)	O'Neill	Cork	Saint John	133
1852	n/k	*Mary Ann*	n/k	Londonderry	Saint John	138

Passenger list: Olive Tree website.

1853	05	*Mary Ann*	n/k	Londonderry	Saint John	226

Passengers were mostly women and children. Passenger list: Olive Tree website.

1853	05	*Mary* (bg)	n/k	Cork	Saint John	n/k
1853	05	*Merkur* (bk)	n/k	Londonderry	Saint John	n/k
1853	05	*Speed* (s, 1,009 tns)	n/k	Liverpool	Saint John	60

Ten cabin and fifty steerage passengers. They included a number of labourers who planned to work on the St. Andrews railroad.

1853	06	*Patience* (bk)	Straud	Londonderry	Saint John	145
1853	07	*Liberia* (875 tns)	n/k	Liverpool	Saint John	110
1853	07	*Swan* (234 tns)	n/k	Cork	Saint John	129
1853	n/k	*Mary Ann*	n/k	Londonderry	Saint John	220

Passenger list: Olive Tree website.

1854	04	*Blanche*	Mc Laughton	Liverpool	Saint John	319

Ten cabin and 309 steerage passengers. There were thirty-five deaths from disease on the crossing. For the names of the deceased, who included Germans, see the Ships List website.

Year	Month	Vessel	Master	Departure Port	Arrival Port	Passenger Numbers
1854	07	*Jessie* (bg)	n/k	Youghall (County Cork)	Saint John	78

Passengers included eleven boys and ten girls from the Foundling Hospital at Cork. They were to work as apprentices.

1854	n/k	*Mary Ann*	n/k	Londonderry	Saint John	209

Passenger list: Olive Tree website.

1854	n/k	*Mary Ann*	n/k	Londonderry	Saint John	137

Passenger list: Olive Tree website.

1854	n/k	*Miner*	n/k	Londonderry	Saint John	119

Passenger list: Olive Tree website.

1855	04	*Middleton* (s)	Deleney	Liverpool	Saint John	110

Eleven of the passengers and one crew member arrived with typhus.

1855	n/k	*Mary Ann*	n/k	Londonderry	Saint John	120

See Mitchell, *Irish Passenger Lists, 1847–71.*

1855	n/k	*Superior*	n/k	Londonderry	Saint John	41

See Mitchell, *Irish Passenger Lists, 1847–71.*

1856	07	*Mary Ann*	Hattrick	Londonderry	Saint John	170

See Mitchell, *Irish Passenger Lists, 1847–71.*

1857	n/k	*Elizabeth*	n/k	Londonderry	Saint John	98

Passenger list: Olive Tree website.

1857	n/k	*Mary Ann*	n/k	Londonderry	Saint John	144

See Mitchell, *Irish Passenger Lists, 1847–71.*

1857	n/k	*Mary Ann*		Londonderry	Saint John	101

Year	Month	Vessel	Master	Departure Port	Arrival Port	Passenger Numbers
1858	n/k	*Elizabeth*	n/k	Londonderry	Saint John	25
Passenger list: Olive Tree website.						
1859	n/k	*Elizabeth*	n/k	Londonderry	Saint John	19
Passenger list: Olive Tree website.						
1859	n/k	*Mary Ann*	n/k	Londonderry	Saint John	80
See Mitchell, *Irish Passenger Lists, 1847–71.*						
1860	n/k	*Argentinus*	n/k	Londonderry	Saint John	52
1860	n/k	*Elizabeth*	Mason	Londonderry	Saint John	14
Passenger list: Olive Tree website.						
1861	05	*Argentinus*	McDaid	Londonderry	Saint John	113
Passenger list: Ships List website, or Mitchell, *Irish Passenger Lists, 1847–71.*						
1861	06	*Irvine* (bk, 502 tns)	Cask, John	Greenock	Saint John	134
There were three deaths on the voyage.						
1861	n/k	*Elizabeth*	Gillespie	Londonderry	Saint John	55
Passenger list: Olive Tree website.						
1862	04	*Elizabeth* (s, 770 tns)	Gillespie	Londonderry	Saint John	123
See Mitchell, *Irish Passenger Lists, 1847–71.*						
1862	06	*Olympia* (bk, 532 tns)	Tobias	Glasgow	Saint John	253
1862	07	*Elizabeth* (s, 770 tns)	Gillespie	Londonderry	Saint John	34
1862	09	*Hiawatha* (bk, 271 tns)	Mc Donough	Galway	Saint John	42

Year	Month	Vessel	Master	Departure Port	Arrival Port	Passenger Numbers
1863	05	*Elizabeth*	n/k	Londonderry	Saint John	167

Passenger list: Olive Tree website.

Year	Month	Vessel	Master	Departure Port	Arrival Port	Passenger Numbers
1863	05	*Margaret* (bg, 180 tns)	Watson, James	Galway	Saint John	66

1863	05	*Marvel* (bg, 171 tns)	Morrison, A.	Galway	Saint John	22

1863	06	*Joseph Newlay* (bg, 204 tns)	Yorke, Peter	Galway	Saint John	40

Thirty two of the passengers thanked the captain for his kindness during the crossing (letter printed in Saint John *Morning Freeman*, June 9, 1863). Their names are shown in Punch, *Erin's Sons*, 4: 125.

1863	10	*Nubia* (834 tns)	Little, William	Londonderry	Saint John	38

Passenger list: Olive Tree website.

1864	05	*Doctor Kane* (bk, 606 tns)	McLaughlin	Londonderry	Saint John	278

There were two deaths on the voyage.

1864	06	*Margaret* (bg, 180 tns)	Peterson, James	Galway	Saint John	89

1865	04	*Britannia* (ss, 1350 tns)	Ferrier	Glasgow	Saint John	43

1865	07	*Ariel* (bk, 355 tns)	McDonagh, John	Galway	Saint John	119

1865	08	*Rubicon* (s, 834 tns)	P. McLaughlin	Londonderry	Saint John	30

1865	10	*Britannia* (ss, 1350 tns)	Ferrier	Glasgow	Saint John	33

Thirty-three passengers landed at Saint John. Another 440 passengers went on to New York.

Year	Month	Vessel	Master	Departure Port	Arrival Port	Passenger Numbers
1865	10	*Ocean Child* (bk, 288 tns)	Morgan, David	Galway	Saint John	23
1866	04	*Venezia* (ss, 507 tns)	Smith, William	Glasgow	Saint John	29
1867	05	*Doctor Kane* (bk, 606 tns)	n/k	Londonderry	Saint John	37

APPENDIX III

Ship Crossings from Ireland to Prince Edward Island, 1771–1848

The following table lists the year, month of sailing, and number of passengers carried by each ship identified as having left Ireland for Prince Edward Island between 1771 and 1848. It provides details of eighty-five sea crossings, involving a total of 6,539 Irish passengers, showing the different Irish ports from which they embarked and their arrival ports in Charlottetown.

Ship-crossing data has been obtained from the following documentary sources:

Edward G. MacDonald, *New Ireland: The Irish in PEI*
(Charlottetown: PEI Museum and Heritage Foundation, 1990).
J. Orlo and D. Fraser, "Those Elusive Immigrants, Parts 1 to 3," *The Island Magazine* 16 (1984): 36–44; 17 (1985): 32–37; 18 (1985): 29–35.
Douglas Fraser, "More Elusive Immigrants." *The Island Magazine* 26 (Fall/Winter, 1989): 35–40; 27; (Spring/Summer, 1990): 38–41.
PEI Ships Database: www.islandregister.com.

See "Explanatory Notes" on pages 217–18 for an explanation of the shipping terms used in this listing.

For details of the quality of the ships that brought the Irish to Prince Edward Island, see Tables 10 and 11.

Year	Month	Vessel	Master	Departure Port	Arrival Port	Passenger Numbers
1771	n/k	Hopewell	n/k	Ireland	North of Charlottetown	n/k

Passengers included nine families.

| 1772 | n/k | John and James | n/k | Belfast | Charlottetown | 188 |

Vessel also called at Newry.

| 1772 | n/k | Yaward | n/k | Belfast | Charlottetown | n/k |

Vessel called at Newry and carried fifty families.

| 1775 | n/k | Elizabeth | n/k | Cork | Charlottetown | n/k |

Vessel came originally from London with fourteen passengers. An unknown number boarded at Cork. Vessel was wrecked off Lot 11.

| 1793 | 06 | Union | Landry | Cork | Charlottetown | n/k |

| 1817 | 07 | Sarah | n/k | Limerick | Charlottetown | 18 |

| 1817 | 08 | Harriot | n/k | Dublin | Charlottetown | n/k |

Passengers included John Large, plus others.

| 1818 | 06 | Nelson | n/k | Cork | Charlottetown | 3 |

| 1819 | 06 | Two vessels | n/k | Ireland | St. Andrews | 600 |

Arrived at St. Andrews, PEI, with six hundred passengers. However, this is unlikely since no other evidence supports this claim. They probably went to St. Andrews, NB.

| 1820 | 05 | Carron (228 tns) | Short, R. | Cork | Charlottetown | 11 |

Lieutenant Samuel Holland plus ten steerage passengers.

| 1820 | 05 | Jane (140 tns) | McGrath, W. | Waterford | Charlottetown | 57 |

Year	Month	Vessel	Master	Departure Port	Arrival Port	Passenger Numbers
1820	06	*Alexander* (142 tns)	Hogg, J.	Limerick	Charlottetown	93
1820	n/k	*Quebec Trader*	n/k	Dublin	Charlottetown	2

Passengers were A. Willock, Theophilus Chappell, Jr.

Year	Month	Vessel	Master	Departure Port	Arrival Port	Passenger Numbers
1821	n/k	*Quebec Trader*	n/k	Waterford	Charlottetown	3

Passengers were Mr. Connery, Richard Goff, and Miss Goff.

Year	Month	Vessel	Master	Departure Port	Arrival Port	Passenger Numbers
1822	07	*Devonshire*	n/k	Waterford	Charlottetown	42
1822	n/k	*San Domingo* (140 tns)	Lewis, David	Ross	Charlottetown	87

Vessel called at Newfoundland.

Year	Month	Vessel	Master	Departure Port	Arrival Port	Passenger Numbers
1823	06	*General Elliott* (399 tns)	Frank, J.	Cork	Charlottetown	113
1823	08	*John* (317 tns)	Wall, R.	Bristol	Charlottetown	n/k

Vessel sailed from Bristol and collected passengers in the south of Ireland. They settled in Lots 48 and 49.

Year	Month	Vessel	Master	Departure Port	Arrival Port	Passenger Numbers
1826	n/k	*Martin*	n/k	Limerick	Charlottetown	n/k

Passengers went to Seven Mile Bay.

Year	Month	Vessel	Master	Departure Port	Arrival Port	Passenger Numbers
1827	07	*Hannah*	Murphy	Ross	Charlottetown	43

Vessel arrived via Newfoundland.

Year	Month	Vessel	Master	Departure Port	Arrival Port	Passenger Numbers
1828	05	*Benjamin Shaw*	n/k	Waterford	Charlottetown	181

Passengers included John Morris plus 180 steerage passengers.

Year	Month	Vessel	Master	Departure Port	Arrival Port	Passenger Numbers
1828	06	*Hannah*	n/k	Wexford	Charlottetown	45

Vessel came via Newfoundland.

Year	Month	Vessel	Master	Departure Port	Arrival Port	Passenger Numbers
1829	05	*Benjamin Shaw*	n/k	Waterford	Charlottetown	n/k

Vessel arrived via Newfoundland. Passengers included John Morris plus settlers in steerage.

Year	Month	Vessel	Master	Departure Port	Arrival Port	Passenger Numbers
1829	05	*Pandora* (147 tns)	Baldwin	Waterford	Charlottetown	n/k

Mr. R. Goff plus settlers.

Year	Month	Vessel	Master	Departure Port	Arrival Port	Passenger Numbers
1829	11	*Collina*	n/k	Dublin	Charlottetown	1

Passenger was Mr. Henry Cowley.

Year	Month	Vessel	Master	Departure Port	Arrival Port	Passenger Numbers
1830	05	*Corsair* (273 tns)	Hamilton	Greenock	Charlottetown	207

Rev. John McDonald plus 206 settlers bound for Fort Augustus. Passengers were mainly from the north of Ireland.

Year	Month	Vessel	Master	Departure Port	Arrival Port	Passenger Numbers
1830	06	*Favourite*	Cowman	Dublin	Charlottetown	3

Mr. Connery plus two others.

Year	Month	Vessel	Master	Departure Port	Arrival Port	Passenger Numbers
1830	06	*Hannah*	n/k	Ross	Charlottetown	30

Vessel came via Newfoundland. Passengers were settlers.

Year	Month	Vessel	Master	Departure Port	Arrival Port	Passenger Numbers
1830	07	*Don*	Anderson	Waterford	Charlottetown	n/k

Passengers went to Orwell Bay.

Year	Month	Vessel	Master	Departure Port	Arrival Port	Passenger Numbers
1830	07	*Saltern's Rock*	Mollard	Cork	Charlottetown	n/k

Year	Month	Vessel	Master	Departure Port	Arrival Port	Passenger Numbers
1830	11	*Quebec Trader*	n/k	Dublin	Charlottetown	2

Passengers were A. Willock and Theophilus Chappell Jr.

Year	Month	Vessel	Master	Departure Port	Arrival Port	Passenger Numbers
1831	05	*Quebec Trader*	n/k	Waterford	Charlottetown	3

Passengers were Mr. Connery, Mr. Richard Goff, Miss Goff.

Year	Month	Vessel	Master	Departure Port	Arrival Port	Passenger Numbers
1831	06	*Hannah*	n/k	Wexford	Charlottetown	22

Vessel came via Newfoundland. Passengers from Wexford.

Year	Month	Vessel	Master	Departure Port	Arrival Port	Passenger Numbers
1831	08	*Venus*	n/k	Dublin	Charlottetown	40

Vessel was bound for Quebec. One hundred and fifty passengers remained on board for Quebec. The forty who disembarked went to Three Rivers, P.E.I.

Year	Month	Vessel	Master	Departure Port	Arrival Port	Passenger Numbers
1831	11	*Quebec Trader*	n/k	Dublin	Charlottetown	19

Year	Month	Vessel	Master	Departure Port	Arrival Port	Passenger Numbers
1832	05	*Pandora* (147 tns)	n/k	Waterford	Charlottetown	106

Year	Month	Vessel	Master	Departure Port	Arrival Port	Passenger Numbers
1832	09	*Pandora* (147 tns)	n/k	Waterford	Charlottetown	19

Vessel anchored at the quarantine ground on arrival.

Year	Month	Vessel	Master	Departure Port	Arrival Port	Passenger Numbers
1832	11	*George & Henry*	n/k	Dublin	Charlottetown	n/k

Year	Month	Vessel	Master	Departure Port	Arrival Port	Passenger Numbers
1833	05	*Pandora* (147 tns)	n/k	Waterford	Charlottetown	34

Mr. Thomas plus thirty-three steerage passengers.

Year	Month	Vessel	Master	Departure Port	Arrival Port	Passenger Numbers
1834	05	*Pandora* (147 tns)	n/k	Waterford	Charlottetown	76

Mr. George Conroy plus seventy-five steerage passengers.

Year	Month	Vessel	Master	Departure Port	Arrival Port	Passenger Numbers
1834	09	*Pandora* (147 tns)	n/k	Waterford	Charlottetown	9

Year	Month	Vessel	Master	Departure Port	Arrival Port	Passenger Numbers
1834	11	*Anna*	n/k	Cork	Charlottetown	1

Passenger was T.B. Tremaine.

Year	Month	Vessel	Master	Departure Port	Arrival Port	Passenger Numbers
1835	05	Grace	n/k	Belfast	Charlottetown	196

The passengers included sixty-three children under seven years old. Twenty-four children and one adult died from measles during the voyage.

Year	Month	Vessel	Master	Departure Port	Arrival Port	Passenger Numbers
1835	05	Pandora (147 tns)	n/k	Waterford	Charlottetown	35

Miss Conroy, Mr. N. Conroy, Mr. Foran, plus thirty-two in steerage.

Year	Month	Vessel	Master	Departure Port	Arrival Port	Passenger Numbers
1835	06	Molly Moore	Henley	Waterford	Charlottetown	12

The vessel called at Halifax. The twelve passengers went to Crapaud.

Year	Month	Vessel	Master	Departure Port	Arrival Port	Passenger Numbers
1835	n/k	Margot	n/k	Belfast	Charlottetown	80
1836	05	Agitator	n/k	Belfast	Charlottetown	310
1836	05	Consbrook (423 tns)	n/k	Belfast	Charlottetown	308

Mainly from county Monaghan. To settle on Rev. John MacDonald's lands.

Year	Month	Vessel	Master	Departure Port	Arrival Port	Passenger Numbers
1836	06	Pandora (147 tns)	n/k	Waterford	Charlottetown	47

Thomas Conroy, Cochrane Doyle, Miss O'Farrel, plus forty-four in steerage.

Year	Month	Vessel	Master	Departure Port	Arrival Port	Passenger Numbers
1836	09	Thomas Hanforth	n/k	Cork	Charlottetown	15

Simon Dodd plus fourteen in steerage.

Year	Month	Vessel	Master	Departure Port	Arrival Port	Passenger Numbers
1836	n/k	Argyle	n/k	Waterford	Charlottetown	n/k
1837	06	Pandora (147 tns)	Power, John	Waterford	Charlottetown	20
1837	07	Lady Anne of Newcastle (bg, 286 tns)	Simms, James	Belfast	Charlottetown	35

Forty-eight people from county Monaghan sailed from Belfast to Wallace, Nova Scotia. Thirty-five of them then travelled in a sloop to Charlottetown.

Year	Month	Vessel	Master	Departure Port	Arrival Port	Passenger Numbers
1837	09	*William Alexander*	n/k	Porthall, Co. Donegal	Charlottetown	n/k
1837	10	*Hibernia*	n/k	Dublin	Charlottetown	n/k

Some passengers went to Crapaud.

1839	05	*Agitator*	n/k	Belfast	Charlottetown	310
1839	05	*Consbrook* (423 tns)	Pollock, J.	Belfast	Charlottetown	308

Mainly from county Monaghan. Went to Fort Augustus (Lot 36).

1839	08	*Grecian*	n/k	Waterford	Charlottetown	n/k
1840	05	*Argyle*	n/k	Waterford	Charlottetown	62
1840	06	*Lawrence Forestal*	n/k	Waterford	Charlottetown	21
1840	06	*Rose Bank* (308 tns)	Liget	Belfast	Charlottetown	208

Chiefly from county Monaghan. To settle at Fort Augustus, Kinkora, Millvale, and Kelly's Cross.

1840	09	*Ellen Stewart*	n/k	Limerick	Charlottetown	n/k
1841	05	*Margaret Pollock* (917 tns)	Pye, John	Belfast	Charlottetown	685

Twenty-eight passengers died of measles. Most passengers from county Monaghan.

1841	05	*Sir James McDonnell*	Kelly	Cork	Charlottetown	131

Year	Month	Vessel	Master	Departure Port	Arrival Port	Passenger Numbers
1841	05	*Thomas Gelston* (442 tns)	Donald, John	Belfast	Charlottetown	139

Mainly Monaghan people.

Year	Month	Vessel	Master	Departure Port	Arrival Port	Passenger Numbers
1841	08	*Sir James MacDonald*	n/k	Cork	Charlottetown	n/k

Went to Malpeque.

Year	Month	Vessel	Master	Departure Port	Arrival Port	Passenger Numbers
1842	05	*Morgiana* (bk, 354 tns)	n/k	Belfast	Charlottetown	145

Came from county Monaghan.

Year	Month	Vessel	Master	Departure Port	Arrival Port	Passenger Numbers
1842	05	*Thomas Gelston*	n/k	Belfast	Charlottetown	280

Mainly Monaghan people.

Year	Month	Vessel	Master	Departure Port	Arrival Port	Passenger Numbers
1842	08	*St. George*	n/k	Cork	Charlottetown	n/k

Vessel came via Liverpool and Newfoundland.

Year	Month	Vessel	Master	Departure Port	Arrival Port	Passenger Numbers
1842	09	*Morgiana* (bk, 354 tns)	Hetherington	Belfast	Charlottetown	66

Year	Month	Vessel	Master	Departure Port	Arrival Port	Passenger Numbers
1843	05	*Antelope*	n/k	Dublin	Charlottetown	16

Vessel came via Liverpool.

Year	Month	Vessel	Master	Departure Port	Arrival Port	Passenger Numbers
1843	05	*Chieftain* (325 tns)	Legate	Belfast	Charlottetown	208
1843	05	*Mary Jane*	n/k	Dublin	Charlottetown	n/k
1843	05	*Rose Bank*	n/k	Belfast	Charlottetown	150

Year	Month	Vessel	Master	Departure Port	Arrival Port	Passenger Numbers
1844	06	*Independence* (584 tns)	McCappin	Belfast	Charlottetown	156

Had sailed from Belfast with 360 passengers. The remainder to go on to Quebec. Passengers wrote a letter of commendation to the captain for ensuring a safe crossing (*Royal Gazette*, August 1, 1844). Most to settle at Fort Augustus.

Year	Month	Vessel	Master	Departure Port	Arrival Port	Passenger Numbers
1844	09	*Antelope*	n/k	Dublin	Charlottetown	n/k
1844	09	*Mary Jane*	n/k	Dublin	Charlottetown	n/k
1844	n/k	*Antelope*	n/k	Dublin	Charlottetown	40
1844	n/k	*Margoretta*	n/k	North of Ireland	Charlottetown	n/k
1845	05	*Fanny*	n/k	Liverpool	Charlottetown	n/k
1846	05	*Antelope*	Jones	Liverpool	Charlottetown	40

Passengers mainly from the north of Ireland.

Year	Month	Vessel	Master	Departure Port	Arrival Port	Passenger Numbers
1847	04	*Lady Constable* Garbutt (bg, 613 tns)		Liverpool	Charlottetown	444

Thirty-three died on the voyage from disease. The sick were taken to the quarantine hospital and many others died in the summer.

Year	Month	Vessel	Master	Departure Port	Arrival Port	Passenger Numbers
1848	10	*Douglas*	Jones, Thomas	Dublin	Charlottetown	14

NOTES

Chapter 1: Fish, Timber, and Hope

1. W.F. Ganong, "Monograph of the Origins of Settlements in the Province
    of New Brunswick," *Transactions of the Royal Society of Canada* 2nd series
    (10), sections 1–2 (1904): 77.
2. A detailed study of the causes of the Great Irish Famine and the exodus
    from Ireland that followed, is to be found in a 710-page definitive study
    encapsulating all aspects of the disaster: John Crowley, William J. Smyth,
    and Mike Murphy, *Atlas of the Great Irish Famine* (Cork: Cork University
    Press, 2013).
3. David A. Wilson, *The Irish in Canada* (Ottawa: Canadian Historical
    Association, 1989).
4. T.P. Power, *The Irish in Atlantic Canada, 1780–1900* (Fredericton: New
    Ireland Press, 1991), 7–12.
5. Kerby Miller argues that Irish immigrants, once settled in North America,
    regarded themselves as exiles. Kerby A. Miller, *Emigrants and Exiles:
    Ireland and the Irish Exodus to North America* (Oxford: Oxford University
    Press, 1985), 4, 6, 107.
6. Irish emigration to all parts of the world, from the seventeenth century
    to the present, is covered in Patrick Fitzgerald and Brian Lambkin,

Migration in Irish History, 1607–2007 (New York: Palgrave Macmillan, 2008). For an overview of Irish immigration to North America, see Miller, *Emigrants and Exiles*. For an overall study of Irish immigration to Canada, see Cecil J. Houston and William J. Smyth, *Irish Emigration and Canadian Settlement: Patterns, Links and Letters* (Toronto: University of Toronto Press, 1990) and Donald MacKay, *Flight from Famine: The Coming of the Irish to Canada* (Toronto: Dundurn, 2009).

7. PANB MC2618: Laurence Hughes fonds.

8. PANB MC41: McCarthy family fonds.

9. Terrence M. Punch, "Irish Immigrants to Atlantic Canada, 1832–1846," *The Irish Genealogist* 7 (1989): 642–48.

10. See Lucille H. Campey, *An Unstoppable Force: The Scottish Exodus to Canada* (Toronto: Natural Heritage, 2008), 17–41 for details of the proprietors who assisted Highland Scots to immigrate to the Maritimes.

11. *Sketch of the Province of New Brunswick Published for the Use of Emigrants by the Limerick Emigrants' Friend Society* (Limerick, Ireland: Printed by C. O'Brian, publisher to the Limerick Emigrant's Friend Society, 1832), 5.

12. MCFMS (Ulster-American Folk Park): G.J. in Fredericton to his cousin David Carse, living in county Down, June 28, 1847.

13. PANB MCI387 MS3F: T.B.B. to Samuel Bacon, August 14, 1821.

14. Terrence Punch has demonstrated that the presumed Irish predilection for heavy drinking and violence, compared with the Scots and English, was not reflected in the official crime statistics for Halifax between 1846 and 1861. Terrence M. Punch, "Anti-Irish Prejudice in Nineteenth Century Nova Scotia: The Literary and Statistical Evidence" in Thomas P. Power, *The Irish in Atlantic Canada*, 13–22.

15. *Morning Freeman*, August 30, 1859.

16. John Francis Maguire, *The Irish in America* (New York, Montreal: D. and J. Sadler, 1868.), 2.

17. Phillip Buckner and John G. Reid (eds.), *The Atlantic Region to Confederation: A History* (Toronto: University of Toronto Press, 1993), 107–08, 160–61, 216–17.

18. PANL MG318: Fishery servant's agreement, Trinity, October 17, 1811, between Thomas Verge, Ship Master and Robert George, fisherman.

19. Houston and Smyth, Irish Emigration and Canadian Settlement, 67–78, 191–204.

20. Andrew Hill Clark, *Three Centuries and the Island: A Historical Geography of Settlement and Agriculture in Prince Edward Island, Canada* (Toronto: University of Toronto Press, 1959), 89–91.

21. The development of transatlantic passenger services is discussed in William Forbes Adams, *Ireland and Irish Emigration to the New World from 1815 to the Famine* (New Haven: Yale University Press, 1932) 68–127.

22. Houston and Smyth, *Irish Emigration and Canadian Settlement*, 31–34, 188–204. Dublin was involved with Quebec's timber trade but not with the Saint John trade.

23. Immigration to the region eventually took place from the four Irish provinces of Ulster, Leinster, Connaught, and Munster (see Map 1).

24. Peter Michael Toner, "The Irish of New Brunswick at Mid Century: The 1851 Census," in *New Ireland Remembered: Historical Essays on the Irish in New Brunswick*, edited by P.M. Toner (Fredericton: New Ireland Press, 1988), 106–32.

25. Irish urban dwellers are discussed in Lahey Doyle, "The Irish Experience in Halifax, Nova Scotia, Saint John, New Brunswick, and St. John's, Newfoundland: A Comparative Analysis," MA thesis, St. Mary's University, NS (2010).

26. Terrence M. Punch, "Finding Our Irish," *Nova Scotia Historical Review* 6, no. 1 (1986): 57–62.

27. Norman MacDonald, *Canada, Immigration and Settlement 1763–1841* (London: Longmans & Co., 1939), 512–25.

28. "The Society, in connection with the Established Church of Scotland, for Promoting the Religious Interests of Scottish Settlers in British North America" was founded in 1825. Having been established by Glaswegians, it later came to be known by its condensed name — "The Glasgow Colonial Society."

29. The work of the Society for the Propagation of the Gospel in promoting the interests of the Anglican Church in Atlantic Canada is discussed in Lucille H. Campey, *Planters, Paupers, and Pioneers: English Settlers in Atlantic Canada.* (Toronto: Dundurn, 2010), 70, 75. 81, 84, 103, 141, 199, 205–23.

30. In 1881 the province of Ulster was nearly 50 percent Catholic, 22 percent Church of Ireland, and 26 percent Presbyterian. Munster and Connaught provinces were strongly Catholic (more than 90 percent) as was Leinster (86 percent). Angela McCarthy, *Irish Migrants in New Zealand, 1840–1937: "The Desired Haven"* (Belfast: The Boydell Press, 2005), 239–40.

31. In 1861, New Brunswick's Irish were 60 percent Catholic and 40 percent Protestant. Around 15 percent were Anglican and 15 percent were Presbyterians, with the remainder being Baptist, Methodist, and other nonconformist faiths. See Toner, "The Irish of New Brunswick at Mid Century: The 1851 Census," 106–32.

32. Houston and Smyth, *Irish Emigration and Canadian Settlement*, 169–77.

33. LAC MG25-G271 Vol. 16 #17a: "Truly Canadian," by James McGivern. Memorial windows were dedicated to John McGivern at St. Martin's Church in St. George and at Christ Church in the neighbouring parish of Pennfield, where he had also served the Anglican community.

34. United Society for the Propagation of the Gospel, Series E 1845–1855, quoted in Campey, *Planters, Paupers, and Pioneers*, 141.

35. PANB MC1387: Samuel Bacon fonds.

36. Samuel Delbert Clark, *Church and Sect in Canada* (Toronto: University of Toronto Press, 1948), 234–44.

37. NSARM Acc2011-028: Richey family fonds. *DCB* 11 (Matthew Richey).

38. Maguire, *The Irish in America*, 4.

39. Ibid., 32–33.

40. PAPEI Acc 4495: Reverend David Fitzgerald fonds. Sermon delivered at St. Paul's Anglican Church, Charlottetown, August 20, 1871.

41. James M. Whalen, "Almost as Bad as Ireland: The Experience of the Irish Immigrant in Canada, Saint John, 1847," in Robert O'Driscoll and Lorna Reynolds (eds.), *The Untold Story: The Irish in Canada*, Vol. I, 155–70.

42. The rebellion of Catholics in 1641 against English rule was brutally suppressed by Oliver Cromwell's English army in 1649–50.

43. For example, Tim Coogan argues that the British government was complicit in genocide. Tim Pat Coogan, *The Famine Plot: England's Role in Ireland's Greatest Tragedy* (New York: Palgrave Macmillan, 2012).

Chapter 2: Early Irish Settlers

1. Marjorie Whitelaw (ed.), *The Dalhousie Journals* (Ottawa: Oberon, 1978–82), 60.

2. The Ulster settlers originated from counties Antrim, Armagh, Down, Fermanagh, Londonderry, and Tyrone in Northern Ireland and counties Cavan, Donegal, and Monaghan in the Republic of Ireland.

3. John Robinson and Thomas Rispin, *A Journey Through Nova Scotia: Containing a Particular Account of the Country and Its Inhabitants; with Observations on the Management in Husbandry, the Breed of Horses and Other Cattle, and Everything Material Relating to Farming; to Which Is Added an Account of Several Estates for Sale in Different Townships of Nova-Scotia, with Their Number of Acres and the Price at Which Each Is Set* (York: Printed for the authors by C. Etherington, 1774), 17.

4. Brian Mitchell, *Derry-Londonderry: Gateway to a New World: The Story of Emigration from the Foyle by Sail and Steam* (Londonderry, Northern Ireland: Clearfield Co., 2014), 3–4.

5. J.G. Leyburn, *The Scotch-Irish: A Social History* (Chapel Hill: University of North Carolina Press, 1962).

6. For background information on the political, economic, and religious tensions in Ulster in the seventeenth century, see R.J. Dickson, *Ulster Emigration to Colonial America, 1718–1775* (London: Routledge & Kegan Paul, 1996), 1–17.

7. The largest group of settlers came from the east end of London. Peter L. McCreath and John G. Leefe, *A History of Early Nova Scotia* (Tantallon, NS: Four East Publications, 1990), 196–203.

8. Around 45 percent of the 2,547 settlers who arrived in 1749 were reported to have left the area. Esther Clark Wright, *Planters and Pioneers* (Wolfville, NS: the author, 1982), 8–11.

9. Campey, *Planters, Paupers, and Pioneers*, 83–84.

10. In 1752 the Acadian population was estimated to be between 10,000 and 15,000. Buckner and Reid, *Atlantic Region*, 131, 144–47, 164–65, 198–99.

11. The Mi'kmaq declared war on Britain in 1749, in retaliation for the creation of a British military presence and settlement at Halifax. Despite attempts by the British to bring this war to an end by treaty, the conflict continued until 1760, when a series of treaties brought peace. Meanwhile, with the defeat of the French at Louisbourg in 1758, the Mi'kmaq had been forced to surrender to British control, and from then on they were progressively removed from their hunting grounds to make way for European settlers and to accommodate Britain's defence needs.

12. Some Acadians escaped deportation in 1755 by fleeing to Île Royale (renamed Cape Breton) and the Island of St. John (renamed Prince Edward Island), then still under French control. But when Britain acquired these islands another round of deportations followed in 1858. With the ending

of hostilities in 1763 many Acadians returned to the eastern Maritimes, although they were confined to mainly remote areas and to relatively poor land. W.S. MacNutt, *The Atlantic Provinces: The Emergence of Colonial Society, 1712–1857* (London: McClelland and Stewart, 1965), 62–63, 113; Buckner and Reid, *Atlantic Region*, 144–47, 164–65, 198–99.

13. *Planter* is an old English term for colonist.

14. Buckner and Reid, *Atlantic Region*, 151–52, 162–63.

15. McNutt was born in Londonderry, in the north of Ireland. He immigrated to Virginia around 1750 and later moved to Londonderry, New Hampshire.

16. W.O. Raymond, "Colonel Alexander McNutt and the Pre-Loyalist Settlements of Nova Scotia," *Proceedings and Transactions of the Royal Society of Canada*, 3rd series, 5 (1911) section 2: 69.

17. For a detailed description of McNutt's negotiations with officials, see Dickson, *Ulster Emigration to Colonial America*, 134–52.

18. The people who went to Truro were mainly from New Hampshire while those destined for Onslow came mainly from Massachusetts. J.M. Murphy, *The Londonderry Heirs: A Story of the Settlement of the Cobequid Townships of Truro, Onslow, and Londonderry, in Nova Scotia, Canada, by English-Speaking People in the Period 1760 to 1775* (Middleton, NS: Black Print Co., 1976), 64–67.

19. Ibid., 66–67.

20. Thomas Chandler Haliburton, *An Historical and Statistical Account of Nova Scotia*, vol. 2 (Halifax: J. Howe, 1829), 39.

21. *Belfast Newsletter*, April 24, 1761.

22. Indentured servants received their passage and provisioning in return for working for a specified number of years.

23. Dickson, *Ulster Emigration to Colonial America*, 140–43. See *Belfast Newsletter*, June 2, 1761, for an advertisement stating that the *Jupiter* was preparing to sail to Halifax.

24. Murphy, *The Londonderry Heirs*, 77–85. A log church, built by the Ulster settlers in 1767 at Londonderry, was replaced by a frame church in 1794. The Reverend David Smith, recruited from Scotland in 1769, served as minister, becoming the first permanently settled Presbyterian minister in Canada.

25. NAB CO 218/6, 153-60: Privy Council to the Board of Trade, April 8, 1762, quoted in Dickson, *Ulster Emigration to Colonial America*, 192.

26. The 1762 groups sailed from Londonderry to Halifax in the *Hopewell* and *Nancy*.

27. The letter printed in *Belfast Newsletter*, March, 11, 1762, was signed by the following people: Andrew Ross (Ballyrashane Parish, Antrim), William Moore (Fahan Parish, Donegal), William Henderson (town of Rathmullan Parish, Donegal), William McNutt (Mevagh Parish, Donegal), John Mahon (Drumhome Parish, Donegal), Joseph Crawford (town of Rathmelton, Donegal), Robert Spencer (Clondahorky Parish, Donegal), John Morrison (Tullaghobegley Parish, Donegal), Benjamin McNutt (Kilmacrenan Barony, Donegal), Mark Patton (Faughanvale Parish, Londonderry), John McNutt (Ballynascreen Parish, Londonderry), Daniel Cochran (Derrykeighan Parish, Antrim), Robert Smith (Drumachose Parish, Londonderry), Anthony McLean (town of Letter Kenny, Donegal), John Clark (Tamlaght Finlagan Parish, Londonderry), John Barnhill (Leck Parish, Donegal).

28. Ester Clark Wright, *Planters and Pioneers* (Wolfville, NS: the author, 1982), 18–20.

29. See *Belfast Newsletter*, April 19, 1768, for an advertisement of the *Nancy* sailing.

30. *DCB*, vol. 5, Alexander McNutt. McNutt's name appears in the 1771 census for Truro.

31. For the Onslow inhabitants' petition to the Nova Scotia government for aid in 1762, see: NSARM MG1 vol. 258, no. 19.

32. Extract from Morris's report in Raymond, "Colonel Alexander McNutt and the Pre-Loyalist Settlements of Nova Scotia," 72. The full report is printed in *Report Concerning Canadian Archives for the Year 1904* (Ottawa: S.E. Dawson, 1905), Appendix F (NSARM: call no. F80/C16R/1904). Also see Donald MacKay, *Flight from Famine: The Coming of the Irish to Canada* (Toronto: Natural Heritage, 2009), 24.

33. The Truro group had originated mostly from New England while the Londonderry families came from Ireland.

34. *Nova Scotia Census*, 1770. See the Irish-born entries, which are summarized in Terrence M. Punch, *Erin's Sons: Irish Arrivals in Atlantic Canada, 1761–1853*, vol. 1 (Baltimore, MD: Genealogical Publishing Co., 2008), 172–79.

35. Haliburton, *An Historical and Statistical Account of Nova Scotia*, 47, 49.

36. Dickson, *Ulster Emigration to Colonial America*, 148.

37. Ibid., 149. In 1761–1762 only four vessels left Londonderry for Nova Scotia while thirteen left for the American colonies.

38. A census of 1767, taken in what is now the Maritime provinces, revealed a total population of only 13,374. Bernard Bailyn, *Voyagers to the West:*

Emigration from Britain to America on the Eve of the Revolution (New York: Alfred A. Knopf, 1986), 372.

39. Although appointed lieutenant governor in 1769, Desbrisay waited a decade before taking up his appointment.

40. The proprietors were to get land, upon payment of a quit-rent (a small rent paid in lieu of services that might otherwise be required) assessed at rates ranging from two shillings to six shillings per hundred acres, and had to agree to settle their lands within ten years, at the rate of one hundred people per township. It was also agreed that the quit-rent revenues would be used to finance the island's government, which was established some two years later, in 1769. The condition that the new government's expenses would be paid from the proceeds of quit-rents was not honoured by the proprietors in spite of repeated attempts to force them to pay. F.W.P. Bolger (ed.) *Canada's Smallest Province: A History of Prince Edward Island* (Halifax: Nimbus, 1991), 38–43; J.M. Bumsted, *Land Settlement and Politics in Eighteenth Century Prince Edward Island* (Kingston: McGill-Queen's University Press, 1987), 12–26.

41. The leasehold system was only completely abolished in 1873 when Prince Edward Island entered the Canadian Confederation. Bumsted, *Land Settlement and Politics*, 196–200.

42. Dickson, *Ulster Emigration to Colonial America*, 152–64.

43. *Belfast Newsletter*, February 1, June 21, December 31, 1771.

44. The nine tenants were Barnaby McGuire (a tailor), William Read (a farmer), William McCracken (a blacksmith), and James McCullum (a farmer), all from county Antrim; John Brown, William Crosby, and Nelthorp Carson, all farmers from county Down; James Irwin, a farmer from county Monaghan; and Patrick MacDonell, a mariner from county Down. The names of settlers who signed leases with Thomas Desbrisay or purchased land from him have been compiled from documents held with the Selkirk Papers (LAC MG19-E1). For further details, see Edward MacDonald, *New Ireland: The Irish in Prince Edward Island* (Charlottetown: PEI Museum and Heritage Foundation, 1990), 34–35.

45. *Belfast Newsletter*, July 26, August 13, 1771.

46. Examples of the advertisements are given in Stephen A. Royle and Caitriona Ni Laoire, "Desbrisay's Settlers," *Island Magazine* 51 (2002): 19–23.

47. In addition to the nine tenants identified as having sailed in 1771, the list compiled from the Selkirk Papers reveals that the following tenants

were included among the 188 people who arrived in 1772: John Druitt, Edward Hodskiss, Charles Hyndman, Samuel Kennedy, Thomas McCrow, Edward Rogers, Joseph Johnson, and George Thompson and possibly James Cregg from county Antrim; John Beaty, William and Joseph Corry, John Fullerton, John Hamilton, William McKee, James Mollone, James and Alexander Patterson from county Armagh; Elias Harrison and Robert McConnell from county Down; Robert Lowry from county Tyrone.

48. Falling linen prices in 1771 may have helped to stimulate emigration. See Richard K MacMaster, "Emigration from Ulster to Prince Edward Island, 1770–1790," *Familia* [Ulster Historical Foundation] No. 12 (1996): 14–32.

49. *Belfast Newsletter*, November 8, 1771; Dickson, *Ulster Emigration to Colonial America*, 157.

50. Part of the letter, which was printed in Faulkner's *Dublin Journal*, January 7, 1773, is quoted in Dickson, *Ulster Emigration to Colonial America*, 160.

51. *Belfast Newsletter*, April 30, 1773.

52. Generally, the British government turned a blind eye to the recruitment of British settlers for the colonies, but in this case it took offence to Desbrisay's actions in seeking settlers from a government minister's estate.

53. In addition to the nine families Desbrisay recruited in 1771 and the 188 people in 1772, he brought out a few more in 1773. For the latter group see Dickson, *Ulster Emigration to Colonia America*, 161–63.

54. In 1772, ten Ulster people purchased one-hundred-acre farms from Desbrisay: Thomas Belshaw, John Bunteen, Thomas Hyde, Daniel Maguire, John Morrow, Richard Rogers, Philip Thornton, William Walker, and George Wattson, all from county Antrim, and Charles McNely from county Down. They were all farmers and tradesmen. See Royle and Ni Laoire, "Desbrisay's Settlers," 23.

55. Brendan O'Grady, *Exiles and Islanders the Irish Settlers of Prince Edward Island* (Montreal: McGill-Queen's University Press, 2004), 15–18.

56. Campey, *Planters, Paupers, and Pioneers*, 37–59, 92–97, 128–30.

57. Campey, *An Unstoppable Force*, 65–96.

58. They settled in what became Upper Canada, when the separate provinces of Upper and Lower Canada were created in 1791.

59. Buckner and Reid, *Atlantic Region*, 184–209.

60. Neil MacKinnon, *This Unfriendly Soil: The Loyalist Experience in Nova Scotia 1783-1791* (Kingston, ON: McGill-Queen's University Press, 1986), 158–79.

61. The British Army consisted of British regulars (professional soldiers who served wherever they were needed, usually for life), the provincial corps, and the militia (non-professional soldiers who were responsible for local defence in times of emergency). The soldiers in the provincial corps were organized and trained much like the British regulars but were recruited in North America for service only in that region.

62. The King's Orange Rangers included Irish immigrants who had been recruited in Newfoundland.

63. The Volunteers of Ireland and British Legion regiments sought British recruits, including the Irish-born. See Stuart Salmon, "The Loyalist Regiments of the American Revolutionary War, 1775–1783," Ph.D. dissertation, University of Stirling (2009) 32, 55, 61, 74, 86, 97, 146.

64. Esther Clark Wright, *The Loyalists of New Brunswick* (Fredericton, NB: 1955), 4–6, 151–55.

65. Marion Gilroy, *Loyalists and Land Settlement in Nova Scotia* (Halifax: PANS Publication, No. 4, 1937).

66. Graeme Wynn, "A Region of Scattered Settlements and Bounded Possibilities: North Eastern America 1775–1800," *Canadian Geographer* 31: 319–38.

67. Loyalist concentrations along the north shore at Pictou and Merigomish were principally Scottish.

68. A number of units serving in the Island of St. John had been merged with Timothy Hierlihy's group to form the Nova Scotia Volunteers. Hierlihy had commanded British troops in New York during the American War of Independence.

69. Hierlihy himself was not a Catholic.

70. MacKinnon, *This Unfriendly Soil*, 44. The area then in Sydney County was later renamed Guysborough and Antigonish Counties.

71. Anthony Johnston Angus, *A History of the Catholic Church in Eastern Nova Scotia*, Vol. 1 (Antigonish: St. Francis Xavier University Press, 1960), 126.

72. Reverend James Jones to the Bishop of Quebec, April 27, 1781, Archiepiscopal Archives of Quebec, quoted in Edna C. Wilson, "The Impact of a Century of Irish Catholic Immigration in Nova Scotia (1750–1850)" Ph.D. dissertation, University of Ottawa, 1961, 54.

73. For example, John Hammond and Patrick O'Neil, both disbanded Irish-born soldiers, and the Irish-born John Higgins, a Loyalist who relocated from the United States to the Maritimes in 1784, sought land grants in Cape

Breton in 1803. Their land grant applications appear in the Cape Breton Land Papers. For further details, see Punch, *Erin's Sons*, vol. 1: 89, 90, 93.

74.   O'Grady, *Exiles and Islanders*, 21.

75.   The allocation of land to the Loyalists who settled in Prince Edward Island is discussed in Bumsted, *Land Settlement and Politics*, 98–138.

76.   Clark, *Three Centuries and the Island*, 57–58, 61; Bolger, *Canada's Smallest Province*, 59–64.

Chapter 3: The Newfoundland Irish

1.   Doyle, "The Irish Experience in Halifax, Nova Scotia, Saint John, New Brunswick, and St. John's, Newfoundland," 111.

2.   Cyril Byrne, "The First Irish Foothold in North America," in *The Untold Story: The Irish in Canada*, eds. Robert O'Driscoll and Lorna Reynolds (Toronto: Celtic Arts of Canada, 1988), 1: 171–74.

3.   St. John's had emerged as the colony's principal fishing centre by 1650.

4.   For details of the early English influx to Newfoundland see Campey, *Planters, Paupers, and Pioneers*, 190–223.

5.   Keith Matthews, "A History of the West of England-Newfoundland fishery," unpublished Ph.D. thesis, University of Oxford (1968), 14.

6.   Kildare Dobbs, "Newfoundland and the Maritimes: An Overview," in O'Driscoll and Reynolds, *The Untold Story*, 1: 175–94.

7.   The "Old English Shore" extended between Trepassey on the south to Greenspond on the north.

8.   The extent to which English merchants exercised control over Newfoundland's affairs is discussed in David J. Starkey, "Devonians and the Newfoundland Trade," in *The New Maritime History of Devon*, ed. Michael Duffy et al. (London: Conway Maritime Press in association with the University of Exeter, 1992), 1: 163–71.

9.   Joseph Bouchette, *The British Dominions in North America: A Topographical and Statistical Description of the Provinces of Lower and Upper Canada, New Brunswick, Nova Scotia, the Islands of Newfoundland, Prince Edward Island and Cape Breton*, 2: 181–85. Despite official discrimination against Roman Catholics in Protestant England, Calvert, who himself had converted to the Catholic faith, allowed a Roman Catholic priest to reside in Ferryland.

10.   Dobbs, "Newfoundland and the Maritimes," 175.

11. Wages in Newfoundland were considerably higher than for equivalent work in Ireland. The yearly migration of Irish workers was highly organized and well-administered. John Mannion, *Tipperary Trails to Newfoundland: The Story of Emigration from Tipperary to Newfoundland During the 18th and 19th Centuries* (Tipperary: Ireland Newfoundland Connections Festival, 2012), 4–9.

12. WORO 705:1059/9600/26(i)/ 3: Bishop of Newfoundland, December 4, 1866.

13. Matthews, "A History of the West of England-Newfoundland Fishery," 334–39.

14. By the early eighteenth century the French and British components of the resident population were roughly equal. J.M. Bumsted, *The Peoples of Canada: A Pre-Confederation History* (Toronto: Oxford University Press, 1992), 1: 56–59; Buckner and Reid, *Atlantic Region*, 53–56.

15. Buckner and Reid, *Atlantic Region*, 55–77. W. Gordon Handcock, "English Migration to Newfoundland," in *The Peopling of Newfoundland: Essays in Historical Geography*, edited by John J. Mannion (St. John's: Institute of Social and Economic Research, Memorial University of Newfoundland, 1978), 15–48.

16. The agreement required France to relocate Newfoundland's French inhabitants to Île Royale (later Cape Breton) and to desist from maintaining any fortifications.

17. The French had made Placentia their capital in 1655. Once Britain gained control of Newfoundland the French residents of Placentia were forced to relocate to Louisbourg (Cape Breton).

18. The Irish were less well represented in Trinity Bay, Bonavista Bay, and Notre Dame Bay, which the English continued to dominate.

19. C.W. Doody, "The Irish in Newfoundland," in *The Untold Story: The Irish in Canada*, eds. Robert O'Driscoll and Lorna Reynolds (Toronto: Celtic Arts of Canada, 1988), 1:195–201.

20. Frederick W. Rowe, *History of Newfoundland and Labrador* (Toronto: McGraw-Hill Ryerson, 1980), 214–15.

21. Planters had to pay for supplies at prices determined by the merchants and their earnings were also controlled by the merchants.

22. Census, Newfoundland, 1794–1795. For a list of the Irish householders see Punch, *Erin's Sons*, 4: 80–82.

23. Rowe, *History of Newfoundland and Labrador*, 217.

ATLANTIC CANADA'S IRISH IMMIGRANTS

24. John J. Mannion (ed.), *The Peopling of Newfoundland: Essays in Historical Geography*, Social and Economic Papers No. 8 (St. John's: Institute of Social and Economic Research, Memorial University of Newfoundland, 1978), 1–13.

25. Matthews, "A History of the West of England-Newfoundland Fishery," 549.

26. STRO D3388/23/3: William Dyott to his brother Richard in Lichfield, Staffordshire, July 1787. Dyott had sought refuge at Cape Broyle Harbour.

27. Having arrived in 1784, Father O'Donel founded four parishes at St. John's, Harbour Grace, Placentia, and Ferryland, which were then the main centres of Irish populations.

28. PANL GN 5/4/C/1, Box 1. The names of the men receiving the various punishments are listed in Punch, *Erin's Sons*, 2: 122–25.

29. Doyle, "The Irish Experience in Halifax, Nova Scotia, Saint John, New Brunswick, and St. John's, Newfoundland," 32, 79, 80, 116.

30. The regiment, founded in 1795, was known as His Majesty's Royal Newfoundland Regiment of Foot. For details of the 1800 rebellion see Michael J. McCarthy, *The Irish in Newfoundland 1600–1900: Their Trials, Tribulations and Triumphs* (St. John's: Creative Publishers, 1999), 99–110.

31. John Edward Fitzgerald, "The United Irish Rebellion in Newfoundland, 1799–1800," lecture presented to the Irish Newfoundland Association, St. John's, October 28, 1998.

32. Brigadier-General John Skerrett court-marshalled twelve of those taken, five of whom were sentenced to be hanged and seven of whom were shot.

33. Cyril J. Byrne, "Ireland and Newfoundland: The United Irish Rising of 1798 and the Fencible's Mutiny in St. John's, 1799," *Newfoundland Historical Society Lecture* 37 (November 9, 1977): 4.

34. "Irish Newfoundland Association: Souvenir Programme and Order of Proceedings for the Unveiling of the Historic Plaque Marking the Site of the United Irish Rising in Newfoundland," Belvedere Street, St. John's, Saturday, June 17, 2000.

35. A low-key description of the uprising appeared in the *Sun*, a London newspaper (June 26, 1800).

36. Waldegrave to St. John's Magistrates, August 31, 1797, quoted in Matthews, "A History of the West of England-Newfoundland Fishery," 593.

37. D.W. Prowse, *A History of Newfoundland, from the English, Colonial, and Foreign Records* (London: Eyre and Spottiswoode, 1896), 378.

38. NLI CSO/RP/1821/1228: Petition of Peter Strange requesting government employment, August 20, 1821.

39. SOAS LMS, Jacket B, Folder 2 /45, March 4, 1818.

40. DRO 5592Z/Z/4 Extracts of letters, March 4–31, 1817.

41. Ibid.

42. However, serious problems being caused by the decline in trade and rising poverty of the people still had to be addressed: DRO 5592Z/Z/6 "Brief Considerations on the Nature, Importance and Existing Difficulties of the Newfoundland Trade Presented by a Deputation of Merchants to Lords Liverpool and Bathurst at the Board of Trade, 1817."

43. Prowse, *A History of Newfoundland*, 404–06.

44. PANL Mildred Howard Collection: *Royal Gazette and Newfoundland Advertiser*, 1810–14.

45. Punch, *Erin's Sons*, 1: 105.

46. John J. Mannion, "Old World Antecedents, New World Adaptation: Inistioge (Kilkenny) Immigrants in Newfoundland," *Newfoundland Studies* 5, no. 2 (1989): 112, 121–23, 162.

47. "19th Century Passenger List to Newfoundland," in *An Nasc, Newsletter of the D'Arcy McGee Chair of Irish Studies* 1, no. 2. St. Mary's University, Halifax (Summer 1988): 6–7. The passenger list is taken from NAB CO 194/71, 322–23.

48. Mannion, "Old World Antecedents, New World Adaptations," 103–75.

49. Doyle, "The Irish Experience in Halifax, Nova Scotia, Saint John, New Brunswick, and St. John's, Newfoundland," 86–87.

50. *DCB*, vol. 7. Pierce Sweetman, from county Wexford, came from a prosperous and high status Roman Catholic family. He became a formal partner in the Saunders and Sweetman Company in 1788. Returning to Ireland in 1796, he took over one of his father's large farms and entrusted the Placentia business to a relative, although he continued to manage shipping operations from Waterford.

51. PANL MG49.40: Letter Book of Pierce Sweetman, 1785–1804. Thomas Saunders to his brother, May 11, 1786.

52. PANL MG49.40, List of boat owners, June 2, 1789.

53. John J. Mannion, "Irish Merchants Abroad: The Newfoundland Experience, 1750–1850," in *Newfoundland Studies* 2, 2: 168–78.

54. John J. Mannion, *Irish Settlements in Eastern Canada: A Study of Cultural Transfer and Adaptation* (Toronto: University of Toronto Press, 1974), 15–32.

55. PANL Mildred Howard Collection, 1: 10.

56. The Jerseyside community, just to the north of Placentia, is a lasting reminder of the influx from the Channel Islands, which also occurred at this time.

57. Bouchette, *The British Dominions in North America*, 2: 185.

58. Between 1858 and 1860 nearly 1,800 Irish immigrants arrived in Newfoundland, reflecting an expansion of the province's industrial economy. See Helen Cowan, *British Emigration to British North America: The First Hundred Years* (Toronto: University of Toronto Press, 1961), Appendix B, 290.

59. Census, Newfoundland, 1857. The Protestant to Catholic ratio (virtually synonymous with English to Irish) was around 64,500 Protestants compared with around 57,000 Catholics, suggesting that the English and Irish were present in roughly equal numbers.

60. Edward Wix, *Six Months of a Newfoundland Missionary's Journal from February to August, 1835* (London: Smith, Elder, 1836), 143. Wix was educated at Oxford University and served as an Anglican clergyman in Newfoundland in the 1830s. He was also a member of the St. John's Committee of the Society for Promoting Christian Knowledge, distributing prayer books, bibles, and tracts. He helped to organize a temperance society that met in St. John's and returned to England in later life. See *DCB*, vol. 9 (Edward Wix).

61. Ibid., 6.

62. Ibid., 143–44.

63. NSARM RG1, vol. 337, doc. 20: Clement Hubert to Lt. Gov. Maitland, October 15, 1830.

64. Sean T. Cadigan, *Newfoundland & Labrador: A History* (Toronto: University of Toronto Press, 2009), 128–29.

65. Joseph Arthur de Gobineau, *Voyage a Terre-Neuve* (Paris, 1862), quoted in Dobbs, "Newfoundland and the Maritimes," 177.

66. In the mid-eighteenth century, Newfoundland had a permanent population of 7,500 of whom 4,795 were Catholics, and they were mostly Irish.

Chapter 4: Nova Scotia's Irish and Their Links with Newfoundland

1. Punch, "Finding Our Irish," 49.

2. J.S. Martell, *Immigration to and Emigration from Nova Scotia, 1815–1838* (Halifax, NS: PANS, 1942), 8–9. Because the shipping records are incomplete, it is likely that immigrant numbers were significantly higher.

3. In 1758 the Nova Scotia Assembly decreed that Catholics could not hold public office or acquire land unless it had been granted by the Crown. The province's anti-Catholic legislation was repealed in 1827. Nevertheless, before this, laws forbidding Catholics to hold land were not usually enforced and thus could be ignored with relative impunity.

4. Terrence M. Punch, "The Irish in Halifax, Nova Scotia, before 1830," *Canadian Genealogist* 1, no. 3 (1979): 173–80.

5. Owen Fitzgerald, *The Fitzgerald Family* (Halifax: published by author, February 1984).

6. Terrence M. Punch, "Gentle as the Snow on a Rooftop: The Irish in Nova Scotia to 1830," in *The Untold Story: The Irish in Canada*, eds. Robert O'Driscoll and Lorna Reynolds (Toronto: Celtic Arts of Canada, 1988), 215–29.

7. NAB CO217, vol. 80, no. 135, quoted in Wilson, "The Impact of a Century of Irish Catholic Immigration in Nova Scotia," 57.

8. Punch, "Finding Our Irish," 57–62.

9. The early Ulster settlements are described in Chapter 2.

10. Martell, *Immigration to Nova Scotia, 1815–38*, 42–52.

11. *Acadian Recorder*, October 10, 1818.

12. NAI CSO/OPMA/820 Philip Martin, December 30, 1835.

13. Nova Scotia census, 1871.

14. Andrew H. Clark, "Old World Origins and Religious Adherence in Nova Scotia," *Geographical Review* 1 (1960): 329.

15. Maribelle Smith Smiley, *History of the Smiley Family of Hants County, Nova Scotia* (Nova Scotia: published by author, n.d.), 3; *The Nova Scotian*, July 31, 1828. The *Dispatch* had carried two hundred passengers of whom 142 were rescued. John and Joseph Smiley were former weavers.

16. Another group to arrive in 1828 were 233 Irish people who formed part of a two-thousand-strong Brazilian expedition that had failed. Some also ended up in Saint John. As was the case in Halifax, they arrived in a destitute state and needed to be supported by public funds. See Koral Lavorgna, *New Brunswick as a Home for Immigrants*, 6–7, which can be found at the New Brunswick Irish Portal: www.archives.gnb.ca/Irish/databases_en.html.

17. John Mulholland was the principal of King's College at Windsor in 1849. The Anglican college had been founded by Loyalists in 1789.

18. PRONI D 1424/11/1: J.G. Mulholland to G. Kirkpatrick, March 21, 1849.

19. See "Cumberland County Settlers from Ireland," in Punch, *Erin's Sons*, 2: 112–13. This list reveals that the Cumberland Irish originated from counties Kilkenny, Cork, and Sligo in the south and from Ulster in the north.

20. Overcrowding had been particularly excessive during the great surges of Highland emigration to Nova Scotia and Prince Edward Island in the late eighteenth and early nineteenth centuries. The 1803 Passenger Act was intended to curb such abuses, although its ultimate impact was to cause fares to rise sharply. The formula, stipulating the minimum space requirement, allowed one person for every two tons burthen, an allocation that far exceeded earlier limits. For further details of transatlantic passenger legislation, see Lucille H. Campey, *Fast Sailing and Copper-Bottomed: Aberdeen Sailing Ships and the Emigrant Scots They Carried to Canada* (Toronto: Natural Heritage, 2002), 99–113.

21. Adams, *Ireland and Irish Emigration*, 86–87.

22. On October 16, 1816, the *Royal Gazette and Newfoundland Advertiser* carried a notice stating that fifty-nine passengers, who had travelled in the *Speculator* in the previous year, had to pay their passages by November 10 or legal action would be taken against them. The names are listed in Punch, *Erin's Sons*, 3: 78–79.

23. With the easing of space restrictions in the 1817 Passenger Act, it was cheaper for immigrants to sail to British America than to the United States, whose ships had to allow passengers more space. As a result, many immigrants destined for New York, Philadelphia, and other places to the west could economize on their fares by travelling via Quebec and New Brunswick.

24. Terrence M. Punch, "The Irish in Halifax: 1815–1867: A Study in Ethnic Assimilation" (Halifax: Dalhousie University, M.A. thesis, 1976), 74.

25. Punch, "The Irish in Halifax, Nova Scotia before 1830," 178.

26. Angus Anthony Johnston, *A History of the Catholic Church in Eastern Nova Scotia* (Antigonish: St. Francis Xavier University Press, 1960), 2 vols., 145.

27. Wilson, "The Impact of a Century of Irish Catholic Immigration in Nova Scotia," 47–48.

28. NSARM MG3, vol. 6190: Thomas Maher fonds.

29. NAB CO217/99, 7–10: Surveyor-General Morris to Dalhousie, December 13, 1816. Mice ate large quantities of grain and other food and contaminated the rest, the latter representing ten times the amount consumed. As a consequence of frosts and a considerable loss of food stocks, these settlers suffered severe hardship.

30. Ibid.
31. For details of Shelburne's demise, see Campey, *Planters, Paupers, and Pioneers*, 68–72, 90.
32. *Acadian Recorder*, August 8, 1818. Letter written by "Agricola," the pen-name of John Young, a Halifax merchant.
33. Ninety-nine of the disbanded soldiers were from the Newfoundland Fencibles and 172 were from the Nova Scotia Fencibles.
34. J.S. Martell, "Military Settlements in Nova Scotia after the War of 1812," *Nova Scotia Historical Society Collection* 24 (1938): 75–106.
35. In addition to New Ross, attempts were made to found two other military settlements, but these were equally unsuccessful. One was located at Dalhousie and the other at Wellington, both being situated along the proposed road from Annapolis to Halifax.
36. The Dublin tradesmen sailed to St. John's in the *Concord* and later sailed to Halifax in the *Kitty*. Those people who sailed in the *Kitty* are listed in NAB CO 194/160, 175. The list has been reproduced in Punch, *Erin's Sons*, vol. 1, 70–71.
37. NAB CO 217/98: Dalhousie to Bathurst, January 2, 1817.
38. NSARM RG1, vol. 305, doc. 121: Michael Tobin and Samuel Cunard to Dalhousie, February 9, 1818.
39. Martell, *Immigration to Nova Scotia, 1815–1838*, 22–23.
40. Adams, *Ireland and Irish Emigration*, 87.
41. Martell, *Immigration to Nova Scotia, 1815–1838*, 97.
42. NSARM RG1, vol. 230, doc. 132: Sir Charles Hamilton to Sir James Kempt, December 8, 1821.
43. Adams, *Ireland and Irish Emigration*, 152–53.
44. Around 1,800 Irish people are recorded in official documents as having arrived in Halifax from Newfoundland between 1815 and 1838. However, various contemporary reports indicate that the actual figure must have been much larger.
45. *Acadian Recorder*, January 25, 1817.
46. *Acadian Recorder*, January 4, January 25, and February 8, 1817.
47. NAB CO 217/101, 441.
48. *Royal Gazette & Newfoundland Advertiser*, August 16, 1831.
49. *Acadian Recorder*, October 10, 1818.
50. Mitchell, *Derry-Londonderry: Gateway to a New World*, 6–8.
51. Minutes of the Nova Scotia Council, June 3, 1831, quoted in Martell, *Immigration to Nova Scotia, 1815–1838*, 18.

52. NSARM RG1, vol. 307, doc. 124: Sir James Kempt to Lord Goderich, September 7, 1827.

53. Terrence Punch's reconstituted partial passenger list for the crossing of the *Cumberland* to Halifax in 1827 reveals a startling death toll immediately after the crossing. See Punch, *Erin's Sons*, 1: 97–99.

54. Martell, *Immigration to Nova Scotia, 1815–1838*, 23–29.

55. Wynne, "A Region of Scattered Settlements," 323–24; MacKinnon, *This Unfriendly Soil*, 30–31.

56. Ann Wallace, *Life in the Irish Salmon River District* (Antigonish: Casket Printing and Publishing, 1992), 9, 17.

57. Harriet Cunningham Hart, *History of the County of Guysborough* (Belleville, ON: Mika, 1975), 72.

58. Nova Scotia census, 1818. The Irish census data is reproduced in Punch, *Erin's Sons*, 1: 77–81.

59. Stephen J. Hornsby, *Nineteenth Century Cape Breton: A Historical Geography* (Montreal: McGill-Queen's University Press, 1992), 4–15, 85–95.

60. Cape Breton was separated from Nova Scotia in 1784 and was re-annexed to it in 1820. During this period Cape Breton was made an adjunct colony of Nova Scotia, seriously weakening the island's ability to organize its own affairs. It had an appointed council, but no elected House of Assembly, and the island did not have a system of taxation in place.

61. While Newfoundland's fishery became less reliant on the seasonal labour being imported from southwest England and Ireland from the early nineteenth century, largely because jobs could be filled by permanent residents, the situation was different in Cape Breton. Here, the Channel Island companies, which owned the fishery, maintained their grip and continued to bring some of their workforce to the fishing stations on a temporary basis each year.

62. Census of Nova Scotia, 1871.

63. Hornsby, *Nineteenth Century Cape Breton*, 15–18.

64. Johnston, *History of the Catholic Church in Eastern Nova Scotia*, 123, 150, 179, 182, 295.

65. J.S. Martell, "Early Coal Mining in Nova Scotia," in *Cape Breton Historical Essays*, eds. Don MacGillivray and Brian Tenyson (Sydney, NS: College of Cape Breton Press, 1981), 169.

66. Kenneth Donovan, "Mary Grace Barron and the Irish of Ingonish, Cape Breton, 1822–1999," *The Nashwaak Review* 6–7 (Fall 1999): 177–237.

67. NSARM RG 20/B/5/1128, /2124 quoted in Hornsby, *Nineteenth Century Cape Breton*, 59.

68. Hornsby, *Nineteenth Century Cape Breton*, 95–110.

69. Ibid., 121–22, 132–33,186.

70. Settlers paid £3 to £5 initially for a one-hundred-acre lot. It was subject to an annual quit-rent of 2 s., payable after two years; but in practice, quit-rents were never collected. Hornsby, *Nineteenth Century Cape Breton*, 48–53.

71. NSARM RG20"B": Cape Breton Land Papers, 1794–1839. The names of the Irish people listed have been transcribed in Punch, *Erin's Sons*, 1: 82–97.

72. Haliburton, *An Historical and Statistical Account of Nova Scotia*, 210.

73. Angus Anthony Mackenzie, *The Irish in Cape Breton* (Antigonish: Formac, 1979), 31–36, 48–53. By 1871 there was also a small Irish community at Neil's Harbour.

74. James Kiley of Wexford, Ireland, and Baddeck, Cape Breton: www.genealogy.com?users/k/i/l/Colin-Kiley.

75. Moses H. Doyle, *The Irish Pioneers of Margaree, Cape Breton Island, Nova Scotia* (Ottawa: published by author, 1994), i–xi.

76. Morse, "Immigration to Nova Scotia, 1839–51," 72.

77. See Chapter 7.

78. *The Nova Scotian*, May 24, 1847.

79. *Acadian Recorder*, May 29, 1847.

80. LAC MG24-I122/7: Patrick Nowlan fonds.

81. NSARM RG1, Vol. 116: Falkland to Stanley, December 21, 1841, quoted in Martell, *Immigration to Nova Scotia, 1815–1838*, 14.

82. Mackenzie, *The Irish in Cape Breton*, 103–07. The Cape Breton Land Papers also reveal that a sizeable number of Irish people originated from Kilkenny.

83. Melon Centre for Migration Studies: letter dated November 18, 1831.

Chapter 5: New Brunswick's Irish and the Timber Trade

1. Thomas Moore, *The Life and Death of Lord Edward Fitzgerald* (London: Longman, Rees, Orme, Brown and Green, 1831), 43–44.

2. In spite of widespread and repeated complaints within Britain over the high cost of timber, the protective tariffs remained in place until 1860. Ralph Davis, *The Industrial Revolution and British Overseas Trade* (Leicester:

Leicester University Press, 1979), 48–49. Duties increased from 25s. per load in 1804 to 54s. 6d. per load in 1811.

3.   Graeme Wynn, *Timber Colony: An Historical Geography of Early Nineteenth-Century New Brunswick* (Toronto: University of Toronto Press, 1981), 11–53.

4.   The Loyalist settlements extended from the mouth of the Saint John River to above Woodstock (now in Carleton County). For a detailed account of Loyalist settlements, see W.F. Ganong, "Monograph of the Origins of Settlements in the Province of New Brunswick," *Transactions of the Royal Society of Canada*, 2nd series (10), sections 1–2 (1904): 52–73.

5.   Bouchette, *The British Dominions in North America*, 2: 235.

6.   Most of the customs records were lost in 1877 in the great fire of Saint John. They only survive for 1815, 1832, 1833–34, and 1837–38.

7.   Ganong, "Settlements in New Brunswick," 75. A total of 1,312 immigrants arrived at Saint John from Londonderry in 1819.

8.   The emigrant societies were formed in 1820 with funds raised locally by individuals with only a small level of support from the provincial purse. They were the primary source of relief to immigrants for the following decade.

9.   NAI CSO/RP/1822/66. Twenty-four names were listed in the petition: Robert Parker, Joseph Cattney, Arthur Sumerville, Alexander Komafrem, Isaac Larmon, James Thompson, John Thompson, James McCalister, John Redmond, Charles Fleming, James Anderson, George Barnet, Thomas Wright, William Sinclair, Andrew Rankin, William Irwin, Thomas Amos, William Gounde, Robert Gibson, Robert Maxwell, John Mitchell, James Maxwell, John Maxwell, and George Ashmore.

10.   Lucille H. Campey, *With Axe and Bible: The Scottish Pioneers of New Brunswick, 1784–1874* (Toronto: Dundurn, 2007), 3–94.

11.   Ganong, "Settlements in New Brunswick," 73–94. Immigrant numbers peaked in 1847 at 14,879, the overwhelming number being Irish.

12.   J.S. Buckingham, *Canada, Nova Scotia, New Brunswick & Other British Provinces in North America: With a Plan of National Colonization* (London, Paris: Fisher & Sons, 1843), 428.

13.   Peter Fisher, *History of New Brunswick* (Saint John, NB: reprinted jointly by the Government of New Brunswick and W.S. Fisher under the auspices of the New Brunswick Historical Society, 1921 (originally published 1825), 85.

14.   Ibid., 76.

15.   New Brunswick census, 1871.

16. Data on the people from county Londonderry who immigrated to North America between 1833 and 1839 was collected by the Ordnance Survey of Ireland. It includes immigrant destinations, religious affiliations, parish of origin, age, and year of immigration. See Brian Mitchell, *Irish Emigration Lists, 1833–1839: Lists of Emigrants Extracted from Ordnance Surveys of the Counties of Londonderry and Antrim* (Baltimore: Genealogical Publishing Company, 1989). The collection has been digitized.

17. The Ordnance Survey data for county Antrim reveals that more than 80 percent of immigrants who went to North America between 1835 and 1839 carried some money with them. Cecil J. Houston and William J. Smyth, *Irish Emigration and Canadian Settlement: Patterns, Links, and Letters* (Toronto: University of Toronto Press, 1990), 59, 71–72, 227.

18. By 1785, Charlotte County had acquired 20 percent of New Brunswick's Loyalists. T.W. Acheson, "A Study in the Historical Demography of a Loyalist County," *Social History* 1 (April 1968): 53–65.

19. "*Dorcas Savage* Passenger List, 1818," *Generations, Journal of the New Brunswick Genealogical Society* 36, no. 1 (Spring 2015): 66.

20. Immigrant ship arrivals at St. Andrews from Belfast have been taken from the *Belfast Newsletter*. A few arrivals from Londonderry were recorded as well. No doubt, passenger arrivals at Saint John from both Londonderry and Belfast were considerable at this time, but the ship names and passenger numbers are not known due to the loss of customs records.

21. J. Hannay, *History of New Brunswick: Its Resources and Advantages* (Saint John: John A. Bowes, 1909), 1: 353.

22. Abraham Gesner, *New Brunswick with Notes for Emigrants: Comprehending the Early History, Settlement, Topography, Statistics, Natural History, Etc.* (London: Simmonds and Ward, 1847), 315–16.

23. PRONI T3032/1/1: Henry Coulter to Rev. William Moreland, June 14, 1820. In his letter, Henry Coulter voiced his disapproval of the continuing use of slaves in the southern United States.

24. Baillie was named after Thomas Baillie, the surveyor general of New Brunswick.

25. Ganong, "Settlements in New Brunswick," 113, 177.

26. Wynn, *Timber Colony*, 162.

27. Ibid., 44–45, 95–96.

28. John Higgins to John Ward, November 5, 1822, quoted in Wynn, *Timber Colony*, 45.

29. Wynn, *Timber Colony*, 32–33.

30. NAB CO 188/75, 229–31.

31. Acheson, "Historical Demography of a Loyalist County," 58–61.

32. With a steadily deteriorating timber trade, many of Charlotte County's residents were leaving for Upper Canada and the United States, where better land and job prospects were available.

33. PRONI D3305/1/3: William Gamble to his brother, March 23, 1857.

34. PRONI D3305/1/6: William Gamble to his brother, September 1, 1862.

35 PRONI D3305/1/11: Malcolm Gamble to his brother and sister, May 30, 1869.

36. SOAS MMS, W. Bennett, November 16, 1804.

37. Buckner and Reid, *Atlantic Region*, 295–96, 337–38.

38. Doyle, "The Irish Experience in Halifax, Nova Scotia, Saint John, New Brunswick, and St. John's, Newfoundland," 41. T.W. Acheson, "The Irish Community in Saint John, 1815–1850," in *New Ireland Remembered: Historical Essays on the Irish in New Brunswick*, ed. P.M. Toner (Fredericton, NB: New Ireland Press, 1988), 29–54.

39. Peter Michael Toner, "The Origins of New Brunswick Irish, 1851," *Journal of Canadian Studies* 23: 1–2 (1988), 104–19, quoted in Houston and Smyth, *Irish Emigration and Canadian Settlement*, 68–69.

40. Houston and Smyth, *Irish Emigration and Canadian Settlement*, 204. Acheson, "The Irish Community in Saint John, 1815–1850," 41.

41. Peter Michael Toner, "The Irish of New Brunswick at Mid Century: The 1851 Census," in *New Ireland Remembered: Historical Essays on the Irish in New Brunswick*, ed. P.M. Toner (Fredericton, NB: New Ireland Press, 1989), 106–32.

42. PRONI T2125/7/2: Robert McClory to David McClory, November 15, 1819 (also held by LAC as MG40-R92 & R93).

43. PRONI Mic 6/127: James Ward to his father, August 17, 1834 (microfilmed with permission of the Royal Irish Academy).

44. Ganong, "Settlements in New Brunswick," 141. In 1866, Irishtown was a fishing community with approximately twenty-five families, see www.newirelandnb.ca.

45. The group of two hundred who settled at Saint John's Lower Cove included people from counties Armagh and Down. The group sailed in 1834 from Newry in the *Cupid* of Londonderry. Peter Murphy, *From Ireland to Saint John: Together in Exile* (Saint John: Lingley Printing, 1990), ix–xx. For the passenger list, see www.theshipslist.com.

46. 1851 census of New Brunswick. County Louth arrivals in the 1830s included Ellen and Peter Casely, James Murphy, James and Sarah Quinn, Stephen Thompson, and Mary, Patrick, and Thomas Trainor.

47. 1851 census of New Brunswick.

48. Johnston, *Notes on North America*, 1: 117.

49. Ibid., 124–25.

50. 1871 census of New Brunswick.

51. Ganong, "Settlements in New Brunswick," 175.

52. Rev. W. Christopher Atkinson, *An Historical and Statistical Account of New Brunswick, British North America with Advice for Emigrants* (Edinburgh: Printed by Anderson & Bryce, 1844), 88, 93.

53. LAC MG25–G320: Howe family collection; county origins in the New Brunswick census, 1851.

54. Gesner, *New Brunswick with Notes for Emigrants*, 148.

55. LAC M-1352: Glasgow Colonial Society Papers: Welsh to Rev. Burns, December 10, 1829.

56. Atkinson, *An Historical and Statistical Account of New Brunswick*, 90–91. Ganong, "Settlements in New Brunswick," 145.

57. Ganong, "Settlements in New Brunswick," 127, 142, 145.

58. Ibid., 133.

59. PANB MC2106: Robinson family collection.

60. The Henderson settlement included Baptists who built their first church in 1855. See www.drh24.wordpress.com/2009/12/14/henderson-settlement; Ganong, "Settlements in New Brunswick," 138.

61. Ganong, "Settlements in New Brunswick," 170.

62. Ibid., 134, 141.

63. Ibid., 130, 148. Enniskillen is in county Fermanagh.

64. Ibid., 171.

65. Ibid., 144.

66. Gesner, *New Brunswick with Notes for Emigrants*, 152–53.

67. PANB MC1847: An account by Alexander Machum of New Jerusalem.

68. PANB MC1401: Alexander Machum fonds. Alexander wrote an account of his life when aged seventy-four. It covers the period from September 17, 1845, to March 15, 1850, and February 9 to May 12, 1864.

69. Ibid., 19. The Orange Order's role in maintaining the solidarity of Protestants in Atlantic Canada is discussed in Chapter 9.

70. Another Irishman made good was George Inch, whose parents originated from Fermanagh. Born in Gagetown in 1825, he became a merchant in

Kings County, although he was buried in New Jerusalem where his parents and siblings resided. See PANB MC3293: George Inch fonds.

71. Letter of David Moore, New Jerusalem, to his brother in Carndonagh, Donegal, June 28, 1840, reproduced in Marion Gilchrist Reicker, *A Time There Was: Petersville and Other Abandoned Settlements in Queens County, N.B., 1815–1953* (Jemseg, NB: Queens County Historical Society, 1984), 17–19 (PANB MC80–1038). David had a third brother who settled along the Salmon River (Chipman Parish), joining others who had come from his home parish in Donegal.

72. Irish immigrants formed the Boland Settlement in 1848. Ganong, "Settlements in New Brunswick," 118.

73. Fredericton had been selected as the capital because it was the highest point on the Saint John River that was navigable for ocean-going vessels.

74. The 1871 census reveals that the city of Fredericton accommodated about one-third of York's Irish residents, while the remaining two-thirds lived in rural parishes.

75. Many of Laurence Hughes's brothers and sisters emigrated, but most went to the United States.

76. PANB MC2618: Laurence Hughes fonds, MS1A, Thomas Hughes to Laurence, January 24, 1837.

77. Ibid., MS1B, John Jackson to Laurence, February 17, 1848; MS1C, March 28, 1850; MS1D, November 24, 1851; MS1E, Edward Hughes to Laurence, July 11, 1852.

78. Ibid., MS1F, Patrick Hughes to Laurence, May 29, 1851; MS1G, July 18, 1851.

79. Ganong, "Settlements in New Brunswick," 137.

80. The company, founded in 1831, purchased a tract of around six hundred thousand acres in York County north of Fredericton. For details of the company's prospectus, see NAB CO 384/41, 319–20. The land company published extensive publicity. See, for example, New Brunswick and Nova Scotia Land Company, *Sketches in New Brunswick in the Year 1833 ... and ... the Operations of the Association During the Years 1834 and 1835* and *Practical Information Respecting New Brunswick for the Use of Persons Intending to Settle Upon the Lands of the New Brunswick and Nova Scotia Land Company* (London: Pelham Richardson, 1843).

81. J.F.W. Johnston, *Notes on North America: Agricultural, Economical and Social* (Edinburgh: William Blackwood & Sons, 1851), 2: 177. The New Brunswick and Nova Scotia Land Company's two major settlements were

located at Harvey and Stanley. Both attracted English and Scottish settlers. For further details, see Campey *Planters, Paupers, and Pioneers*, 144–56.

82. Ganong, "Settlements in New Brunswick," 155, 173.

83. While Newmarket and Smithfield bring to mind English place names, it is possible that Newmarket might commemorate Newmarket in county Cork and Smithfield may have been named after Smithfield in Dublin.

84. Ganong, "Settlements in New Brunswick," 147. New Brunswick census, 1861.

85. The Cork settlement was formerly called the Teetotal Settlement. Ganong, "Settlements in New Brunswick," 125.

86. Johnston, *Notes on North America*, 1: 175–76.

87. Petition of Miles O'Leary and thirty-three others, dated December 10, 1841, Wilmot to Lieutenant-Colonel Sir W.M.G. Colebrooke, Lieutenant Governor of New Brunswick, December 2, 1841, in PP 1842(373)XXXI. The settlers were required to build part of the St. Andrews Road in exchange for their land grants, which were located on the eastern side of the road.

88. PANB RS24: Journals of the House of Assembly, 1843, xcvi–xcvii. Report of Hon. L. A. Wilmot, Commissioner for the Teetotal Settlement. Mr. Perley's report provides the names of the thirty-five heads of households living in the settlement in 1843.

89. Carleton County was created from York County circa 1831.

90. William P. Kilfoil, *Johnville: The Centennial Story of an Irish Settlement* (Fredericton: published by author, 1962).

91. A similar scheme, involving Scottish Presbyterians from the northeast of Scotland, was launched by the Reverend Charles Glass in 1861. Named after its founder, Glassville was located just to the south of Johnville in Carleton County. For further details, see Campey, *Axe and Bible*, 114–17.

92. Statement issued by Bishop Sweeney in 1861 quoted in Kilfoil, *Johnville*, 13.

93. Similar schemes to assist poor Irish people living in Saint John to obtain land for settlement were also offered in Westmorland, Sunbury, Queens, and Kings Counties. However, they were unsuccessful owing to their remote locations and poor land.

94. Kilfoil, *Johnville*, 24. The early petitioners for land are listed on pages 28–29.

95. T.C.L. Ketchum, *A Short History of Carleton County* (Woodstock, NB: Sentinel, 1922), 67.

96. Maguire, *The Irish in America*, 56.

97. Ibid., 66–67.

98. PANB RS24 1837/peFile 7 #22: Petition to Sir John Harvey, July 6, 1837. Names: John Bedwin JP, Richard Witcham JP, John Dibbler JP, James Kitchen JP, A.I. Garden JP, A.I. Carman JP, J.M. Garden, Joseph Phillips, Laban Stoddard, Daniel Foster, Ralph Kitchener, Hezekiah Stoddard, Richard Dibbler, Joseph Haney, John Harper, W. Jenning, S. Grosvenor, John Burtin, George Williams, O. Dibbler, Samuel D. Lee Street (Rector of Woodstock), Richard English, Thomas G. Cunliffe, Charles Raymond, William Suly, John Winchan, W.S. Newham, John Bedell, JP, Avner Bull, George Bedell, Walter Bedell, and A.K. Medislertrudy.

99. Ganong, "Settlements in New Brunswick," 141.

100. Ketchum, *History of Carleton County*, 58. The Newburg settlers included Martin Hale, Peter Gallagher, William Monahan, John Martin, Frank Montague, Charles Cunningham, John McGuire, and Frank McCarron.

101. Wicklow, carved from Kent Parish, might have been named after county Wicklow, Ireland, but its relatively small Catholic population suggests otherwise.

102. Richmond Parish was created from Woodstock Parish in 1853.

103. Gloucester and Kent Counties were created from Northumberland County in 1826.

104. Bouchette, *The British Dominions in North America*, 2: 132.

105. Houston and Smyth, *Irish Emigration and Canadian Settlement*, 197, 203.

106. Bouchette, *The British Dominions in North America*, 2: 135.

107. PANB MC1729: Valentine Gibbs fonds, Dooly to Gibbs, August 3, 1832. Valentine Gibbs, also from county Kilkenny, probably emigrated with his parents and initially settled in the Miramichi area. The family had moved to Lower Pokemouche in Gloucester County by 1820. Gibbs, a farmer/lumberman, was instrumental in founding the Gloucester County Agricultural Society. He died in 1847 from "immigrant fever" while assisting newly arrived settlers.

108. Ibid., Silvester Dooly to Valentine Gibbs, August 16, 1836.

109. The 1851 census reveals that significant numbers from counties Kilkenny, Tipperary, Limerick, Waterford, and Monaghan also settled in Northumberland County.

110. William Davidson, a Scot, was the region's first timber trade entrepreneur. He was prepared to take risks, and had tremendous business acumen and great qualities of endurance. Campey, *Axe and Bible*, 20–25, 50–59.

111. PANB MC1753/MS1/E: Harley family collection. Article on the life of Mary Ann Harley (Henry) published in the *Portland Daily Press*, February

7, 1898. Mary was the sister of John Harley, who became a shipbuilder. She married John Henry and they had eight children.

112. The Miramichi newspaper account of the fire that appeared on October 11, 1825, was reported in John MacGregor, *Historical and Descriptive Sketches of the Maritime Colonies of British America* (London: Longman, Rees, Orme, Brown and Green, 1828), 169–72.

113. Robert Cooney, *A Compendious History of the Northern Part of the Province of New Brunswick and of the District of Gaspe in Lower Canada* (Chatham, NB: D.G. Smith, 1896), 78.

114. Ganong, "Settlements in New Brunswick," 114. The Glasgow-based Gilmour, Rankin & Co. controlled timber operations on the Miramichi River. The company owned the largest shipping fleet in Britain, with many of their vessels being built at Douglastown.

115. Gesner, *New Brunswick with Notes for Emigrants*, 193. Ganong, "Settlements in New Brunswick," 117. Blackville attracted Loyalists who had moved to it from the Saint John area.

116. Gesner, *New Brunswick with Notes for Emigrants*, 194.

117. PANB MC41: McCarthy family fonds. John's son Edward became a prosperous farmer and acquired property in Chatham.

118. Johnston, *Notes on North America*, 1: 111.

119. W.S. MacNutt, *New Brunswick: A History, 1784–1867* (Toronto: Macmillan, 1984), 180.

120. William A. Spray, "The Irish in Miramichi," in *New Ireland Remembered: Historical Essays on the Irish in New Brunswick*, ed. P.M. Toner (Fredericton: New Ireland Press, 1988), 57.

121. *Royal Gazette*, April 6, 1824.

122. NAB CO 188/35: Campbell to Goderich, February 14, 1832.

123. Cooney, *History of Northern New Brunswick*, 120.

124. Joseph A. King, *Ireland to North America: Emigrants from West Cork* (LaFayette: K & K Publications, 1995), 44–72.

125. NAS GD 45/3/159/2: Sir Howard Douglas, Lieutenant Governor of New Brunswick to Lord Dalhousie, October 19, 1825.

126. Ibid.

127. Fisher, *History of New Brunswick*, 39.

128. Bouchette, *The British Dominions in North America*, 2: 132.

129. Wynn, *Timber Colony*, 36. The cutting of trees also stimulated settlement in the Saint John River Valley and in the Richibucto region.

130. *DCB*, vol. 10 (John Harley). PANB MC1753: Harley family collection.

131. *DCB*, vol. 13 (George Burchill).

132. Wynn, *Timber Colony*, 36–39.

133. Ganong, "Settlements in New Brunswick," 116, 141.

134. Alexander Munro, *New Brunswick with a Brief Outline of Nova Scotia and Prince Edward Island* (Belleville, ON: Mika Studio, 1972), 194 (first published 1855 by Richard Nugent, Halifax, NS).

135. Ganong, "Settlements in New Brunswick," 141, 153.

136. Margaret Hunter, *Pioneer Settlers in the Bay of Chaleur in the Nineteenth and Twentieth Centuries* (Sackville, NB: Tribune Press, 1978), 17–21. The petitioners included: Jeremiah Ahern, Thomas Madden, James Madden, Richard Coombs, Joseph Coombs, Patrick Riordon, Samuel Salter, Matthew Crimmin, Patrick Sisk, Patrick Foley, Daniel Coholan, Bartholomew Whelton, Jeremiah Cowhig, Cornelius Coughlan, Jeremiah Murphy, Jeremiah Fitzpatrick, Margaret Hillock, Timothy McCarthy, and widow Ellen Crowly.

137. The 1871 census reveals that the Irish represented 45 percent of New Bandon's population.

138. Cooney, *History of Northern New Brunswick*, 186–87.

139. Johnston, *Notes on North America*, 2: 16.

140. PANB MC651: Robert Eddy fonds.

141. Ganong, "Settlements in New Brunswick," 180.

142. PANB MC3710 MS1C: Martha (Moorhead) Ellis fonds, death notice February 9, 1935. Martha Moorhead was born in Londonderry in 1851. She and her brother James immigrated to New Brunswick in 1873.

143. Wynn, *Timber Colony*, 164–65.

144. John Meahan, a Roman Catholic, represented Gloucester in the Legislative Assembly of New Brunswick from 1862 to 1870. In 1860 he contributed funds toward the establishment of schools in Omagh, Ireland. See PANB MC3075: Meahan family collection.

145. Stanley T. Spicer, *Masters of Sail: The Era of Square-Rigged Vessels in the Maritime Provinces* (Toronto: McGraw-Hill Ryerson, 1968), 110.

146. LAC MG24 D50, Daniel McGruar fonds: letter dated July 4, 1859.

147. NLI Ms 20,628: Studdert Papers:/MS1Browne to Michael Studdert in county Clare, July 23, 1843. A copy of the Studdert Papers is held by PANB; (See MC3028: John Browne Letters).

148. Ibid., /MS2, Feb 8, 1848, /MS3, January 16, 1849.

149. Another Irish community formed just south of South Branch called Balla Philip, named after Ballyphilip in county Down (Ulster). The Murphy Settlement sprouted to the south of Balla Philip, and southwest of it, Sweeneyville appeared. It was named after Bishop John Sweeney. The bishop secured lands for Irish settlers in 1864, but the land was boggy and few of them remained. "The Irish of Kent," at www.newirelandnb.ca/Communities.

150. Johnston, *Notes on North America*, 2: 56. Ganong, "Settlements in New Brunswick," 131, 134.

151. PANB MC2688: William Martin fonds. His list of Irish people in receipt of land grants by 1831 includes: Alexander Boyle (800 acres), Mundleville and Main River (Weldford); John Brown (55), East Branch; Samuel Brown (200), South Branch; James Brown (100), East Branch; Mary Brown (200), Targettville; Sarah Brown (100), South Branch;, James Burns (100), South Branch; Terrence Curran (100), South Branch; Terrence Curran (200), Targettville; John Curran (200), South Branch; Francis Curran (200), South Branch; William Fitzgerald (200), Main River; Alex Fraser (100), Rexton; Pat Hanrahan (100), Mundleville; Andrew Hudson (200), South Branch; Thomas Hudson (180), South Branch; William Martin (200), Main River; Pat Phelan (200), East Branch; John and Robert Kinsella (each 200), South Branch; Patrick Fahey (200), South Branch; James Fawey (100), Targettville; Thomas and Moses McDermott (each 200), Targettville; William Rowett (100), Targettville; Thomas Park (200) Main River; and Martin Walsh (100), Main River.

152. *DCB*, vol. 12 (Henry O'Leary). O'Leary represented Kent County as a Liberal in the New Brunswick legislature. He also controlled lobster canneries in Prince Edward Island.

153. Albert County was created from Westmorland County in 1845. It contains the original parishes of Hillsborough and Hopewell, part of Salisbury, and the later parishes of Coverdale and Harvey.

154. Alma Parish was carved out of Harvey Parish in 1851.

155. Heather Long, *Good Green Hope: The Irish Catholic Settlers of Albert County, New Brunswick* (Halifax: published by author, 1995) (see also: PANB MC80 2014).

156. Johnston, *Notes on North America*, 2: 109.

157. Morrissey, Beulah, and others, "The Irish of Albert County," see the Irish Canadian Cultural Association of New Brunswick website: www.newirelandnb.ca.

158. Census of New Brunswick, 1871.
159. For details of Westmorland County's settlers, see the Irish Canadian Cultural Association of New Brunswick website: www.newirelandnb.ca.
160. Houston and Smyth, *Irish Emigration and Canadian Settlement*, 195–201. Evidence from the 1851 census suggests that a good many of the Westmorland arrivals originated from county Kilkenny.
161. Packet 11, Item 34, in the New Brunswick Historical Society Papers stored in the New Brunswick Museum, Saint John, which is quoted in Houston and Smyth, *Irish Emigration and Canadian Settlement*, 199. The collection is entitled Cape Tormentine Emigrant Settlement in the District of Westmorland; Location tickets and records of sale to emigrants during the 1820s.
162. Houston and Smyth, *Irish Emigration and Canadian Settlement*, 197–200. These Irish settlers had to accept interior locations owing to their relatively late arrival, since the much-preferred shorelines sites were the first to have been taken.
163. Ganong, "Settlements in New Brunswick," 141.
164. PANB MC80/924: Warren Schella and Lawrence Gillespie, "The History of Irishtown," Moncton: n.d.
165. Munro, *New Brunswick*, 222.
166. Ganong, "Settlements in New Brunswick," 132.

Chapter 6: Prince Edward Island's Irish Communities

1. Houston and Smyth, *Irish Emigration and Canadian Settlement*, 196.
2. Bruce Elliott, "Irish Protestants," in *The Encyclopedia of Canada's Peoples*, ed. Paul Robert Magocsi (Toronto: Published for the Multicultural History Society of Ontario by the University of Toronto Press, circa 1999), 770.
3. Mark G. McGowan, "Irish Catholics," in ibid., 739.
4. Even by as late as 1841, less than a quarter of the land in more than half of the townships was freehold. The leasehold system was only completely abolished in 1873 when Prince Edward Island entered the Canadian Confederation. Bumsted, *Land Settlement and Politics*, 196–200.
5. There were settlements at Charlottetown, Malpeque (Lot 18), Covehead (Lot 34), New London (Lot 21), Tryon and Cape Traverse (Lot 28), Tracadie (Lot 36), and Three Rivers (Lot 59). Daniel Cobb Harvey (ed.), *Journeys to the Island of Saint John or Prince Edward Island 1775–1832* (Toronto: Macmillan, 1955), 76–77.

6.   Lucille H. Campey, *A Very Fine Class of Immigrants: Prince Edward Island's Scottish Pioneers, 1770–1850* (Toronto: Natural Heritage, 2001), 16–31.

7.   Census data reveals that immigrants arrived on the island from Great Britain and Ireland between 1821 and 1832, but few of their ship crossings were recorded (see the introduction to J.L. Lewellin's "Emigration," in Harvey, *Journeys to the Island of Saint John or Prince Edward Island 1775–1832*), 177.

8.   Clark, *Three Centuries and the Island*, 89–90, 207–08.

9.   Roman Catholics had to wait until 1832 before they could vote.

10. Ian Ross Roberston, "Highlanders, Irishmen, and the Land Question in Nineteenth-Century Prince Edward Island," in *Interpreting Canada's Past*, Vol. 1, ed. J.M. Bumsted (Toronto: Oxford University Press, 1986), 359–73.

11. LAC MG19-F10, Edward Walsh fonds: Journal of a Voyage from Portsmouth to Quebec, 1803: 112, 116.

12. Ibid., 19.

13. McGregor, *Sketches of the Maritime Provinces*, 69.

14. John C MacMillan, *The Early History of the Catholic Church in Prince Edward Island* (Quebec: Evenement Print Co., 1905), 108–09.

15. See Chapter 3.

16. *A True Guide to Prince Edward Island, Formerly Saint John's, in the Gulph of Saint Lawrence, North America* (Liverpool: Printed by G.F. Harris for Woodward and Alderson, 1808), 14. This "Immigrant Guide" of 1808, which extolled the advantages of Prince Edward Island, also warned British people not to be deceived by overly optimistic reports.

17. MacMillan, *The Early History of the Catholic Church in Prince Edward Island*, 163–64.

18. Ibid., 227–28.

19. PAPEI RG5/S4/39/673.

20. Peter Gallant, *From Ireland to Prince Edward Island: A List Compiled from Newspapers, Obituary Notices, and Cemetery Transcriptions* (Charlottetown:, PEI Genealogical Society, 1990), 1.

21. Ibid., 39.

22. Ibid., 9.

23. Ibid., 12.

24. PAPEI RG5/S4 /37/605. James Leonard served in the 14th Dragoons Regiment.

25. O'Grady, *Exiles and Islanders*, 142.

26. Adams, *Ireland and Irish Emigration*, 147–48.

27. *Belfast Newsletter*, March 19, 1819.

28. Ibid., July 13, 1819.

29. *Belfast Newsletter*, February 23, 1830.

30. Another botched attempt to bring immigrants to Prince Edward Island happened in 1842 when the British American Association chartered a ship to take them, but irregularities over funding caused a delayed departure. Caught in severe storms in the North Atlantic in December, the ship was forced back to Cove, Ireland, and eventually the ship and immigrants returned to London. See *Belfast Newsletter*, November 1, 1842. W.S. Shepperson, *British Emigration to North America: Projects and Opinions in the Early Victorian Period* (Oxford: Blackwell, 1957), 45–46.

31. For further details of the island's shipbuilding industry, see Campey, *Planters, Paupers, and Pioneers*, 172–80.

32. No Irish were located in Kings County in 1798. The Irish heads of households listed in the 1798 census are printed in Punch, *Erin's Sons*, 4: 78–79.

33. The 1848 census, Prince Edward Island. About two-thirds of the Irish lived in Queens County.

34. Reginald Porter, "The First Irish Settlers in Tignish," *Abegweit Review* (Spring 1983): 27–33.

35. O'Grady, *Exiles and Islanders*, 80–86.

36. Punch, *Erin's Sons*, 3: 153.

37. O'Grady, *Exiles and Islanders*, 74–79.

38. PAPEI Acc 2353#258: Reverend Burke papers. The earliest Irish Catholic settlers were: Thomas Doyle, Patrick O'Reilly, Michael White, Thomas Dalton, Maurice Griffen, Robert Howard, Maurice O'Halloran, Lawrence Butler, Garret O'Reilly, and Patrick O'Reilly.

39. John Cousins, "James H Fitzgerald and Prince Edward Island, Adieu," *Island Magazine* 8 (Fall/Winter 1980): 27–31.

40. *Summerside Progress*, December 24, 1867, quoted in John Cousins, "The Irish of Lot Seven," in *Abegweit Review* 4, no. 1 (Spring 1988): 35–40.

41. Hunt was a colonel of the 28th Regiment of Foot, which had served in Nova Scotia.

42. PAPEI Acc 2353#252: Reverend Burke papers. Large was intending to sail for Quebec, but following disturbances over the outbreak of fever and lack of provisions on his ship he and the other passengers disembarked at New London. Large liked what he saw and remained on the island.

43. The Lot 11 settlers may have sailed in the *General Elliott* (see Appendix 3), Robert S.P. Jardine, and L. Ann Coles, *Some Immigrants from Offaly and Laois* (Kensington, PEI: Offaly and Laois Family History Society, 1992).

44. J. Clinton Morrison, *Along the North Shore: A Social History of Township 11, PEI, 1765-1982* (St. Eleanor's, PEI: published by the author, 1983), 1: 8-13.

45. O'Grady, *Exiles and Islanders*, 28-48.

46. John MacDonald of Glenaladale had supervised the founding of Catholic Highland communities at Lots 35 and 36 in Queens County in 1772. For further details, see Campey, *A Very Fine Class of Immigrants*, 22-31.

47. Father John MacDonald had been ordained in 1825 as a Roman Catholic priest at St. Andrews Church in Glasgow, located in a deprived area that included the towns of Airdrie and Hamilton.

48. Brendan O'Grady, "The Monaghan Settlers," *Abegweit Review* 4, no. 1 (Spring 1983): 50-75.

49. The names of many of the *Corsair*'s passengers are listed in O'Grady, *Exiles and Islanders*, 148.

50. *Glasgow Chronicle*, April 2, 1830. Their arrival was reported in the *Prince Edward Island Register*, May 25, 1830.

51. *DCB*, vol. 10 (John MacDonald).

52. O'Grady, *Exiles and Islanders*, 142-50.

53. Mount Mellick in Lot 49 is named after a county Laois parish.

54. However, before this, there are indications that settlers from counties Wexford and Waterford had come to Kelly's Cross in the 1820s. They had been employed as labourers by William Lord of Tryon who ran a major shipbuilding enterprise in the area. A merchant, property owner, and shipbuilder, he provided passages in his ships for immigrant labourers. Mary Brehaut (ed.), *Pioneers on the Island* (Charlottetown: PEI Historical Society, 1959), 2: 94.

55. O'Grady, *Exiles and Islanders*, 162-65.

56. Peter McGuigan, "From Wexford and Monaghan: The Lot 22 Irish," *Abegweit Review* 5, no. 1 (Winter 1985): 61-96. Cemetery transcriptions and death notices reveal that Wexford settlers began arriving from the 1820s. See Gallant, *From Ireland to Prince Edward Island*.

57. O'Grady, *Exiles and Islanders*, 84.

58. The first Catholics to settle at Kinkora included John Brenan, John Keefe, Michael Cahill, Edward Wynn, James Walsh, and Andrew Glen, who arrived in 1835 from the south of Ireland; Patrick Murphy, John Smith,

Philip Regan, and Owen Shreenan, who arrived in 1839 from the north of Ireland; Valentine Shreenan and Felix Mulligan, who came in 1841 from the north; and Mathew Kelly, Leslie Kelly, Patrick Young, James Farmer, and John McGarvill, who came in 1847, also from the north. PAPEI Acc2353#250: Reverend Burke papers.

59. O'Grady, *Exiles and Islanders*, 167–73. Some of the settlers originated from county Armagh.

60. Lot 27 had been granted in the 1767 lottery to James Searle and Russell Spence, both merchants. By the 1830s it was partly owned by Searle's daughter, who had married Horatio Mann. In 1849 she in turn bequeathed it to her daughter, Mrs. Gillean, who married a lawyer in Philadelphia. The Gillean family (who were Catholics) sold their share of Lot 27 to the Pope family in 1865.

61. D.A. MacKinnon and A.B. Warburton, *Past and Present of Prince Edward Island* (Charlottetown: B.F. Bowen, 1906), 84.

62. PAPEI Acc2353#250: Reverend Burke papers.

63. Mackinnon and Warburton, *Past and Present of Prince Edward Island*, 290–91.

64. O'Grady, *Exiles and Islanders*, 64, 98.

65. Ibid., 94–104.

66. PAPEI Acc3005: William Creed fonds. Creed was elected to the PEI Legislative Assembly and is buried in the Old Protestant Cemetery on University Avenue in Charlottetown.

67. Peter McGuigan, "The Lot 61 Irish: Settlement and Stabilization," *Abegweit Review* 6, no.1 (Spring 1988): 33–63.

68. *Journal of the Legislative Assembly*, 1863, quoted in ibid., 33.

69. Born in county Queens, Brennan came to the island in 1823 at the age of twenty-seven. A Roman Catholic, he became a successful merchant and prominent politician, serving as both an elected member of the legislature and later as an appointed member of the executive council.

70. Maguire, *Irish in America*, 32–33.

71. Ibid., 33–34.

72. MacMillan, *Early History of the Catholic Church in Prince Edward Island*, 292.

73. Robertson, "Highlanders, Irishmen and the Land Question," 359–73.

74. Clark, *Three Centuries and the Island*, 125.

75. Edward MacDonald, "The Ill and the Dying," *Island Magazine* 36 (Fall/Winter 1994): 35–39.

Chapter 7: Emigration During the Great Irish Famine

1.   Houston and Smyth, *Irish Emigration and Canadian Settlement*, 4.

2.   James S. Donnelly, Jr., *The Great Irish Potato Famine* (Stroud: Sutton Publishing, 2001).

3.   By 1846, potatoes formed a large part of the diet of the average Irish family. The fungus (*phytophthora infestans*) that attacks the leaves and tubers of potatoes destroyed the crops, making thousands of people vulnerable to malnutrition and severe destitution.

4.   Miller, *Emigrants and Exiles*, 280–344.

5.   Houston and Smyth, *Irish Emigration and Canadian Settlement*, 39, 216–18.

6.   Toner, "The Irish of New Brunswick at Mid Century: The 1851 Census," 1–4.

7.   Spray, "'The Difficulties Came Upon Us Like a Thunderbolt': Immigrants and Fever in New Brunswick in 1847," 107–26.

8.   Whalen, "Almost as Bad as Ireland," 155–70.

9.   Letter from Ference McGowan, October 13, 1847: *Third Report from the Select Committee on Colonization from Ireland*, 122–32.

10. NAB CO 188/102, 92–101: Report to the Saint John Council, October 9, 1847, quoted in Spray, "'The Difficulties Came Upon Us Like a Thunderbolt': Immigrants and Fever in New Brunswick in 1847," 114.

11. Carrier and Jeffrey, *External Migration: A Study of the Available Statistics, 1815–1950*, 95–96.

12. The Irish Poor Law gave powers to parishes to collect a poor rate as a form of taxation to support local workhouses.

13. Letter from John Mullawny, July 4, 1847: *Third Report from the Select Committee on Colonization from Ireland*, 122–32.

14. MacKay, *Flight from Famine*, 266.

15. Letter from the committee (passengers) of the *Aeolus* dated June 5, 1847: *Third Report from the Select Committee on Colonization from Ireland*, 122–32.

16. Ibid., Letter from Michael Driscoll, June 13, 1847.

17. A "Card of Thanks" to the captain, signed by Farrel Brogan, Walter Long, Richard McGee, Billy McCownly, William Brogan, Francis Coglan, Robert McJunkin, and Condy Breslin, was printed in the *New Brunswick Courier*, July 19, 1847.

18. Spray, "'The Difficulties Came Upon Us Like a Thunderbolt': Immigrants and Fever in New Brunswick in 1847," 114.

19. *New Brunswick Courier*, July 31, 1847.

20. Whalen, "Almost as Bad as Ireland," 155–70.

21. *Papers Relative to Emigration to the British Provinces in North America*, HC 1847–48 (932), xlvii, 110; Ibid., HC 1847–48 (50), xlvii, 90.

22. Moran, *Sending Out Ireland's Poor*, 102, 108–09, 112.

23. *Papers Relative to Emigration to the British Provinces in North America*, HC 1847–8 (932) xlvii, 54–55.

24. Resolution of the Saint John Council dated November 4, 1847, quoted in Moran, *Sending Out Ireland's Poor*, 105.

25. *Saint John Albion*, November 13, 1847.

26. *Papers Relative to Emigration to the British Provinces in North America*, HC 1847–8 (932) xlvii, 48.

27. When they recovered, the children later found work as domestic servants and labourers. The Emigrant Orphan Asylum closed in 1849.

28. Moran, *Sending Out Ireland's Poor*, 65–66, 95 102–09, 112.

29. Spray, "'The Difficulties Came Upon Us Like a Thunderbolt': Immigrants and Fever in New Brunswick in 1847," 114.

30. A reconstructed passenger list for the crossing of the *Star* from New Ross in 1848 is provided in Rees, *Surplus People: From Wicklow to Canada*, 131–37.

31. NLI MS3987: Letter book of Robert Chaloner, 216.

32. *Papers Relative to Emigration to the British Provinces in North America*, HC 1847–8 (971) xlvii, 16.

33. PANB RS555 B2b5.

34. The rail link between Quebec City and St. Andrews provided Upper and Lower Canada with access to the Atlantic Ocean during the winter months when the St. Lawrence was frozen over.

35. Rees, *Surplus People: From Wicklow to Canada*, 84–116.

36. The quality of the shipping services provided during the famine years is discussed in Chapter 8.

37. PANB RS555B2b4.

38. Ibid., Perley to John Partelow, November 16, 1850.

39. PP 1851 XL (348). See www.theshipslist for the passengers listed as having travelled in the *Susan* in 1850 from Cork.

40. Letter from Catherine Bradley, October 6, 1847: *Third Report from the Select Committee on Colonization from Ireland*, 122–32.

41. Ibid., Letter from Bryan Clancy and his sister, November 17, 1847.

42. Ibid., Letter from the Henigans, March 17, 1848.

43. See PANB: "The Irish Portal" for the arrival years of the Sligo immigrants.

44. Thomas Power, "The Palmerston Estate in County Sligo: Improvement and Assisted Emigration," in *To and From Ireland: Planned Migration Schemes c 1600–2000*, eds. Patrick J. Duffy and Gerard Moran (Dublin: Geography Publications, 2004), 105–36.

45. PANB RS555/B4b/2: John Doran to J.S. Saunders, November 27, 1847.

46. Rees, *Some Other Place than Here*, 62–65.

47. Rees, *Surplus People: From Wicklow to Canada*, 109–13.

48. Landlord assistance was provided to 1,582 Gore-Booth tenants, 405 Palmerston tenants, and 375 Fitzwilliam tenants, giving a total of 2,362. The total number of Irish arrivals at Saint John was around 17,000 and at least 547 Irish immigrants arrived at St. Andrews.

49. See Appendix 2 for the individual ship crossings.

50. Morse, "Immigration to Nova Scotia, 1839–51," 120–21. The immigrant total, taken from official sources, records the number of people who had sailed from Irish ports to Halifax in 1847. Only 120 Irish had arrived in 1845 and 190 in 1846.

51. Flewwelling (Morse), "Immigration to and Emigration from Nova Scotia, 1839–51," 80–97.

52. See Appendix 2 for the individual ship crossings.

53. See Chapter 4.

54. NSARM RG 5, Series "p," vol. 7, item 31. For the list of petitioners see Punch, *Erin's Sons*, 4: 164–65.

55. *Armagh Guardian*, April 27, 1847.

56. O'Grady, *Exiles and Islanders*, 180–81.

57. Ibid., 133–36.

58. See Chapter 6.

59. Doyle, "The Irish Experience in Halifax, Nova Scotia, Saint John, New Brunswick, and St. John's, Newfoundland," 99–100.

60. Deegan, "A List of Passenger Shipping from Waterford Port to America and Canada, 1845–1850," 49–55.

61. PANB MC1401: Alexander Machum fonds, 27.

62. Buckner and Reid, *Atlantic Region*, 315–16.

Chapter 8: Sea Crossings

1. *Reports from the Select Committee Appointed to Inquire into the Expediency of Encouraging Emigration from the United Kingdom, 1826, IV; 1826–27, V; A384.*

2.   Ibid., A385.

3.   Davis, *The Industrial Revolution and British Overseas Trade*, 48–49. Between 1814 and 1843, Baltic timber was sometimes shipped to North America and then back to Britain, as the saving of duty more than compensated for the double freight. Despite widespread complaints in Britain over the high cost of timber, the protective tariffs remained in place until 1860.

4.   Arthur R.M. Lower, *Great Britain's Woodyard: British America and the Timber Trade 1763–1867* (Montreal: McGill-Queen's University Press, 1973), 67–75.

5.   *Information Published by His Majesty's Commissioners for Emigration Respecting the British Colonies in North America* (London: J. Hartnell, 1832), 6–7.

6.   Oliver Macdonagh, *A Pattern of Government Growth 1800–1860, The Passenger Acts and Their Enforcement* (London: 1961), 150–51. Oliver MacDonagh, "Emigration and the State, 1833–55: An Essay in Administrative History," *Transactions of the Royal Historical Society* 5, fifth series (London: The Royal Historical Society, 1955), 133–59. Edwin C. Guillet, *The Great Migration: The Atlantic Crossing by Sailing Ships since 1770* (Toronto: T. Nelson, 1963), 13–19.

7.   Mitchell, *Derry-Londonderry: Gateway to a New World*, 7.

8.   *Information Published by His Majesty's Commissioners for Emigration*, 6, 7.

9.   *Belfast Newsletter*, August 17, 1819.

10. *Acadian Recorder*, June 4, 1836.

11. Ibid., June 30, 1838.

12. Ibid., June 22, 1839.

13. Smith Smiley, *History of the Smiley Family of Hants County, Nova Scotia*, 2. Another account of the shipping disaster, written by an anonymous passenger and printed in the *Nova Scotian*, July 31, 1828, states that the *Dispatch* carried two hundred passengers and of these, fifty-eight died.

14. PANL MHC: *Royal Gazette and Newfoundland Advertiser*, July 8, 1834. The record of events was provided by Dr. Henry Downs, one of the few survivors.

15. The survivors were: Captain Ladler; Robert S. Ladler (his brother); Henry Downs (surgeon); Thomas Enwright (carpenter); James Cook (seaman); Peter Lily Wall and James Clarke (apprentices); Mary Hastings; Andrew Young; James Sheehan; and Edmund Curry (or Cody).

16. *New Brunswick Courier*, July 7, 1832.

17. Ibid., May 20, 1837; June 22, 1844.

18. *The Nova Scotian*, August 4, 11, 1831.

19. PANL MHC: *Royal Gazette and Newfoundland Advertiser*, August 30, 1831.

20. PRONI Mic 112/1: "Extracts from the Letter Books of J & J Cooke, merchants in Londonderry concerning the Emigrant Trade to America, 1837–47," 3. A formula was used for calculating passenger numbers that treated passengers who were under the age of sixteen as a fraction of an adult.

21. The physical characteristics of a vessel greatly affected sailing performance as well as passenger comfort and safety. For an analysis of the different types of Aberdeen-registered vessels that were used to transport emigrants to North America, see Campey, *Fast Sailing and Copper-Bottomed*, 80–98.

22. PRONI Mic 112/1: Extracts from the Letter Books of J & J Cooke, 13.

23. Mitchell, *Derry-Londonderry: Gateway to a New World*, 7.

24. The *Lloyd's Shipping Register* is available as a regular series beginning in 1775, apart from the years 1785, 1788, and 1817.

25. Still in use today and run by a Classification Society with a worldwide network of offices and administrative staff, the *Lloyd's Register* continues to provide standard classifications of quality for shipbuilding and maintenance.

26. An honest and open inspection was vital to an insurer's risk assessment, and the shipowner's ability to attract profitable trade hinged on the classification given to his ships.

27. The number of years that a ship could hold the highest code varied according to where it was built.

28. The letters were followed by the number 1 or 2, the former signifying that the vessel's equipment was satisfactory and the latter that it was not. George Blake, *Lloyd's Register of Shipping 1760–1960* (London: Lloyd's, 1960), 12–13, 26–27.

29. The inability to find a Lloyd's code does not necessarily cast doubt on the quality of a vessel. For instance, the *Envoy* of Londonderry and the *Londonderry* were both owned by John Cooke, a shipping magnate who had no need to insure his vessels with Lloyd's.

30. The impact of immigrant transport legislation on voyages to the Maritime ports is discussed in Oliver Macdonagh, *A Pattern of Government Growth 1800–1860: The Passenger Acts and Their Enforcement* (London: MacGibbon & Kee, 1961), 54–69, 180–92.

31. The Passenger Act of 1817 specified a space allocation of one and a half tons per person in the steerage, while the 1828 act required a passenger to tonnage ratio of three passengers for every four tons. Space regulations

were made slightly more generous in 1835 when the ratio was increased to three passengers for every five tons.

32. NAB CO 188/35, August 1, 1827, quoted in Cowan, *British Emigration to British North America*, 148. By 1828 the New Brunswick Agricultural and Emigrant Society dropped the word *Emigrant* from its name, and from then on were dedicated solely to agricultural pursuits.

33. The Fredericton Emigrant Society, formed in 1820 to help destitute immigrants, was the first institution of its kind in the province. See Ganong, "Settlements in New Brunswick," 75–77.

34. *Information Published by His Majesty's Commissioners for Emigration*, 4–5; *Information for Emigrants to British North America* (London: C. Knight, 1842), 7–8. The fare for an adult sailing in the *Hornet* of Limerick to Saint John in 1848 was £3, a sum that included food, water, and the immigrant tax (PP 1847–48 [985] XLVII, 19–20).

35. The land company's promotional literature stated that "owing to the number of ships which go out in ballast for timber, passages are generally more moderate to Saint John or Chatham on the Miramichi than to any other part of America." New Brunswick and Nova Scotia Land Company, *Practical Information Respecting New Brunswick for the Use of Persons Intending to Settle Upon the Lands of the New Brunswick and Nova Scotia Land Company* (London: Pelham Richardson, 1843), 9.

36. NAB CO 217/147: Kempt to Goderich, September 7, 1827, quoted in Cowan, *British Emigration to British North America*, 147.

37. *New Brunswick Courier*, May 28, June 16, 1831.

38. Ibid., May 28, 1831. The *Billow*, sailing from Newry that year, also arrived with passengers suffering from fever.

39. Martell, *Immigration to Nova Scotia, 1815–38*, 23–29.

40. PANL GN2.17: Quarantine letter books (1832–36).

41. Two thousand of the 1846–47 arrivals died later. See MacNutt, *New Brunswick*, 303–04.

42. Daniel F. Johnson, *The St. John County Alms and Work House Records* (Saint John: published by author, 1985).

43. Harold E. Wright, "Partridge Island: Re-Discovering the Irish Connection," in *The Irish in Atlantic Canada, 1780–1900*, ed. T.P. Power (Fredericton: New Ireland Press, 1991), 127–49.

44. The nineteenth-century graveyard on Partridge Island was destroyed by later building and by military operations during the Second World War.

Information, supplied by Harold E. Wright, an expert on the history of Partridge Island, is gratefully acknowledged.

45. Partridge Island Research Project, Quarantine File, 1847, quoted in Wright, "Partridge Island: Re-Discovering the Irish Connection," 141.

46. PP 1854–55 XXXIX (109). The names of those who died in the *Blanche* crossing can be found on The Ships List website.

47. *Royal Gazette*, May 25, 28, 1847.

48. *New Brunswick Courier*, July, 4, 11, 25, 1847.

49. Ibid., July 3, 1847.

50. Ibid., August 21, 1847.

51. Ibid., August 29, 1846.

52. Thomas P. Power, "The Emigrant Ship: The Transportation, Regulation and Reception of Irish Immigrants in New Brunswick, 1815–1855," in *Celtic Languages and Celtic People*, edited by Cyril Byrne and others (Halifax: Saint Mary's University, 1989), 691.

53. Spray, "'The Difficulties Came Upon Us Like a Thunderbolt': Immigrants and Fever in New Brunswick in 1847," 109.

54. *New Brunswick Courier*, July 12, 1847.

55. Ibid., August 15, 1846.

56. Ibid., August 21, 1847. The names of the thirty-two passengers who signed the letter are printed.

57. Ibid., October 2, 1847.

58. Thirteen of the forty-one vessels had an 'A' ranking, ten were 'AE,' and fourteen were 'E.' Four vessels were owned by reputable shipping firms whose large resources meant that they could insure vessels themselves. It can be assumed that they offered top-quality shipping.

59. The only doubtful ship was the *Thomas Gelston*, ranked as 'E2.' For details of the county Monaghan crossings, see Appendix 3.

60. Power, "The Emigrant Ship: The Transportation, Regulation and Reception of Irish Immigrants in New Brunswick, 1815–1855," 683–705.

Chapter 9: The Irish in Atlantic Canada

1. Harold E. Wright, *The Diary of Nellie McGowan, Partridge Island Quarantine Station, 1902* (Saint John: Partridge Island Research Project, 1904), 4.

2. Wright, "Partridge Island: Re-Discovering the Irish Connection," 127–49.

3. Séamus J. King, *The Clash of the Ash in Foreign Fields: Hurling Abroad* (Tipperary: Cashel, 1998), 85.

4. William J. Kirwin, "The Planting of Anglo-Irish in Newfoundland," in *Focus on Canada*, ed. Sandra J. Clarke (Amsterdam: John Benjamins, 1993), 68.

5. Campey, *An Unstoppable Force*, 17–41.

6. Proinsias Mac Aonghusa, "Reflections on the Fortunes of the Irish Language in Canada, With Some Reference to the Fate of the Language in the United States," in *The Untold Story: The Irish in Canada*, eds. Robert O'Driscoll and Lorna Reynolds (Toronto: Celtic Arts of Canada, 1988), 2: 711–17.

7. The festival was established by the author Louise Manning, who was asked by Lord Beaverbrook to collect and document folk music. See www.miramichifolksongfestival.com.

8. Terry McDonald, "Where Have All the (English) Folk Songs Gone?" *British Journal of Canadian Studies* 14, no. 2 (1999): 180–92.

9. Michael Whelan's father, William, had been born in county Laois and worked as a farmer and lumberman while his mother, Mary Keary, was New Brunswick–born.

10. *Moncton Times*, October 9, 1980.

11. PANB MC971: Michael Whelan collection.

12. *Saint John Morning Freeman*, February 4, 1864.

13. Ibid., August 2, 1864.

14. Ibid., February 4, 1864.

15. The Orange Order is an international Protestant organization, based in Northern Ireland, with a significant presence in the Scottish Lowlands and across North America. It was founded in county Armagh in 1795, during a period of Protestant-Catholic sectarian conflict, as a Masonic-style brotherhood sworn to uphold the interests of the Protestant faith.

16. The Irish component of the Orange Order membership in Prince Edward Island was only about 10 percent. O'Grady, *Exiles and Islanders*, 237–40.

17. Ibid., 72, 75.

18. Cecil J. Houston and William J. Smyth, *The Sash Canada Wore: A Historical Geography of the Orange Order in Canada* (Toronto: University of Toronto Press, 1980), 82.

19. Ibid., 139.

20. Acheson, "The Irish Community in Saint John, 1815–1850," 47. However, troops were needed in 1846 to quell a major riot.

21. Scott W. See, *Riots in New Brunswick: Orange Nativism and Social Violence in the 1840s* (Toronto: University of Toronto Press, 1993), 190–210.

22. Acheson, "The Irish Community in Saint John, 1815–1850," 50.

23. See, *Riots in New Brunswick*, 195–97.

24. Ibid., 210.

25. Moore, *The Life and Death of Edward Fitzgerald*, 43–44.

26. NSARM MG1, vol. 3586: Patrick Gallagher papers #2 Copy Letterbook 1837–1840, October 12, 1839.

27. *New Brunswick Courier*, April 3, 1841.

28. Maguire, *Irish in America*, 83.

29. NSARM MG1, Vol. 3586: Patrick Gallagher papers, #3 Copy Letterbook, 1846–1848, circa October 1846, to M.J. Walters, Manchester.

30. Gesner, *New Brunswick with Notes for Emigrants*, 388.

31. Abraham Gesner, *The Industrial Resources of Nova Scotia : Comprehending the Physical Geography, Topography, Geology, Agriculture, Fisheries, Mines, Forests, Wild Lands, Lumbering, Manufactories, Navigation, Commerce, Emigration, Improvements, Industry, Contemplated Railways, Natural History and Resources of the Province* (Halifax: A. and W. MacKinlay, 1849), 332–34.

32. Adams, *Ireland and Irish Emigration*, 202, 215.

33. PANB MC2618: Laurence Hughes fonds, John Whelan to Laurence Hughes, September 25, 1854.

34. Donna McDonald, *Illustrated News: Juliana Horatia Ewing's Canadian Pictures, 1867–1869* (Toronto: Dundurn, 1985), 30–31.

35. Many of the abstinence groups were modelled on an Irish temperance movement that had been founded in Cork in 1838 by Father Theobald Mathew. PANB MC41 MS5/2: Liquor abstinence pledge cards, 1841.

36. Ernest J. Dick, "From Temperance to Prohibition in 19th Century Nova Scotia," *Dalhousie Review* 61 (1981): 530–52.

37. O'Grady, *Exiles and Islanders*, 234–36.

38. *New Brunswick Courier*, March 26, 1842. The newspaper reported that 3,327 people in Northumberland County had taken "the total abstinence pledge."

39. The Halifax Charitable Irish Society was founded in 1786 to alleviate poverty among the needy Irish. It later offered help to all of Halifax's poor, including the non-Irish, as long as they did not belong to another national society. Uniacke also promoted an Irish settlement near Lake Shubenacadie, off the road between Halifax and Truro. MacKay, *Flight from Famine*, 25.

40. The Saint John Irish Friendly Society amassed a considerable library, which was lost in the great fire of 1877.

41. *DCB*, vol. 12 (Henry O'Leary).

42. Later, as a member of the Liberal government, Whelan was an advocate of Confederation, although most of his fellow Liberals opposed it. Edward MacDonald, "Edward Whelan and the Election of 1867," *Island Magazine* 52 (Fall/Winter 2002): 19–26.

43. PAPEI Acc. 4262: Edward Whelan fonds.

44. Spray, "The Irish in Miramichi," 55–62. W.D. Hamilton, *Dictionary of Miramichi Biography: Biographical Sketches of Men and Women Born Before 1900 Who Played a Part in Public Life on the Miramichi Northumberland County, New Brunswick, Canada* (Saint John: W.D. Hamilton, 1997), 287.

45. Terrence M. Punch, "Irish Repealers at Halifax, Nova Scotia, in 1843," *The Irish Ancestor* 10, no. 1 (1978): 6–13. The repeal movement was also well supported in Newfoundland and Prince Edward Island. See O'Grady, *Exiles and Islanders*, 189–91.

46. *Armagh Guardian*, December 4, 1885.

BIBLIOGRAPHY

PRIMARY SOURCES (MANUSCRIPTS)

Devon Record Office (DRO)

5592Z/Z/4: Extracts of letters written in March 1817 from St. John's, Newfoundland, concerning extreme poverty.

5592Z/Z/6: "Brief Considerations on the Nature, Importance, and Existing Difficulties of the Newfoundland Trade Presented by a Deputation of Merchants to Lords Liverpool and Bathurst at the Board of Trade, 1817."

Library and Archives of Canada (LAC)

M-1352: Glasgow Colonial Society Papers.

MG19-E1: Thomas Douglas, Fifth Earl of Selkirk fonds.

MG19-F10: Edward Walsh fonds.

MG24-158: Lists of immigrants from parishes in Londonderry contained in the original Ordnance Survey of Ireland (1833–1836).

MG24-D50: Daniel McGruar fonds.

MG 24-I122/7: Patrick Nowlan fonds.

MG25-G271, Vol. 16#17a: "Truly Canadian" by James McGivern.

MG25-G320: Howe family collection.

MG40-102: Notice of sailing in 1847 of the *Lady Caroline* to Saint John.

MG40-R92 & R93: Letters from Robert McClorg [McClory], 1819, 1820.

Mellon Centre for Migration Studies, Ireland (MCFMS)

Letter from G.J. in Fredericton to his cousin David Carse, living in county Down, 1847.

Letter from Johnston Keys to William Keys in county Fermanagh, 1831.

National Archives of Britain, Kew (NAB)

CO 188: New Brunswick original correspondence.

CO 194: Correspondence, Newfoundland.

CO 217: Nova Scotia and Cape Breton original correspondence.

CO 384: Colonial Office papers on emigration concerning North American settlers.

National Archives of Ireland (NAI)

CSO/OPMA/820: Philip Martin, 1835.

CSO/RP/1818/593: Petition of Daniel Smith and others in Limerick, March 8, 1818.

CSO/RP/1821/1228: Petition of Peter Strange requesting government employment, August 20, 1821.

CSO/RP/1821/1228: Petition of Philip Murphy.

CSO/RP/1822/66: Petition of one hundred passengers on board *Commerce* of Workington.

CSO/RP/1822/2048: John and Elizabeth Farrol, October 18, 1822.

QRO/4/3/1/214: Petition of Denis Leary in Charlotte County, NB, June 19, 1843.

National Archives of Scotland (NAS)

GD 45/3/159/2: Sir Howard Douglas, Lieutenant Governor of New Brunswick to Lord Dalhousie, 1825.

National Library of Ireland (NLI)

MS 3987: Letter book of Robert Chaloner.

MS 20628: Studdert Papers.

MS 4974/4975 (m/f 934): Emigration books, 1848, Earl of Fitzwilliam's estates, county Wicklow.

Nova Scotia Archives and Records Management (NSARM)

Acc2011-028: Richey family fonds.

MG1 Vol. 258: Isaac Deschamps fonds.

MG1 Vol. 3586: Patrick Gallagher papers.

MG3 Vol. 6190: Thomas Maher fonds.
RG1: Bound Volumes of Nova Scotia Records.
RG5: Records of the Legislative Assembly.
RG20 "B": Cape Breton Land Papers, 1794–1839.

Public Archives and Records Office of Prince Edward Island (PAPEI)

Acc 2353#258: Reverend Burke papers.
Acc 3005: William Creed fonds.
Acc 4262: Edward Whelan fonds.
Acc 4495: Rev. David Fitzgerald fonds.
RG5 Series 4: land petitions.

Public Archives of New Brunswick (PANB)

MC41: McCarthy family fonds.
MC80-924: Schella, Warren, and Lawrence Gillespie. *The History of Irishtown.* Moncton: n.d.
MC80-1038: Reicker, Marion Gilchrist. *A Time There Was: Petersville and Other Abandoned Settlements in Queens County N.B., 1815-1953.* Jemseg, NB: Queens County Historical Society, 1984.
MC80-2014: Long, Heather. *Good Green Hope: The Irish Catholic Settlers of Albert County, New Brunswick.* Halifax: published by author, 1995.
MC651: Robert Eddy fonds.
MC971: Michael Whelan collection.
MC1387: Samuel Bacon fonds.
MC1401: Alexander Machum fonds.
MC1729: Valentine Gibbs fonds.
MC1753: Harley family collection.
MC1847: An Account by Alexander Machum of New Jerusalem.
MC2106: Robinson family collection.
MC2618: Laurence Hughes fonds.
MC2688: William Martin fonds.
MC3028: John Browne letters.
MC3075: Meahan family collection.
MC3293: George Inch fonds.
MC3710 Martha (Moorhead) Ellis fonds
RS24: Journals of the House of Assembly.
RS555: Provincial Secretary: Immigration Administration Records.

Public Archives of Newfoundland and Labrador (PANL)

GN2.17: Quarantine letter books.

GN 5/4/C/1, Box 1: Rioters at Ferryland, 1788.

MG49.40: Letter Book of Pierce Sweetman, 1785–1804.

MG318: Fishery servant's agreement, Trinity, October 17, 1811, between Thomas Verge, [Ship] Master, and Robert George, fisherman.

MHC: Mildred Howard Collection (taken from Newfoundland newspapers).

Public Record Office, Northern Ireland (PRONI)

D1424/11/1: Rev. J.G. Mulholland in Windsor, Nova Scotia, to Rev. G. Kirkpatrick, Craigs Rectory, March 21, 1849.

D2892/1/1–14: J. & J. Cooke fonds, 1847–67.

D2892/2/2; William McCorkell letter book, 1826–33.

D3305/1/3: William Gamble to his brother, 1857.

Mic 6/127: James Ward to his father, 1834 (microfilmed with permission of the Royal Irish Academy).

Mic 112/1: Extracts from the letter books of J. & J. Cooke, merchants in Londonderry.

T2125/7/2: Robert McClory to David McClory, 1819.

T3032/1/1: Letter from Henry Coulter to Rev. William Moreland, county Down, 1820.

University of London School of Oriental and African Studies (SOAS)

LMS: London Missionary Society Papers.

MMS: Methodist Missionary Society Papers.

Staffordshire County Record Office (STRO)

D3388: Dyott family papers.

Worcestershire Record Office (WORO)

705:1059/9600/26(i)/ 3: Letter from Bishop of Newfoundland, 1866.

PRINTED PRIMARY SOURCES AND CONTEMPORARY PUBLICATIONS

Anonymous. *A True Guide to Prince Edward Island, Formerly St. John's in the Gulph of St. Laurence, North America.* Liverpool: Printed by G.F. Harris for Woodward and Alderson, 1808.

———. *Information for Emigrants to British North America*. London: C. Knight, 1842.

———. *Information Published by His Majesty's Commissioners for Emigration Respecting the British Colonies in North America*. London: Charles Knight, publisher to the Society for the Diffusion of Useful Knowledge, 1832.

———. *Report Concerning Canadian Archives for the Year 1904*. Ottawa, Printed by S.E. Dawson, 1905.

———. *Sketch of the Province of New Brunswick Published for the Use of Emigrants by the Limerick Emigrants' Friend Society* (Limerick, Ireland: Printed by C. O'Brian, publisher to the Limerick Emigrants' Friend Society, 1832).

Atkinson, Rev. W. Christopher. *An Historical and Statistical Account of New Brunswick British North America with Advice for Emigrants*. Edinburgh: Printed by Anderson & Bryce, 1844.

Baillie, Thomas. *An Account of the Province of New Brunswick Including a Description of the Settlements, Visitations, Soil and Climate of That Important Province with Advice to Emigrants*. London: J.G. & F. Rivington, 1832.

Bouchette, Joseph. *The British Dominions in North America: A Topographical and Statistical Description of the Provinces of Lower and Upper Canada, New Brunswick, Nova Scotia, the Islands of Newfoundland, Prince Edward Island and Cape Breton*. Vols. 1 and 2. London: Longman, Rees, Orme, Brown, Green and Longman, 1832.

Brown, Richard. *A History of the Island of Cape Breton*. (London: Sampson Low, Son and Marston, 1869).

Buckingham, J.S. *Canada, Nova Scotia, New Brunswick and Other British Provinces in North America: With a Plan of National Colonization*. London, Paris: Fisher & Sons, 1843.

Campbell, Duncan. *History of Prince Edward Island*. Charlottetown: Bremner Bros., 1875.

Census of New Brunswick, 1851, 1861, 1871.

Census of Newfoundland, 1794–95, 1857.

Census of Nova Scotia, 1770, 1818, 1871.

Census of Prince Edward Island, 1848, 1881.

Cooney, Robert. *A Compendious History of the Northern Part of the Province of New Brunswick and of the District of Gaspe in Lower Canada*. Chatham, NB: D.G. Smith, 1896.

de Gobineau, Joseph Arthur. *Voyage a Terre-Neuve*. Paris: 1862.

Edgar, James. *New Brunswick as a Home for Emigrants: With the Best Means of Promoting Immigration and Developing the Resources of the Province.* Saint John, NB: Barnes & Co., 1860.

Gesner, Abraham. *The Industrial Resources of Nova Scotia : Comprehending the Physical Geography, Topography, Geology, Agriculture, Fisheries, Mines, Forests, Wild Lands, Lumbering, Manufactories, Navigation, Commerce, Emigration, Improvements, Industry, Contemplated Railways, Natural History and Resources of the Province.* Halifax: A. and W. MacKinlay, 1849.

————. *New Brunswick with Notes: For Emigrants, Comprehending the Early History, Settlement, Topography, Statistics, Natural History, Etc.* London: Simmonds and Ward, 1847.

Guillet, Edwin C. *The Great Migration: The Atlantic Crossing by Sailing Ships since 1770.* Toronto: T. Nelson, 1963.

Haliburton, Thomas Chandler. *An Historical and Statistical Account of Nova Scotia.* 2 vols. Halifax: J. Howe, 1829.

Hill, S.S. *A Short Account of Prince Edward Island Designed Chiefly for the Information of Agriculturists and Other Emigrants of Small Capital by the Author of the Emigrant's Introduction to an Acquaintance with the British American Colonies.* London: Madden, 1839.

Johnston, J.F.W. *Notes on North America: Agricultural, Economical and Social,* 2 vols. Edinburgh: William Blackwood & Sons, 1851.

Lloyd's Shipping Register 1775–1855.

MacGregor, John. *Historical and Descriptive Sketches of the Maritime Colonies of British America.* London: Longman, Rees, Orme, Brown and Green, 1828.

Maguire, John Francis. *The Irish in America.* New York, Montreal: D. and J. Sadler, 1868.

Martin, R. Montgomery. *History of Nova Scotia, Cape Breton, the Sable Islands, New Brunswick, Prince Edward Island, the Bermudas, Newfoundland.* London: Whittaker & Co, 1837.

Moore, Thomas. *The Life and Death of Lord Edward Fitzgerald.* London: Longman, Rees, Orme, Brown and Green, 1831.

New Brunswick and Nova Scotia Land Company. *Practical Information Respecting New Brunswick for the Use of Persons Intending to Settle Upon the Lands of the New Brunswick and Nova Scotia Land Company.* London: Pelham Richardson, 1843.

————. *Sketches in New Brunswick in the Year 1833 ... and ... the Operations of the Association During the Years 1834 and 1835* and *Practical Information Respecting New Brunswick for the Use of Persons Intending to Settle Upon the Lands of the New Brunswick and Nova Scotia Land Company.* London: Pelham Richardson, 1843.

Perley, Moses Henry. *A Handbook of Information for Emigrants to New Brunswick.* Saint John, NB: H. Chubb, 1854.

————. *On the Early History of New Brunswick.* Saint John, NB: published by author, 1891.

Prowse, D.W. *A History of Newfoundland, from the English, Colonial, and Foreign Records.* London: Eyre and Spottiswoode, 1896.

Robinson, John, and Thomas Rispin. *A Journey Through Nova Scotia: Containing a Particular Account of the Country and Its Inhabitants; with Observations on the Management in Husbandry, the Breed of Horses and Other Cattle, and Every Thing Material Relating to Farming; to Which Is Added an Account of Several Estates for Sale in Different Townships of Nova-Scotia, with Their Number of Acres and the Price at Which Each Is Set.* York: Printed for the authors by C. Etherington, 1774.

Society for the propagation of the Gospel in foreign parts. *Annual reports.*

Stevenson, Benjamin R. *Report on Immigration to New Brunswick in 1873.* Saint John, NB: Daily Telegraph Printing, 1874.

Stewart, John. *An Account of Prince Edward Island, in the Gulph of St. Lawrence, North America: Containing its Geography, a Description of Its Different Divisions, Soil, Climate, Seasons, Natural Productions, Cultivation, Discovery, Conquest, Progress and Present State of the Settlement, Government, Constitution, Laws, and Religion.* London: W. Winchester, 1806.

Wix, Edward. *Six Months of a Newfoundland Missionary's Journal from February to August, 1835.* London: Smith, Elder, 1836.

PARLIAMENTARY PAPERS

Papers Relative to Emigration to the British Provinces in North America, HC 1847–8 (932) xlvii.

Papers Relative to Emigration to the British Provinces in North America, HC 1847–8 (964) xlvii.

Papers Relative to Emigration to the British Provinces in North America, HC 1847–8 (971) xlvii.

Reports from the Select Committee Appointed to Enquire into the Expediency of Encouraging Emigration from the United Kingdom, 1826, IV, 1826–27, V.

Third report from the Select Committee of the House of Lords on Colonization from Ireland: Together with Minutes of Evidence HC 1849 (86) vi.

CONTEMPORARY NEWSPAPERS

Acadian Recorder (Halifax)
Armagh Guardian
Belfast Newsletter
Cork Examiner
Glasgow Chronicle
Halifax Herald
Moncton Times
New Brunswick Courier
The Nova Scotian
Portland Daily Press
Prince Edward Island Register
Royal Gazette (New Brunswick)
Royal Gazette and Newfoundland Advertiser
Saint John Albion
Saint John Morning Freeman
Saint John Weekly Freeman
Sun (London, England)

CONTEMPORARY MATERIAL OF LATER PRINTING

Fisher, Peter. *History of New Brunswick*. Saint John, NB: reprinted jointly by the Government of New Brunswick and W.S. Fisher under the auspices of the New Brunswick Historical Society, 1921(originally published 1825).

Munro, Alexander. *New Brunswick with a Brief Outline of Nova Scotia and Prince Edward Island*. Belleville, ON: Mika Studio, 1972. (First published 1855 by Richard Nugent, Halifax, NS.)

Whitelaw, Marjorie (ed.). *The Dalhousie Journals*. Ottawa: Oberon, 1978–82.

SECONDARY SOURCES

Acheson, T.W. "The Irish Community in Saint John, 1815–1850." *New Ireland Remembered: Historical Essays on the Irish in New Brunswick*, edited by P.M. Toner. Fredericton: New Ireland Press, 1988, 29–54.

———. "A Study in the Historical Demography of a Loyalist County." *Social History* 1 (April 1968): 53–65. Adams, William Forbes. *Ireland and Irish Emigration to the New World from 1815 to the Famine*. New Haven: Yale University Press, 1932.

Angus, Anthony Johnston. *A History of the Catholic Church in Eastern Nova Scotia*. Vol. 1. Antigonish: St. Francis Xavier University Press, 1960.

Anonymous. "19th Century Passenger List to Newfoundland." In *An Nasc: Newsletter of the D'Arcy McGee Chair of Irish Studies* 1, no. 2 (Summer 1988). Halifax: St. Mary's University.

———. "*Dorcas Savage* Passenger List, 1818." In *Generations, Journal of the New Brunswick Genealogical Society* 36, no. 1 (Spring 2015).

———. Irish Newfoundland Association: Souvenir Programme and Order of Proceedings for the Unveiling of the Historic Plaque Marking the Site of the United Irish Rising in Newfoundland. Belvedere Street, St. John's, Saturday, June 17, 2000.

———. Passengers to New Brunswick: The Custom House Records: 1833: 34, 37, 38. Saint John: New Brunswick Genealogical Society, 1987.

Aonghusa, Proinsias Mac. "Reflections on the Fortunes of the Irish Language in Canada, With Some Reference to the Fate of the Language in the United States." In *The Untold Story: The Irish in Canada, Volume 2*, edited by Robert O'Driscoll and Lorna Reynolds, 711–17. Toronto: Celtic Arts of Canada, 1988.

Bailyn, Bernard. *Voyagers to the West: Emigration from Britain to America on the Eve of the Revolution*. New York: Alfred A. Knopf, 1986.

Bitterman, R. *Rural Protest on Prince Edward Island: From British Colonization to the Escheat Movement.* Toronto: University of Toronto Press, 2006.

Bittermann, Rusty, Robert A. MacKinnon, and Graeme Wynne. "Of Equality and Interdependence in the Nova Scotian Countryside 1850–70." *Canadian Historical Review* 64 (1993): 5–12.

Blake, George. *Lloyd's Register of Shipping 1760–1960.* London: Lloyd's, 1960.

Bolger. F.W.P. (ed.). *Canada's Smallest Province: A History of Prince Edward Island.* Halifax: Nimbus, 1991.

Brehaut, Mary (ed.). *Pioneers on the Island.* Charlottetown: Prince Edward Island Historical Society, 1959.

Brown, R. *The Coal Fields and Coal Trade of Cape Breton.* London: Sampson, Low, Marston, Low & Searle, 1869.

Buckner Phillip. *Peoples of the Maritimes: English.* Tantallon, NS: Four East Publications, 2000.

———. "The Transformation of the Maritimes: 1815–1860." *The London Journal of Canadian Studies* 9 (1993): 13–30.

Buckner, Phillip, and John G. Reid (eds.). *The Atlantic Region to Confederation: A History.* Toronto: University of Toronto Press, 1993.

Bumsted, J.M. *Land Settlement and Politics on Eighteenth-Century Prince Edward Island.* Kingston: McGill-Queen's University Press, 1987.

———. *The Peoples of Canada: A Pre-Confederation History.* Vol. 1. Toronto: Oxford University Press, 1992.

Byrne, Cyril J. "The First Irish Foothold in North America." In *The Untold Story: The Irish in Canada, Volume 1,* edited by Robert O'Driscoll and Lorna Reynolds, 171–74.

———. "Ireland and Newfoundland: The United Irish Rising of 1798 and the Fencible's Mutiny in St. John's, 1799." Newfoundland Historical Society Lecture No. 37 (November 9, 1977).

Cadigan, Sean T. *Newfoundland and Labrador: A History.* Toronto: University of Toronto Press, 2009.

Callbeck, Lorne C. *The Cradle of Confederation: A Brief History of Prince Edward Island from Its Discovery in 1534 to the Present Time.* Fredericton, NB: Brunswick Press, 1964.

Campey, Lucille H. *"A Very Fine Class of Immigrants": Prince Edward Island's Scottish Pioneers, 1770–1850.* Toronto: Natural Heritage, 2001.

———. *After the Hector: The Scottish Pioneers of Nova Scotia and Cape Breton, 1773–1852.* Toronto: Natural Heritage, 2004.

————— . *Fast Sailing and Copper-Bottomed: Aberdeen Sailing Ships and the Emigrant Scots They Carried to Canada.* Toronto: Natural Heritage, 2002.

————— . *Planters, Paupers, and Pioneers: English Settlers in Atlantic Canada.* Toronto: Dundurn Press, 2010.

————— . *An Unstoppable Force: The Scottish Exodus to Canada.* Toronto: Natural Heritage, 2008.

————— . *With Axe and Bible: The Scottish Pioneers of New Brunswick, 1784–1874.* Toronto: Dundurn Press, 2007.

Carrier, N.H., and J.R. Jeffrey. *External Migration: A Study of the Available Statistics 1815–1950.* London: HMSO, 1953.

Carrigan, D. Owen. "The Immigrant Experience in Halifax, 1881–1931." *Canadian Ethnic Studies* 20, no. 3 (1988): 28–41.

Clark, Andrew H. "Old World Origins and Religious Adherence in Nova Scotia." *Geographical Review* 1 (1960): 317–44.

————— . *Three Centuries and the Island: A Historical Geography of Settlement and Agriculture in Prince Edward Island, Canada.* Toronto: University of Toronto Press, 1959.

Clark, Samuel Delbert. *Church and Sect in Canada.* Toronto: University of Toronto Press, 1948.

Conrad, Margaret, with Alvin Finkel and Cornelius Jaenen. *History of the Canadian Peoples.* Vol. 1: *Beginnings to 1876.* Toronto: Copp Clark Pitman, 1993.

Coogan, Tim Pat. *The Famine Plot: England's Role in Ireland's Greatest Tragedy.* New York: Palgrave Macmillan, 2012.

————— . *Whenever Green Is Worn: The Story of the Irish Diaspora.* London: Random House, 2006.

Cousins, John. "The Irish of Lot Seven." *Abegweit Review* 4, no. 1 (Spring 1988): 35–40.

————— . "James H. Fitzgerald and Prince Edward Island, Adieu." *Island Magazine* 8 (Fall/Winter 1980): 27–31.

Cowan, Helen. *British Emigration to British North America: The First Hundred Years.* Toronto: University of Toronto Press, 1961.

Crowley, John, William J. Smyth, and Mike Murphy. *Atlas of the Great Irish Famine.* Cork: Cork University Press, 2013.

Cushing, J. Elizabeth, Teresa Casey, and Monica Robertson. *A Chronicle of Irish Emigration to Saint John, New Brunswick, 1847.* Saint John: New Brunswick Museum, 1979.

Daley, Louis J. *A Doyle Family of Prince Edward Island.* Charlottetown: printed by author, 1992.

Dallison, Robert. *Hope Restored: The American Revolution and Founding of New Brunswick*. Fredericton: Goose Lane Editions and the New Brunswick Military Heritage Project, 2003.

Davis, Ralph. *The Industrial Revolution and British Overseas Trade*. Leicester: Leicester University Press, 1979.

De Jong, Nicholas, and Marven E. Moore. *Shipbuilding on Prince Edward Island: Enterprise in a Maritime Setting, 1787–1920*. Hull: Canadian Museum of Civilization, 1994.

Deegan, Tommy. "A List of Passenger Shipping from Waterford Port to America and Canada, 1845–1850." *DECIES: The Journal of the Waterford Historical and Archaeological Society* 51 (1995), 49—55.

Dick, Ernest J. "From Temperance to Prohibition in 19th Century Nova Scotia." *Dalhousie Review* 61 (1981), 530—52.

Dickson, R.J. *Ulster Emigration to Colonial America, 1718–1775*. London: Routledge & Kegan Paul, 1996.

Dictionary of Canadian Biography. Toronto: University of Toronto Press, 1979–85.

Dingfelder, Dorothy Rines. *Irish Emigrants in the Emigrant Hospital, Saint John, NB, April 30, 1848–Jan. 1, 1849*. Chico, CA: printed by author, 1983.

Dobbs, Kildare. "Newfoundland and the Maritimes: An Overview." In *The Untold Story: The Irish in Canada, Volume 1*, edited by Robert O'Driscoll and Lorna Reynolds, 175–94. Toronto: Celtic Arts of Canada, 1988.

Donnelly, James S. Jr. *The Great Irish Potato Famine*. Stroud: Sutton Publishing, 2001.

Donovan, Kenneth. "Mary Grace Barron and the Irish of Ingonish, Cape Breton, 1822–1999." In *The Nashwaak Review* 6/7 (Fall 1999): 177–237.

Doody, C.W. "The Irish in Newfoundland." *The Untold Story: The Irish in Canada, Volume 1*, edited by Robert O'Driscoll and Lorna Reynolds, 195–201. Toronto: Celtic Arts of Canada, 1988.

Doyle, Lahey. "The Irish Experience in Halifax, Nova Scotia, Saint John, New Brunswick, and St. John's, Newfoundland: A Comparative Analysis." M.A. thesis, St. Mary's University, Nova Scotia, 2010.

Doyle, Moses H. *The Irish Pioneers of Margaree Cape Breton Island Nova Scotia also Known as the "Long-Tailed Family" Mogue Doyle — Myles (McDaniel: Doyle — McDaniel — Tompkins — Burns — Carroll — Coady — Dunn — Fitzgerald — Fortune — Hayes — Kiley (Kieley) — McGarry — Miller — Murphy and others*. Ottawa: published by author, 1994.

Drudy, P.J. (ed.). *The Irish in America: Emigration, Assimilation and Impact.* Cambridge, NY: Cambridge University Press, 1985.

Duffy, Patrick J., and Gerard Moran (eds.). *To and From Ireland: Planned Migration Schemes c 1600–2000.* Dublin: Geography Publications, 2004.

Elder, Annie E. *History of New Jerusalem.* Fredericton: Ufsdell Printing, 1953.

Elliott, Bruce. "Irish Protestants." In *The Encyclopedia of Canada's Peoples,* edited by Paul Robert Magocsi, 763–83. Toronto: Published for the Multicultural History Society of Ontario by the University of Toronto Press, circa 1999.

Evans, Eric J. *The Forging of the Modern State: Early Industrial Britain, 1783–1870.* Harlow, UK: Pearson Education, 2001.

Fitzgerald, John Edward. "The United Irish Rebellion in Newfoundland, 1799–1800." Typescript monograph of a lecture presented to the Irish Newfoundland Association, Salon B, Hotel Newfoundland, St. John's, October 28, 1998.

Fitzgerald, Owen. *The Fitzgerald Family.* Halifax: published by author, February 1984.

Flewwelling, Susan Longley (Morse). "Immigration to and Emigration from Nova Scotia 1839–51." *Nova Scotia Historical Society (Collections)* 28 (1949): 66–97.

Fraser, Douglas. "More Elusive Immigrants." *The Island Magazine* 26 (Fall/Winter, 1989), 35–40; no. 27 (Spring/Summer 1990): 38–41.

Gallant, Peter. *From Ireland to Prince Edward Island: A List Compiled from Newspapers, Obituary Notices and Cemetery Transcriptions.* Charlottetown: PEI Genealogical Society, 1990.

Ganong, W.F. "Monograph of the Origins of Settlements in the Province of New Brunswick." In *Transactions of the Royal Society of Canada,* 2nd series (10), sections 1–2 (1904): 1–185.

Gilroy, Marion. *Loyalists and Land Settlement in Nova Scotia.* Halifax: Public Archives of Nova Scotia, 1937.

Guillet, Edwin C. *The Great Migration: The Atlantic Crossing by Sailing Ships since 1770.* Toronto: University of Toronto Press, 1963.

Hamilton, W.D. *Dictionary of Miramichi Biography: Biographical Sketches of Men and Women Born Before 1900 Who Played a Part in Public Life on the Miramichi Northumberland County, New Brunswick, Canada.* Saint John: W.D. Hamilton, 1997.

Hammond, Linda. "Irish Immigration into Newfoundland." Typescript monograph of essay submitted for the geography course, BA Memorial University, Newfoundland, 1967.

Handcock, W. Gordon. "English Migration to Newfoundland." In *The Peopling of Newfoundland: Essays in Historical Geography*, edited by John J. Mannion, 15–48. St. John's: Institute of Social and Economic Research, Memorial University of Newfoundland, 1978.

———. "Spatial Patterns in a Trans-Atlantic Migration Field: The British Isles and Newfoundland During the Eighteenth and Nineteenth Centuries." In *Proceedings of the 1975 British-Canadian Symposium on Historical Geography. The Settlement of Canada: Origins and Transfer*, edited by Brian S. Osborne. Kingston, ON: Queen's University (Dept. of Geography), 1976.

Hannay, J. *History of New Brunswick: Its Resources and Advantages*. 2 vols. Saint John: John A. Bowes, 1909.

Hart, Harriet Cunningham. *History of the County of Guysborough*. Belleville, ON: Mika, 1975.

Harvey, D.C. "Early Settlement and Social Conditions in Prince Edward Island." In *Dalhousie Review* 11, no. 4 (1932): 448–61.

Harvey, Daniel Cobb (ed.). *Journeys to the Island of Saint John or Prince Edward Island, 1775–1832*. Toronto: Macmillan, 1955.

History Committee, St. Ann's Parish, P.E.I. *St. Ann's Parish History, Hope River, PEI, 50th Anniversary, 1843–1993*. Hope River, PE: The History Committee, 1993.

Hornsby, Stephen J. *Nineteenth Century Cape Breton: A Historical Geography*. Montreal: McGill-Queen's University Press, 1992.

Houston, Cecil J., and William J. Smyth. *Irish Emigration and Canadian Settlement: Patterns, Links and Letters*. Toronto: University of Toronto Press, 1990.

Houston, Cecil J., and William J. Smyth. *The Sash Canada Wore: A Historical Geography of the Orange Order in Canada*. Toronto: University of Toronto Press, 1980.

Hunter, Margaret. *Pioneer Settlers in the Bay of Chaleur in the Nineteenth and Twentieth Centuries*. Sackville, NB: Tribune Press, 1978.

Hynes, Leo J. *Catholic Irish in New Brunswick, 1783–1900*. Moncton, NB: published by author, 1992.

Jardine, Robert S.P., and L. Ann Coles. *Some Immigrants from Offaly and Laois*. Kensington, PE: Offaly and Laois Family History Society, 1992.

Johnson, Daniel F. *Irish Emigration to New England Through the Port of Saint John, NB, 1841–1849*. Baltimore, MD: Clearfield, 1997.

———. *The St. John County Alms and Work House Records*. Saint John: published by author, 1985.

Johnson, Stanley C. *A History of Emigration from the United Kingdom to North America, 1763–1912*. London: G. Routledge, 1913.

Johnston, Angus Anthony. *A History of the Catholic Church in Eastern Nova Scotia*. 2 vols. Antigonish, NB: St. Francis Xavier University Press, 1960.

Kelly, E.T. "The Coming of the Newfoundland Irish." In *Newfoundland Quarterly* 65 (1967): 18–20.

Ketchum, T.C.L. *A Short History of Carleton County*. Woodstock, NB: Sentinel, 1922.

Kilfoil, William P. *Johnville: The Centennial Story of an Irish Settlement*. Fredericton: published by author, 1962.

King, Joseph A. *Ireland to North America: Emigrants from West Cork*. LaFayette: K & K Publications, 1995.

King, Séamus J. *The Clash of the Ash in Foreign Fields: Hurling Abroad*. Tipperary: Cashel, 1998.

Kirwin, William J. "The Planting of 'Anglo-Irish' in Newfoundland." In *Focus on Canada*, edited by Sandra J. Clarke, 65–84. Amsterdam: John Benjamins, 1993.

Leyburn, J.G. *The Scotch-Irish: A Social History*. Chapel Hill: University of North Carolina Press, 1962.

Long, Heather. *Good Green Hope: The Irish Catholic Settlers of Albert County, New Brunswick*. Halifax: published by author, 1995.

Lower, Arthur R.M. *Great Britain's Woodyard: British America and the Timber Trade 1763–1867*. Montreal: McGill-Queen's University Press, 1973.

MacDonagh, Oliver. "Emigration and the State, 1833–55: An Essay in Administrative History." In *Transactions of the Royal Historical Society*, fifth series, 5: 133–59. London: Royal Historical Society, 1955.

———. *A Pattern of Government Growth 1800–1860: The Passenger Acts and Their Enforcement*. London: MacGibbon & Kee, 1961.

Macdonald, C. Ochiltree. *The Coal and Iron Industries of Nova Scotia*. Halifax: Chronicle, 1909.

MacDonald, Edward. "Edward Whelan and the Election of 1867." *Island Magazine* 52 (Fall/Winter 2002), 19–26.

———. "The Ill and the Dying." *Island Magazine* 36 (Fall/Winter 1994): 35–39.

———. *New Ireland: The Irish in Prince Edward Island*. Charlottetown: PEI Museum and Heritage Foundation 1990.

Macdonald, Ernest (ed.). *The Burke Chronicles: The Story of the Beginnings of the Roman Catholic Parishes in Prince Edward Island to 1885*. PEI: published by author, 2007.

Macdonald, Heidi. "Developing a Strong Roman Catholic Social Order in Late Nineteenth Century Prince Edward Island." *Canadian Catholic Historical Studies* 69 (2003): 34–51.

MacDonald, Norman. *Canada, Immigration and Settlement 1763–1841.* London: Longmans & Co., 1939.

MacKay, Donald. *Flight from Famine: The Coming of the Irish to Canada.* Toronto: Natural Heritage, 2009.

Mackenzie, Angus Anthony. *The Irish in Cape Breton.* Antigonish: Formac, 1979.

MacKinnon, D.A., and A.B. Warburton. *Past and Present of Prince Edward Island.* Charlottetown: B.F. Bowen, 1906.

MacKinnon, Neil. *This Unfriendly Soil: The Loyalist Experience in Nova Scotia 1783–1791.* Kingston, ON: McGill-Queen's University Press, 1986.

MacLaren, George. *The Pictou Book: Stories of Our Past.* New Glasgow, NS: Hector, 1954.

MacMaster, Richard K. "Emigration from Ulster to Prince Edward Island, 1770–1790." *Familia* 12 (Ulster Historical Foundation), (1996): 14–32.

MacMillan, John C. *The Early History of the Catholic Church in Prince Edward Island.* Quebec: Evenement, 1905.

MacNutt, W.S. *The Atlantic Provinces: The Emergence of Colonial Society 1712–1857.* London: McClelland & Stewart, 1965.

———. *New Brunswick, a History: 1784–1867.* Toronto: Macmillan, 1984.

Magosci, Paul Robert (ed.). *The Encyclopedia of Canada's Peoples.* Toronto: Published for the Multicultural History Society of Ontario by the University of Toronto Press, circa 1999.

Mannion, John J. "Irish Merchants Abroad: The Newfoundland Experience, 1750–1850." *Newfoundland Studies* 2, no. 2 (1986): 127–90.

———. *Irish Settlements in Eastern Canada: A Study of Cultural Transfer and Adaptation.* Toronto: University of Toronto Press, 1974.

———. "Old World Antecedents, New World Adaptation: Inistioge (Kilkenny) Immigrants in Newfoundland." *Newfoundland Studies* 5, no. 2 (1989): 103–75.

———. (ed.). *The Peopling of Newfoundland: Essays in Historical Geography.* Social and Economic Papers No. 8. St. John's: Memorial University of Newfoundland, Institute of Social and Economic Research, 1978.

———. *Tipperary Trails to Newfoundland: The Story of Emigration from Tipperary to Newfoundland During the 18th and 19th Centuries.* Tipperary: Ireland Newfoundland Connections Festival, 2012.

Martell, J.S. "Early Coal Mining in Nova Scotia." In *Cape Breton Historical Essays*, edited by Don MacGillivray and Brian Tenyson, 165–71. Sydney: College of Cape Breton Press, 1981.

———. *Immigration to and Emigration from Nova Scotia, 1815–1838.* Halifax, NS: PANS 1942.

———. "Military Settlements in Nova Scotia after the War of 1812." *Nova Scotia Historical Society Collection* 24 (1938): 75–106.

Matthews, Keith. "A History of the West of England-Newfoundland Fishery." Ph.D. thesis, University of Oxford, 1968.

McCarthy, Angela. *Irish Migrants in New Zealand, 1840–1937: "The Desired Haven."* Belfast: The Boydell Press, 2005.

McCarthy, Michael J. *The Irish in Newfoundland 1600–1900: Their Trials, Tribulations and Triumphs.* St. John's: Creative Publishers, 1999.

McCreath, Peter L., and John G. Leefe. *A History of Early Nova Scotia.* Tantallon, NS: Four East Publications, 1990.

McDonald, Donna. *Illustrated News: Juliana Horatia Ewing's Canadian Pictures, 1867–1869.* Toronto: Dundurn Press, 1985.

McDonald, Terry. "Where Have All the (English) Folk Songs Gone?" *British Journal of Canadian Studies* 14, no. 2 (1999): 180–92.

McGowan, Mark G. "Irish Catholics." In *The Encyclopedia of Canada's Peoples*, edited by Paul Robert Magocsi. Toronto: Published for the Multicultural History Society of Ontario by the University of Toronto Press, circa 1999.

McGuigan, Peter. "From Wexford and Monaghan: The Lot 22 Irish." *Abegweit Review* 5, no. 1 (Winter 1985): 61–96.

———. "The Lot 61 Irish: Settlement and Stabilization." *Abegweit Review* 6, no.1 (Spring 1988): 33–63.

Miller, Kerby A. *Emigrants and Exiles: Ireland and the Irish Exodus to North America.* Oxford: Oxford University Press, 1985.

Mitchell, Brian. *Derry-Londonderry: Gateway to a New World: The Story of Emigration from the Foyle by Sail and Steam.* Londonderry, Northern Ireland: Clearfield, 2014.

———. *Irish Emigration Lists, 1833–1839: Lists of Emigrants Extracted from Ordnance Surveys of the Counties of Londonderry and Antrim.* Baltimore: Genealogical Publishing Company, 1989.

———. *Irish Passenger Lists, 1847–1871: Lists of Passengers Sailing from Londonderry to America on Ships of the J & J Cooke Line and the McCorkell Line.* Baltimore: Genealogical Publishing Co., 1988.

Moir, John S. *The Church in the British Era: From the British Conquest to Confederation, Volume Two of the History of the Christian Church in Canada.* General editor John Webster Grant. Toronto: McGraw-Hill Ryerson, 1972.

Moran, Gerard. *Sending Out Ireland's Poor: Assisted Emigration to North America in the Nineteenth Century.* Dublin: Four Courts, 2004.

Morrison, J. Clinton. *Along the North Shore: A Social History of Township 11, PEI, 1765–1982.* St. Eleanor's, PE: published by author, 1983.

Morse, Susan Longley. "Immigration to Nova Scotia 1839–51." Halifax, NS: Dalhousie University (unpublished M.A.), 1946.

Murphy, J.M. *The Londonderry Heirs: A Story of the Settlement of the Cobequid Townships of Truro, Onslow, and Londonderry, in Nova Scotia, Canada, by English-Speaking People in the Period 1760 to 1775.* Middleton, NS: Black Print Co., 1976.

Murphy, Peter. *From Ireland to Saint John: Together in Exile.* Saint John, NB: Lingley, 1990.

Murphy, Peter D. *Poor Ignorant Children: Irish Famine Orphans in Saint John NB.* Halifax, NS: D'Arcy McGhee Chair of Irish Studies, Saint Mary's University, 1999.

New Brunswick Genealogical Society. *Passengers to New Brunswick: Custom House Records — 1833, 34, 37 & 38.* Saint John, NB: 1987.

O'Driscoll, Robert, and Lorna Reynolds (eds.). *The Untold Story: The Irish in Canada,* 2 vols. Toronto: Celtic Arts of Canada, 1988.

O'Flaherty, P. *Lost Country: The Rise and Fall of Newfoundland.* St. John's, NL: Long Beach, 2005.

————. *Old Newfoundland: A History to 1843.* St. John's, NL: Long Beach, circa 1999.

O'Grady, Brendan. *Exiles and Islanders the Irish Settlers of Prince Edward Island.* Montreal: McGill-Queen's University Press, 2004.

————. "The Monaghan Settlers." *Abegweit Review* 4, no. 1 (Spring 1983): 50–75.

O'Reilly, J.W. "Newfoundland and Its Irish Settlers," parts 1 and 3. *Donahoe's Monthly Magazine* 23, no. 3 (1890): 201–08; vol. 23, no. 5 (1890): 434–48.

Orlo, J., and D. Fraser. "Those Elusive Immigrants," parts 1 to 3. *The Island Magazine* 16 (1984): 36–44; no. 17 (1985): 32–37; no. 18 (1985): 29–35.

Porter, Reginald. "The First Irish Settlers in Tignish." *Abegweit Review* (Spring 1983): 27–33.

Power, Thomas P. "The Emigrant Ship: The Transportation, Regulation and Reception of Irish Immigrants in New Brunswick, 1815–1855." In *Celtic*

Languages and Celtic People, edited by Cyril Byrne et al., 683–705. Halifax: Saint Mary's University, 1989.

———. *The Irish in Atlantic Canada, 1780–1900*. Fredericton: New Ireland Press, 1991.

———. "The Palmerston Estate in County Sligo: Improvement and Assisted Emigration." In *To and from Ireland: Planned Migration Schemes c 1600–2000*, edited by Patrick J. Duffy and Gerard Moran, 105–36. Dublin: Geography Publications, 2004.

Punch, Terrence M. *Erin's Sons: Irish Arrivals in Atlantic Canada, 1761–1853*. 4 vols. Baltimore, MD: Genealogical Publishing, 2008.

———. "Finding Our Irish." *Nova Scotia Historical Review* 6, no. 1 (1986): 57–62.

———. "Gentle as the Snow on a Rooftop: The Irish in Nova Scotia to 1830." In *The Untold Story: The Irish in Canada*, edited by Robert O'Driscoll and Lorna Reynolds, 215–29. Toronto: Celtic Arts of Canada, 1988.

———. "Irish Immigrants to Atlantic Canada, 1832–1846." *The Irish Genealogist* 7 (1989): 642–48.

———. "The Irish in Halifax: 1815–1867: A Study in Ethnic Assimilation." M.A. thesis, Dalhousie University, Halifax, 1976.

———. "The Irish in Halifax, Nova Scotia Before 1830." *Canadian Genealogist* 1, no. 3 (1979): 173–80.

———. "Irish Repealers at Halifax, Nova Scotia, in 1843." *The Irish Ancestor* 10, no. 1 (1978): 6–13.

———. "Ships from Ireland to Nova Scotia, 1765–1850." *An Nasc* 13 (Spring 2001): 3–10.

Rayburn, Alan, *Geographical Names of Prince Edward Island: Toponymy Study*. Ottawa: Department of Energy, Mines, and Resources, 1973.

Raymond, W.O. "Colonel Alexander McNutt and the Pre-Loyalist Settlements of Nova Scotia." *Proceedings and Transactions of the Royal Society of Canada*, 3rd series, no. 5 (1911), section 2: 23–115.

Reicker, Marion Gilchrist. *A Time There Was: Petersville and Other Abandoned Settlements in Queens County, N.B., 1815–1953*. Jemseg, NB: Queens County Historical Society, 1984.

Rees, Jim. *Surplus People: From Wicklow to Canada*. London: Collins Press, 2014.

Rees, Ronald. *Some Other Place than Here: St. Andrews and the Irish Emigrant*. Fredericton: New Ireland Press, 2000.

Roberston, Ian Ross. "Highlanders, Irishmen and the Land Question in Nineteenth-Century Prince Edward Island." In *Interpreting Canada's Past*, edited by J.M. Bumsted, 1: 359–73. Toronto: Oxford University Press, 1986.

Rowe, Frederick W. *History of Newfoundland and Labrador*. Toronto: McGraw-Hill Ryerson, 1980.

Royle, Stephen A., and Caitriona Ni Laoire. "Desbrisay's Settlers." *Island Magazine* 51 (2002): 19–23.

Salmon, Stuart. "The Loyalist Regiments of the American Revolutionary War, 1775–1783." Ph.D. dissertation, University of Stirling (2009).

Schella, Warren, and Lawrence Gillespie. *The History of Irishtown*. Moncton: n.d.

See, Scott W. *Riots in New Brunswick: Orange Nativism and Social Violence in the 1840s*. Toronto: University of Toronto Press, 1993.

Sharpe, Errol. *A People's History of Prince Edward Island*. Toronto: Steel Rail, 1976.

Shepperson, W.S. *British Emigration to North America: Projects and Opinions in the Early Victorian Period*. Oxford: Blackwell, 1957.

Shortt, A., and A.G. Doughty (eds.). *Canada and Its Provinces: A History of the Canadian People and Their Institutions* (written by "one hundred associates"). Vols. 13 and 14. Toronto: Publishers Association of Canada, 1913–17.

Siebert, Wilbur Henry. "The Loyalists in Prince Edward Island." *Transactions of the Royal Society of Canada*, series 3, vol. 4, section 2 (1910): 109–17.

Smith, Leonard H., and Norma H. Smith. *Nova Scotia Immigrants to 1867*. Baltimore: Genealogical Publishing, 1992.

Smith Smiley, Maribelle. *History of the Smiley Family of Hants County, Nova Scotia*. Nova Scotia: published by author, n.d.

Spicer, Stanley T. *Masters of Sail: The Era of Square-Rigged Vessels in the Maritime Provinces*. Toronto: McGraw-Hill Ryerson, 1968.

Spray, William A. "'The Difficulties Came Upon Us Like a Thunderbolt': Immigrants and Fever in New Brunswick in 1847." In *The Irish in Atlantic Canada, 1780–1900*, edited by Thomas P. Power, 107–26. Fredericton, NB: New Ireland Press, circa 1991.

————. "The Irish in Miramichi." In *New Ireland Remembered: Historical Essays on the Irish in New Brunswick*, edited by P.M. Toner, 55–62. Fredericton: New Ireland Press, 1988.

Starkey, David J. "Devonians and the Newfoundland Trade." In *The New Maritime History of Devon*, edited by Michael Duffy et al., 1: 163–71. London: Conway Maritime Press in association with the University of Exeter, 1992.

Stewart, Herbert Leslie. *The Irish in Nova Scotia: Annals of the Charitable Irish Society of Halifax.* Kentville: Kentville Publishing, 1949.

Taylor, Thomas Griffith. *Newfoundland: A Study of Settlement with Maps and Illustrations.* Toronto: Canadian Institute of International Affairs, 1946.

Toner, Peter Michael. "Another New Ireland Lost: The Irish of New Brunswick." In *The Untold Story: The Irish in Canada,* edited by Robert O'Driscoll and Lorna Reynolds, 1: 231–36. Toronto: Celtic Arts of Canada, 1988.

————. "The Irish of New Brunswick at Mid Century: The 1851 Census." In *New Ireland Remembered: Historical Essays on the Irish in New Brunswick,* edited by P.M. Toner, 106–32. Fredericton: New Ireland Press, 1989.

————. "Occupation and Ethnicity: The Irish in New Brunswick." *Canadian Ethnic Studies* 20, no. 3 (1988): 155–65.

————. "The Origins of New Brunswick Irish, 1851." *Journal of Canadian Studies* 23, nos. 1–2 (1988): 104–19.

Wallace, Ann. *Life in the Irish Salmon River District.* Antigonish: Casket Printing & Publishing, 1992.

Warburton, A.B. *A History of Prince Edward Island: From Its Discovery in 1534 Until the Departure of Lieutenant Governor Ready in AD 1831.* Saint John, NB: Barnes & Co., 1923.

Whalen, James M. "Almost as Bad as Ireland: The Experience of the Irish Immigrant in Canada, Saint John, 1847." In *The Untold Story: The Irish in Canada,* edited by Robert O'Driscoll and Lorna Reynolds, 1: 155–70. Toronto: Celtic Arts of Canada, 1988.

————. "Social Welfare in New Brunswick, 1784–1900." *Acadiensis* 2, no. 1 (Autumn 1972): 54–64.

White, Mary Ann. "Irish Emigration to Newfoundland During the 18th and 19th Centuries." Essay, Memorial University, St. John's (1982).

Wilson, David A. *The Irish in Canada.* Ottawa: Canadian Historical Association, 1989.

Wilson, Edna C. "The Impact of a Century of Irish Catholic Immigration in Nova Scotia (1750–1850)." Ph. D. dissertation, University of Ottawa (1961).

Wright, Esther Clark. *The Loyalists of New Brunswick.* Fredericton, NB: E.C. Wright, 1955.

————. *Planters and Pioneers.* Wolfville, NS: published by author, 1982.

Wright, Harold E. *The Diary of Nellie McGowan, Partridge Island Quarantine Station, 1902.* Saint John: Partridge Island Research Project, 1904.

————. "Partridge Island: Re-Discovering the Irish Connection." In

The Irish in Atlantic Canada, 1780–1900, edited by T.P. Power, 127–49. Fredericton: New Ireland Press, 1991.

Wynn, Graeme. "A Region of Scattered Settlements and Bounded Possibilities: North Eastern America, 1775–1800." *Canadian Geographer* 31 (1987): 319–38.

————. *Timber Colony: An Historical Geography of Early Nineteenth Century New Brunswick*. Toronto: University of Toronto Press, 1981.

ONLINE RESOURCES

www.archives.gnb.ca/Irish/databases_en.html
www.newirelandnb.ca
www.drh24.wordpress.com/2009/12/14/henderson-settlement
www.folkways.si.edu/folksongs-of-the-miramichi-lumber-and-river-songs-from-the-miramichi-folk-fest-newcastle-new-brunswick/world/music/album/smithsonian www.genealogy.com?users/k/i/l/Colin-Kiley
www.theshipslist.com

IMAGE CREDITS

93   *Photograph by Geoff Campey.*

106   *Courtesy Provincial Archives of New Brunswick, Peter Murphy Collection: P408–63.*

111   *Photograph by Geoff Campey.*

113   *Courtesy Provincial Archives of New Brunswick, Keswick Historical Society Collection: P421-21.*

126   *Courtesy Provincial Archives of New Brunswick. MC3710.*

134   *Courtesy Public Archives and Record Office of Prince Edward Island, Acc.2320/5-11.*

142   *Courtesy Public Archives and Record Office of Prince Edward Island, Acc.2763/72.*

144   *Courtesy Public Archives and Record Office of Prince Edward Island, Acc. 3466/HF78.131.781.29.1.*

147   *Photograph by Geoff Campey.*

155   *Courtesy Library and Archives Canada C-008744.*

159   *Courtesy Harold E. Wright, Saint John, New Brunswick.*

160   *Courtesy New Brunswick Museum, New Brunswick, Canada William Francis Ganong Collection 1987.17.485.*

186   *Courtesy Provincial Archives of New Brunswick.*

187   *Courtesy New Brunswick Genealogical Society, Miramichi Branch.*

194   *Courtesy Deputy Keeper of Records, Public Record Office of Northern Ireland. T1498/1.*

206   *Courtesy Nova Scotia Archives, Tom Connors Collection, 1987-218 No. 790.*

209   *Courtesy Library and Archives Canada, PA-132965.*

210   *Courtesy Provincial Archives of New Brunswick, Peter Murphy Collection, P408–53.*

214   *Courtesy Provincial Archives of New Brunswick, Peter Murphy Collection, P408–48.*

215   *Courtesy Nova Scotia Archives, Charitable Irish Society of Halifax Photograph Collection.*

216   *Courtesy Harold E. Wright, Saint John, New Brunswick.*

Author photo   *The Portrait Place, Priory Square, Salisbury, U.K.*

Front cover   *Courtesy of the Art Gallery of Nova Scotia. Gift of the Halifax Chamber of Commerce, 2007.*

Back cover   *Reproduced courtesy of the National Library of Ireland ET B38.*

INDEX

Nova Scotia Regiment, 47
Nowlan, John, 92, 341
Nowlan, Patrick, 92

O'Brien, Smith, 208
O'Donel, Bishop James Louis, 57, 58, 334
Offaly, county (Ireland), 141, 355
Ogden, Nova Scotia, 86
O'Halloran, Maurice, 354
O'Leary, Henry, 128, 215, 351
O'Leary, John Francis, 28
O'Leary, Miles, 347
O'Neil, Patrick, 331
O'Reilly, Garret, 354
O'Reilly, Patrick, 354
Onslow Township (Nova Scotia), 29, 37, 40, 42, 327, 328
Ontario. *See* Upper Canada
Orange Order, 206, 345, 364
   New Brunswick, 109, 169, 208, 210
   Newfoundland, 208, 209
   Nova Scotia, 208
   Prince Edward Island, 35, 208, 364
Ordnance Survey Memoirs, 98, 343
Overcrowding (on ships), 79, 84, 178, 185, 188, 189, 203, 286, 287, 338

Palmerston, Lord (Henry John Temple, 3rd Viscount), 157, 158, 160, 162, 202, 296–98, 359
Parrsboro, Nova Scotia, 34
Partridge Island (New Brunswick), 154, 155, 186–88, 205, 249, 256, 282, 286, 294, 299, 301, 362, 363

Passamaquoddy Bay (New Brunswick), 95, 101
Passenger Act regulations (Atlantic crossings)
   1803, 79, 184, 338
   1817, 184, 338, 361
   1828, 184, 361
   1835, 362
   1842, 175
Passenger fares (Atlantic crossings), 44, 79, 84, 138, 163, 171, 173, 184, 185, 338
Passenger lists, 62–64, 66, 102, 219, 237, 248–63, 288–90, 292, 296, 297, 299, 300, 302, 303, 305–10, 335, 340, 343, 344, 358, 359
Patterson, Alexander, 330
Patterson, Governor Walter (Prince Edward Island), 44
Paupers/the poor/poverty, 21, 22, 25, 28, 30, 34, 35, 51, 59, 61, 70, 73–75, 79, 81, 82, 84, 86, 92, 93, 96, 101, 109, 114, 122, 125, 135, 138, 143, 153, 155, 159–61, 163, 166, 167, 169, 171, 172, 207, 212, 227, 335, 347, 365
Pennfield Parish (New Brunswick), 163, 325
Pennsylvania, State of (United States), 25, 38, 42, 43, 47, 112, 213
Perley, Moses, 114, 153, 154, 156–58, 160, 161, 188, 189, 193, 203, 204, 292, 347, 358, 374
Petersville Parish (New Brunswick), 108
Petitcodiac River region (New Brunswick), 130

ABOUT THE AUTHOR

Ottawa-born Dr. Lucille Campey began her career in Canada as a scientist and computer specialist, having previously obtained a degree in chemistry from Ottawa University. Following her marriage to her English husband, Geoff, she moved to England. Lucille gained a master's degree at Leeds University based on a thesis that dealt with medieval settlement patterns. She subsequently gained a doctorate at Aberdeen University on a study that focused on the regional links associated with Scottish emigration to Canada. Between 2001 and 2008 Lucille wrote eight books about Scottish emigration to Canada, all published by Dundurn. Lucille then turned her attention to the English who came to Canada. Between 2010 and 2014 Dundurn published three books on this topic.

Lucille is now focusing on the Irish; this book is the first of three books about Irish emigration to Canada. The second and third books will be published in 2018 and 2020.

Lucille's work has recently been recognized by the academic community. In 2016 she was awarded the prestigious Prix du Quebec, which is provided by the Quebec government and administered by the British Association for Canadian Studies.

Lucille and Geoff travel regularly in Canada in connection with Lucille's writing and to keep in touch with family and friends. They live near Salisbury in Wiltshire.

Visit us at

Dundurn.com
@dundurnpress
Facebook.com/dundurnpress
Pinterest.com/dundurnpress